# Violent Sensations

# Violent Sensations

SEX, CRIME, AND UTOPIA IN
VIENNA AND BERLIN, 1860–1914

SCOTT SPECTOR

The University of Chicago Press
Chicago and London

Scott Spector is professor of history and German studies at the University of Michigan.

The University of Chicago Press, Chicago 60637
The University of Chicago Press, Ltd., London
© 2016 by The University of Chicago
All rights reserved. Published 2016.
Printed in the United States of America

25  24  23  22  21  20  19  18  17  16        1  2  3  4  5

ISBN-13: 978-0-226-19664-0 (cloth)
ISBN-13: 978-0-226-19678-7 (paper)
ISBN-13: 978-0-226-19681-7 (e-book)
DOI: 10.7208/chicago/9780226196817.001.0001

Library of Congress Cataloging-in-Publication Data

Spector, Scott, 1959– author.
Violent sensations : sex, crime, and utopia in Vienna and Berlin, 1860–1914 /
Scott Spector.
    pages cm
  Includes bibliographical references and index.
    ISBN 978-0-226-19664-0 (cloth : alk. paper) — ISBN 978-0-226-19678-7 (pbk. : alk.
paper) — ISBN 978-0-226-19681-7 (e-book)    1. Sex crimes—Europe, Central—
History—19th century.    2. Sex crimes—Press coverage—Europe, Central—
History—19th century.    3. Sex crimes—Austria—Vienna—History—19th century.
4. Sex crimes—Germany—Berlin—History—19th century.    5. Sex crimes in
literature.    6. Homosexuality—Europe, Central—History—19th century.    7. Lust
murder—Europe, Central—19th century.    8. Blood accusation—Europe,
Central—History—19th century.    9. Marginality, Social—Europe, Central—
History—19th century.    10. Civilization, Modern—19th century.    I. Title.
HV6593.E8515S66 2016
364.15'3094315509034—dc23

                                                        2015030353

*This book is for*
MICHAEL STEVEN BOYCE
*1982–2015*

# Contents

# On the Border

When we call the period around 1900 the "fin de siècle" or describe its cultural tendencies as "decadent," we invoke a glamorously censorious appraisal of the turn of the twentieth century in metropolitan Europe. The mood evoked by these terms is confirmed by a constellation of familiar and sensational images associated with the period: femmes fatales and sensational slashers, destitute and dangerous new urban districts, criminal violence and sexual excess. An equally strong instinct drives us to associate the urban European milieu of the turn of the twentieth century with a spirit of triumph of science and reason, with the emergence of new expert knowledges, and with a prideful confidence, bordering on arrogance, in "progress." Both of these mental pictures—the sensational and the scientific—were strongly and simultaneously present in the self-image many urban central Europeans had about the lives they were living. How are these apparently opposing visions linked as part of a single way of looking at the world and one's place in it? Instead of concurrently running but contradictory clichés of modernity, taken together these strands and the tensions among them have the character of a single myth: a way of seeing others and oneself through a symbolically laden system of image and narrative suggesting origins, essences, and destinies.

What was perceived at the time as the "new" metropolis—the great city as a life experience different from the way life had ever been lived before—is the stage for this study, and the metropolises in particular focus are Vienna and Berlin.[1] These two were very different and yet both crucial sites in the

---

1. The *locus classicus* for a contemporary statement on this status of the metropolis has become Georg Simmel's essay "The Metropolis and Mental Life"—actually a lecture delivered in 1902 that then appeared in print in Thomas Petermann, ed., *Die Großstadt: Vorträge und Aufsätze*

development of modern conceptions of gender and sexuality, as well as of the political emancipation movements these conceptions inspired. One thinks for instance of the birth of the science of sexology, the earliest articulations of homosexuality as an identity, the concomitant movement to abolish persecution of sexual minorities, and the "first-wave" feminisms of the turn of the century, to name a few. At the same time, these cities became host to fantasies of violence associated with what may be called marginal, liminal, or "border" figures: the pervasive image of the dangerous and erotic femme fatale, reports and fictions of sexual murder and the violent underworld of prostitution, the surprising and forceful reemergence of the blood libel, scandals involving the homosexuality of public figures, and representations of homosexual rings or secret associations. These prurient fantasies hold a startlingly prominent place in the period's high culture (including literature and philosophy), science (especially sexology, urban sociology, and criminology), and popular culture (including fiction writing as well as sensational court cases reported in the popular press). This book is an attempt at a synthetic analysis of this explosion of disparate but intricately linked discourses.

The phrase "violent sensations" refers most directly to the cultural fantasies contained in dramatic courtroom scenes, scandals, and broadly disseminated tales of serial, sexual, or ritual murder. It is meant, at the same time, to signal a new-fashioned apprehension of an interior, unconscious self that was subject to violent feeling—furtive but powerful, even insurmountable sexual or criminal impulses. These fantasies of a primal self take many different forms in the chapters that follow. Similarly, exactly how and to what degree producers and consumers of these fantasies were engaged with this figure of the violent self differ from text to text as they do among genres and periods.

To regard these disparate and contradictory phenomena together, as part of a single and complex cultural moment, promises to cast them all in a different light, but it can also be expected to raise difficult questions. It may even begin to suggest the counterintuitive question of what positive work these texts and practices may be doing. What affirmative or even utopian potential could be entailed in the creation of liminal figures and the production of fantasies of radical violence pertaining to them? The more intuitive assumption of the role such figures played is that as marginal figures, they served to validate and empower "centered" identities—the normal, the respectable, the

---

zur *Städteausstellung* (Dresden: Gehe-Stiftung, 1903), 185–206. A reading of this essay that intends to rescue it as something more complex than a diagnosis of this kind is offered in chap. 1.

productive, and disciplined.[2] The elaborate and repetitive marking of such others—especially sexualized ones, such as the homosexual, the prostitute, and the Jew—is easily explained by this thesis. The association of such figures with fantasies of radical violence, on this view, is not only a feature of this marking process but an ominous indication of where all this cultural work was heading. It is obviously not possible to disprove this kind of interpretation, and there is clearly something valuable to the observation that damaging sexist and homophobic fantasies emerge out of patriarchal societies. But this functionalist view—let us call it the "marginalization thesis"—obscures many of the most prominent and also most surprising features of the historical phenomena analyzed in the pages that follow.

It will take a book to persuade a reader of the degree to which the marginalization thesis is an insufficient explanation of the cultural meaning of these fantasies or, for that matter, their function. Their intimate bonds to the enlightenment projects of the same period in which they emerged also requires more ample illustration, analysis, and argument than a preface can manage. The chapters below each explore a complex of such linkages, paradoxes, and mutual reflections; to introduce the themes to come it will be useful to outline them in brief.

## Border Stations

This book, then, argues for the productivity of a dual analytic encompassing "enlightened" and "decadent" practices and representations associated with the self-image of central European modernity. An analytic of this sort requires the comparison of a deep reserve of very different registers of discourse: scientific and other specialized texts from the disciplines of law, medicine, and the social sciences; professional records and manuals for police, jurists, and detectives in addition to court records; high-cultural texts from philosophy and literature meant for an educated public; popular culture ranging from pulp fiction to lampoon; sensational genres of crime reportage from newspapers of record to new crime and detective genres; emancipation movement literature and archival records; and finally, the rare documents that record the self-experience of sexual and criminal subjects, including court or police interrogation testimony, private writings, and letters to friends, doctors, or

---

2. Richard Evans made a powerful case for this interpretation, which can be said to undergird many accounts. See, e.g., Richard J. Evans, *The German Underworld: Deviants and Outcasts in German History* (London: Routledge, 1988) and *Tales from the German Underworld*.

newspaper editors. This is not to say that all these disparate texts are to be weighed equally or even considered in the same way. To the contrary, the methods used for interpreting these different kinds of sources need to be specific to their types just as they need to be contextualized within their own genres; but positioning them in relation to one another — reading the rhetorics of liminal identity and violence across genres — offers another, revealing context that has not been deeply explored.

The chapters below offer a set of sites, stations, or moments where these intricate connections come into view. The first, "Dark City, Bright Future," explores the fin-de-siècle discourses of the city and the criminal to get at what has just been described as the dual contexts of modernity: on the one hand, the explosion of popular and social-scientific discourses reflecting anxiety relating to the urban sphere (theories of degeneration, atavism, and violence); on the other hand, the enlightenment optimism inherent in criminal science as well as the "constructive" identity projects of gender and sexuality. The "metropolis" (*Großstadt*) — or modern great city — serves as the setting for all of these conflicting discourses. Drawing on texts from the years around 1900 (most all date roughly from 1893 to 1903, in fact), one of the key objectives in this chapter is the interpretation of a proliferation not only of texts, but also of genres relating to what was perceived as the novel experience of urban modernity. These include writings on these cities and this urban experience itself and also ethnographic writing on the new breeds that inhabit it. This is also the high-water mark of debates within criminology (and, specifically, criminal anthropology) about criminal "types," whose origins may be inborn or environmental. But the question of whether the origins of urban criminality are biological or social may in part mask a more profoundly historical question concerning the emergence of this very question of origins as well as a particular conceptualization of the subject, criminal and otherwise.

In the second chapter, the issue of the origins of marginal identity and its connection to violence will be explored through an earlier moment and a complex of relations relating to the early formation of homosexual identity. We go back to the 1860s and early writings on homosexual identity and emancipation by Hanoverian lawyer Karl Heinrich Ulrichs and his counterpart in Austria-Hungary, Karl Maria Kertbeny. The medical discourse on sexuality emerging out of medical forensics along with the criminal studies that linked social and sexual degeneracy both obliquely defined the normal bourgeois subject through the definition of deviancy. These writers' papers, letters, and published works, along with the transcripts of a central court case involving a homosexual murder, mark the emergence of a shared language of identity in the work by early sexologists and criminologists as well as in the first homosexual rights activists. The 1860s may seem too far a leap back for a book that is really seeking to come to terms with the fin de siècle, and yet the episode of "urning" identity foreshadows, influences, and exposes *in nuce* the cluster that will blossom a quarter century hence. The connection of deviant sexual identity to the notion of sexuality as such, the search for the origins of this new sexuality, and its immediate association with an imaginary of violence are all part of the chapter "Identical Origins."

In the next chapter, "Sensation and Sensibility," we turn to a dual study of turn-of-the-century explorations of homosexuality and emancipation efforts alongside a series of sex scandals involving highly placed public figures.[3] The Viennese literary figure Karl Kraus offers a theoretical grounding for the analysis of these particular sensations.[4] Rather than focusing on transformative, apocalyptic, or redemptive violence, the stories pouring out of the crossroads of sexual science, emergent identity politics, and newspaper sensation concerned the boundary between the interior sphere of sexuality and the world of social and political concern. How was it that this newly defined realm of sexuality—private by definition—could be seen to hold the key to secrets of the public sphere and the political and social worlds? The material presented in this chapter helps shed light on the complex relationships among three realms: sexual identity as experienced by male homosexuals involved in emancipation efforts; medical, juridical, and police definitions of sexual deviance; and cultural fantasies of homosexual conspiracy. The role of experts drawn from the community of sexual science and emancipation in some of the early twentieth century's most notable scandals is one more link between new notions of sexual sensibility and sensational fantasy.

The context of the "woman question" is another major axis along which many of the same questions can be mapped. Some of the thinking of the Austrian and German feminists Rosa Mayreder, Grete Meisel-Hess, and Helene Stöcker is set against Otto Weininger's influential misogynist work *Sex and Character* in chapter 4 alongside medical, social-scientific, and journalistic work arguing for the centrality of gender to a modern "crisis." From a parallel exploration of the identification of the prostitute and the sex murderer as counterpart criminal "types," the chapter titled "Utopian Bodies" moves on to the textual analysis of reports, police files, and case records relating to the sexual murder of prostitutes. Parallel with these, several texts by Robert

---

3. Two articles based on material from this chapter have been published: Spector, "Personal Fate"; "Wrath of the 'Countess Merviola.'"
4. Karl Kraus, *Sittlichkeit und Kriminalität*.

Musil and Otto Weininger are read alongside these events to explore how sensationalist violent fantasy was linked to a critique of European civilization.

The uncanny reemergence of the charge that Jews abducted and killed Christian children for ritual purposes—in the form of a veritable spate of accusations leading to court cases in central Europe—is the focus of the fifth chapter. If the revitalized late nineteenth-century attacks on the Jewish minority in central Europe were based on the association of the Jews with modernization, as is often assumed, then why did this cultural fantasy identify them instead with a primitive and savage past? "Blood Lies" relates urban debates on accusations of Jewish ritual murder and ensuing sensational trials to the themes of modernization and enlightenment, degeneracy and social progress, and race and gender that have run through the discourses on sexuality and violence in the previous chapters. The particular roles of expert knowledge and an unstable discourse of the criminal subject in these cases constitute a vortex in which the sensational ritual murder cases converge with the sensational discourses on lust murder in particular, resonating as well with other fantasies of criminality and sexuality seen earlier in the book. If the modern central European cultural imaginary had an ambivalent relationship to its community of "internal others," this pointed to a self-reflection that is obscured by most interpretations of episodic antisemitism, and the primitive self was as much in play in these representations as an unproblematically modern other.

## Border Figures

There are several recurring figures throughout these different sites, or "border stations": some are actors, some are images, some are arguments. Central to each of the chapters, for instance, is the person of the expert and the notion of expert knowledge. These knowledges took different forms and competed with one another: medical knowledge was central, to be sure, and its main competitor in the context of sensational cases that led to court was juridical expertise. The search for knowledge of the deviant body, character, and crime also brought forth the kinds of expertise already commanded by or hailed by the needs of police inspectors, detectives, and investigating magistrates. This profile of knowledge is discernible in the field of criminal investigations by police, in the literature that they produced for a general public, and in the growing expert literature designed to train them in the detection of crime. Of course, many of the texts belonged to specialized literature of various kinds. Much of what can be culled from archival documents was never meant for public consumption at all. Yet from its inception, there was a consciousness of the potential prurient interest of all of these new modes of knowing the modern subject. This is evident in the ways in which academic and professional discourses were hidden from public view or else coded to restrict access and otherwise minimize the potential for vicarious and unsanctioned pleasure. Obversely, other texts barely disguise their double function to serve specialized professionals just as they marketed these vocations as links to the worlds of sex, crime, and violence. All of these texts betray a keen awareness of the threat and promise that they might themselves spill over into the sensational.

And what of sensational discourse itself? If expert and scholarly and professional training discourses were not meant for public consumption, then how did these knowledges become disseminated throughout the general culture? An answer comes in the form of a genre, the *sensation*—whether a scandal, a moral panic, or another medium of exploiting the potential for intensive attention and excitement that marginal and violent figures could count on producing.[5] Chief among these media are the genres associated with the mass press. These include the proliferating cheap broadsides as well as the press organs considered most respectable, the newspapers of record, and so forth; they also include other kinds of publications, including pamphlets and full-scale books, exhibiting the excesses of crime, sex, and violence in various kinds of detail. Categories such as "homosexuality" and "sadism," practices of commercial sex and of crime detection, as well as melodramatic narratives of fallen souls, were all brought to the popular consciousness through these more than any other mode of knowledge production and distribution. This book will consider the ways in which such genres represent an underexplored register of expertise that self-consciously competed with—just as it depended on and supported—other registers of liminal knowledge.

Further, as will be discussed below, there is the knowledge of the self, or the self-knowledge of the subject, not unconnected to these more disciplinary forms of knowing. As subjects came to recognize themselves within the abject categories decried and celebrated in this host of fin-de-siècle texts, they also used these identities as platforms for emancipation. That is why liberation movements such as the fractious women's movement, the struggles for the decriminalization of homosexuality, and the bourgeois enlightened movements against the promulgation of superstition about Jews and other strang-

---

5. Both the history and an interpretation of the sensation are offered in Joy Wiltenburg, "True Crime." The sociological literature on the moral panic, as discussed since the mid-1970s, offers a set of ways to interpret phenomena discussed in more than one chapter below. See esp. Cohen, *Folk Devils*.

ers in the midst of European civilization all belong to the discursive apparatus explored in this book. This is not to implicate all progressive discourse in the machinery of oppressive identity discourse any more than it is to take a stand on the question of whether or not identity science has ultimately served to marginalize or to liberate subjects relegated to beyond the horizon of the normal. To offer sight of the mutual reflections and common trajectory of these disparate and often conflicting elements is to begin to grasp a highly ramified and self-contradictory cultural project that has had a remarkably central place in Austria and Germany.

The rhetoric of borders is powerful and complex in many cultural traditions and has a particular intricacy in central Europe. Some of this surely has to do with the fact that the late nineteenth century was a period of border drawing (the unification of the German Empire, in particular) and contestation (to the south, the struggle for ethnic autonomy in the Habsburg Empire).[6] The frontiers of both central European empires enclosed ethnically mixed populations, a fact that was handled in very different ways in the north and the south. The German term *Grenze* contains a built-in ambivalence due to the way it connotes connection and association (as in the verb form *grenzen an*, to border on) as well as the manifest connotation of bounding off, delimiting, protecting (*begrenzen*). Hegel exploited this implicit ambivalence of the notion of the border as an illustration of a dialectical opposition governing the process of identification and its limits in the relationship of self and other.[7] In most of the instances examined here, the relationship of an implied centered, normative self—either the professional observer or a normative subject against which the deviant is measured—is more appropriately said to be in a dialectical than a diacritical relation to the "limit figure" or "other." In either case, the obsessive attention to limit figures would betray a self-reflection; but what seems to be consistent in each of the cases studied here is a powerful if conflicted identification with the marginal figures and scenes of violence captured by authoritative discourse, whether medical, juridical, journalistic, or investigative.

In light of what's been said so far, it is tempting to place this inquiry within the field of "modernity studies," but it is important to note that this book does not concern itself with the historical novelty of an experience of

6. The latter was the subject of Spector, *Prague Territories*.

7. In the *Phenomenology of Spirit*. Admittedly, this is Hegel filtered through Lacan and offered up by Žižek, *For They Know Not What They Do*, esp. 109–12. For a clear definition of the distinction between boundary and limit (*Grenze* and *Schranke*), see "limit, restriction and finitude" in Michael Inwood, ed., *A Hegel Dictionary* (Oxford: Blackwell, 1992).

modernity per se, nor does it take a position on the effects of changing material conditions of life on consciousness; the reflection of central European society on its own state of evolution, on the other hand, is a very important feature of the cases explored below. Cognates of "modernity" were less likely to signal this self-reflection than *Aufklärung* (Enlightenment), or references of various kinds to civilization. Decades later, just as German fascism was beginning to cast its shadow, Norbert Elias's "very simple discovery" would be that the whole notion of civilization is no more than an expression of "the self-consciousness of the West"—it is a diacritical concept that condemns the uncivilized periphery to beyond its borders in order to define itself.[8]

In the German-language context, the opposition between notions of "civilization" (technical, superficial, Western, modern) and "culture" (artistic, grounded, German, historical) made this concept complex in different ways, which Elias does much to outline. For our purposes, the distinction of *Kultur* and *Zivilisation* (which gains ground particularly during World War I) is less significant than that between civilization broadly understood— whether as "culture" or as "enlightenment"—and savagery, the wild and natural independence from the constraints of the civilized. To be sure, this figure could be identified with outsiders or with liminal members of society or in civilization's own savage past. Its remnants could live on in the unpredictable appearance of an atavism—the throwback, the return of a repressed unevolved (or pre-evolved) genetic refuse—living within modern society. Or it could persist in fragments within an individual consciousness, not so much awakened as emergent when waking life is interrupted by a "twilight condition" (*Dämmerzustand*), as the physicians would come to call a series of phenomena—"border states" (*Grenzzustand*) between volition and reflex, conscious and unconscious life. Somnambulism, epileptic seizure, amnesia, blackouts, and fits of rage are a few among many such states receiving special attention in this period. The culture's deep investment in such marginal states, as well as in the liminal figures sometimes subject to them, is one underexamined aspect of cultural history that emerges in the chapters that follow.

## Musil, on the Border

Robert Musil's unfinished master work of European modernism, *The Man without Qualities*, stands in a special position, but a problematic one, with regard to these questions. As a product of interwar Europe, it may be seen

8. Elias, *The Civilizing Process*, 5.

to have more to do with the environment of that period—a product of the senseless brutality of World War I, a harbinger of the radical violence of the coming regime that was implicit in the interwar ideologies—than of the fin de siècle. Yet, the setting of the novel is fin-de-siècle Vienna, and he is the first commentator to do the work this book sets out to do, namely, to read the deep structure of the fantasies of the period for themselves at the same time as our view of them is refracted by the moment of Germany's Weimar Republic and by what was to come after. *The Man without Qualities* is useful here, therefore, as a unique kind of source, primary and secondary at once; the storyteller-philosopher Musil seems to be, with fellow Austrians such as the misogynist psychologist-philosopher Otto Weininger and the master of detective science Hanns Gross, a paradigmatic figure of what is studied here, and yet he is also the one who sees most clearly what *Violent Sensations* is also trying to discern.

In chapter 4, we will have a chance to look closely at the character Musil names Moosbrugger, a serial murderer of prostitutes modeled half after the Austrian murderer Christian Voigt, whose atrocities were committed proximate to the time of the action of the novel, and half after the Weimar killer Fritz Haarmann, whose case unfolded as Musil was writing. Moosbrugger is not a main character of the novel, but as a figure in it—particularly in its first volume—he is central. Ulrich, the "man without qualities," comes to take on the murderer's cause, and other main characters are swept up in the fantasy that he should be pardoned or released, that Moosbrugger's insanity is an exaggerated sense of justice, or even "no more than a distortion of our own elements of being. Cracked and obscure it was; it somehow occurred to Ulrich that if mankind could dream as a whole, that dream would be Moosbrugger."[9]

The reason Musil's novel can serve a double function for this book is that these statements are intended to revivify a utopian and constructive fantasy that can now only be seen as decadent and destructive; at the same time, they diagnose the pathology of a culture that would conjure such dreams. Elsewhere, Musil described the fin de siècle as the "last great moment of hope" in central Europe, a moment of extraordinary promise that was merely masked by a "veneer of decadence."[10] Such promise, for Musil, is linked precisely to the openness, formlessness, or void left in rare periods of disorientation, ideological interregna.[11] It is hence not without recognition of the danger of

---

9. Robert Musil, *Man without Qualities* (hereafter *MwQ*), 76–77.

10. Robert Musil, "Der Deutsche Mensch als Symptom" [1923], in *Gesammelte Werke*, 1353.

11. The figure of the void is Patrizia McBride's; see McBride, *Void of Ethics: Robert Musil and the Experience of Modernity* (Evanson, Ill.: Northwestern UP 2006), 3–12. The cultural historian

a utopian fantasy of Moosbrugger's virtually messianic pathology and other such dreams that he revives the sense of promise in them that is lost once a certain amorphousness of an age "without qualities" hardens in the crucible of war into something else, where ethereal possibilities yield to brutal inexorabilities. And nonetheless, a hopeful civilization that dreams murder must, in spite of itself, be doomed.

Ulrich is not the character who is most affected by Moosbrugger in the novel in spite of his initial passion.[12] It is the passionate, Nietzschean soul Clarissa who falls deeper and deeper into an obsession with freeing Moosbrugger, with seeing him, and with all he represents; her visits to the mental asylum where he is interned bring Clarissa herself to the brink of madness. Indeed, the "borderline" condition is toyed with in the text in a late scene where she finds herself in the asylum in conversation with a group of psychiatric experts who are observing Moosbrugger in order to come to a determination of his degree of accountability for his own actions (the important category discussed in chap. 1 and thereafter as *Zurechnungsfähigkeit*, criminal responsibility). The patient clearly appears to be "half-mad," collapsing at least at particular moments into dementia or fits of paranoia, a "borderline personality" (*Grenzfall*). The more passionately Clarissa argues for the necessity of a determination of deficient responsibility, the more she begins to seem to the physicians (suddenly noting the "stigmata of heightened nervousness"—"but who doesn't display such stigmata nowadays!") a candidate for the asylum herself. When accused after an outburst of being insane, she self-righteously trumpets a demand for courage and action where it is not clear to whom and what it applies—her own insanity, the doctors' required action, or Moosbrugger's: "One has to have the courage for it, if the world is to be put right again! From time to time human beings must appear who do not go along with the lies!"[13]

In Musil's notes relating to this volume of the novel, we can see his investment in the figure of gruesome violence and its promise of overcoming an impossible present. In notes headed "All *Border-Crossings*" and qualified by "with violence—atrocity," we find telegraphic clues—"Unity of value,

---

who has been most engaged with Musil as a symptom of his context has been David S. Luft, most recently in Luft, *Eros and Inwardness*.

12. Moosbrugger is replaced by "another monster," in Stefan Jonsson's excellent reading, in the last volume of the novel: Ulrichs's sister Agathe, figured as a feminine twin of himself. Ulrich's incestuous relationship with Agathe provides the redemptive moment previously imagined in relation to Moosbrugger's "twilight state" of murderous rampage. See Jonsson, *Subject without Nation*, esp. 197–208.

13. Musil, *Der Mann ohne Eigenschaften* (hereafter *MoE*), 2:1369.

eventually through violence. . . . Redemption through violence"—and references traceable to the character of Clarissa— "The relationship to atrocity is oriented toward Nietzsche . . . first visit to asylum . . . Clarissa's pessimism . . . N[ietzsche]'s proposal: Is there a p[essimism] of the strong? . . . Is madness perhaps not necessary degeneration? That is the foundation of the transition to the attraction of madness"—and later, in a paragraph of its own, "Not to shy from violence."[14]

Here Musil seems certainly to be dancing on the border of concurrent interwar discourses justifying and ultimately celebrating violence.[15] At the same time, Musil's position is also one of critique, even if, as this brief discussion suggests, it is an ambivalently sympathetic one. A conclusion about the complicity of representations of violence with violent action is not necessary to embark on an exploration of them. *Violent Sensations* sets out from the assumption that there is something to be gained from setting aside the critical position that dismisses or else summarily condemns violent representations and instead takes them seriously, as Musil suggests, and explores how they operated culturally and historically.

## Historical Agendas

The current study locates itself within several developing collective scholarly projects. The most general of these is central European sociocultural and intellectual history, which has in the last years moved toward many of the questions and themes explored in these chapters: identity and social critique, modern subjectivity, and the relations of these to gender and sexuality. Yet it has been the primary sources referenced in the chapters below—the medical and juridical tracts, the newspaper scandals, the police and court records, the fiction and the high culture of the period, all circulating about these figures, stations, and fantasies—that truly shaped the analysis that follows. The collection of those sources began in earnest more than a dozen years ago, although the inspiration began some years before that, it the crossroads of very different kinds of texts: Musil's *Man without Qualities* and *Young Törless*, Otto Weininger's *Sex and Character*, and a draft paper presented in the standing history seminar at the Johns Hopkins University on a particular sensational exposé of child prostitution in Victorian London, which the *Pall Mall*

---

14. Cf. *MoE*, 1:196, and Musil, *Der literarische Nachlass*, 1:128.

15. Such as those discussed by Dominick LaCapra, "Toward a Critique of Violence," in LaCapra, *History and Its Limits*, 90–122. More on this below.

*Gazette* editor William Stead would title "The Maiden Tribute of Modern Babylon." That paper was of course to become one of the central chapters of Judith Walkowitz's *City of Dreadful Delight*.[16] Walkowitz's marvelous work of history is so grounded in the contexts of a social field rife with conflict among "new social actors" and facing new political challenges that its nod toward literary theory is easily overlooked, but at that table the historian was asked to provide a definition of the foreign term *discourse* and to justify the importation of a critical concept from literary theory (which she, unflappable, accomplished with spontaneous alacrity). The engagement with texts that follows differs in method and style from that of *City of Dreadful Delight*, and its attention to social space is understated in comparison; but Weininger and Musil took on new dimensions in light of this innovation of sociocultural history. Around the same time, "new historicist" and cultural studies proponents (generally found in academic departments of literature) began to offer nuanced "literary" readings of historical material, including nonliterary texts, episodes, and so on. Their reach into the historical record was highly selective, and it is difficult to maintain a rigor of interpretive practice and at the same time cover vast reaches of cultural practice. But all of these methodological precursors have informed the present work.

It is the nature of a wide-reaching study that it treads on fields to which others dedicate their entire books or whole careers. Such is certainly the case for fields with substantial bibliographies, such as the histories of psychiatry, criminology, sexuality, and so on, but it is also the case for smaller topics, such as the social phenomena of sexual murder or the blood libel. In each of these cases, the history told here might not be the one sought by specialists in each area. Those bibliographies have nonetheless been useful to the very different purposes these historical objects are put to in this book, but it will make more sense to refer to them as the chapters unfold than to do justice to them at the outset.

Innumerable studies in central European cultural history informed the agenda below in different ways, but one particular problem in the overall shape of that body of work helped powerfully to shape it. There seems to be a gulf between a historiographical image of either "decadence" or a turn-of-the-century disengaged aestheticism, on the one hand (Vienna 1900 is an important component of this image), and, on the other hand, an interwar scene of explicit violence and frank sexuality (typified by the image of Weimar Berlin). In spite of the widespread reception of Klaus Theweleit's pathbreaking study

16. Walkowitz, *City of Dreadful Delight*.

of the violent imaginary of the Weimar Republic era, *Male Fantasies*, the history of the fin-de-siècle roots of this paradigm remains unwritten.[17] In fact, although *Male Fantasies* was also a primary inspiration for the study of the fin-de-siècle sources discussed below, it has generally, and ironically, served to deflect attention from these texts of the nineteenth and early twentieth centuries and to lure the gaze of cultural historians to the violent spectacle of World War I.[18] Central Europeans marched into that war—so the cliché goes—naively, optimistically, driven by a "war enthusiasm" that took for granted easy victory and never anticipated apocalyptic violence.[19] The bloody outcome of the war *produced* the violent fantasies (sexualized, to be sure, we learn from Theweleit's presentation of radical-right "free corps" paramilitary fantasies of the 1920s), and these partially latent fantasies would be ready to bubble to the surface once again as the "crisis" of the Weimar Republic reached a head.[20]

But what do we do with this causal trajectory if the fantasies of apocalyptic, redemptive violence latent in the self are littered all about the decades preceding the Great War? What if these fantasies can be shown to be other than peripheral, excessive exercises of the "decadent" imaginary of restless aesthetes, but instead are central to the positive agendas of people we do not picture in smoky cafés thinking of ways to shock a public beset with ennui? These might include enlightened reformers, scientists, or marginalized groups fighting for rights of citizenship—and they might include the likes of Musil as well as Weininger. In other words, what if the War would have to be seen not as a cause but as a symptom—or even an effect of this violent cultural imaginary?

A central question to come out of the research into the ever-repeating association of liminal figures with fantasies of violence was the conceptualization of the self emerging in new form in the nineteenth century, and a key

17. Theweleit, *Männerphantasien*.

18. In this sense, the war can be seen as a temporal as well as an imperial boundary within the historiography: on one side is an aestheticist and erotic "garden," see Schorske, *Fin-de-Siècle Vienna* and on the other side is the ominously political violent sexual imaginary of interwar Berlin, as in the work of Theweleit or Maria Tatar. A recent example of this latter position that is bound to become a classic is Anton Kaes, *Shell Shock Cinema: Weimar Culture and the Wounds of War* (Princeton, NJ: Princeton University Press, 2011).

19. This historiographical cliché (or myth, as the author calls it) is dispatched by Verhey, *Spirit of 1914*.

20. One historian who has richly demonstrated the transformation of fin-de-siècle tropes of violence in the interwar period, chiefly in France, has been Carolyn Dean. Dean acknowledges that the interwar representations were actual innovations of the fin de siècle but that they are transformed by the experience of World War I. This is discussed in chap. 4.

place to locate this process is in the fields of the history of sexuality and of criminality. Michel Foucault's contributions have clearly been of immeasurable influence on both. His last major work, *History of Sexuality*, insisted on the connections between sexual subjectivity or self-understanding, emancipation movements, and potentially oppressive authoritative medical and juridical discourses, but its actual analysis focused almost exclusively on the last of these sets.[21] Many authors have written on some aspect of "medico-moral discourse," but Foucault's provocative suggestion about the connection of these to sexual subjectivity has not been worked through empirically.[22] The crucial German contribution to the specific science of sexology is well known, although a comprehensive survey of this science field and its relation to society is yet to be written in any language.[23] A systematic study of the centrality of this complex of sexuality and violence to the cultural imagination of this place and time has not been undertaken. Further, work in this area tends to focus either on popular discourses or on canonical artistic and literary representations. By setting popular sensations against scientific, political, and philosophical discourses, *Violent Sensations* makes it possible to regard some of the puzzling obsessions of the late nineteenth and early twentieth centuries differently and to consider the ways in which this complex apparatus functioned as a cultural project or as a self-critical discourse on and of modernity.

Dominick LaCapra, in much recent work, and most pointedly in his book *History and Its Limits*, has offered several perspectives on some of the ques-

---

21. Foucault, *History of Sexuality*, individually published as *The Will to Knowledge* (or, in the American edition, *The History of Sexuality I: An Introduction*), *The Use of Pleasure*, and *The Care of the Self* between 1976 and 1984. Interestingly, the problem of sexual subjectivity is approached in the latter two volumes, focusing on Greek and Roman antiquity; the operation of a sexual subjectivity as part of the uniquely modern apparatus of "sexuality" is suggested in the first volume but not demonstrated. The specific political context of the first volume is one possible ground for this omission and for the greater emphasis on "disciplinary discourse." The grounds for an ethical objection to a particular investigation of subjectivity is suggested in Foucault's influential edited volume on the killer Pierre Rivière, consisting of a series of archival documents on the medico-juridical pathologization of the accused along with a remarkable narrative by the subject himself. In the preface, Foucault explains that the research team deliberately decided not to interpret the ego document so as not to reproduce the disciplinary gesture of all the expert discourse in the rest of the dossier. See Foucault, *I, Pierre Rivière*, xiii.

22. See, e.g., Mort, *Dangerous Sexualities*. For an attempt to focus on the previously underemphasized implications of Foucault's late work, see Spector, Puff, and Herzog, eds., *After the History of Sexuality*.

23. An attempt at such a survey has recently been made, and it is not surprising that this, too, emerged in the German cultural field by sexologist Volkmar Sigusch. See Sigusch and Grau, *Geschichte der Sexualwissenschaft*.

tions tackled here. He is acutely aware, first of all, of the problem of what in contemporary psychoanalytic language is called the jouissance connected to such experience and the reproduction of it of culture-historical work—the problem, as he puts it, of working through these connections without repeating them compulsively and unproductively.[24] He has also been invested in the critique of any position validating this surplus, this pleasure or jouissance in the liminal, amounting to a kind of rationalization of sensation and ultimately of violence.[25] The focus in the present cultural history is somewhat different in that it is not expressly on the high cultural texts complicit in this "liminal logic" but in the historical connections between those high cultural discourses (philosophical or critical, aesthetic or literary, scientific and social scientific) and theorizations of the subject taking place "on the ground." These "ground-level theorizations" include practices of police, activists, murderers, and "ordinary people," such as they were, who were having or seeking or avoiding sex, engaging in, reproducing, or attempting to quell cultural fantasies of excess associated with figures designated as liminal. To recover this saturated historical moment is to grasp the complicity of each strand with the others—it is not possible, in other words, to "take the side" of rational Enlightenment and to expurgate its perilous dalliances with its own apocalyptic other. To tell this history, even carefully, is to awaken the beast. But there is a difference, as LaCapra suggests, following Freud, between an implicitly destructive repetition compulsion (acting out) and an engagement that is analytical and critical (working through). One can only hope to remain vigilant enough to maintain analytic precision in the face of the seductive spectacle of the fantasies of sensational violence that follow.

24. LaCapra, *History and Its Limits*, esp. 1–12.
25. Especially in "Toward a Critique of Violence," in ibid., 90–122.

# 1

# Dark City, Bright Future: Utopian and Dystopian Urban Genres around 1900

Whether, how, or when modern metropolitan life became radically different from all forms of life that came before are questions that are impossible to answer. The far more interesting and puzzling question, and the genuinely historical question that these ponderings mask, is how this way of thinking itself emerged and what functions it served. If the presupposition of the utter novelty, unprecedented hope, and implicit and dire danger of the contemporary urban world was at least to a degree illusory, its effects were real and remarkable. The cultural innovation responding to this thesis was immense in German-speaking central Europe as well as elsewhere, ranging from innovation in the visual arts and architecture to literary genres, new branches of learning, disciplinary institutions, and areas of scientific research.

Even a strict definition of the fin de siècle as the short period from the early 1890s to about 1905 hardly helps restrict the number of representations and practices that can be seen as central to this inquiry; points of focus need to be identified. One of these is the figure of the modern city or "metropolis" (*Großstadt*), which was at the center of this thinking about the unprecedented character of the experience of modernity. The self-affirming confidence in civilization and progress on the one hand and fear and anxiety about decay, illness, and danger on the other both found validation in the big city. A cultural imaginary of the threat and promise (or darkness and light) of the "new" metropolis posited a set of oppositional relations—town and country, civilization and nature, and many more—that concealed as much as it revealed. The figure of crime developed in such close proximity to that of the city that the two seemed at times to be artlessly affiliated with one another;

sustained, controversial reflection on the nature of the criminal mirrored the dark and light shadings of the urban picture.[1]

A toolbox useful for an analysis of these disparate things would attend to several different figures that often seem to drive the most innovative moments of what must be seen as a revolutionary cultural production. The figures guiding our inquiry include the following: *location*, the mapping of crime within the city, the search for origins; further, linked to the notion of location, *identification* and the problem of identity; on the rhetorical level we attend to the recurrence of *irony*, paradox, or the unity of opposites; *genre*, the production of novel forms to respond to what seem to be novel conditions; and *procedure*, an attention to method and system as well as an impulse to abandon previously conventional procedures.

## Paradox Metropolis

The opposition of darkness and clarity is powerfully at work in Hans Ostwald's 1904 book, *Dark Corners of Berlin*, but it paints those dark corners in color. "One of the darkest corners of Berlin, by the Oranienburg Gate, has the brightest illumination, the most colorful action."[2] The insight that "dark deeds do not always shy from the light" is all the more reason to bathe the streets in them, as he hopes his books will do. "Our modern science," Ostwald ventures, "our modern outlook has so thrived, that we may now be permitted confidently to open our eyes to things that until now have been taboo."[3] Part of the contradiction that the fascination with the "dark city" contained has to do with the Enlightenment confidence in the success of a modernity of knowledge and outlook, so that things too awful to have been looked at earlier may now be coolly regarded. This book (fig. 1) was the first of a set of what would be fifty-one studies called the "Documents of the metropolis" (*Großstadt-Dokumente*), intended, according to Ostwald, the founder and editor of the series, to "shed light" on these dark quarters and provide a "pathfinder through the labyrinth of the metropolis," where various experts would lead the curious reader through the chaos of the modern great city. But this previously unspeakable chaos—the world of prostitution and pandering,

---

1. Cf. Williams, *Country and the City*; see esp. "Cities of Darkness and of Light" and "The Figure in the City," 215–47. Another important source is Schivelbusch, *Disenchanted Night*, esp. 81–134.

2. Hans Ostwald, *Dunkle Winkel in Berlin*. Großstadt-Dokumente 1 (Berlin: Seemann, 1904), 31. All translations are mine unless otherwise stated.

3. Ostwald, *Dunkle Winkel*, "Vorwort," [4].

FIGURE 1. Cover of the first book in the *Großstadt-Dokumente* series, Ostwald's *Dunkle Winkel in Berlin*. The *Jugendstil* cover design is by poster artist Paul Haase.

perversion and gender disorder, gambling, lewd diversions, bohemianism
and crime—seemed not only enabled but produced by the "dark corners"
of the great cities in which they were found. The taboo was not an ancient
prohibition against speaking of eternal unspeakables but a ban on naming
the other half of civilization, just as much a product of modern culture as was
science and art. As another author in the series would have it, "Rome was not
built in a day, and Berlin did not become the metropolis it is overnight."[4] If
Paris was the City of Light of the nineteenth century, world consensus held
that no nights were as enticing as Berlin's. Beyond comparisons to Paris and
London that were common in such texts, this author recalled ancient Rome,
and all other capitals of humanity as such, which were also overcome with the
"rapture of sensuality" of Berlin at the moment that they shone most brightly
as beacons of world culture.[5] If the modern metropolis was the apogee of
civilization, it was also the site of world-historically novel horrors.

There is nothing unfamiliar about the cohabitation of pride in the progress of civilization and simultaneous elaborately staged disgust (perhaps
paired with a vicarious thrill) for the urban underworld. In Wilhelmine Germany and late Habsburg Austria—the period in central Europe contemporary with the age the Anglo-American world called "Victorian"—the positions were stereotypes of a kind and were certainly not seen as contradictory.
Yet it might be worthwhile to recover and interrogate the strangeness of what
is arguably a paradox: the optimistic claim that our civilization has advanced
to the point that it is now equipped to face its own degenerate state. The efflorescence of images and texts attesting to the decay of the age embodied in
the modern city was accompanied by an array of other genres, instruments,
disciplines, and institutions confident in modernity's ability to heal these
wounds of its own making.[6] The intimate but complicated relation between
these impulses may bear meaning that could not be discerned by rending
them from one another or by dismissing them. The same could be said of the
implicit sensationalism of Ostwald's ostensibly scientific impulse to appre-
hend the seedy underbelly of urban life.

What emerges from an analysis of the cultural operation of prurient practices of urban narrative if one wants to take them seriously and as something

4. Satyr [Richard Dietrich], *Lebeweltnächte der Friedrichstadt*, Großstadt-Dokumente 30
(Berlin: Seemann, 1906), 7.

5. Satyr, *Lebeweltnächte*, 7–8.

6. A subset of the voluminous scholarly literature on discourses on the city attends to the
gender dimensions of these discourses, the imaginary that identified as feminine the city of mystery, sexuality, and crime as against masculinist fantasies of scientific mastery. See, e.g., Ankum,
*Women in the Metropolis*, and Felski, *Gender of Modernity*.

more than symptoms of a pathologically patriarchal culture? What positive
work could these texts and practices be doing, or can they be seen as nothing
other than novel forms of normative policing mechanisms and instruments
of marginalization? In focusing on the function of these manifestations as
social control, there is the risk that they may be read as reductively as it seems
on first glance the city itself was read in these texts. The interpretation that
these texts were chiefly means of stigmatizing "others," for instance, ironically leads to little more than reiteration of the same coarse stigmatization of
the texts and their authors.

One of the biggest methodological problems associated with unpacking
the complexity of this system of texts on crime, sexuality, and the metropolis
is the difficulty of analyzing such texts without simply recasting them. It is
thus surprisingly awkward to begin a chapter on the discourse of the big city
in central Europe without talking about the material changes of the last third
of the nineteenth century that turned such cities as Berlin, Hamburg, Vienna,
and Budapest into metropoles: the urbanization of national populations, the
growth of the big cities, electrification and the revolutions of communication
and transport, the explosion of newspaper media, and so forth. Histories of
the discourse on the big city seem structurally bound to reproduce it: life really *was* different, rather suddenly, from the way life was experienced by all
generations that came before.[7]

The most-cited text from the period in any such discussion must be the
Berlin sociologist Georg Simmel's dense lecture "The Metropolis and Mental Life."[8] Simmel certainly and brilliantly argued that modern urban life
was quintessentially different from the forms of life that had preceded it, and
his essay is full of quotable phrases that seem to confirm a chain of causation: radically new material conditions produced the metropolis and with it
a novel form of life in which unique sensory experiences have unprecedented
effects on subjects. Memorably, "the psychological foundation of the metro-

---

7. For a critique of the academic use of the category of modernity, see Cooper, *Colonialism
in Question*, 113–52. A list of academic works on discourses of modernity that begin with a list
of material changes driving the discourse would be embarrassingly long. An unusual but telling case is Detlev Peukert's brilliant work on the Weimar Republic (Peukert, *Weimar Republic*),
where the self-possession of German interwar society by a discourse of modernity is the subject
of the ingenious essay, and yet the author is compelled to include three short pages densely
cataloging such changes (see pp. 81–5).

8. The lecture was delivered in Dresden on the occasion of an exhibition on the metropolis,
and the text was somewhat refined and expanded for publication as "Die Großstädte und das
Geistesleben," in Bücher, *Die Großstadt*, 185–206. Translations here adapted from Wolff, *Sociology of Georg Simmel*, 409–24.

politan type of individuality consists in the *intensification of nervous stimulation* which results from the swift and uninterrupted change of outer and inner stimuli."[9] But to draw this chain of causation from the lecture does violence to its rhetorical power and effects.[10] The essay has been called non-sociological or at least "nonsystematic" by latter-day sociologists because of its refusal to make methodological claims and apparent inconsistencies of its argument.[11] The dichotomy at its core is modern metropolitan life against what is named at one point as town or agrarian life (lumped together). Yet the binary categories are unstable, shifting among ancient and modern cities, premetropolitan great cities, the state of nature, and so on, and the qualities of the metropolis (from division of labor to facile communication) are often more broadly modern, shared by inhabitants of many places beyond the relatively few great cities designated as *Großstädte*.[12] The city is both cause and effect in the essay; it was product and producer, a creation of modern civilization and the source of pressure causing the persons in it to change. This circularity, with the modern subject rather than the city at its center, takes precedence over the causal or linear argument that seems to be made at various points. While the English translator converted the text into an essay format organized in paragraphs, the original text appears as a series of theses or aphorisms, chains of clauses separated by semicolons or dashes. It has probably been argued that the lecture performs the overstimulated and distracted intellectualism it describes as the condition of the modern urban subject. Such a diagnosis was surely not beyond Simmel's own insight and intentions. In spite of this self-reflexivity and irony, the author still acts on the same "basic motive" of the individual agreed on by Marx and Nietzsche, and that is the "resistance of the subject to be leveled down and used up within a socio-technical mechanism."[13]

---

9. Bücher, "*Die Großstadt*," 3; Wolff, *Sociology of Georg Simmel*, 409–10.

10. An example of this reification of the material foundation of the city in Simmel is in Rémy, *Georg Simmel*, esp. Rémy's introduction, 7–15, and Stéphane Jonas, "La 'Groszstadt' Métropole européenne, dans la sociologie des père fondateurs allemands" and "La métropolisation de la société dans l'oeuvre de Georg Simmel," 19–36, 51–60.

11. Heinrich Rickert defended this nonsystematicity in Rickert, *Die Philosophie des Lebens*, 26. Cf. Jazbinsek, "Metropolis and the Mental Life of Georg Simmel, 104–6.

12. This whole aspect of the essay is a clear reference to Tönnies's binary of community and society; see Tönnies, *Gemeinschaft und Gesellschaft*. The term *Großstadt* was formally defined as any conglomeration of at least 100,000 people, yet the translation "metropolis" is more appropriate for the use to which Simmel and Ostwald, among many other contemporaries, were using the term.

13. Simmel, "Die Großstädte," 185.

Simmel's great urban paradoxes have been described with the trope of *coincidentia oppositorum* (coterminosity of opposites), a notion rescued by psychoanalysis from medieval theology and philosophy.[14] For Simmel, the city is the place where the great post-Enlightenment conflict between universality and individualism becomes both extreme and manifest; the metropolis itself is, at once, its material manifestation, the conglomeration of subjects of a novel type, and the creation of a new kind of subject confected out of conflicting and cohabiting impulses toward individuation and massification.

We may see in Simmel a proleptic revision of Michel de Certeau, who considered the opposing kinds of vision and experience embodied in the "city," one represented by the objective, abstracting, scientific, mapping gaze from above, as it were, and the other by the rich and uneven texture of the city as experienced on the street.[15] The "concept-city," the theoretical creation visualized (through the mathematically driven Renaissance perspective) even before it could technically be seen, is not only a different place but a different kind of place from the walked city ruled by irregularity, texture, and diversity. These seem to constitute not only distinct but arguably opposed kinds of knowledge. Our reading of Simmel's metropolis troubles this opposition by raising a different question: What if these two are fully conscious of each other in the period under study—what if the concept-city and the street-level experience, the planned and the "dark" city, are of a piece?

## The Generic City: Writing the Großstadt

One of the problems with strictly segregating positive and negative assessments of the turn-of-the-century metropolis is that the urban underworld is picturesque. Representing the metropolis without criminals, prostitutes, and perverts is rather like imagining the countryside without landscape. Such was the dilemma of a weekly gazette in Berlin, *The Illustrated Weekly Review of Berlin Life* (*Illustrirte Wochenrundschau über das Berliner Leben*), which committed itself to a positive image of the burgeoning life of the new capital. In its third issue it ran an article by a certain A. von Zerbst on criminals in the city that argued more confidently than coherently about the perception of crime in the city.[16] First, Zerbst argued that crime was actually not increas-

14. Jazbinsek uses "conincidentia oppositorium [*sic*]"; Jazbinsek, "Metropolis and the Mental Life of Georg Simmel," 106.

15. Certeau, *Practice of Everyday Life*, , esp. 91–114.

16. A. v. Zerbst, "Berliner Verbrecher," *Illustrirte Wochenrundschau über das Berliner Leben* 1, no. 3 (1894): 20–22.

ing as much as it seemed because the apparent rise was proportionate to the booming population. Second, a scholar was quoted to demonstrate how natural economic cycles prove that increasing criminality is actually a result of the financial boom of the founding of a unified Germany (hence, crime is a sign of success). And finally, the author turned to a lengthy description of a proliferating new popular genre: the "backstairs novel," penny fictions of a sensational nature, "teeming with crimes of the most insane, ingenious, gruesome kind," often serialized and hand-delivered to subscribers. The editor chimed in with a tsk-tsk to signal his disapproval of the profit motives of unscrupulous authors and publishers whose work was clearly linked to the appearance of the very such crimes in the city as they depicted: "the fantasy is aroused." Zerbst leapt from representation to fantasy to social reality as effortlessly as he concealed his own place among the new sensational genres he described.

The proliferation of sensationalist texts on the city's shadow side was widely acknowledged, often in ways (as in the Zerbst article) that reproduced the prurient interest it reported. The tendency can be seen everywhere, from pulp fiction to criminal newspapers, from police circulars to the mainstream press. Newspapers of record engaged in sensational practice merely more subtly than more popular organs, where headlines such as "Murder? A Mysterious Incident in Darkest Berlin" echoed criminal fiction (fig. 2).[17] The article actually offered a diagrammatic map of the urban district in question to guide its readers through this particular dark corner. The underworld depicted in these texts was rich and diverse, chaotically random in its potential violence and yet meticulously stratified and ordered. It was, as Zerbst implied in his exposé on Berlin criminals, a reflection of the modern metropolis itself, even a realm of unparalleled human endeavor and productivity: "All criminals work on the artful expansion of their system, which is so interesting and dangerous to the public precisely because of the way no single criminal of a particular species can achieve the goal but must count on the support of several accomplices."[18] A report from a later issue of the same illustrated paper offered a tour of Berlin's various penal institutions and their inhabitants. The social system within the walls of these penitentiaries was reminiscent of the

17. The reporter dramatically described the pimps and prostitutes involved in the case as "dangerous perpetrators" who "have so often played the principal roles in Berlin murder trials." *Berliner Morgenpost* no. 242 (October 16, 1900); the case file including this clipping is in the Landesarchiv, formerly BBLHA, rep 30 bln c tit 198B no. 37, p. 242.

18. Zerbst, "Berliner Verbrecher," 20–22.

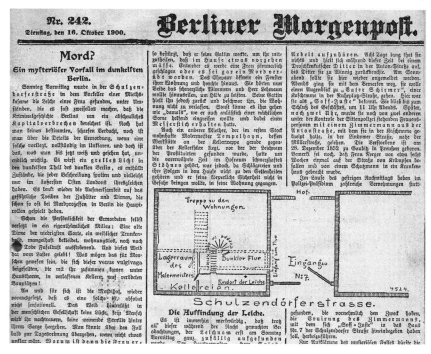

FIGURE 2. *Berliner Morgenpost* story of murder "in darkest Berlin" with diagram of the crime scene.

hierarchies of the city of millions: every social station is represented, with delegates of each punished for crimes specific to its function.[19] Hence, post and court officials are interned for embezzlement, teachers for lewdness or disciplinary excesses, merchants for swindles, down to the maiming butchers, gambling bakers, thieving servants, and finally waiters with the host of crimes suggested by their intercourse with the public. The tour of the prisons was not atypical of voyeuristic texts on the city's shadow side that displayed an unknown world no more than it exposed the barely concealed essence of the known one: a corruption of official and economic life, an abusive educational system, a meanness, lasciviousness, and greed that characterized the world readers knew as much as that which was beyond their sight.

The point has often been made that depictions of the criminal underworld in this period provided a mirror image of bourgeois society just as the staple image of the professional crook was an inverse image of the respect-

19. A. v. Zerbst, "Ein Blick in die Berliner Gefängnisse," *Illustrirte Wochenrundschau über das Berliner Leben* [1], no. 6 (1894): 43–44.

able burgher.[20] This narrative structure is clearly at work, and it seems just as clear that authors and readers at the time were aware of it. This observation, however, does not justify a reduction of the significance of these texts to moral lessons produced by a disciplinary authority for the purpose of shaping an obedient or productive citizenry. How readers' processes of identification and disidentification might have operated and what motivated these repetitive yet complex fantasies are valuable questions that do not make for conveniently simple answers; they demand closer readings of a wide range of cultural products, beginning with the new genres of metropolis literature.[21]

One of the most expansive novel venues of the sensational exposure of the urban underworld is the series of studies edited by Hans Ostwald with which this chapter began.[22] Ostwald, an autodidact from the working classes, a vagabond artisan turned journalist, conceptualized a series of studies that would bring this unseen, taboo world to light.[23] In the fifty-one volumes of the *Großstadt-Dokumente* initially published between 1904 and 1908, insider-experts offered their curious audience views chiefly of Berlin and Vienna that were at once intimate and scientific. The official position of the series with regard to the moral balance of the modern city was ambivalence:

> The last decades have created those imposing conglomerations of men that we name "metropolis." Even those who recognize and despise her abhorrent faults will not be able to deny it a certain cultural value. And whoever treasures her cultural value will not be able to overlook her faults.[24]

The topics of the first ten volumes, all published by 1905, included Ostwald's inaugural pamphlet on Berlin's dark corners quoted above followed by theater adviser and critic Julius Bab's study of the life of Berlin bohemians. Next came sexologist Magnus Hirschfeld's pathbreaking ethnography of

20. See, e.g., Evans, *Tales from the German Underworld*, and Becker, *Verderbnis und Entartung*, esp. 177–248.

21. The literary genres of crime and detective fiction, penny dreadfuls, and so on are intimately connected with those that follow here and have been discussed elsewhere at length. For a bibliography of the classic standard literature up to 1978, see, e.g., Hügel, *Untersuchungsrichter, Diebsfänger, Detektive*, 340–53. An excellent recent treatment of the connection between genre and its impact on literature is Herzog, "Crime Stories," 34–61.

22. Portions of this chapter appeared in German as Scott Spector, "Die Großstadt schreiben: Zur literarischen Unterwelt der Städte um 1900," in *Kriminalliteratur und Wissensgeschichte: Genres—Techniken—Medien*, ed. C. Peck and F. Sedlmeier, 115–27 (Bielefeld: Transcript, 2015).

23. See Peter Fritzsche, "Vagabond in the Fugitive City: Hans Ostwald, Imperial Berlin and the Grossstadt-Dokumente," *Journal of Contemporary History* 29, no. 3 (1994): 385–402, and Thies, *Ethnograph des dunklen Berlin*.

24. Ostwald, *Dunkle Winkel*, "Vorwort," [3].

Berlin's "third sex," same-gender-loving men. Then came separate studies of dance locales and procurers, both by Ostwald, with further studies of religious sects, coffee houses, banks, underground anarchism, and sport. A set of Vienna volumes followed, also covering topics on the underworld of the glittering bourgeois city, especially crime and sexuality, as well as the varied experience of the higher classes. This alternation emphasizes a tension present in many of the self-descriptions of the new central European *Großstädte*, where the peculiar character of the individual cities was at odds with the generic character of the big city as such. Berlin was hence a unique product of its history and particular stock characters just as it was fast coming to resemble the quintessential *Großstadt* London; Vienna was stuck in its more traditional hierarchies just as it was becoming a new Berlin. Volume 20, a 1906 report on lesbian life in Berlin, was subject to censorship leading to a court case, ultimately to be replaced with a volume on Berlin educators; Ostwald and his publisher seem otherwise to have been relatively cautious about avoiding trouble with the state even as they forged new ground in the interest of finding best sellers.[25] Between 1905 and 1907, Ostwald also put out a series of ten volumes—planned as twenty—on prostitution in Berlin that were stylistically similar if not quite identical to the *Großstadt-Dokumente*.[26]

Ostwald wandered into the series (or into a position to market it to an editor) after having received critical acclaim and popular success through an "autobiographical novel" titled *Vagabonds*, depicting his life as a transient laborer.[27] Published in 1900, the work was written in a colorful and readable style and was of interest in part for its ethnographic representation of a society of homeless and poor, a world with its own customs of communication and interaction and of course its own modes of subsistence. He was hence in the role of an observer-participant, both inside and outside of the exotic world he depicted.[28] The volumes of the series were explicitly not to belong to *belles-lettres*, but would be a mixed genre: no work of art could "master the violent material," and "some things would always remain unanswered," so he came to the idea of presenting short and concise representations of the material while not eschewing the artistic altogether.[29] At times he seemed to wish only to report the "raw material" of the urban underworld, leaving

---

25. Thies, *Ethnograph des dunklen Berlin*, 129–31.

26. Titled *Das Berliner Dirnentum*.

27. Klaus Bergmann, introduction to Ostwald, *Vagabunden*, 5–33.

28. For the topic of the metropolis, he may also be thought of in a mixed role of outsider and insider, having been raised in the working-class north of Berlin and then moved for a critical period of youth to a country town in Mecklenburg, West Pomerania.

29. Ostwald, *Dunkle Winkel*, "Vorwort," [3].

actual scholarly analysis to the more formally trained. That raw material was hardly so raw, of course—the first volume consisted of episodes constituted by different dark corners of the city where supposedly overheard conversations (in a stylized, comprehensible version of Berlin dialect, or in one case Yiddish) became literary vignettes of homelessness, crime, prostitution, and pandering. On the other hand, as a group this collection of texts provided the most complete ethnographic work on the city in this period. It was part of a tradition that can be traced back much further, but it advanced the genre not only in scope and in volume but in depth. A reading of any of these slim volumes today is guaranteed to emphasize the comically prurient and patriarchal registers of the texts that are everywhere apparent. But this, after all, is what was conventional about the books, what makes them recognizable as part of a genre developing over the nineteenth century and since at least the century previous.[30] The work of the publicists involved in the series more closely resembles later texts of cultural anthropology and urban sociology on account of the insider status of the observers (Julius Bab, Magnus Hirschfeld, and others) as well as the use of reports from the street, overheard conversations, extensive quotations of interviewed subjects or correspondents, and other first-person digests. The sometimes montage-like effect of this fragmentary material presented alongside other texts, from newspaper clippings to calling cards, seems to have belonged to a unique if unarticulated methodology poised between naturalist literature, journalist reportage, and urban ethnography. The very notion of the *Documents* was to document—to claim to present the material in the raw, as in the introduction to one of the volumes, a memoir of a migrant laborer and convict, where Ostwald "deliberately refrain[ed]" from analysis, leaving it to experts and antagonists to "extract the pulp from the rind."[31] The volumes vary widely in this regard, and even where Ostwald himself was the author, he did not generally shy from moralizing or from positing typologies. His review of male prostitution in Berlin included transcripts of seven blackmail letters of homosexual prostitutes followed by a brief characterology of the "most common types of male prostitutes: the intelligent and energetic, the tenderly self-offering, the con-

---

30. Most discussed have been the studies of London, notably Mayhew, *London Labour*; Mearns, *Bitter Cry*; Charles Booth, *Life and Labour of the People in London* (London: Macmillan, 1889–97); William Booth, *In Darkest England and the Way Out* (New York: Funk and Wagnalls, 1890). Gareth Stedman Jones, *Outcast London: A Study in the Relationship between Classes in Victorian Society* (Oxford: Clarendon, 1971); Williams, *Country and the City*, 221–22; Walkowitz, *City of Dreadful Delight*, 24–39.

31. Ostwald in Schuchardt, *Sechs Monate Arbeitshaus*, translated in Jazbinsek, "Metropolis and the Mental Life of Georg Simmel," 116.

stantly homeless one, who only threatens and threatens, the position seeker, the cautious . . . and the one who works with an accomplice."[32] No one could disagree with Peter Fritzsche's insight that the "fragmentary," "provisional," "carnivalesque," "kaleidoscopic," and "fugitive" character of Ostwald's metropolis made it a quintessentially modernist production.[33] The representations of the city in the series nonetheless constantly returned to systems of classification: the functional stratification of Berlin cafés, the characterological types of prostitutes under the regulatory surveillance of the Berlin police on the basis of their life trajectories, the real-life encounter of the needy with Vienna's charitable organizations, the fourteen types of girls and women of Vienna, or the ethnic and national makeup of criminal specialization in that imperial capital.[34] The texts' impulse toward systematicity and their sympathy with the multiplicity and individuality of the lived experience of the city may seem to be at odds with one another (put differently, they strike a reader today as neither rigorous nor sympathetic). Both impulses are nonetheless as central to the project as is their common feuilletonistic style.[35]

Little research had been conducted on Ostwald until recently, but some scholars have now suggested that the *Großstadt-Dokumente* project was kin to if not a direct precursor of the Chicago School of urban sociology. Wirth acknowledged it specifically in his "Bibliography of the Urban Community," even if its direct impact on the Chicago School is hard to reckon.[36]

32. The letters were provided by series contributor Magnus Hirschfeld of the Scientific-Humanitarian Committee (for decriminalization of homosexuality). Hans Ostwald, *Männliche Prostitution, Das Berliner Dirnentum*, vol. 5 (Leipzig: Spohr, 1906), repr. Ostwald, *Männliche Prostitution im kaiserlichen Berlin*, 55.

33. Fritzsche, "Vagabond," 385, 391, 394–95, 397–98.

34. Ostwald, *Großstadt-Dokumente* (hereafter GD), vol. 7; Wilhelm Hammer, *Zehn Lebensläufe Berliner Kontrollmädchen und zehn Beiträge zur Behandlung der geschechtlichen Frage*, GD 23; Max Winter, *Das goldene Wiener Herz*, GD 11; Alfred Deusch-German, *Wiener Mädel*, GD 17; Emil Bader, *Wiener Verbrecher*, GD 16.

35. An interesting parallel could be made to a competing series published by the Pan-Verlag and edited by Hans Landsberg, also beginning in 1904 under the title *Moderne Zeitfragen* (Questions of modern times). Like Ostwald's series, the ten or so volumes of this series explored a canonical curriculum of topics concerning the modern world, including urban engineering, penal law, education and church, prostitution, unions, the proletariat, perversion, fashion, sex, and gender. While some of these were written by leading thinkers in their fields and were important, the series did not possess the same unity of project, from methodology to tone, that is found in the *Großstadt-Dokumente*, although it may be seen as a symptom of a similarly synthetic impulse.

36. See Louis Wirth, *A Bibliography of the Urban Community*, University of Chicago Studies in Urban Sociology, vol. 1 (Chicago: University of Chicago Press, 1925). Fritzsche suggests this kinship is greater than that to the more distant and patronizing treatments of Charles Booth

But it should not be surprising that this mode of apprehending urban life was valued by academic researchers. The volumes were reviewed and closely watched in scholarly journals in the nascent fields of sexology and criminology as well as in the more established disciplines of psychiatry and penology, and Ostwald even claimed to have been offered to be put up for an honorary degree and academic position by the leading light in progressive criminal law in central Europe, Franz von Liszt.[37] The claim is unsupported by evidence, but the very possibility of making such a claim in an Imperial Germany obsessed with credentials attests to the power of this field to shake up established boundaries of knowledge.

It is impossible to decouple the scientific value of the *Großstadt-Dokumente* series from its prurience, so that the practice of deigning the project popular or scholarly is certainly beside the point. The books in the series brought into dual focus the urban underworld as milieu—life on the streets and in bordellos, the social world of homosexuals and their private moments with each other, the languages of crime and practices of swindle—and the big city as an assemblage of personages, characters, or types: the prostitute, her procurer, the hustler, the swindler, the queer, the easy girl, the vagrant, the player. This can be seen as a continuation of genres of urban literature that had existed for some time or as a culmination of them that so intensified their tendencies that the result must be considered novel. But whether focusing on milieu or on the types that constituted it, the *Großstadt-Dokumente* documented urban life on the ground. In taking big city life as its subject, it consistently turned to the subjects of urban life. In this respect, the varying registers of analysis in the volumes—sensational or scientific, naturalist or characterological—were never as much at odds with one another as they were in concert. Writing the *Großstadt* was, for these contributors, writing its inhabitants.

---

et al.; see Fritzsche, *Reading Berlin 1900*, "Vagabond in the Fugitive City," 396, and 401–2n37; Ralf Thies and Dietmar Jazbinsek, "The Berlin 'Großstadt-Dokumente': A Forgotten Precursor of the Chicago School of Sociology," Wissenschaftszentrum Berlin für Sozialforschung, Discussion Paper FS II 01–502 (Berlin, 2001), http://skylla.wz-berlin.de/pdf/2001/ii01-502.pdf; "Berlin: Das europäische Chicago: Über ein Leitmotiv der Amerikanisierungsdebatte zu Beginn des 20. Jahrhunderts," in Zimmermann and Reulecke, *Die Stadt als Moloch*, 53–94; R. Thies, *Ethnograph des dunklen Berlin*, 210–13. Thies and Jazbinsek fall just short of drawing a definitive genealogy from Ostwald to Park and Wirth.

37. Thies, *Ethnograph des dunklen Berlin*, 114n. Ostwald's volumes were reviewed in the most prestigious scholarly journals.

## The Subject of Criminality

By the time the *Großstadt-Dokumente* were being published, the realm of criminal science had been not only reformed but totally transformed, albeit still somewhat disputed. That transformation can be periodized in different ways, but most would agree that the revolution in the modern Western discursive complex relating to crime and the intervention that condensed this complex into a discipline was the positivist or "positive" school of criminology emerging out of newly united Italy under the leadership of the medically trained scholar Cesare Lombroso. It is difficult to gauge the influence of this school and the discipline of "criminal anthropology" it grounded in part because so many people engaging in the discourse disagreed substantially and often vehemently with Lombroso and rejected his chief claims. Yet the differences among those entering the arena may be less great than they themselves held and than has been held by their historians.

The self-proclaimed "positive school" was formed in self-conscious opposition to the so-called classical school, those theorists who currently held academic positions and the greatest sway in penal policy in every European country. The principles of this earlier school, in as much as it was one, were seen to have been descended directly from the Enlightenment principles of penology inscribed most famously by Beccaria—there should be a measured, rational, and consistent relationship between offences and punishments, and so forth.[38] Lombroso and his cohort insisted on turning the attention from the abstracted crime and theory-based law to the criminal him- or herself. This was a key moment in the medicalization of the criminal,[39] to be sure— part of the process by which, as Foucault has it, criminality and pathology are bound up together.[40] Seen differently, though, this moment was also the condensation of procedures bridging practical knowledge of the criminal person with theoretical reform of penal law. It represented a turn to the subject of criminality—the criminal—even as it objectified him and made him an ob-

---

38. Imanuel Baumann points out that the latest representatives of the field, against whom the positivists were initially arguing also had adopted biological models of thought; see Baumann, *Dem Verbrechen auf der Spur*, 43.

39. The linked but distinct Weberian notion of "scientification"(*Verwissenschaftlichung*) is explored on the field of German criminology in Galassi, *Kriminologie im Deutschen Kaiserreich*.

40. Michel Foucault et al., *Abnormal*, esp. 92–108. As with other Foucauldian periodizations, the move to medicine is not for him a radical change in direction as much as an intensification of a process of pathologization underway in juridical/moral interpretations of criminal behavior. Cf., "The Dangerous Individual," in Foucault, *Politics, Philosophy, Culture*, 125–51.

ject of physical measurement and statistics.[41] In the context of diverse concurrent genres of urban danger literature such as the *Großstadt-Dokumente*,
Lombroso and his academic opponents seem closer to each other, just as they
seem less remote from the sensational genres themselves.

Lombroso's criminal anthropology is understandably known today as an
extreme form of biological determinism and the example par excellence of a
pseudoscience, a system of power disguised as objective knowledge.[42] To read
the volumes published under the titles *Criminal Man* and *Criminal Woman*
today is to enter a world not merely of exaggeration and hyperbole (as Lombroso's critics usually held) but of delirium and fantasy.[43] It is a world where
criminals "nearly always" have "something strange" about their appearance
and where perpetrators of particular types of crimes universally share a corporeal anomaly or other—swollen lips (for rapists); thick, close eyebrows
(for thieves); a hawklike nose and filmy eyes (for murderers); an unnatural
softness of skin (for arsonists)—and where just about all criminals share a
family resemblance marked by "jug ears, thick hair, thin beards, pronounced
sinuses, protruding chins, and broad cheekbones."[44] Yet we may too easily ex-
oticize our own readings of these many exoticizing passages, congratulating
ourselves too early on our rejection of transparently patriarchal accounts.[45]

The principal storyline today's readers are compelled to see in the rise and
fall of Lombroso in particular and the history of criminology in general is the
struggle between the nature and nurture explanation. Indeed, this moment
must be an important one for anyone interested in tracking a genealogy of
the stark opposition, unknown in most historical cultures and periods but
fundamental to our contemporary conceptions, of inheritance and environment. Lombroso and his colleagues came to refer to and even privilege a
category of congenital delinquency, the "born criminal," which became the

41. This is not as contradictory as it may appear to be to Peter Becker's argument that as a result of this discursive transition, criminals "lost their subjectivity." Peter Becker, "Criminological Language and Prose from the Late Eighteenth to the Early Twentieth Centuries," in Srebnick
and Lévy, *Crime and Culture*, 27–30. In fact the dual processes of objectification and attention to
criminals as subjects is the dialectical process we are trying to get at here.

42. Mary S. Gibson's work in particular has offered a much more differentiated view of
the Lombrosian project; see, e.g., *Born to Crime*; "Cesare Lombroso and Italian Criminology:
Theory and Politics," in Becker and Wetzell, *Criminals and Their Scientists*, 137–58.

43. Lombroso, *L'uomo delinquente*, with further editions in 1878, 1884, 1889, 1891, and 1896–
97; Lombroso and Ferrero, *La donna delinquente*.

44. All from the first edition of Lombroso's *L'uomo delinquente*; Lombroso, *Criminal Man*,
51–53.

45. Gould, *Mismeasure of Man*, 173–75.

object of bitter dispute. The struggle was explicit in the period in which the positive school vied for theoretical dominance of crime science so that the record of the International Congresses on Criminal Anthropology initiated by Lombroso himself reflect on their surface nothing more than a debate between biological determinists, mainly the Italians, on the one side and French proponents of sociological or environment arguments on the other.[46]

By turning a blind eye to this issue, however, something can be learned that seems most salient. The traditional way of looking at the landscape of criminality studies at the turn of the century is too schematic — not only because it is manifestly not true that social environmental theories won out whereas congenital theories were put to rest.[47] Close analysis of both sides shows much more in common than we assume. It is also too easy to read back onto Lombroso our notion of biological determinism. Lombroso was no more obsessive about the determinative power of physical signs (called *stigmata*), such as forehead shape, than stigmata such as tattoos, which he collected just as obsessively.[48] How could the category of physical signs of degeneration so comfortably include features that we think of as inherited and immutable (e.g., cranium form) and marks on the body so deliberately acquired? In discussions of particular cases, Lombroso not infrequently resorted to explanations relating to social environment alongside ones relating to inherited degeneration and outright racism.[49] While it is customary to consider as distinct (if not oppositional) the connotations of physical or biological and ethnographic or cultural senses of "anthropology," Lombroso himself was a dedicated folklorist, and his approach to the criminal is decidedly colonial and ethnographic.[50] This is abundantly clear in his full-length study of graffiti, tattoos, and the drawings and writings of prison inmates, for

46. See *Actes du premier Congrès international d'anthropologie criminelle: Biologie et sociologie (Rome, novembre 1885)* (Turin: Bocca, 1887); cf. *Actes du troisième Congrès international d'anthropologie criminelle tenu à Bruxelles en août 1892 sous le haut patronage du gouvernement: Biologie et sociologie* (Brussels: Hayez, 1893). The narrative arc described here was influentially forged by Robert A. Nye in the important article "Heredity or Milieu," 334–55.

47. Gould, *Mismeasure of Man*, 173–75, and Horn, *Criminal Body*.

48. Witness the images of tattoos alongside physical anomalies in editions of *L'uomo delinquente*; cf. Cesare Lombroso, "The Savage Origin of Tattooing," *Popular Science Monthly* 48 (1896), 793–803, cited in Horn, *Criminal Body*, 48–51.

49. Gibson uses the terms *ambiguity, inconsistent,* and *contradictory* while also recognizing this may "not have confused readers"; see Mary S. Gibson, "Science and Narrative in Italian Criminology, 1880–1920," in Srebnick and Lévy, *Crime and Culture*, 42.

50. The connection of the context of the colonialist European state, the discipline of anthropology, and the discipline of criminal anthropology is explored in Broekmann, "Visual Economy of Individuals." A relevant discussion of figures of savagery and civilization in relation

instance, where the criminal anthropologist comes forth as a kind of archae-
ologist. That is Lombroso's explicit metaphor, at any rate, as he compares
his study of the "prison palimpsests" to those of antiquity and prehistory,
his own project the assembly of a "codex" of these inscriptions of foreign-
ness, human races living among us without our consciousness of what dif-
ferentiates us from them.[51] The new direction of criminology was, to be sure,
positivist in its avowed reliance on quantitative data (criminal statistics), but
it relied on qualitative description throughout. The emphasis on stigmata
reminds us that this was more of a semiotic (and therefore interpretive) practice than an etiological one.[52] It was ultimately less invested in origins than it
was in meanings.

Nonetheless, there pertained a conflict between a group of mostly Italian, self-identified positivists who insisted on a criminal morphology that
was clearly a sign of evolutionary atavism and mainly French challengers raising inconsistencies in the data set and the underestimated influence of social
environment. What the two "schools" shared throughout their battle over
three successive international congresses was the question of the criminal—
the person of the criminal as a question to which causes, answers, and solutions could be attributed.[53] Criminology emerged as a system of producing
questions and answers literally and figuratively to locate the criminal and her
criminality. The twin critical processes of interpretation (reading signs) and
navigation (identifying criminals, criminal districts, questions) haunt texts
on both sides of what we take to be the nature/nurture divide.

The debate in question took place among a different set of experts than
those discussing crime before the advent of the positivist school. Jurists
maintained steady sway in most aspects of penal practice and participated
in discussions about the nature of criminality, but the interlocutors with the

---

to violence in Victorian newspaper reporting is Judith Rowbotham, "Criminal Savages? Or
'Civilizing' the Legal Process," in Rowbotham and Stevenson, *Criminal Conversations*, 91–105.

51. Lombroso, *Kerker-Palimpseste*, iii–iv.

52. This claim is clearly related to what Carlo Ginzburg has famously called the "conjectural
paradigm" (*paradigma indiziario*); see Ginzburg, *Clues*.

53. This statement supports a modified Foucauldian thesis positing a relative shift of inquiry
from the subject of a penal system to criminal subjects. Piers Beirne offers readings of earlier
texts on crime and punishment as far back as Beccaria's classical text and then Adolphe Quéte-
let's important work in social statistics, arguing that *homo criminalis* is implicit in them; Beirne,
*Inventing Criminology*. The presence of an implicit subject notwithstanding, there is evidence
to support an interpretation of a novel emphasis on the subject in the nineteenth century, and
recognition of this emphasis is not incompatible with a rejection of a social control thesis.

most prestige and the most new to say were men of general medicine, psychiatry, or anthropology proper. In the German literature, one of the most
important responses came from Adolf Baer, chief physician for the prison at
Plötzensee near Berlin.[54] Baer wrote as an authority with medical expertise
(he served as a state official adviser on public health) and a large sample of
subjects against which to assess Lombroso's claims, virtually all of which are
found wanting—there is no "born criminal" in his professional view. Yet the
book itself, in structure and rhetoric as well as in the assumptions it makes
about criminal subjects, closely resembles the work of his object of criticism.
His book is divided into sections on "the Physical Composition of the Criminal," "The Mental Composition of the Criminal," and "The Born Criminal"
and is accompanied by lavish appendices of foldout statistical tables and catalogs of criminal tattoos (fig. 3), some in color. Like the tables in Lombroso's
own editions of *Criminal Man* (in the later editions to consume their own
separate volume, which he significantly named the "atlas"), Baer's tattoos are
ordered according to their location on criminal bodies and cross-referenced
by the offender's crimes, sentence, and recidivism. In disciplinary terms—
and simply in terms of the categories employed, the questions posed, the evidence presented, and the modes of argument—the criminal anthropology of
Lombroso and of Baer are in the same class.

It is not that it should be regarded as insignificant that Baer offers socioenvironmental explanations in place of Lombroso's theory of the "born
criminal" and that he saw this polemic as central to his book. But looking at
the ground on which this position is argued ought to make clear their shared
territory. In his conclusion, he responds to Lombroso's collaborator Ferri,[55]
who proposed "that the criminal is the result of three factors that are in effect
simultaneously, and that these three causes are of individual (i.e., anthropological), somatic, and social nature,"[56] that he holds Ferri's three factors to be
expressions of a single cause, social environment, as he notes Ferri himself has
recognized. The debate would seem to have been seen as an extension of the
Enlightenment struggle for immanent over transcendent explanation (with
immanence here understood as deriving from environment, as opposed to

54. Baer, *Der Verbrecher*. Abraham Adolf Baer (b. 1834) had been appointed physician to the
public health (Geheimer Sanitätsrat) in 1879 and had made special contributions to the field of
alcoholism and crime.

55. Enrico Ferri (1856–1929), lawyer and later politician, actually coined the term *born
criminal*. In this period he was a socialist, as was Lombroso, but would later move over to the
Fascists.

56. Baer, *Der Verbrecher*, 410.

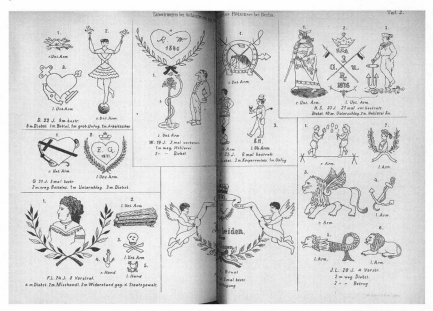

FIGURE 3. From A. Baer, *Der Verbrecher in anthropologischer Beziehung* (Leipzig: Thieme, 1893).

an innate atavism). The French school is represented in the person of Adolphe Prins, who argues "criminality consists of elements of human society itself. . . . One can see in it a kind of degeneracy of the social organism. . . . The criminal and the honest man each derive from his environment."[57] Indeed, Baer's great contribution to this debate, as he understood it, was to show Lombroso's methodological error in not recognizing that the physiological stigmata he identified were common to people who were not criminals— such signs of degeneration were common to members of the social class from which the prison criminals were drawn.[58] Lombroso's data were fiercely disputed by psychiatrist Paul Näcke, who considered it absurd to apply an innate character to something as culturally defined as crime and yet whose refutations consisted of elaborations of the conflation of degeneracy, mental illness, and criminality.[59] With opponents like this, the Lombrosians hardly had need

57. Adolphe Prins, "Criminalité et repression: Essai de science pénale," cited in Baer, *Der Verbrecher*, 410.

58. See Baer, *Der Verbrecher*, 186–93, cf. Wetzell, *Inventing the Criminal*, 50.

59. Paul Näcke, *Verbrechen und Wahnsinn beim Weibe: Mit Ausblicken auf die Criminal-Anthropologie überhaupt* (Vienna: Braunmüller, 1894), and "Degeneration, Degenerationszei-

for advocates. In fact the debates were vociferous, but the categories in play may not have been those projected onto them by later observers.[60]

Lombroso's most dedicated and important follower in German speaking lands was surely Hans Kurella (1858–1916), head psychiatrist of a Silesian provincial asylum and translator and German editor of many of Lombroso's works.[61] His 1893 *Naturgeschichte des Verbrechers: Grundzüge der criminellen Anthropologie und Criminalpsychologie* (Natural history of the criminal: outlines of criminal anthropology and criminal psychology) asserted an orthodox view of Lombrosian atavism theory and morphology long after followers had modified their appropriations of the theory, indeed after Italian criminal anthropology itself had modified itself somewhat.[62] Even Kurella's intended criminal-anthropological orthodoxy wavers in its definition of the origins of the elusive criminal "disposition" (*Anlage*), a product of degeneration that nonetheless may be a product of environmental conditions, specifically those of modern slums. The host of criminal psychologists between Kurella and Näcke (or the presumed poles of the born criminal and the socially produced criminal) stayed within the categories of the criminal subject consistent throughout—the criminal was a vulnerable subject, compromised by either an inborn degenerate constitution or a moral depravity produced by social environment, by alcoholism or by epilepsy.[63]

---

chen und Atavismus," *Archiv für Kriminal-Anthropologie und Kriminalistik* 1 (1899), 200–21, among other articles. Bondio points out that the dispute broke out at the Fourth Congress of Criminal Anthropology in Geneva; see Mariacarla Gadebusch Bondio, "The Impact of Lombrosian Theory in Germany," in Becker and Wetzell, *Criminals and Their Scientists*, 192n50.

60. The common assertion that Lombroso and his followers were definitively dispatched in 1913 with the publication of Charles Goring's *The English Convict: A Statistical Study* is a continuation of this misunderstanding, so that one finds oneself agreeing with Enrico Ferri, who recognizes that "the contentions of the positive school are corroborated by persons who call themselves opponents." See Enrico Ferri and Robert Ferri, "The Present Movement in Criminal Anthropology," 224–27.

61. He also edited a significant journal, the *Centralblatt für Nervenheilkunde und Psychiatrie*, and an interesting series of pamphlets published under the title *Grenzfragen des Nerven und Seelenlebens: Einzel-Darstellungen für Gebildete aller Stände*. The series was intended to introduce a general educated audience to a broad range of issues touching on modern investigations of the psyche, especially sexuality and gender, crime, and art, or how "nervous conditions" relate to modern urban life. It can thus be usefully compared with the more sociologically oriented *Großstadt-Dokumente*.

62. Hans Kurella, *Naturgeschichte des Verbrechers*.

63. Such as Robert Sommer, Julius Koch, and Eugen Bleuler, discussed by Wetzell in *Inventing the Criminal*, 53–60. Wetzell, however, often seems to focus on the differences between

History-of-science approaches to the texts of criminology, focusing on the specificities of disagreement among discussants within the field, tend to understate the foundation of assumptions these discussants shared, but they miss something far more important as well, that is, the way the new criminal science was a new and spectacular *medium*. Its consensus on what it was authorized to investigate and display, to what purpose, and what ancillary purposes were acceptable was as important as its internal disagreements about origins and causes. It is in this regard telling that Lombroso's opening chapter in the first edition of *Criminal Man* was titled "Criminal Craniums (Sixty-six Skulls)."[64] The presentation of the criminal body as an exhibit had the sensational value it continues to hold—witness the reproduction of Lombroso's collection of skulls, the tables of criminal faces, the charts of tattoos, and so on, throughout the historiography of criminological discourse (figs. 4, 5).

The statistical data on which the research was supposed to have relied may have been sparse and flawed, but it was laid out on page after page of flowing tables appealing to a related if unrecognized kind of scopophilia. The First International Congress of Criminal Anthropology in Rome was not only the site of the nascent conflict between Italian positivists and French social environmentalists, it was also the occasion for the exhibition of over 300 skulls and anatomical casts, hundreds and even thousands of photographs and drawings of epileptics and offenders, specimens of brains and cross sections of brains and body parts conserved in gelatin, all in splendid display at the Roman Palace of Fine Arts concurrent with the congress.[65] If Lombroso's influence in central Europe is measured by the number of followers who accepted his findings wholesale and by the length of time they did so, he must be considered unimportant. In fact, his significance as a symptom of a way of thinking about criminality is immeasurable. Lombroso was certainly speaking a language more Foucauldian than Linnaean when he taught that "crime is a species."[66]

---

these authors' views of the origins of criminal character even as he often exposes their common characterology and even inherent biologism.

64. Lombroso, *Criminal Man*, 45.

65. A. Broekmann, "Visual Economy of Individuals"; Morrison, "Lombroso," in Ferrell et al., *Cultural Criminology Unleashed*, 67–80. Morrison sees positivist criminology as "cultural production" informed by international flows of information. The connection between the exhibition here described and the colonial exhibits is deeply relevant here.

66. "Moral insanity is a genus of which crime is a species"; Lombroso, *Criminal Man*, 217 (from the third edition of *L'uomo deliquente*).

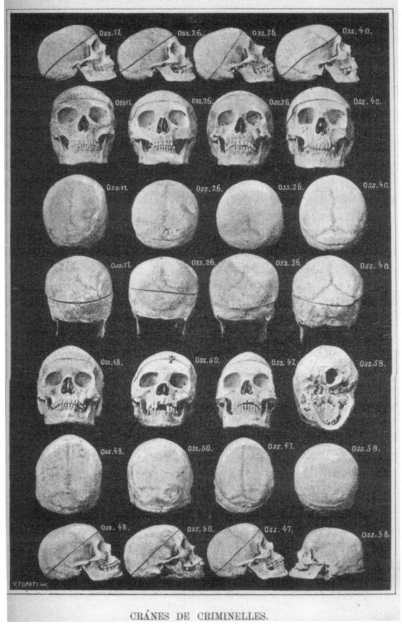

CRÂNES DE CRIMINELLES.

FIGURE 4. Images of skulls of Italian criminals from Lombroso's "Atlas," the illustrated appendix to later editions of *Criminal Man.* Taken from the French edition, César Lombroso, ed. Félix Alcan, *L'homme criminel: Atlas* (Paris: Ancienne Librairie Germer Baillière, 1887), plate 26.

PORTRAITS DE CRIMINELS ALLEMANDS,

FIGURE 5. Images of faces of Italian criminals from Lombroso's "Atlas," the illustrated appendix to later editions of *Criminal Man.* Taken from the French edition, César Lombroso, ed. Félix Alcan, *L'homme criminel: Atlas* (Paris: Ancienne Librairie Germer Baillière, 1887), plate 10.

## Accounting for the Criminal

If the secret of crime is to be found in the criminal, the principle by which it becomes a secret—something known only with difficulty that, however, must become known—is that of accountability. In German the terms taking on increasing relevance and under regular contest are *Zurechnung* and *Zurechnungsfähigkeit* (conversely, *Unzurechnungsfähigkeit*, criminal irresponsibility). Derived from the metaphor of arithmetic, the roots are also biblical—the accounting of sins, or of the sins of Adam.[67] At issue is the concept of criminal law known in a more restricted form in the English tradition under the name criminal responsibility and in all cases touching on the question of responsible agency and, by extension, free will.[68] These categories seem to have been in place to some degree in classical German-language juridical thinking, but the category became increasingly important throughout the nineteenth century.[69] For Georg Simmel, *Zurechnung* is the factor binding act, agent, and cause, for it establishes the conditions under which will and criminal act can be traced to the same "address"—causality is hence the key concept for locating the crime as well as the criminal.[70]

The question of free will is explicit in the legal definition in place in both Germany and Austria in this period as defined in Paragraph 51 of the German penal code: "A culpable act is not present if the perpetrator at the time of commission of the act found himself in a state of unconsciousness or morbid disturbance of mental faculties interfering with his free will."[71] Before the nineteenth, or at the earliest the late eighteenth century, the category of the responsible or irresponsible individual was not in play, but rather the conditions of particular acts at the moments in which they occurred. Hence the maturity, perception, or rage of a perpetrator were discussed, but the person

67. Jacob Grimm and Wilhelm Grimm, *Deutsches Wörterbuch*, 32 vols. (Leipzig: Hirzel: 1854–1960), s.v. "Zurechnung," "Zurechnungsfähig," "Zurechnungsfähigkeit."

68. See S. J. Hucker and K. DeFreitas, "Criminal responsibility," in *Encyclopedia of Forensic and Legal Medicine* (Amsterdam: Elsevier Academic, 2005).

69. Cf. Kant's definition of someone as agent (*Urheber/causa libera*) of her actions, after Christian Wolf's definition of *causa libera*; see Eisler, *Wörterbuch*, 841–43. The 1803 dictionary includes "Zurechnung" but not "Zurechnungsfähigkeit" or its derivatives.

70. Georg Simmel, *Einleitung in die Moralwissenschaft*, vol. 2, chap. 6, "Die Freiheit," 131–306; see 210–11.

71. As worded in the penal code for member states of the German Kaiserreich, the Reichsstrafgesetzbuch [RStrGB]. The Austrian Paragraph 56 is arguably looser: "An act is not of a criminal nature when the individual who has committed it found himself in a state of unconsciousness or morbid inhibition or disturbance of mental faculties which made it impossible for him to determine his will freely or to understand the culpability of his actions."

herself as responsible for her act or as capable of that responsibility was not the point. Forensic guides from the early nineteenth century stress that the medical expert is not to establish responsibility or irresponsibility, as this lies within the competency of judge and jurist, but rather the question of whether the accused was, at the time of committing the act, mentally sane or mentally ill. The hereditary disposition and the physical and mental development of the individual is to be precisely recorded followed by a thorough *physical examination* that should encompass all organs. Deformities, for example, of the skull, ears, teeth, and so on, are to be particularly attended to. The medical examination should note in particular those factors likely to be relevant to the establishment of accountability, such as epileptic seizures, alcoholism, and withdrawal symptoms.[72] The proliferating discussion of the category of accountability corresponds to the struggle for authority among juridical and medical experts.[73] The passage from the "classical" to the "positive" school was seen by proponents of the new criminology to be a move from the moral-juridical categories of determination of accountability through specific criteria to the so-called biological method, where a psychiatric determination of a condition of *Unzurechnungsfähigkeit* suffices.[74] But physiological and juridical definitions of accountable states and their subjects were at times at odds with one another—indeed, in these decades of shifting definitions, they were often at odds with themselves.

This dilemma of *Zurechnungsfähigkeit* within juridical discourse is the subject of a bitingly satirical chapter of the Musil's epic satire *Man without Qualities*. One of the gravitational centers of the novel's first volume is the case of the sexual murderer Moosbrugger, to whose cause several characters are drawn, including the man without qualities himself, Ulrich. Ulrich's father, as it happens, is a prominent jurist currently sitting on the imperial

72. "It would be too much to ask for one to require the court physician to study penal law textbooks in order to acquire the fundaments on which criminal accountability and penal responsibility [*Zurechnung und Zurechnungsfähigkeit*] are based or the shifting variations of the latest criminalistic theory"; Albrecht Meckel, *Lehrbuch der gerichtlichen Medizin*, quoted in *Heidelberger Jahrbücher der Literatur* 50, n.s. 2, no. 2 (July–December 1882): 664–76; see 666. This is still the argument in the 1880s; see Mendel, "Zurechnungsfähigkeit," in Albert Eulenburg, *Real-Encyclopädie der gesammten Heilkunde*, 15:302–26.

73. The definitive account of this struggle is Ylva Greve, "Richter und Sachverständige: Der Kompetenzstreit über die Beurteilung der Unzurechnungsfähigkeit im Strafprozeß des 19. Jahrhunderts," in Berding, Klippel, and Lottes, *Kriminalität und abweichendes Verhalten*, 69–104. See also Christian Müller, *Verbrechensbekämpfung im Anstaltsstaat*, esp. 35–52.

74. H. Gross, "Besprechung: Die geisteskranken Verbrecher im Strafverfahren und Strafvollzuge: Referat von Prof. Dr. Ad. Lenz in Freiburg (In den Verhandlungen des schweizerischen Juristenvereins 1899)," *GKA*, 1:351.

committee assigned to review the penal code. The problem is that the legal mind cannot accommodate a category of insanity that may and may not apply to the same person, even at the same time ("to jurists there are no half-insane men" or, as the newer translation has it, "insanity is an all-or-nothing proposition").[75] The chapter, in tandem with the committee debate it describes, devolves into a shrill cacophony of hairsplitting semantic and logical contortions to create a legal model of accountability that would be applicable to actual persons and acts that alternate between moments of control, volition, and reason and their opposites. What is more, the behavior of the distinguished members of the reform committee begins to resemble the subjects of its regulation: failing to agree on a definition, they rashly descend into intemperance, illogic, willful misunderstanding, and a lapse of standards. The committee dissolved into factions and splinter groups of these factions: the "and" and "or" factions, then separate and competing "Zurechnungsfähigkeit" and "Zurechnung" parties, yielding theoretical refinements offering various fractionations of the juridical subject himself, all in order to make the category of legal responsibility legible, if inapplicable, to actual actors.

In the face of this intractable problem and the unraveling of the committee, Ulrichs's father

took what he called his sensational turn to social thought. The social view holds that the criminally "degenerate" individual must be judged not morally, but only insofar as he is likely to harm society as a whole. Hence the more dangerous he is, the more responsible he is for his actions [daß er desto zurechnungsfähiger sein muß, je schädlicher er ist], with the inescapable logical consequence that those criminals who seem to be the most innocent—the mentally sick, who are by nature least susceptible to correction by punishment—must be threatened with the harshest penalties, harsher than those for sane persons, so that the deterrent factor of the punishment be equal for all.[76]

The competition between juridical and medical experts for authority in the courtroom in this period has been the subject of some discussion. Often lost in this discussion is the place of popular perceptions of a category such as accountability and the role of the press in mediating those perceptions. These relations will be central in later chapters, but for the moment it is useful to mention the example of a somewhat sensational murder case

75. Musil, *MoE*, 1:534–39; *MwQ*, 583–88.
76. *MwQ*, 587.

from this period, the 1886 knifing of stationmaster Karl Schippek in a suburb of Vienna.[77] The accused murderer, Rudolf Nagel, was the son of a dismissed station agent, and he might have felt that the stationmaster was responsible for his father's loss of employment and the ensuing family misery. Standard press reports produced the sort of melodramatic storytelling that had become common in journalism of the late nineteenth century.[78] But the central significance of the category of criminal responsibility appeared in other reports and emerged crucially throughout the investigation and trial on the part of many actors. The investigating magistrate and the chief of police were mindful of circumstances that could bear on the question of criminal responsibility: before his death, the victim was asked for confirmation of the identity of the perpetrator as well as his state of mind, particularly drunkenness (he was sober); questions to the accused followed suit. The perpetrator's initial confession demonstrated a consciousness of possible ways out of the charges, especially self-defense (the attacked man was unarmed, but Nagel claimed the victim leapt on him), that he did not "apply violence" nor intend to, and, significantly, that at the time of the crime he was in a state of "great agitation." In the course of the investigation, however, it emerged as the professional opinion of psychiatrist expert witnesses that the accused suffered from epilepsy, and "that with consideration of that fact the assumption appears justified that the accused at the time of the deed had not been fully conscious of his actions."[79] These elements were easily assimilated in the most innovative and sensationalist reports, where readers were introduced to medical terms such as *epilepsy* and *neurasthenia*, emphasized in the text, along with the category of criminal unaccountability (*Unzurechnungsfähigkeit*). The juridico-medical drama being played out intersected with the melodramatic narrative of capture, producing a social dilemma:

> The gallows seemed [the accused's] certain fate. At the last moment the asylum doctors were called, and they explained that the murderer Nagel, according to observations made of him at the inquisition hospital, is to be treated as an individual afflicted with *epilepsy* and a *neurasthenic*. And so the situation changed. In the case of *epileptics*—the physicians agree on this—complete criminal responsibility [Zurechnungsfähigkeit] is out of the question. According to our laws, however, criminal unaccountability excludes the possibility of penalty, and the judges would find themselves forced into the certainly un-

77. Kaiser-Ebersdorf since 1892 incorporated into the city and is now part of its eleventh district, Simmering.

78. See, e.g., "Gerichtshalle: Wien, 8. März," *Volksblatt für Stadt und Land* 17, no. 10 (1886): 3.

79. "Der Mord," *Wiener illustrirte Kriminal-Zeitung* 2, no. 11 (March 12, 1886): 4–7.

comfortable position of having to release a proven, confessed murderer—to return *this sort* of individual to society.[80]

The paper—belonging to the new, sensational European genre of illustrated detective and crime newspapers—took an interest in the academic reconsideration of the categories of criminal responsibility, citing an unpublished lecture a certain Dr. Benedikt had recently delivered at the Juridical Society.[81] This brief example skims the surface of what an inquiry into the reflexive relations among popular and expert discourses on the subject might look like.

Lombroso's German deputy Hans Kurella, in a book explicitly linking criminal accountability, degeneration, and criminal anthropology, makes clear the central place of the forensic psychiatrist, who represents both scientific precision, regularity, and necessity at the same time as he protects the principle of free exercise of the human will.[82] Here as elsewhere we see the expert as hero, and one who is a mirror image of his object of study—his role lies in the ability to capture the object's reflection, the picture of a subject incapable of rationality, control, and free will. Simmel perceptively reverses the direction of the gaze at the criminal subject's accountability: clearly it is the punishment, whether aimed at retribution or rehabilitation, that drives the category. The subject incapable of correction or being punished is retroactively diagnosed as irresponsible. The free individual is hence defined by his ability to respond to discipline.[83]

As in the literary urban genres, the question of accountability inevitably led legal theorists to liminal states of marginal figures: the criminal, the prostitute, the pervert. Every substantial statement on the problem of *Zurechnungsfähigkeit* resorts to examples from criminality as well as sexuality; we will see more on this linkage in the following chapter. For now, it is useful to

80. "Der Meuchelmörder Rudolf Nagel aus Kaiser-Ebersdorf," *Wiener illustrirte Kriminal-Zeitung* 2, no. 11 (March 12, 1886): 1.

81. This was certainly Moriz Benedikt (1835–1920), the Vienna neurology professor active in this period in offering moderate alternatives to Lombrosian theories; see, e.g., Benedikt, *Anatomische Studien*. Similar to Baer, Benedikt was a self-described freethinker whose revisionist theory of a seat in a particular region of the brain for "moral insanity" shared in this quest more than it rejected from criminal anthropology. See Jan Verplaetse, "Localization of Morality," 305–28.

82. "[The forensic psychiatrist] is in one and the same thought process the representative of the presentation of strict legality and necessity and at the same time deputy of the study of freedom of will. He—theoretician of human action—should at the same moment treat actions as causally determined and autonomous"; Kurella, *Die Grenzen der Zurechnungsfähigkeit*, 2–3.

83. Simmel, *Einleitung in die Moralwissenschaft*, 213–15.

locate the source of that linkage in a single figure, and that is what doctors—
but not only doctors—denoted with the term *degeneration*.

## Becoming Other: Discourses of Degeneration

When scholars from Kurella to Weininger to Lombroso to Krafft-Ebing
spoke of *degeneration*, they were referring not to a specific and well-defined
natural process described by a coherent scientific explanation on which there
was consensus. The term may have been ubiquitous in the late nineteenth
century, but it was as nonspecific as it was appealing. In German as in English, the term refers to a variation that implies a departure from the genus,
a migration from one's own kind to something other (in German, *Entartung*,
*ent-* implying an undoing, *Art* being one's kind). Karl Birnbaum, in his discussion of the psychopathic criminal, acknowledged the popularity of the
concept of degeneration in all fields and posited a psychiatric definition that
he considered much more narrow and precise: it referred only to "those *ad-
verse deviations from the normal type* that are substantially due to *abnormal
predisposition*."[84] A later, longer definition is similarly tautological, stressing
nonetheless that psychic degeneration in the psychiatric sense is always con-
stitutional, based in an abnormal predisposition that has been inherited or
caused by hereditary contamination, often but not always accompanied by
physical signs of degeneration.[85] Diagnosticians of degeneration in all fields
spoke a language itself descended from evolutionary theory—just as certain
adaptations will over millennia move the species forward, other aberrations
represent throwbacks, atavisms. Thus, cultural historians have noted, the
metaphor of degeneration was irresistible to a civilization whose vistas of
endless progress were clouded by its own smokestacks in an era that donned
the world-weary name "fin de siècle" and clothed itself in an art known as
"decadence."[86] The vague and unsystematic nature of the term was commented on at the time and by its users, so to point out that it was not a "real"
medical theory is not really much of an analytical statement.

*Degeneration* was not just a biological term that was adopted in many
other fields because of its great metaphorical potential. The network of mutual borrowings of the term among medicine, evolutionary biology, an-

84. The definition is of course not technically precise and is somewhat tautological. Karl
Birnbaum, *Die psychopathischen Verbrecher*, 12, emphasis in original. As a relatively late intervention, this text distinguishes itself as a more specific, medical (psychiatric) definition.

85. Birnbaum, *Die psychopathischen Verbrecher*, 14.

86. See, e.g., Daniel Pick, *Faces of Degeneration*, and Chamberlin and Gilman, *Degeneration*.

thropology, and social critique was so dense that it is not easy to determine which of its uses was *not* metaphorical. Did it ramify from mythical crypto-Darwinian origins to all branches of theoretical science and practical medicine to the human sciences? Or was the sense of an exhausting century more than just a favorable medium for the concept (if it is one)? Famously, it was a Budapest-born physician, Max Nordau (1849–1923), who brought it to cultural criticism. Nordau's biting attack on modern culture, first published in 1892 under the simple title *Degeneration,* offered a dedication of several pages to Lambroso, wherein the author promised fealty to apply the vision and method of the great criminal anthropologist to contemporary culture and the arts.[87] Nordau was not yet the Zionist he would become, famous for promoting "muscle Judaism" to reverse both stereotype and reality of the bookish and intellectualized Jewish people in the Diaspora.[88] He had already made a name and some trouble for himself trying his hand at cultural and political criticism, especially in the tract *The Conventional Lies of Our Civilization,* where he analyzed the inherent dissimulation in every aspect of modern politics and social life on account of its outmoded institutions.[89] He was hence never a strict traditionalist but rather favored programmatic adaptation even as he condemned the cultural vanguard's disposal of long-held aesthetic and moral values.

By the end of Nordau's rant against modernism in all its forms, he comes out as a physician, and one rather sure of his diagnosis: degeneration—a "mental disorder affecting modern society"—has consumed all civilized humanity (i.e., the educated upper classes) and consumed them with tendencies toward mysticism and irrationality, egomania, and a false realism masking pessimism and licentiousness; all of these symptoms of a brain incapable of normal operation, a feebleness of will, inattention, predominance of emotion and yet absence of sympathy—"medically speaking," these are all symptoms of a generalized *exhaustion* ranked in the genus *melancholia,* the psychiatric manifestation of an exhausted central nervous system. As a doctor, Nordau must postulate on the etiology of the condition, and to do so he offers a history of the *Großstadt.* He compares the material conditions of an educated

---

87. Nordau, *Entartung.* If apologists for criminal anthropology would blame Lombroso's exaggerations for the discredit to the discipline, Lombroso's apologists would blame Nordau for distorting the ideas of the master. While vulnerable to an unreconstructed stigmatization thesis, the rhetorical analysis of Nordau's dedication is useful here; see Kaiser, *Rhetorik der Entartung,* 21–49.

88. Hans-Peter Söder, "A Tale of Dr. Jekyll and Mr. Hyde? Max Nordau and the Problem of Degeneracy," in Käser and Pohland, *Disease and Medicine,* 56–69; Söder, "Disease and Health," 473–87.

89. Nordau, *Die conventionellen Lügen.*

traveler one generation previous to one of his own generation; he measures the kilometers of railway in Europe in 1840 against 1891, the number of travelers, the number of posted letters per capita, newspapers and books published, and so on—in short he produces the introduction that was so hard for us not to reiterate above. In doing so he comes to a thesis not unlike the one culled by literal-minded readers of Georg Simmel's metropolis essay—that these conditions have affected the nervous system of people under its sway (as in Simmel's essay, Nordau slips from speaking about the city to the altered experience of all modern individuals). Degeneration and hysteria are the consequences of these conditions, and their symptoms in turn are everywhere to be seen in modern culture and are not the "heralds of a new era" they claim to be but, like Lombroso's atavisms, "point backward to times in the past."[90]

In further editions, Nordau denies that he has claimed that degeneration and hysteria are products of the modern age. Instead, he argues, these have always existed, but in sporadic manifestations that did not have importance for the collective life of the community. Like a bacillus that survives within a population for generations only to become an epidemic when conditions are ripe, the success of civilization itself has created the conditions of its undoing: the endless series of discoveries and innovations thrust abruptly on a single generation have "created favorable conditions under which these maladies could gain ground enormously, and become a danger to civilizations."[91] He then provides a picture of a future dystopia where every aberration is the norm, overrun by drugs, deviance, and violence and where nervous irritability and sensitivity is universal; but this eccentric fantasy is followed by the promise that this phantasmic end will not be reached because of the inability of degenerates to adapt. The better elements of the race will either adapt to be able to withstand the ever-increasing barrage (of transportation, communication, sociability, overcrowding, and so on), or, if the exploding civilization outstrips these potential adaptive powers, humanity has another option. It is what Lombroso named *misoneism*, or inherent resistance to innovation and change.[92] The aversion to progress is hence "inherited" by civilization, and it

90. Nordau, *Entartung*, 1:63–81; *Degeneration*, 34–44.

91. Nordau, *Entartung*, 2:522–23; *Degeneration*, 536–37. A concise survey of nineteenth-century theories of mental degeneration caused by civilization itself is Volker Roelcke, "'Gesund ist der moderne Culturmensch keineswegs . . .': Natur, Kultur und die Entstehung der Kategorie 'Zivilisationskrankheit' im psychiatrischen Diskurs des 19. Jahrhunderts," in Barsch and Hejl, *Menschenbilder*, 215–36.

92. Lombroso uses this neologism in several places, sometimes referring to it as a characteristic of normal individuals often absent in criminals; see Lombroso, *Criminal Man*, 300, 315, and esp. 396n13. He sometimes described it as an aberrant quality found in degenerates or

will save civilization from itself: "Humanity has, today as much as ever, the tendency to reject all that it cannot digest."[93]

Particularly vulnerable to misoneism is the special kind of human who is otherwise capable of producing the very sort of radical innovation that he himself would reject, and that is the genius. It was Lombroso who ascribed to the genius this attribute, but the treatment of genius as a positive outcome of the processes of degeneration was shared by many and widely discussed.[94] To capture what is really interesting and important about the theory linking genius and criminal insanity as twin degenerate phenomena, it takes recalling that the authors of such theory—Lombroso and Nordau, arguably, but in a very self-conscious way the misogynist psychologist-philosopher Otto Weininger, of whom more below—self-identified with the genius group. It is not just the speculation on genius but the category of degeneration itself that must be considered as an autodiagnostic discourse, and in many ways.

We are beginning to see many forms of what Robert Nye in a narrower context has called the "irony of progress," the persistent consciousness of the tenuousness and vulnerability of progress at its moments of greatest success.[95] In Nye's example of sociology, the Lamarckian heritage (so often ignored or forgotten, and strongest in the French social sciences) lent for the easy translation of theories of Victorian hygiene (sloth and indulgence of working classes) to degeneration theory and then to thought about urban degeneration (the conditions of urban poverty cause idleness, improvidence, etc.). Contemporary readers want to relegate Nordau and the cultural obsession with degeneration generally to a cultural pessimism that would lead to later twentieth-century marginalizations and purges. Such an easy reading misses the connection of a particular view of progress to a branch of Enlightenment optimism, and with it to a civilizational narrative that was current at the turn of the century. On the other hand, the connections between these narratives of civilizational progress and utopian fantasies of violence are not incidental.

Responding to an 1899 "sociomedical" tract on prostitution, for example, the seminal Graz criminologist Hanns Gross (later to modernize the spelling of his Christian name to Hans) was content to see in the evidence presented "the full proof of the value of the Lombrosian lesson of the connections

geniuses—Nordau is more likely to be referring to this use in Lombroso's work on genius; see Lombroso, *Man of Genius*, 17–18.

93. Nordau, *Entartung*, 2:530–31; *Degeneration*, 542.

94. See Lombroso, *Entartung und Genie*; Otto Weininger, *Geschlecht und Charakter*, 131–44, 212–38; for a rebuttal see Hirsch, *Genius and Degeneration*.

95. R. Nye, "Sociology and Degeneration: The Irony of Progress," in Chamberlin and Gilman, *Degeneration*, 49–71.

among degeneration, crime, and prostitution."[96] Gross was more of an innovator of techniques of detection than a criminological theorist. As we shall soon see, his contribution lay precisely in the breakdown of this particular theory/practice distinction. Yet Gross provided elegant formulations of the laws of degeneration in the context of urban civilization. Nature and culture oppose one another not only in their essence but in their effects: while natural selection improves the race, civilization selects to maintain and breed the unfit for the degradation of the races: "Nature creates fit, culture creates degenerate individuals."[97] In a 1906 lecture to the Vienna Association for Psychiatry and Neurology on the question of when it is medically and legally appropriate to "interrupt" the pregnancy of neurotics or psychotics, he exclaimed, "Let us not forget that our culture breeds degeneration because it so violently resists the natural selection processes as nature moves them forward."[98] In a word, degeneration is the reverse of selection, a perfect inversion of nature's perfecting laws. As a criminal scientist, Gross's interest in all this theory was the problem of the innate and degenerate criminal (although not all criminals are degenerate and not all degenerates criminal, he reminds his readers).[99] If modern civilization and the current penal code conspired to multiply degenerate criminality, the solution lay in the segregation of degenerate criminals from society: Gross argued for the isolation of hereditary criminals from the healthy population and for their forced deportation to penal colonies for life.[100]

### There's No Place Like Crime

The whole question of the origin of criminality can be thought of in terms of spatial location: *where* was criminality to be found? Was it to be located in the body of the born criminal? Or was the city itself, especially the conditions of its depraved districts, actually producing crime? Scholarly discussions of urban criminality may be seen on the one hand as landmarks of the hardening of a broad "nature or nurture" debate familiar to modern readers, but it

96. Gross, *GKA*, 1:352.

97. Gross, "Die Degeneration und das Strafrecht," *GKA*, 2:1–11, p. 4; "Kriminalpsychologie und Strafpolitik," *Archiv für Kriminal-Anthropologie und Kriminalistik* 26 (1903), 67.

98. Gross, *GKA*, 2:64; Lamott, *Die vermessene Frau*, 208–9.

99. Gross, *GKA*, 2:71.

100. Gross, "Degeneration und Deportation," *GKA*, 1:70–77. This essay has been cited as a source in reference to Kafka's story "In the Penal Colony," since, while on the law faculty at the German half of the Charles University in Prague, Gross was one of Kafka's favorite teachers—he was registered for sixteen hours of class a week with him; see Binder, *Kafka-Handbuch*, 1:291.

is equally striking how fluidly they moved between these nascent categories or how easily they were mapped on to one another.

An interesting case where these tendencies can be seen is the group of contributions to the forensic literature between about 1894 and 1910 on the problem of homesickness and crime. If this pairing seems alien to the modern reader, this strangeness itself may be useful for bringing into view what was at stake for scientists when they sought crime's origins, whether in social conditions or in innate dispositions. By the mid-1890s there was an acute awareness of what had been a critical shift in the diagnosis of criminal causality. The recognition of degenerate conditions such as epilepsy and alcoholism and the influence of these on socially pathological behavior had emerged within recent memory, and it was presumed that many more yet unidentified such conditions must exist. Homesickness (*Heimweh*) appeared as just such a condition. But naming this origin of crime did not yet answer the questions about what kind of a causal factor this was. Whom did it afflict? Was it the trigger of an innate pathology, or did it create one? Was the person whose criminal acts were caused by homesickness a willful agent responsible for her own actions? To the contemporary ear, it is hard to ignore the ring of a peculiarly modern form of alienation in an excuse for criminality that finds itself in displacement.

By the time Hanns Gross published his nearly 700-page survey *Criminalpsychologie* (*Criminal Psychology*) in 1898, he was able to conclude that the connection of nostalgia and crime had been well researched.[101] According to his reading of this literature, homesickness was mostly the province of children and childlike persons, such as the mentally impaired, and it was a primary cause for these to fall into crime, particularly arson.[102] Uneducated people from solitary, strongly defined regions such as mountain ranges, plains,

---

101. Gross, *Criminalpsychologie*, 95–97; cf. Gross, *Kriminal-Psychologie*, 2nd ed. (Leipzig: Vogel, 1905), 91–93. The 1898 edition is virtually identical to the 1905 edition excepting the addition of two references, one to a newer secondary source and the second to a contemporary case of arson in the news. In spite of citing just one scholarly source in the first edition, Gross claims "man hat sich vielfach damit befasst" and expresses with certainty the conclusions that follow. The only sustained forensic study appearing before Gross's first edition appears to have been Ferdinand Maack, *Heimweh und Verbrechen: Ein Beitrag zum Strafgesetzbuch* (Leipzig, 1894), but he cites it only in the second edition; in 1898, Gross cites only Meckel's contribution in the *Beiträge zur gerichtlichen Psychologie* (Halle, 1820).

102. Gross's second edition adds "blödsinnige und schwächliche Personen" (imbeciles and weaklings) to those usually affected. Meckel had cited Ernst Platner's *Quaestiones medicinae forensis* (Leipzig, 1797–1817), which identified potential victims of the disease in "children, as well as idiots and madmen on occasion" who might feel "irresistibly driven by a strong sensory stimulus such as that elicited by the eruption of a great flame." Quoted in Meckel, *Beiträge*, 112.

or seacoasts were particularly susceptible. The better-educated portion of the population would appear to be immune on two accounts. First, the relative topographical similarity of the modern metropolis made for their easy transition from city to city. As a second explanation, Gross speculated that social status itself offers its possessor an antidote to homesick depression, since the very cultivation it entails is part of the "home" that its bearer takes abroad.[103]

The spatial displacement of the victim of homesickness from countryside to city mirrors the temporal dislocation of the atavism (the term used by Lombroso and his school, the degenerative throwback). Yet it is civilization itself—here in the form of urbanization and the uprooting of country folk from their roots—that foments the appearance of the precivilized figure in an alien setting. The 1894 source that Gross names in his original entry on the subject, Dr. Ferdinand Maack's *Heimweh und Verbrechen: Ein Beitrag zum Strafgesetzbuch* (Homesickness and crime: A contribution to the penal code), dug up cases and their interpretations from the early 1820s on demonstrating that the homesick condition was a pathological form of autosuggestion and arguing that the stricken should be treated medically rather than penalized by law.[104] Yet, the hypnoid condition in which the nostalgic finds herself would not seem to be transhistorical: Maack introduces his essay with reflection on the problem of weighing different causal factors, noting that the current age, "our half of the [nineteenth] century," could be called the Age of Suggestibility.[105]

The most comprehensive contemporary account of the medico-forensic literature on homesickness and crime was published in Hanns Gross's journal by a 26-year-old Karl Jaspers. While Jaspers (1883–1969) is known for his later twentieth-century contributions to philosophy, his early career was in psychology, launched by his dissertation "Heimweh und Verbrechen" (Homesickness and crime) published in 1909.[106] Gross's brief remarks in the second edition of *Criminal psychology* were noted here; to Gross's deference to the psychiatrist—"the physician is to be consulted whenever homesickness is suspected to be a cause of the crime"—Jaspers expounded that such a diagnosis was not an easy task. The difficult distinction between crimes caused by homesickness and those simply motivated by job dissatisfaction,

103. Gross, *Criminalpsychologie*, 96.

104. Maack, *Heimweh und Verbrechen*, 26–28.

105. Ibid., 3–5. Maack explicitly rejects both the Italian school (physiological etiology) and the sociological explanation, favoring instead an "individual-psychological" model of determining causes of criminality.

106. Jaspers, "Heimweh und Verbrechen."

for instance, is crucial. A violent act with a motive of this sort (escaping from an uncomfortable employment or living situation) is a crime for which the criminal is responsible, but where no such motive is present there is the possibility of a psychic illness possessing the perpetrator so that she cannot be held responsible for her crimes: "if homesickness is the sole cause of a crime on the part of individuals who have been until such a point mentally and morally intact, then the overwhelming probability is that the act was not of free will."[107] Such "pure" cases were perhaps rare, Jaspers thought, but clearly this was the ideal type of the crime and homesickness connection. This is a pattern that will recur broadly in the forensic literature—it is precisely the case that seems utterly without motive that is identified as the pure, the true, or the paradigmatic case even though such cases are the rarest. In the case of homesickness, the motiveless case is crucial to identify in order to get at the nature of the disease, even to establish whether it is in fact its own category of mental illness.

A key text on the subject had been published by the psychiatrist Karl Wilmanns (1873–1945) in 1905 under the title "Heimweh oder impulsives Irresein?" (Homesickness or impulsive insanity?).[108] Wilmanns was the central source for Jaspers's dissertation and an adviser. For Wilmanns as for others, the problem inciting the inquiry, the anomaly producing the question, is the apparent discrepancy in a group of cases between the mental development of the perpetrator and the extremity of the crime. Wilmanns's case study concerns a girl from a family of ten children sent before the age of fourteen to serve as a nanny for a physician several hours from her hometown. After several small incidents of theft, the girl is found to have twice strangled the children in her charge, leading in one case to a near death.

The logic through which Wilmanns arrives at the problem of potential criminal pathology is telling. He explains as "fundamental theses of forensic psychiatry" that every crime is explicable through one of two factors: either the perpetrator—under which is understood her constitution, upbringing, and environment—or else, second, her potential motives. If psychiatric and criminal-psychological investigation reveal no characteristics that would explain a propensity toward crime, and criminological study of the facts shows no sufficient reason for the crime, then the crime is alien to the perpetrator's

107. "Wenn als einziger Grund eines Verbrechens bei intellektuell und moralisch bis dahin intakten Individuen Heimweh vorliegt, so ist die Tat mit überwiegender Wahrscheinlichkeit unfrei"; Jaspers, "Heimweh," 111.

108. Karl Wilmanns, "Heimweh oder impulsives Irresein?" *Monatsschrift für Kriminalpsychologie und Strafrechtsreform* 3 (1905): 136–55.

nature and is incomprehensible from a criminal-psychological perspective. It appears to the investigator as a *puzzle*. Any act or series of acts that remain incomprehensible in this way must lead the investigator at least to the suspicion "that it was committed by the perpetrator while in a state of *abnormal* disturbance of mental capacities."[109] The riddle or puzzle (*Räthsel*) was as we shall see a sort of trope in the medico-forensic literature—it persistently recurs in texts on homosexuality. Here as elsewhere, the metonym transforms persons into puzzles for the investigator, just as the emergence of such puzzles provides the occasion for theory about the nature of crime divorced from personality. The debate about arson or murder attempts inspired by nostalgia, for instance, did not revolve around doubt about whether homesickness was the cause (a conclusion on which experts were prepared to agree) but rather on what the status of homesickness in relation to the perpetrator's psychic processes actually was. In the case examined in detail by Wilmanns, the poles of the argument were represented on the one side by Gross, who saw crime as a pathological reaction directly caused by homesickness in an otherwise normal if susceptible individual, and on the other side by pioneering psychiatrist Emil Kraepelin (1856–1926), who saw such deeds as expressions of an intrinsic, pathological drive: "impulsive insanity." Rather than take one of these sides, Wilmanns was content to conclude that in all events this was a case of morbid manifestations that excluded the possibility of free will determinations. The opinion was apparently shared by the court, and the accused was acquitted of attempted murder.

Wilmanns's interest in homesickness, mental illness, and crime can be seen as an extension of his then pathbreaking work on vagabondage, where the underlying psychopathology of the homeless was the subject of a much-cited treatise he was working on at the same time.[110] The case studies analyzed in this work seemed to suggest the connection of vagrancy to dementia praecox, which following Emil Kraepelin was generally discussed as probably organic in origin and more likely permanent. But the forensic expert's task

---

109. Wilmanns, "Heimweh oder impulsives Irresein?," 144. The case was interpreted psychoanalytically by Wilhelm Nicolini, "Verbrechen aus Heimweh und ihre psycho-analytische Erklärung," *Imago* 22 (1936): 91–120. For comparison, see Boym, *Future of Nostalgia*; Bronfen, *Knotted Subject*, esp. 271–76.

110. Wilmanns, *Psychopathologie des Landstreichers*; "Die Psychosen der Landstreicher," *Zentralblatt der Nervenheilkunde und Psychiatrie* 25 (1902), 729–46. Wilmanns was a lecturer at the University of Heidelberg, and his work on vagabonds was based on the clinical study of 52 criminal vagrants, their case histories, and a tracking of their diagnosis, treatment, and sentencing.

of establishing *Zurechnungsfähigkeit* or lack thereof was as difficult as ever.[111] Rather than locating the possible source of Wilmann's obsession with these formations (e.g., his own biographical displacement, born in Mexico to German merchant parents), it is useful to zero in on what he struck on that was of interest to readers. In the figure of the psychopathologically and criminally homesick and homeless, the psychiatrist identified moments that bound together, rather than disaggregated, the mental state, psychic constitution, and environment of the criminal and his or her crime. These examples specified a locus for the origin of pure criminality that was, at one and the same time, a geographical displacement and a mental dislocation. These contributions were strictly for a scholarly audience, but the "moment" Wilmanns described was one that would hold a mythical fascination for a host of experts and popular readers alike. It was a moment of pure crime, unimpeded by motive, criminal insanity, conspiracy, or corruption.

### Criminal Knowledge: A Hands-On Approach to Delinquency

If you visit the elegantly ornamented assembly hall of the Karl-Franzens University in Graz today, you will find a marble pedestal supporting the bronze bust of Hanns Gross (fig. 6). Gross served on the faculty of penal law and was briefly its dean, but the inscription on the bust reads simply, "Founder of Criminology." This is arguably inaccurate. Historians of criminology would likely place the birth of the discipline at the latest in the last third of the nineteenth century, where efforts at enlightened penal reform and scientific studies of "criminal anthropology" converged.[112] Gross counted himself a follower of the "modern school" of penal studies spearheaded by fellow Austrian Franz von Liszt (1851–1919), a Viennese who had studied in Vienna and Graz before taking chairs at universities in the German Reich, finally Berlin.[113] But it is really Hanns Gross who, as the intellectual historian William Johnston put it, has been the most influential of Austrian social think-

111. See Wilmanns, *Psychopathologie des Landstreichers*, 368–69. For the current views on "dementia praecox," the precursor of schizophrenia, see Emil Kraepelin, *Psychiatrie*.

112. Wetzell points out that the origin of the science is the object of scholarly debate, with some pointing to the development of "moral statistics" or even Enlightenment penal reform discourse, which are clear precursors of the modern discipline. See Wetzell, *Inventing the Criminal*, 15–38; cf. Pasquale Pasquino, "Criminology: The Birth of a Special Knowledge," in Burchell, Gordon, and Miller, *Foucault Effect*, 235–50; Piers Beirne, *Inventing Criminology*.

113. See Wetzell, *Inventing the Criminal*, 33–38.

FIGURE 6. Bust of Hanns Gross in the *Aula* of the Karl-Franzens-Universität Graz. © Alois Kernbauer.

ers, even if his name is little known.[114] The reason, both for this influence and the tendency to neglect Gross as a thinker, is that his lasting contribution was as the "creator of modern crime detection," his role as a real-life Sherlock Holmes. Like the much more famous protagonist of Conan Doyle's creation, Gross believed the solver of crimes had to be a different kind of

114. Johnston, *Austrian Mind*, 94–95. In spite of the underrecognition that persisted long after Johnston's pronouncement, there is a small awakening of Gross scholarship of late, much of it centering on the famous break with his son, the anarchist and important psychoanalyst and analysand of Freud's, Otto Gross. See Dienes and Rother, *Gesetze des Vaters*; Dienes, *Gross gegen Gross*; Vyleta, *Crime, Jews and News*, 20–22.

thinker than an armchair penal theorist. He had to familiarize himself with, if not command, a broad and general knowledge of the modern world: its highest branches of scholarship and the habits, skills, and beliefs of its most common castes. His own knowledge was both theoretical and practical, and it was above all synthetic.

Gross at times advocated not for a transformation of all criminological thought but for the reform of the academic study of crime and the training of officials to include *criminalistics* (*Kriminalistik*)—a term he coined in the 1890s to denote the study of the "actual facts" (*Realien*, realities, facts on the ground, but also "exact sciences") of penal law as opposed to the theoretical workings of law and the textual interpretation of the penal code that dominated the academic study of law.[115] In 1904, in the preface to the fourth edition of the *Handbook*, criminalistics appears as a branch of criminal phenomenology, itself one of three branches of criminology. In this narrow sense, criminology consists of the phenomenology of crime, on the one hand, and the techniques of investigation on the other.[116] Gross returned to the academy from the field, as it were, after more than a decade of experience as investigating magistrate (*Untersuchungsrichter*, the Austrian state officials who were responsible for criminal investigation as well as determination of guilt and sentencing) in the Styrian countryside. His contribution was hence always to reconcile academic theory and the curriculum itself with the actual experience of handling and assessing criminals and their crimes.

By 1914 the popular American magazine *McClure's* reported on Hanns Gross in an entertaining illustrated essay titled "The Crime-Master and How He Works," making much of the by then established myth of inspectors with apparently supernatural detective capabilities and portraying Gross as a master sleuth. In calling him the "Nestor of criminalists," they perhaps offered a left-handed compliment—indeed, the literally encyclopedic quality of his collection of criminalia bordered on the pedantic even as it offered in academic form the same access to the universe of underworld fantasy that other genres did. The author of the essay was also clever to note the originality of this academic contribution was not unrelated to the professor's experience between academic training and hands-on crime work: "a university-taught lawyer who entered the service of the state as a hunter of criminals, eventu-

---

115. See, e.g., Gross's article for the Deutsche Juristen-Zeitung of February 15, 1901, "Kriminalistik," *GKA*, 1:89–93; cf. Christian Bachhiesl, "Hans Gross und die Anfänge einer naturwissenschaftlich ausgerichteten Kriminologie," *Archiv für Kriminologie* 219, no. 1/2 (2007): 46–53.

116. H. Gross, *Handbuch für Untersuchungsrichter als System der Kriminalistik*. 4th ed. (Munich: Schweitzer, 1904), 1:xii.

ally to leave it for the purpose of elevating his profession to the dignity of a science."[117]

In 1896 Gross had attempted to earn the professorial university degree (*Habilitation*) on the basis of his work in this field, submitted under the title "Penal Law Limited to Court Investigation Science (Criminalistics)," but the degree was not granted. Gross was never to receive this advanced degree, but he was nonetheless appointed a regular professorship in penal and trial law at the University of Czernowitz in the eastern Habsburg province of Bukovina in 1899. He was called to the German University at Prague in 1902. In 1905, at the age of 57, Gross was appointed at the university in his hometown of Graz, where he would complete his career.[118] The question of academic legitimacy was never satisfactorily resolved for him, however. His influential supporter, the progressive Berlin jurist Franz von Liszt, favored establishing a university position at Berlin in the "auxiliary sciences" of criminalistics, and the faculty selected Gross but failed to receive approval for the position.[119] Gross also attempted over several years to secure for himself a noble title on the basis of his scholarly achievements, and these efforts brought him frustrations but not fruit.[120] Finally, at the end of his career he did manage to establish what he long held to be the gem in the crown of the discipline he invented: a University Criminalistics Institute, which was intended to house the academic department; the "museum," or collection of objects for pedagogical use; a criminalistics station, equipped with the most sophisticated tools of scientific crime analysis; and the production of the academic organ of the discipline, his *Archiv für Kriminal-Anthropologie und Kriminalistik*.[121] The Criminalistics Institute was the apogee of Gross's career-long efforts at establishing academic legitimacy, and its history is also the history of his always unsatisfied efforts—the rooms allocated to him were wanting in space and in quality, relegated to damp and cold spaces in the basement, and he died under the

117. Waldemar Kaempffert, "The Crime-Master and How He Works," *McClure's* 14, no. 2 (1914): 99–111, 144 (quote on 102).

118. Gross, Hanns, Jurist (Personalakt Hans Gross geb. 26.12.1847), UAG.

119. Karlheinz Probst, *Geschichte der Rechtswissenschaftlichen Fakultät der Universität Graz: Teil 3, Strafrecht, Strafprozessrecht, Kriminologie*. Publikationen aus dem Archiv der Universität Graz, vol. 9/3 (Graz: Akademische Druck- u. Verlagsanstalt, 1987), 54.

120. Documentation of these efforts are in the StLA, partially quoted in material on display at the Kriminalmuseum.

121. H. Gross, "Kriminalistische Universitäts-Institute: Vortrag von Prof. Dr. Hans Groß (Graz) auf der zweiten Tagung der 'Gesellschaft für Hochschulpädagogik' zu München 19. Oktober 1911," *Zeitschrift für Hochschulpädagogik* 3, no. 1/2 (April 1912): 34–44; cf. StLA C 31 e-3259/1909.

pressure of energetically demanding physical space to match the intellectual contribution of practical crime studies.[122] One of the most revealing episodes in Gross's battle for an institute came significantly after his success in getting university backing from within his own field: the faculty and dean (Gross's junior colleague Adolf Lenz [1868–1959], who was soon to be Gross's successor as second director of the institute) objected to Gross's proposals for statutes for the institute, where the position of criminalistics with regard to the rest of penal law was turned on its head. Lenz and supporters endeavored to reinforce the proper hierarchy by renaming the institute (to stress its auxiliary or practical function).[123] The name was to remain University Criminalistics Institute until being changed to University Criminological Institute— the name it retains today—after his death.

In 1893, Gross took the opportunity to publish the catalog of information on investigative techniques that he had compiled over the course of his practical experience as investigating magistrate and then as state attorney and judge. The first edition bore the full title "Manual for Investigating Magistrates, Police Officers, Gendarmes, etc.," although in its English edition it would simply be called *Criminal Investigation*. To its third edition in 1899, Gross would significantly add to the shortened title "Manual for Investigating Magistrates" the further title "as a System of Criminalistics." The play between the particular and practical utility for practitioners on the one hand and the general structure of a system on the other points to some of the unacknowledged complexity of a work that is mainly remembered for its impressive and lasting contribution to the details of criminal investigation. Looking at any edition of the work, it is easy to see how a reader would be first and foremost impressed with the wealth of detail on the particulars of criminal investigation of all kinds, even if one were not aware of

122. Akten betr. des krim. Instituts Studienjahr 1913/14, Jur. Fak, Akten des kriminol. Inst. 1909/10 37/38, and Akten betr. des krim. Instituts Studienjahr 1909/1910 1910/11 1911/12 1912/13, Jur.Fak, Akten des kriminol. Inst. 1909/10 37/38, UAG; C 31 e-3259/1909, StLA.

123. Either the *Erscheinungslehre* (study of physical appearance) of crime or *Hilfswissenschaften* (auxiliary sciences) of penal law studies. In Gross's draft bylaws, the faculty in penal law studies was to fall under the auspices of the institute. Jur. Dek, Juridisches Dekanats-Protokoll Studienjahr 1914/15, Nr. 1677, UAG. Under Lenz's direction, the institute would turn fully to "criminal biology," a successor field to Lombroso's studies on the way to National Socialist eugenics. See Sig 6/1.2 Konvolut: Kriminologisches Universitätsinstitut in Graz (1913–1977), Nr. 76–78, AGSÖ. Copies of Lenz's "criminal-biological examination" forms make the linkage eminently clear; see Sig 6/2.1 Konvolut: Kriminologisches Universitätsinstitut in Graz (1913–1977), Nr. 57–137, AGSÖ. See also Sig 6/1.2 Konvolut: Kriminologisches Universitätsinstitut in Graz (1913–1977), Nr. 76–78, AGSÖ, and S. J. Holmes, "Review of Lenz's *Grundriss der Kriminalbiologie*," *Journal of the American Institute of Criminal Law and Criminology* 18, no. 4 (1928): 611–12.

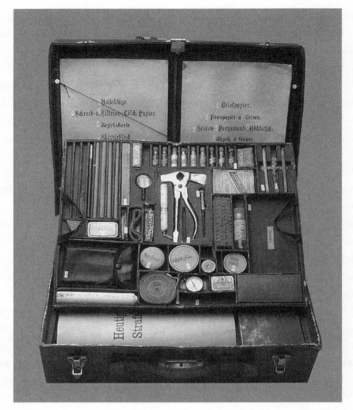

FIGURE 7. Commission case to be brought by the investigating magistrate to the crime scene as assembled according to Hanns Gross's prescriptions. Image reproduced with permission of the Hans-Gross-Kriminalmuseum, Graz.

the originality of such an inquiry. The loving attendance to every conceivable aspect of the practices of criminals and the procedures of criminalists is overwhelming. Gross's construction of the heroic figure of the examining magistrate cannot but have reminded contemporary readers of the fictional British counterpart Sherlock Holmes—the methodological focus on careful procedure, observation of detail, logical reasoning, and intuition for clues is reminiscent of Conan Doyle's hero's remark about a method "founded upon the observation of trifles."[124]

Every reader of Conan Doyle knows that Holmes had his Moriarty—the professor whose mathematical acuity was at the same time (due to degenerate

124. From the "Bocombe Valley Mystery," cited in Wagner, *Science of Sherlock*, 89 (or just as apt, "The world is full of obvious things which nobody by any chance ever observes," 98).

congenital tendency) channeled into criminal genius.[125] Like many a crime story, and in a much more exposed way than in any other criminological text of his period, Gross's criminalistics pits the figure of the investigator against the figure of the criminal, each simultaneously the other's doppelganger and rival. The architecture of the work betrays that the criminal is less the object of construction than the investigating officer: the first chapter of the introductory segment ("General") defines the figure of the *Untersuchungsrichter*, or investigating magistrate, as an ideal type, and parts two and three explore first knowledge and then skills required of him. "Particular Offenses" constitute the last third of the book, although there is no doubt that the immense and various landscape of crime is discussed throughout the sections on the required knowledge and skills of the magistrate. Much of this strikes the reader today as ethnographic: it focuses on criminal practices, including sign systems to communicate with one another, and especially means of dissimulation and disguise; criminal language, receiving its own chapter; superstitious beliefs common to criminals; and a self-consciously anthropological section on "Gypsies."[126]

Above all, the new knowledge was synthetic and what we would call interdisciplinary. Criminal psychology, one of the pillars of the new science, was itself a composite of vast and diverse specialized knowledges. The model of the new jurisprudence generally was to be the natural sciences, medicine in particular. The methodology of the physical sciences ought to rule the criminal scientist's view of law: the observation, collection, and organization of facts.[127]

Criminal psychology was at first understood narrowly as the study of psychic illnesses and liminal mental states as they manifest themselves in criminal behavior.[128] The discipline was hence closely connected to the problem of

125. See Arthur Conan Doyle, "The Adventure of the Final Problem," first published in 1893: "But the man had hereditary tendencies of the most diabolical kind. A criminal strain ran in his blood, which, instead of being modified, was increased and rendered infinitely more dangerous by his extraordinary mental powers." *Strand Magazine* 6 (July–December 1893): 560.

126. H. Gross, *Handbuch für Untersuchungsrichter, Polizeibeamte, Gendarmen u.s.w.*, 2nd ed. (Graz: Leuschner und Lubensky, 1894), 328–49. While in the field in the Styrian countryside, one of Gross's principal occupations was what was known as "Zigeunerbekämpfung," the struggle against gypsies; see Bachhiesl, *Zwischen Indizienparadigma und Pseudowissenschaft*, 161–63. P. Becker argues that Gross ethnicized the earlier juridical category of moral failure through a "strategy of replacement"; see Becker, "The Criminologists' Gaze at the Underworld: Toward an Archaeology of Criminological Writing," in Becker and Wetzell, *Criminals and Their Scientists*, 113–24.

127. H. Gross, "Kriminalpsychologische Aufgaben," *Wiener Zeitung*, May 30, 1900, reprinted in *GKA*, 1:158–63 (see 158–59).

128. Ibid., 159–60.

establishing criminal responsibility (*Zurechnungsfähigkeit*), and this function had by the turn of the century passed to the expert knowledge of psychiatrists and the realm of forensic psychiatry. Gross's adoption of the term represented a self-conscious appropriation of the broadest lessons of "general psychology" by the criminalist and the application of these to every question relating to crime to which it might be useful. The crucial point here is that it is not the special psychology of the criminal that is at issue—in fact, Gross stated explicitly his understanding that the discipline recognized no qualities peculiar to the criminal mind. Psychology was useful for the criminalist not only for the understanding of the psychic capacities and motives of criminals but to help anticipate and interpret the perceptions and mental responses of witnesses, judges, juries, and experts providing testimony. His lengthy volume *Criminal Psychology* was first published by a small university bookstore press in Graz in 1898, but it was soon to be followed by a much more widely distributed edition and several translations. It surprised readers who expected something quite different from a book of its title. It was not about the peculiar and innate psychopathology of the criminal, and in fact the forensic category of *Zurechnungsfähigkeit* that one would expect to be central barely appears in the text at all.[129] Gross's observations about how to glean meanings from what has not been said as well as what is said, tricks of memory and forgetting, strategies of substitution in liars, or even slips of the tongue resemble psychoanalytic insights about the unconscious more than has usually been recognized.[130] But the most striking thing about the structure of the volume is its division into two parts: "Subjective," subtitled "The Psychic Capability of the Investigator," and "Objective," or "The Psychic Activity of the Interrogated." The two halves were unequal, with nearly twice the pages devoted to the latter; further, the categories overlapped significantly, to be sure.[131] The criminal subject, in the last analysis, was unreliable in every

129. Cf. the review in the organ of the German Society for Psychology, the *Zeitschrift für Psychologie und Physiologie des Sinnesorgane* 18, no. 4 (September 1898): 284–95, esp. 284, 291.

130. There are many examples throughout the text. The kinship to psychoanalysis was identified (if passingly) years ago in Ellenberger, *Discovery of the Unconscious*, 495. The first edition of *Criminal Psychology* of course preceded the discovery of the unconscious, strictly taken, and was cited in Freud's *Psychopathology of Everyday Life*; Freud, *Gesammelte Werke*, 4:164n1.

131. While his definitions shift, here is how Gross describes it in the *Deutsche Juristen-Zeitung*, February 15, 1901 (*GKA*, 1:89–93):

"objective criminalistics" refers to criminalistics proper, and "subjective criminalistics" refers to criminal psychology. The latter is purely negative, establishing deficiency and unreliability of perception and reproduction; the former is positive knowledge and the ability to process the artifacts (*Realien*) of crime: criminal language, semiotics, practices, super-

regard; the investigator's task was to nail down that which was by its nature evasive: the crime and the criminal.

Gross hence took an active role in spreading the gospel of the French innovator Alphonse Bertillon, whose vision of a uniform system of personal identification of criminals incorporated the utopian promise of systematically and bureaucratically solving the problem caused by a criminality that was at once international and anonymous.[132] Bertillon's plan involved adopting a system of recording a fixed series of physical measurements of specified bony (and therefore of constant measurement) parts of the body that together could not be identical in two human beings (fig. 8). This anthropometric system vied with the nascent science of dactyloscopy, also called fingerprinting, which was dominant in Britain. Gross reviewed Bertillon's book on the subject and recommended that police prefects uniformly adopt the system, and while he reported that he had first been mocked for the suggestion, he noted that the card system had meanwhile been widely incorporated. Criminals could be taken no more safely at their name than at their word. In a world of increasingly slippery criminals, adopting not only pseudonyms and costumes but even radically altering their physical appearances, the question of criminal identity had become central.[133] Gross reported proudly that between the first of November 1899 and the same day and month of 1901, 23,930 persons were "anthropometrically recorded" in the Viennese identification bureau, 977 inquiries about international criminals were dispatched, and 222 anonymous or pseudonymous persons had been identified. Records show that the Berlin office had approximately twenty-one thousand in the same period, a number that would swell to nearly fifty thousand by 1903.[134]

stition, tools/weapons, identification (Bertillonage), handwriting, forensic photography, expert witnesses, and all possible auxiliary means of the criminalist.

132. Bertillon, *Identification anthropométrique*, reviewed by Hanns Gross in *Allgemeine österreichische Gerichtszeitung* 49 (1894); see *GKA*, 1:124–32.

133. Caplan and Torpey, *Documenting Individual Identity*, and the seminal article by Allan Sekula, "Body and the Archive."

134. I. Rep. 77 CCXXXV, Nr. 1, Bd. 13, "Acta betr. Die Verwaltung der Kriminal-Polizei, sowie der allgemeinen Sicherheitspolizei in der Stadt Berlin," memorandum from Polizei-Präsident to the Minister of the Interior; see document 7297, "Verwaltungsbericht der IV. Abteilung für die Jahre 1901–1903." GSPK. By the end of 1903 Berlin would have 48,786 anthropometric cards in its registry, and suggestions were made to follow cities such as Paris, London, Vienna, and Bucharest in adding measurements of pinky fingers and feet; by this time, however, the dominance of Bertillon's system was no longer assured, as the London police considered moving to fingerprints alone as a simpler and fully reliable system. Galton's research on dactylography was contemporaneous with Bertillon's studies of anthropometry—his book *Finger Prints* came

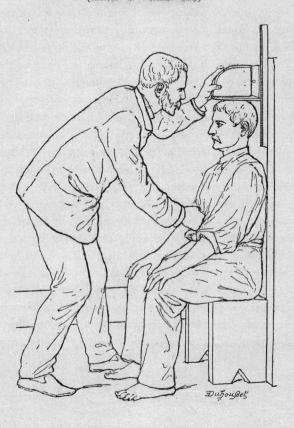

# MENSURATION DU BUSTE

(hauteur de l'homme assis)

Faire asseoir le sujet bien à fond sur le tabouret, veiller à ce qu'il se tienne droit, placer et manœuvrer l'équerre mobile comme pour la taille (*Instr.*, page 20).

FIGURE 8. Alphonse Bertillon's system of anthropometric recording. The diagram instructs users how to make the proper physical measurements.

To be beyond the ecumene of the system was by 1902, for Gross, to live in savagery—in this report he takes as interchangeable synonyms the civilized and the "bertillonized" world.[135]

Indeed, just a few years into the new century, the central European police world would not only be bertillonized but thoroughly saturated with Hanns Gross's way of looking at the solution of crimes, and the techniques he recommended were a kind of bible to aspiring investigators.[136] In 1903, Gross wrote an essay for a broader public where he reflected on the nature of modern criminality.[137] As the times change—as they do so quickly in the modern world, he wrote in "Modern criminals"—perpetrators adapt; in fact, in relative terms, crooks and their means of crime, their talents, knowledges, and their technologies modernize most rapidly. Just when the criminalist masters what tools he can poach from science and what practices he can understand of the criminal, everything changes; technology in modern society creates new venues for crime and new kinds of crime, and the vanguard criminals make use of synthetic knowledge and access to technology just as the model investigating magistrate does. In this rueful essay, the crook is as much a mirror of Gross himself as both are of a certain image of modernity.

## Criminal Exhibitions

The academic prestige of many of these efforts seemed to be in danger of being compromised by their marginally sensational character. The style of reasoning represented by Gross's studies of criminalistics and criminal psychology is one in which prurience, vicarious desire, or sensationalism cannot be separated from the objective study of the criminal and the subjective self-reflection of the investigator or scientist. As was the case in the *Großstadt-Dokumente*, it is counterproductive to disaggregate the scientific from the

---

out in 1892; the British had been slow to adopt the continental system of identification bearing Bertillon's name and early to abandon it.

135. "Die Erkennungsdienst der Wiener Polizei," *GKA*, 1:132–38.

136. The above-cited series of reports to the Imperial German Ministry of the Interior from the Berlin Polizei-Präsidium is an important case in point. The report cited Gross's manual by name, but more impressive than this is the way its descriptions of recommended police procedure follow Gross's manual and articles in the *Archiv* point for point. See, e.g., "Dienstanweisung für das Verhalten des Kriminal-Kommissars vom Dienst bei Kapitalverbrechen" (pp. 31–32), "Anleitung für die Bearbeitung von Kapitalverbrechen (pp. 33–41), and passim, I. Rep. 77 CCXXXV, Nr. 1, Bd. 13, "Acta betr. Die Verwaltung der Kriminal-Polizei, sowie der allgemeinen Sicherheitspolizei in der Stadt Berlin," GSPK.

137. Gross, "Moderne Verbrecher," *Umschau* 12 (March 14, 1903), reprinted in *GKA*, 1:342–52.

literary contribution or the serious inquiry from the exploitative display. The new discipline threatened the protected place of criminological inquiry not only by virtue of its expansive agenda and radical methodological approach. As this discussion has stressed, Gross's central, explicit, and implied claims all insisted on the breakdown of the distance between theoretical knowledge and experience, or between expert and criminal object. The criminalist has awoken from his theoretical slumber and finds himself, so to speak, in the midst of crime itself—he must place himself within the crime scene, he must think like the criminal and speak his language. Seen from this perspective, it is not hard to postulate how Gross easily slipped into visions of social exclusion of criminal elements, even their purge through means as radical as deportation and eugenic measures of sterilization and forced abortion.

In 1908, Paul Langenscheidt launched a series of criminalistics texts—like the *Großstadt-Dokumente* and others we have mentioned, poised between science and popular voyeurism—titled *Enzyklopädie der modernen Kriminalistik* (Encyclopedia of modern criminalistics).[138] One interesting text in this series is the encyclopedia compiled by Hanns Gross and published in 1901. [139] It was really more of a reference manual coming in at just under 100 pages, a catalog of terms ordered alphabetically. The list works in part as a dictionary, with one-word translations of terms (from criminal argot or the language of criminalists) and longer, explanatory entries on topics that will sometimes strike the reader as wildly free ranging and random (dog, cartridge, misunderstanding, sulfur). It is interesting to note the most detailed and lovingly handled articles, such as "Blutspurenbehandlung"—the treatment of traces of blood. The detailed treatment of this entry may be expected in light of its special status as a novel and highly technical forensic measure, but the prurient value of a focus on the unseemly category of blood is made

---

138. The series continued through World War I and into the 1920s, including texts on all branches of forensics including sexology. Titles included (1/2) Staatsanwalt Dr. Erich Wulffen, *Psychologie des Verbrechers*; (3) Prof. Dr. A. Niceforo und Reg.-Rat Dr. H. Lindenau, *Die Kriminalpolizei und ihre Hilfswissenschaften*; (4–6) Prof. Dr. Bruno Meyer, *Sexualgeschichte der Menschheit unter besonderer Berücksichtigung der Kriminalität*; (7) Dr. Franz Helbing, *Die Tortur: Geschichte der Folter in Kriminalverfahren aller Völker und Zeiten*; (8) Staatsanwalt Dr. Erich Wulffen, *Der Sexualverbrecher*; (9) Geh. Med.-Rat Prof. Dr. F. Strassmann, Med.-Rat Dr. H. Hoffmann und Dr. H. Marx, *Gerichtsärzte, Medizin und Strafrecht*; (10) Rechtsanwalt Dr. Max Alsberg, *Justizirrtum und Wiederaufnahme*; (11) Dr. Med. Karl Birnbaum, Anstaltsarzt in der Berliner Städtischen Irrenanstalt Buch, *Die psychopathischen Verbrecher. Die Grenzzustände zwischen geistiger Gesundheit und Krankheit in ihren Beziehungen zu Verbrechen und Strafwesen.*

139. Hanns Gross, *Encyclopädie der Kriminalistik* (Leipzig: Vogel, 1901).

clear in the series of entries dealing with blood in some way: "Blut, Blutegel (an der Vulva, als Abortiv benutzt), Bluterkrankheit (s. Hämophilie), Blut-krystalle, Blutspuren-behandlung, Blutspurenbeseitigung, Blutspurensicherung, Blutstropfen, Blutuntersuchung."[140]

A further book in the series is *Die Kriminalpolizei und ihre Hilfswissenschaften* (The criminal police and their auxiliary sciences), written much along the lines of Gross's handbook but in an illustrated format (including three hundred illustrations after original photographs).[141] The text revels in the idyll of perfect scientific precision in the treatment of crime scenes, criminal identification, the discovery and handling of all sorts of evidence, and other minutiae more than reminiscent of Gross's manual and the articles collected in his *Archiv*. Here, however, the exploitative side of Gross's narrative displays is made explicit, as the three hundred photographs include pornographic images of opened and mutilated bodies found at crime scenes.

The book also contained a detailed description and images of an interesting institution, the Berlin Crime Museum.[142] The municipal police administration had assembled a collection more than ten years earlier; in fact, a report on the exhibition from 1899 already insisted that it was not merely a "Raritätenkabinett" (a cabinet of oddities of prurient value) but rather an educational device for the purpose of training aspiring investigators. Indeed, that was Hanns Gross's intention when he proposed the establishment of such collections wherever investigators were to be trained.[143] In the pedantic pronouncement surrounding the establishment of such a collection in Graz, Gross was explicit about this function: "Paragraph 2. Purpose. The general

140. Gross, *Encyclopädie*, 13–14. The items in the list are blood, leeches (on the vulva for use as an abortive), bloodsickness (see Hemophilia), crystalline derivatives of the blood, treatment of blood traces as evidence, removal of blood traces, securing of blood traces, drops of blood, blood examination.

141. A. Niceforo, *Die Kriminalpolizei und ihre Hilfswissenschaften* (Groß-Lichterfelde-Ost: Langenscheidt, 1910). Alfredo Niceforo (1876–1960), an Italian criminologist associated with the Lombrosian school and active at the time of publication at the University of Naples and the New University at Brussels, had provided much of the text on criminal science, and the text was introduced and expanded by the German Regierungsrat H. Lindenau (indeed, a great deal of the examples are from Berlin, and just as many from Paris).

142. See Niceforo, *Kriminalpolizei*, 394–96. The Berlin police administration reported that the collection had finally found an adequate space for display and use in the fall of 1907; see Acta betr. die Verwaltung der Kriminal-Polizei, sowie der allgemeinen Sicherheitspolizei in der Stadt Berlin [Verwaltungsberichte], Verwaltungsbericht der Abteilung IV für die Jahre 1904–1907, 31/204, GSPK.

143. See H. Gross, "Das Kriminal-Museum in Graz," *Zeitschrift für die gesamte Strafwissenschaften* 16 (1901), reprinted in *GKA*, 1:97–113.

purpose of this museum aims to offer novices in the field of penal law an overview of the facts [*Realien*] of criminalistics so that they may, before they take their own positions as judges or investigating magistrates, achieve clarity on what means serve crime, what the objective effects of culpable behavior are, and what auxiliary means stand at the official's disposal."[144] The collection, at first relatively small, was on display in vitrines in the corridor lobby of the Graz courthouse, although he was eventually to achieve his ambition of having these moved to the university as part of the institute and thereby associated with higher education and the training of crime professionals. In Gross's insistent and detailed demands to the university administration, the need to bring the collections to any future criminalistics institute of the university, the space to display the twenty-two cases (in 1910) of material, and the conditions to maintain them, as well as human resources to catalog and manage them, were all to be seen "in *inseparable unity*" with all other facets of the institute.[145]

While the collection of the Criminal Museum had been assembled and displayed years before the University Criminalistics Institute was close to becoming a reality, the two projects had always been linked.[146] The idea of a criminal museum was mentioned in the first and each subsequent edition of Gross's *Criminal Investigation*, and the first collection of material was gathered within two years of its publication. The museum should serve a chiefly didactic function, and hence should collect and display items that could familiarize aspiring students with the basics of criminalistics, organized in 32

144. Vorschrift für das Criminal-Museum in Graz, May 3, 1895; original held by Hans Gross-Kriminalmuseum, Karl-Franzens-Universität Graz. The text is included in one of the displays and reads

> par. 2. Zweck. Der allgemeine Zweck dieses Museums geht dahin, den Anfängern in der strafrechtlichen Thätigkeit einen Überblick über die Realien der Criminalistik zu bieten, so dass dieselben schon eher, bevor sie selbstständig als Erhebungs- oder Untersuchungs-richter auftreten, sich darüber klar sind, welcher Mittel sich Verbrechen bedienen, was die sachlichen Wirkungen der strafbaren Handlungen sind, und welcher Hilfsmittel sich der erhebende Richter bedienen kann.

145. See esp. C 31 e-3259/1909, "Bericht über den gegenwärtigen Stand der Frage eines Kriminalistischen Instituts" (letter to the Dean's office of the Faculty of Law), June 26, 1910, StLA.

146. H. Gross, "Kriminalistische Universitäts-Institut: Vortrag von Prof. Dr. Hans Groß (Graz) auf der zweiten Tagung der 'Gesellschaft für Hochschulpädagogik' zu München 19. Oktober 1911," *Zeitschrift für Hochschulpädagogik* 3, no. 1/2 (1912): 34–44 (see 38); cf. "Das Kriminal-Museum in Graz," *Zeitschrift für die gesamte Strafrechts-Wissenschaft* 16 (1901/2): 74ff.; reprinted in *GKA*, 1:97–113; *Zeitschrift für die gesamte Strafrechts-Wissenschaft* 14 (1894): 13ff.

categories including, for instance, forensic medicine (damaged bones along-side weapons that had caused the trauma, preserved skin with strangulation marks, etc.); specimens of various kinds, including blood, semen, hair, etc.; poisons, drugs, abortives, etc.; weapons and tools of crime; projectiles, in-cluding bullets and cartridges of every type; blood samples recovered ad hoc; blood samples collected by specific methods; footprints; artifacts of criminal superstition; gypsy artifacts; criminal language samples, and on and on.[147] Gross's frequent references to the medical model of criminalistics suggests the origin for such an idea: throughout the nineteenth century, medical stu-dents across Europe had made use of pathological-anatomical collections where specimens and models of the full range of anatomical peculiarities and corporeal manifestations of illness could be viewed.[148] Any visit to such de-positories, some of which are still available for view today, confirms their sensational character even if some of this has been manufactured more re-cently.[149] As with the pathological-anatomical collections that seem to be their forerunners, the question of the relationship of their pedagogical missions to their character as curiosity cabinets is a crucial one. Gross echoed the defend-ers of any of these collections in his insistence that the aspiring investigator or jurist, as the ideal type of visitor to such a collection, should be as objective and passionless as a doctor upon seeing wounded bodies, mutilated members, or pornographic photographs, and that any sensational effects of such view-ings were either inappropriate or unavoidable by-products of the necessity of facing the realities of crime, as the expert must. This dilemma resembled in some sense the famous catalogs of sexual pathologies published by Gross's colleague and friend in Graz Richard von Krafft-Ebing—lists and narratives

147. "Kriminal-Museum," *GKA*, 1:99–102.

148. One of the finest collections was the Museum des Pathologisch-anatomischen Instituts in Vienna, founded in 1796.

149. Berlin boasts an important collection founded by the pathbreaking scientist Rudolf Vir-chow and attached to the famed Charité hospital, marketed along the lines of medical history, although the feel of the curiosity cabinet is unmistakable. See Krietsch and Dietel, *Pathologisch-Anatomisches Cabinet*; other well-known collections, such as the Hygiene Museum in Dresden, also stress a variety of themes relating to progressive medical enlightenment and political ma-nipulation of health knowledge and policy. The Vienna collection (now the Pathologisches-Anatomisches Bundesmuseum located in the eerie panoptical "madman's tower" on the campus of the old Vienna General Hospital) is both particularly rich and unapologetically sensational, although its particular morbidity seems less altered and manipulated and self-conscious—more "original"—than similar Vienna attractions, such as the Vienna Criminal Museum and the ex-traordinary Bestattungsmuseum (rendered in English as the Funeral Museum). For an overview of this self-thematization of Morbid Vienna see Veigl, *Morbides Wien*.

FIGURE 9. Skulls with labeling from the Hans-Gross-Kriminalmuseum, Graz.

of the unspeakable, obscured by Latin where possible, but nonetheless always threatening to titillate the potential reader.[150] The concern with being taken as lascivious, sensational, or pornographic was a typical one for many of the new knowledge systems discussed in this book, and the background of Gross's struggle for academic legitimacy makes this case typical rather than exceptional. Gross's compulsive systematicity does little to dispel the spirit of the sensational from the work. The more the gruesome objects were measured, documented, categorized, indexed, and so on, the more their objective management itself became an inherent part of their gruesomeness. The index cards in the possession of the current Criminal Museum in Graz and the long listings of museum holdings by group and category in Gross's publications on the collection all confirm the compatibility rather than oppositionality of the twin hyperscientistic and sensational character of the collection.

A good example of this is the excellent collection of damaged skulls and bones assembled and exhibited alongside the instruments that caused their traumas (fig. 9). The exhibit is thus a learning tool, designed so that the student may learn to "read" various fractures and to link them back to likely instruments and potential perpetrators. "These skulls of murdered men," in-

150. Krafft-Ebing, *Psychopathia sexualis*, chap. 2, 4.

sists Gross in a telling disavowal, "are not here because they are the curious
and horrible souvenirs of forgotten assassinations."[151] What appears to be a
curiosity cabinet is precisely not one. Look closely, he continues, and you will
see the subtle differences among these fractured skulls and bones. . . . As at the
crime scene itself, it takes the ice-cold and trained investigator's eye to see the
clue behind the sensation. As was the case for Conan Doyle's concurrent hero
Holmes, the "labyrinthine obscurity and lurid fascination" of the dark city is
the condition of possibility for the emergence of the enlightened detective;[152]
the enlightened law is wrapped in the embrace of darkest criminality.[153]

A few decades before the proliferation of thinking, writing, and practices
relating to the dark city and its criminals, Karl Marx offered a witty reflection
on the productive forces of crime, although it was so unexpectedly prescient
that its wit is usually forgotten. He wrote,

> A philosopher produces ideas, a poet poems, a clergyman sermons, a pro-
> fessor compendia and so on. A criminal produces crimes. If we look a little
> closer at the connection between this latter branch of production and society
> as a whole, we shall rid ourselves of many prejudices. The criminal produces
> not only crimes but also criminal law, and with this also the professor who
> gives lectures on criminal law and in addition to this the inevitable compen-
> dium in which this same professor throws his lectures onto the general mar-
> ket as "commodities." . . . The criminal moreover produces the whole of the
> police and criminal justice, constables, judges, hangmen, juries, etc.; and all
> these different lines of business, which form equally many categories of the
> social division of labor, develop different capacities of the human spirit, cre-
> ate new needs and new ways of satisfying them. Torture alone has given rise
> to the most ingenious mechanical inventions, and employed many honorable
> craftsmen in the production of its instruments. . . . The criminal breaks the
> monotony and everyday security of bourgeois life. In this way he keeps it from
> stagnation, and gives rise to that uneasy tension and agility without which
> even the spur of competition would get blunted. Thus he gives a stimulus to
> the productive forces.[154]

Marx was displaying his most heavy-handed irony to excoriate apologists
of the limitless productive forces of bourgeois capitalism. The irony is often

151. Waldemar Kaempffert, "The Crime-Master and How He Works," *McClure's* 14, no. 2
(1914): 108; cf. Gross, "Kriminal-Museum," *GKA*, 1:106.

152. Quoted in Williams, *Country and City*, 227, cf. 229.

153. In Franz Kafka's brilliant formulation, the authorities do not seek guilt in the population but are drawn or attracted (*angezogen*) to guilt. *Der Process*, "Verhaftung."

154. Karl Marx, *Theories of Surplus Value*, 4 vols. (London: Lawrence and Wishart, 1964),
1:365.

stripped from readings of the passage in contemporary criminology, where it has sometimes been quoted. How could it be otherwise, in a world where penitentiaries replace factories and surveillance cameras are more common than streetlights?[155] Yet Marx's voice in this passage as in others does betray a sense of awe within the biting chord, a pitch of wonder that even the most berating sarcasm cannot dissolve. That remainder of marvel from the previous generation of political economists marks perhaps nothing more than the powerful ambivalence of the Enlightenment legacy.

155. An exceptionally creative and insightful use of Marx's maxim in the contemporary literature is by Michael Zinganel, *Real Crime: Architektur, Stadt und Verbrechen* (Vienna: Selene, 2003).

# 2

# Identical Origins: (Homo)sexual Subjects and Violent Fantasy in the 1860s

We begin with a scandal—the claim that in German-speaking central Europe in the 1860s, the sexual subject in the modern sense emerged. To do so is to revisit a premise made famous—if not notorious—by Michel Foucault, who argued, in an unfortunately quotable phrase, that

> The nineteenth-century homosexual became a personage, a past, a case history, and a childhood. . . . Nothing that went into his total composition was unaffected by his sexuality. . . . It was consubstantial with him, less as a habitual sin than as a singular nature . . . a species.[1]

The claim is scandalous not only because it has been persistently challenged by those who would place the "origins" of homosexual identities (vs. acts) earlier in the nineteenth century, or in the mid-eighteenth century, or even in the medieval or classical periods, or as universal. Foucault posited a relation between the disciplinary discourse embodied in his scant footnote (citing a single essay representing the emergence of a biomedical discourse on sexual deviancy) and the subjective identification of homosexual actors (unnamed), who would produce resistance on the grounds provided by the pathologizing identity.

The prime mover in this liberation movement is Karl Heinrich Ulrichs (1825–95; fig. 10), whose apologies for homosexuality constituted at once a theory of sexuality, an explanation of its origins, and an explicit appeal for political emancipation. Carl Westphal (1833–90; fig. 11) published the 1869/70 essay that Foucault credits as the occasion of the "birth" of the modern psychiatric model of the homosexual. This emerged from a literature of forensic

---

1. Foucault, *History of Sexuality*, 1:43.

FIGURE 10. Karl Heinrich Ulrichs.

medicine (training for physicians to use their knowledge to assist the court in criminal cases), and that evolution is relevant to this study. Another important figure, if less of a self-conscious emancipator than Ulrichs, is the Austro-Hungarian literary critic Karl Maria Benkert/Károly Maria Kertbeny (1824–82; fig. 12), credited with coining the immediate ancestor to the contemporary term *homosexual*.

All these figures and others were unwittingly engaged in the production of a conflicted sometimes self-contradictory complex that can be thought of as the conception of "sexuality." This production process pertained to expert discourses on people designated as deviant, especially males with same-sex at-

FIGURE 11. Carl Westphal. Image courtesy of Universitätsbibliothek, Humboldt-Universität zu Berlin).

tractions; it pertained to surveillance practices, policing, and legal discourses; it pertained as well to the way some people began to recognize and interpret their own feelings and their existence as sexual beings, as persons with and defined by a sexuality. The process also involved a virtually simultaneous cultural fantasy, mediated by press reports of sensational nature, linking the identity of homosexuality to brutal violence.

These registers of articulation of the nature of homosexuality should be seen as parts of a whole but could be differentiated from one another by the designations *disciplinary*, *emancipatory*, and *sensational*. This chapter will show how these articulations of an identity of sexuality itself and a personal

FIGURE 12. Karl Maria Kertbeny.

identity coterminous with one's sexuality were not merely concurrent but rather components of a single process. That is the first of several meanings intended to be denoted by the title phrase "identical origins." Second, the phrase refers to the fact that what emerged from this process was not a homosexual identity but an identity of sexuality in itself, that is, of normative human sexuality. Behind every text describing pathological manifestations is an image of the sexual self as such. "Identical origins" further refers to the history of identity as well as to the identity of searches for origins—the "answers" implied by the stories told of the origins of sexual identity may tell us less than the construction of the question itself. This story hence does not begin with origins, which only emerged as a question in the 1860s. Before the question of origins was the question of nature.

### Second Nature

An extremely important contribution to this transformation was the philosopher Arthur Schopenhauer (1788–1860), whom some might be surprised to see credited as a "theorist of homosexuality."[2] This status was earned on the basis of a six-page appendix to the third edition of his *World as Will and Idea*, published in 1859, the penultimate year of the philosopher's life.[3] The notes on homosexuality in the appendix are third-order commentary: the supplementary second volume of the work takes the form of commentary on the first volume, and Schopenhauer added the appendix to the third edition as an exposition of a passing mention of pederasty in the earlier two editions of the supplement. In the original reference, Schopenhauer had referred to this diversion from reproductive desire as an example of the human's relatively weak instinct in relation to his overdeveloped brain; hence, the suggestion is that our distance from our animal nature—our civilization, our mental hyperdevelopment—is the source of homosexual instincts. (Here the deviation of the instinct is compared to the digressions of the meat fly, whose attraction to rotting meat for a repository of larvae sometimes leads it astray to the stinky dragon lily.)[4]

Schopenhauer's argument in the appendix is easy to consign to simple

2. E.g., Prätorius, "Die Bibliographie der Homosexualität," 345–445. The term *theorist(s) of homosexuality* is taken from Féray and Herzer, "Homosexual Studies," 24, who include in their list all the major figures discussed here.

3. See Arthur Schopenhauer, "Anhang zum vorstehenden Kapitel," in *Die Welt als Wille und Vorstellung*, 8th ed., vol. 2 (Leipzig: Brockhaus, 1891), 643–51.

4. Schopenhauer, *Welt als Wille*, 2:620.

homophobia and pathologization, but this is a misconstrual. It begins with a clear statement that in and of itself, the practice is not merely unnatural but a repulsive and abhorrent monstrosity, and it ends with the sarcastic anticipation that academic opponents will relish attributing to the author the obviously untenable position of having defended pederasty.[5] So the appendix is both begun and concluded with disavowals, and the latter one admits an expectation of opprobrium. From this observation alone we may conclude that the theses that homosexual acts are repugnant and unnatural and that it would be ludicrous for philosophy to defend the practice of pederasty are the background against which Schopenhauer is writing and not his primary position. *Pederasty* was a common name (and a misnomer, as was often noted) for what the law named "unnatural" or, more precisely, "counter to nature."[6] It is too easy to forget that what Schopenhauer concludes above all is that "the complete universality and stubborn ineradicability of the thing show that it proceeds somehow from human nature," and further, quoting Horace, that it is as inevitable as all nature is (*Naturam expelles furca, tamen usque recurret*— you drive nature out with a pitchfork, but it just comes back).[7]

Contemporary readers of Schopenhauer's six-page appendix are apt to focus either on this surface aversion to same-sex desire or on the eccentricity

5. Ibid., 643–44, 651.

6. In Schopenhauer's Prussia it was defined in Paragraph 143 of the penal code as "unnatural indecency exercised between persons of the male sex or humans and animals" (Die widernatürliche Unzucht, welche zwischen Personen männlichen Geschlechts oder von Menschen mit Thieren verübt wird); the Habsburg criminal code deployed the phrase "indecency against nature" (Unzucht wider die Natur) in its Paragraph 129, followed by subsections *a*, with animals, and *b*, with persons of the same sex. "Pederasty" was a catchall phrase of sorts with shifting and unstable referents (not only did it not refer specifically to "boy love" (Knabenliebe), it conflated and shifted among references to anal intercourse between partners of any gender or status (including married couples; see, e.g., W. Pichler and L. G. Kraus, *Compendium der Hygiene: Sanitätspolizei und gerichtlichen Medicin* [Stuttgart: Enke, 1875], 344) to same-sex sexual contact of any kind.

7. Schopenhauer, *Welt als Wille*, 2:645. This primary point will be the one cited by Magnus Hirschfeld's Scientific-Humanitarian Committee in its arguments for the repeal of Paragraph 175 of the German penal code (which was adopted from the Prussian code's Paragraph 143). The signators of the famous petition attribute to Schopenhauer the point that the universal geographical and temporal distribution of same-sex love demonstrates that it is natural ("dass die allgemeine örtliche und zeitliche Ausbreitung der Liebe zu Personen des eigenen Geschlechts ihre Natürlichkeit beweise"); see Wissenschaftllich-humanitäres Komitee, petition "An die gesetzgebenden Körperschaften des Deutschen Reiches" [1901], "Hirschfeld Scrapbook" carton 1, sec. 2, p. 9 (a–d), KIRSGR. By the time the petition was drafted, however, theories of degenerative pathology allowed opponents to decouple the "innate" from the "natural," even calling their conflation "ridiculous." See Schrenck-Notzing, "Beiträge zur forensischen Beurteilung," 7–8.

of the explanation of its relationship to nature. Almost exclusively afflicting the very young and old, Schopenhauer ventures, nature's homosexual impulse protects the species by selecting against weakened or decayed reproductive material. The connection to Darwinism may seem apparent, and this coincidence was noted within a decade.[8] That Schopenhauer, in his seventy-first year of life, identified the unnatural sexual impulse as natural to old age ("a phenomenon of the dying instinct," as he expressed in the year before his own demise), is certainly of some significance. But this subtle confession is merely a facet of the whole gesture of conceptualizing the natural through the manifestly unnatural manifestation. The indecent impulse is a marker of nature—here, one that defines it for the observer.

It is worth returning to the larger context of the chapter on sexual love (once again, drafted as a commentary on the crucial chapter of the first volume, "Affirmation and Negation of the Will") to which the pages on pederasty are appended. Readers of Schopenhauer will recall that the Will is decoupled from and opposed to the Intellect, and it is on account of the human's overdeveloped intellect that deviations (*Irrwege*) take place. In sexual unions, we find a conflict between impulses to unite that are driven by the individual will and those that are driven by the needs of the species. This is deftly illustrated through a discussion of arranged marriages as against love matches. Counterintuitively, Schopenhauer identifies marriages of convenience with the interest of the individual, for they are linked to the real concerns of the present (be they clan loyalty, business interest, or money). Marriages for love, motivated by the illusory force of the will, execute the needs of the species. This is the reason, he argues, that marriages for love are almost always unhappy, whereas arranged matches work out so well by comparison. In love matches one surrenders one's own, immediate happiness, as it were, to the success of future generations.[9]

It is in this light that one should consider the "unprecedented paradox," or unnatural nature, of pederasty. How could the irresistible urge of the pederast be a sign of the human future? It is not a matter of recognizing an exception to the rule of desire, as Gide read Schopenhauer.[10] Just as unions for love express the thing in itself, the will incarnate and uncloaked by the self-interest and reality of society and intellect, so this most vicious of acts is created by nature for her highest purpose: the maintenance and preservation

8. See David Asher, "Schopenhauer and Darwinism," 312–32, 329.

9. Schopenhauer, *Welt als Wille*, 2:607–51.

10. In *Corydon*, quoted in Patrick Pollard, *André Gide: Homosexual Moralist* (New Haven CT: Yale University Press, 1991), 45.

of the race. It is from this point that Schopenhauer seeks how the vice could serve such a purpose, and not yet finding Darwin, whose *Origin of Species* would be published in the same year as this appendix, he finds it in Aristotle.[11] The immature and the decrepit (beyond fifty-four years of age, according to Aristotle) produce compromised offspring. Pederasty is not simply a deviation of the natural instinct, as Schopenhauer had mentioned in passing in his earlier editions. It is natural instinct in purest form. To the philosopher it is of particular force: it reveals nature's hand.

## From Body to Soul: The Sexual Subject Out of the Needs of Forensic Medicine

In what way might we say a "sexual subject" emerged in the 1860s? Clearly—as critics of Foucault have not tired of pointing out—if there were sexual (say "sodomitical" or "pederastic") acts, there must have always been people who did them, knew they did them, sometimes were known to do them, and were punished and even called things because they did them.[12] The term *subject* suggests something more than this, though. For German thinkers such as Kant and Hegel, and then for many thinkers after them, the noun referred to a rational, thinking, and potentially knowing person; one is not born a subject, but rather the term was connected to the ongoing process and goal of becoming fully self-conscious. But the noun *subject* also refers to a being who is subjected to something: an authority, a regime, or any form of observation, disciplining, or surveillance. The term is particularly interesting to use in this historical context, where sexual behavior came to be understood as linked to a deviant psychiatric profile. Both of these senses of the word *subject* are active in a single historical process in which homosexuals were subjected by disciplinary medical, juridical, and investigative modes of knowledge at the same time as they began to articulate a subjective self-identity as well as a subculture. This apparently paradoxical double movement is what is denoted in Foucauldian jargon by the term *subjectivation*.[13]

In both German lands and Austria, identification of evidence of homosexual acts had been the province of forensic physicians (again, doctors employed by the justice system for assistance in the prosecution of crime).

11. In book 7 of the *Politics*; Schopenhauer, *Welt als Wille*, 2:646.

12. See, e.g., Graham Robb, *Strangers: Homosexual Love in the Nineteenth Century* (London: Picador, 2003).

13. For more detailed discussion, see S. Spector, "After the *History of Sexuality*: Periodicities, Subjectivities, Ethics," in Spector, Puff, and Herzog, *After the History of Sexuality*, 1–14.

A survey of manuals aimed at students and practitioners of forensic medicine suggests that discussion of sodomy or pederasty had timid beginnings but was to become standard fare throughout the mid-nineteenth century. Frederick the Great's codification of the common law in Prussia, called the *Preußisches Allgemeines Landrecht*, mentions "sodomy and other like unnatural sins, which cannot be named here on account of their heinousness," which "demand a total extirpation of remembrance" but which jurists as well as physicians understood included "sexual relations of persons with animals, with corpses, with the same sex in unnatural manner, man with man and woman with woman."[14] Prosecuted cases of such unnatural liaisons between members of the same sex were taken to be rare on account of their inherently secret nature. In the literature they were linked not only with bestiality and violation of the dead but especially with violent rape and molestation.[15] These were thought of as linked but distinguished forms of forbidden coition: those counter to law (rape) and those counter to nature (same-sex unions).[16] This early conflation of same-sex and violent sexual practices is notable as a significant precursor to the sensational association of violence and homosexuality in the late 1860s and onward.

The forensic discussions are repetitive in their details about the somatic traces of sodomy or pederasty, so it is clear that they are based on previous such manuals rather than on observation of subjects (or, as the subtitles of these manuals often claimed, from personal observation, "aus eigener Erfahrung"). In line with our thinking about the transition of focus from acts to identities, these texts do aim to identify individual habitual sodomites, but the category is completely absorbed by that of the sexual act itself, specifically anal penetration.[17] The manuals indexed local somatic signs of the crime, including both traces of immediate activity (corresponding to signs of rape

14. G. H. Nicolai, *Handbuch der gerichtlichen Medicin nach dem gegenwärtigen Standpunkte dieser Wissenschaft für Aerzte und Criminalisten* (Berlin: Hirschwald, 1841), 167. Robert Beachy argues for the centrality of this prohibitive code: "The German Invention of Homosexuality," 801–38.

15. Note, e.g., the consistency of a single narrative in this comprehensive 1863 account of the state of forensic medicine in determinations of rape, corpse abuse, pederasty, and bestiality; Ritter, *Zur Geschichte*. The same connection is articulated explicitly in Casper, *Klinische Novellen*, 44–45.

16. "Gesetz- und naturwidrigen Beischlaf"; see, e.g., Bernhard Brach, *Lehrbuch der gerichtlichen Medicin* (Cologne: Eisen, 1846), 629–40.

17. While the definition was famously unstable and would be broadened in the later nineteenth century, pederasty was taken to refer specifically to anal sex: "that the anus of one, the younger as a rule, serves as vagina"; see Brach, *Lehrbuch*, 639.

immediately after the fact) and features thought to be indicative of habitual passive or active pederasts. These, especially the claim that passive partners displayed a pronounced funnel-shaped anus and active partners tapered rods, were constantly repeated from earlier sources. Also typically repeated were the general consequences of the activity, including consumption and emaciation, swelling of the joints, and so forth.[18] As physicians gradually expanded the index of somatic signs of pederasty, they conflated categories of the immediate residues of physical trauma, the physical features they imagined must develop from habitual anal penetration, and those that might explain the origin of the deviance. Small penises were a sign of active pederasty both because they enabled anal penetration and because their possessors would be mocked and shunned by women, for instance. Somatic features could be simultaneously cause and symptom of pederastic behavior. The question of which was cause and which effect did not seem to concern anybody and must have seemed to forensic physicians like a chicken-or-egg puzzle—rather irrelevant. Physicians employed by the state for use in court were focused on traces of crime marked on suspects' bodies, not on the psychic origins of those crimes. The origin, that is, was interesting in the same way that the trace was: both pointed toward the positive fact of the crime event.

The literature in forensic medicine from 1840 into the 1850s did provide a unified, if not entirely consistent, image or identity of pederasty. It was a deviation, it was an abomination, it was a secret, it was a form of violence; it was not yet but was about to become a *riddle*.

It is in this context that leading Berlin medical authority Johann Ludwig Casper (1796–1864) came forth in 1852 with a transformative contribution, but our own understanding of its significance was quite different from his own, and this difference is important not to forget. "On Rape and Pederasty and Their Determination on the Part of the Forensic Physician, Based on Original Observations" continues many of the patterns established in earlier texts: it affiliates violent rape with same-sex unions, it insists on the repugnancy and abhorrence of the latter, and it focuses on telltale signs written on the bodies of passive and active pederasts.[19] Casper thought that basing his article on the actual examination of eleven confirmed pederasts was an important contribution, and he sought to overturn the endlessly repeated misconceptions about forensics in this area. But the text shows no particular recognition of what may seem to today's readers the revolutionary claim of an

18. An influential source is Adolph Henke, *Lehrbuch der gerichtlichen Medicin* (Berlin: Dümmler, 1841), 139.

19. Casper, "Nothzucht und Päderastie," 21–78.

"innate" same-sex "inclination." Forty years hence, Krafft-Ebing would note that Casper could hardly have guessed that the remark would give way to an entire discipline of study. Anticipating what Foucauldians refer to as "acts vs. identities," Krafft-Ebing defines Casper's radical observation "that the uranian sexual orientation is not *perversity*, but *perversion*."[20] Casper may have been the first to suggest the origins of homosexual attraction in pathological, inborn inclination ("in many cases inborn"), but if so, he was witless as to the gravity of this contribution.[21] He made the claim only in passing and did not even deem to include it in his ten-point summary of the major findings of the article. Casper was specifically interested in disproving and dismissing the assumptions of the entire previous forensic literature concerning the diagnostic signs of pederasty, local and general, because most of these are never seen in actual pederasts and may just as well occur in many other people. He substituted instead different somatic markers of passive pederasty previously overlooked in the literature (a particular formation of the buttocks and character of the skin around the anus).[22]

Beyond the authority Casper claimed on the basis of new and original examinations, he was also aware of the importance of a different kind of source he was able to make use of, "completely new and unprecedented in the annals of psychology and criminal justice," an unbelievable find: "the written diaries of a pederast, including daily accounts of his adventures, liaisons, sensations, executed over many years."[23] The journals of one whom Casper calls Count von Cajus (the actual person is thought to have been Baron Heinrich von Maltzan Sr.) had been seized by police officials upon his arrest under suspicion of "unnatural sins."[24] Casper's text is animated by this new kind of

20. See Richard von Krafft-Ebing's forward to Moll, *Die Conträre Sexualempfindung*. This suggests that the historiographical narrative seeking an origin of the search for origins is itself a product of the age of high sexology around the late 1880s and early 1890s.

21. Casper, "Nothzucht und Päderastie," 62. Casper assumed those "unfortunates" burdened with what Krafft-Ebing would later call *krankhafte Veranlagung* (morbid inclination) were in the minority, whereas most of those afflicted with the inclination would be men in later age who had been oversated with vaginal sex. While Krafft-Ebing understood that this assertion of innate homosexuality was not understood by Casper to have been a central contribution of his article, the current literature cannot see it otherwise because it seems so obviously important. Cf. Beachy, *Gay Berlin*, 23.

22. Casper, "Nothzucht und Päderastie," 77–78.

23. Ibid., 67.

24. Hergemöller, *Mann für Mann*, 484. Alternative spellings, e.g., "Malzahn," "Maltzahn," etc., are common. Casper had served as expert witness in the trial of Maltzan, who according to Ulrichs was sentenced to hard time and died in prison, a fact that has been related by Hirschfeld and many others after him but is not verifiable. See Ulrichs, *Forschungen*, 10:88–89.

stimulus, which he understood as both belonging to scientific inquiry and simultaneously threatening to the scientific genre; it drew out the implicit sensationalism of the case study and exposed the fragility of the boundary between Cajus/Maltzan's narrative and his own:

> While I consider it my duty to return to science that which, through a rare fortune by virtue of my official position, I was able to perceive of such a dark province, and yet one that still belongs to science, still I can only offer intimations—for the pen refuse were I to venture to repeat the depictions of orgies from these diaries.[25]

The very existence of the journals is a sign of the pathological constitution of the author. That anyone would commit such confessions to paper, "with greatest naivety and unembarrassed frankness," that he would admit in the very first inquiry to having "surrendered himself" for the last twenty-six years, are all signs of a "feminine-childlike nature" that one cannot grasp without knowing the subject.[26] Hence, the genre of autobiographical narrative of sexual exploits and that of the scientific case study emerge as twins; the scientist is uniquely equipped to read the former, and at the same time, that reading offers the potential for a superior kind of forensic medical description. On the basis of this knowledge of the pathological subject, Casper declares that the individual is capable of responsibility for his actions (here *dispositionsfähig* rather than *zurechnungsfähig*), neither feebleminded nor an idiot, but a clear case of what some have called "sexual insanity." He notes, further, that the subject's pathology cannot easily be identified by external physical features (although inspection reveals anomalies of skin and flesh around the anus mentioned above) or by external bearing or habitus. The diaries offer more insight than any examination would, but they also offer another kind of insight. Casper introduced his long essay on rape and pederasty referring to the milieu of the great city, seat of bitterest poverty with its tragic consequences (rape) as well as the most overrefined luxury with its unnatural deviations (pederasty).[27] The subject's notebooks provide insight into an urban homosexual subculture that is depicted here with odium, to be sure, but also with a picturesqueness that is lacking in the earlier forensic studies, which occasionally referred only to the reported increase of the vice and its vaguely urban character. Casper's article delivered readers a pederast in flesh and blood, and it offered that creature a habitat.

25. Casper, "Nothzucht und Päderastie," 68.
26. Ibid., 67.
27. Ibid., 22.

Had Casper's primary contribution been what he thought it was—debunking received wisdom about local somatic signs of habitual male-male intercourse only to replace it with different and more accurate stigmata—it would not be on the way to disturbing a paradigm at all. But in its presentation of the homosexual case study—in particular its engagement with a homosexual's account of his own sexuality—in his passing suggestion that some pederasts are so, perhaps, not only by habit but perhaps somehow by innate nature—in all these ways he begins to construe a homosexual subject that is nearly ready to emerge as "a personage, a past, a case history," if not in as ossified and literal a form as some of Foucault's most eager readers and vociferous detractors like to take it.[28] Yet for Casper, the fact of innate sexual inclination was, like somatic "facts" on the subject's body, mainly interesting as a sign of the presence of delinquency. The objective of scientific inquiry was for him, as for other forensic physicians, the presence of sexual/criminal acts. Only in retrospect does this mid-nineteenth-century attempt to more accurately identify passive and active sodomite bodies seem such a clear way station on the journey to a homosexual subject.

Casper continued to campaign to reform received knowledge of signs of unnatural indecency, arguing that misconceptions were not surprising in light of the "total absence of any personal observations." Auguste Ambroise Tardieu (1818–79) dubiously claimed to have observed 206 cases, although he detailed only nineteen, just one of which displayed one of the features of the active pederast's organ on which he insisted (a twist and diversion of the urethra caused by repeated pushing against the resistance of the unnatural orifice). The French physician commented too on the "wry mouth, short teeth, thick, turned-in lips" complementing the specific oral vices of two of these subjects, whereas Casper countered that, alas, these vices, as most, left no trace whatsoever.[29] The dispute between Tardieu and Casper brings out the latter's investment in actual homosexual subjects as well as their resistance to display clear signs of their perversions on their bodies. The combination of focus on a class of persons to be identified and the realization that they were not easily recognized by stigmata or even behavior led the forensic physician—the doctor charged with identifying the subjects of this particular crime—to seek a different kind of recognizable attribute. That search came to be assisted by nonacademic readers of scientific texts who recognized themselves in Casper's descriptions; these were in turn used as important

28. See David M. Halperin, "Forgetting Foucault," in *History of Homosexuality*, 24–47.
29. Casper, *Handbook*, 329.

new data by Casper in the 1863 publication with the provocative title *Klinische Novellen zur gerichtlichen Medicin.*[30]

"Novelle" generally has the literary meaning of "novella," although here it also implies an amendment or supplement. Indeed, Casper published the *Klinische Novellen* in 1863 as a supplement to his influential *Handbook* meant to provide more (and more colorful) illustrative detail on "the most interesting and instructive" cases relating to forensic medicine. In response to his original 1852 article on "Rape and Pederasty," Casper received a detailed letter from an anonymous correspondent that accorded with Count Maltzan's diaries to such a degree as to convince the doctor that it must reflect an "inner truth." A long extract from the letter was reproduced in the *Novellen*, wherein the author confirmed, first of all, early childhood memories of same-sex attraction and excitement; feelings of shame and aloneness; his sexual initiation, and so on.

The subject's first sexual encounter with a man was described in the letter as a revelation not only because of the sexual release that had hitherto not been experienced but also in light of the postrelease conversation in which he learned that hundreds of such men existed. The presumption that deviants are "elderly, ugly, spent, exhausted by debauchery" was belied by the informant's experience of a community of young, healthy, attractive, virtuous, and affectionate companions. The idea of a sexual community or subculture is as central to the confession as that of a hidden sexual nature. Indeed, the two are inextricably braided to one another, and not only because the community consists of those of deviant inclination: "Generous nature has provided us with a certain instinct that unites us like a brotherhood: we find each other immediately, in the blink of an eye, like an electric bolt, and has never let me down."[31] These references to secret recognition, signals of a fraternity beyond borders, prove as important to the reporter as the insistence on the innate nature that unites them. This secret and universal brotherhood is linked in the informant's mind to the naturalness of his sexual identity as well as to the promise of emancipation. If, in travels from Italian cities to the Louvre to the Scottish Highlands to Petersburg to arrival at the port of Barcelona the correspondent found people never seen before, "*who in one second were spellbound by me, and I by them,* can that be a crime?"[32]

The contacts are described as fleeting but meaningful affective relations, and the physical liaisons are underplayed; indeed, while not denying that

30. Casper, *Klinische Novellen*, iii–iv.
31. Quoted in Casper, *Klinische Novellen*, 38.
32. Quoted in ibid., 39.

"pederasty" may take place among baser individuals, he denies ever having engaged in it, describing instead tender kissing and caressing. This fact, confirming the claims of von Maltzan and Ulrichs, turns out to be of crucial significance for the evolution of this discussion of the identification of pederasts. The statutes against unnatural indecency had provided the occasion for forensic medicine's explorations of the pederastic subject, but that very inquiry led to the emergence of the idea that such an identity or such a subject did exist. Now it became clear that the subject in question was not a passive or active pederast, marked by complementarily deformed organs suited to or caused by sodomitical acts. The identity of the subject in question would have to be found elsewhere.[33]

This leads us to Westphal's article on "contrary sexual sensibility," cited by Foucault as the precise moment of the "birth" of the modern, "psychological, psychiatric, medical" category of homosexuality.[34] The occasion for Westphal's contribution was a gap in the research literature on what the doctor took to be the principal "symptom" of illness in two cases, one male and one female: an inborn inversion of sexual feeling with consciousness of the morbidity of this manifestation.[35] After Foucault, this has often been identified as the moment of the medicalization of the homosexual, although as we have seen, the whole idea of a "type of person" as opposed to a person who was agent of a vice evolved specifically and necessarily out of the exigencies of the field of forensic medicine, that is, the intersection of juridical, police, and medical logics. In Westphal's text the subject is thoroughly pathologized, to be sure, but the subject is also, more than in any of the previous texts we have discussed or that were in existence, given a subjectivity. In contrast to Casper's eleven cases and Tardieu's claimed hundreds, Westphal presents two case studies in depth. The sources of those studies are varied, and this diversity is central to Westphal's methodology. Westphal's own investigations in the mental ward of the famed Charité hospital in Berlin are given as the

33. This complements Arnold I. Davison's identification of this crucial moment in the transition from what he calls an anatamo-pathological style of reasoning (locating the seat of the morbidity first in the genitals, as we've seen, then in the brain) to the fundamentally novel model of perversion as a functional deviation of the sexual instinct. See Davison, "Closing Up the Corpses: Diseases of Sexuality and the Emergence of the Psychiatric Style of Reasoning," in *Homosexuality and Psychoanalysis*, 59–90.

34. C. Westphal, "Die conträre Sexualempfindung: Symptom eines neuropathischen (psychopathischen) Zustandes," *Archiv für Psychiatrie und Nervenkrankheiten* 2, no. 1 (February 1870). Cf. Foucault, *History of Sexuality*, 1:43.

35. "eine angeborene Verkehrung der Geschlechtsempfindung mit dem Bewusstsein von der Krankhaftigkeit dieser Erscheinung"; Westphal, "Sexualempfindung," 73.

primary source and the one first presented, but the reader is soon led through other accounts: the reports of relatives and of prison personnel on both the histories of the patients' conditions and their behaviors; medical and prison logs; as well as the patients' own accounts to the physician, ego documents including commissioned autobiographical reports, and letters in their own hand. To help explain the conditions reflected in these documents, Westphal produces reports of other documentary evidence of similar pathological subjectivities: the written confessions mailed to Casper and published in the latter's *Klinische Novellen*, the reported account of Count von Cajus (he apparently did not know the source), and, finally, one of the pamphlets published by "Numa Numantius" (Karl Heinrich Ulrichs) under the general title *Forschungen über das Räthsel der mannmännlichen Liebe.*

Taking pathological subjects at their own word was Westphal's methodological gamble in the pathbreaking article (indeed, it is what made the article pathbreaking). While making a clear claim of special authority to recognize and interpret these sources, he was aware that taking them into account at all held risk as well as promise. In the case of "Ha——" (the male case study he selected), the fact of the subject's record of thieving and deception made for particular problems. First, there was the possibility that his cross-dressing primarily served the purpose of disguise, dissimulation, deception, or fraud.[36] In his other example, a thirty-five-year-old woman, too, there was the concern that "the feeling of representing a male being," which the subject reported having experienced since early youth, could be a matter either of deception or of self-delusion. It is here that Westphal noted this could not be the case, for the statements made by the subject are identical ("almost literally match") those of male counterparts with contrary sexual feeling—those reported by Casper's informants and by Ulrichs. First-person reports hence constitute both the data set and the context in which it might be verified.

Westphal's most significant source in this respect was not drawn from the snippets of deviant subjectivity relayed by Tardieu and Casper but by the seventy-two-page pamphlet written by Karl Heinrich Ulrichs but published at first under the pseudonym Numa Numantius.[37] Westphal knew that this pamphlet was the second in a series but had not seen the first, and he seems not to have known about Ulrichs's subsequent volumes, which by the time his article was being published numbered seven (or eight, the last being published in two parts). In light of how important Westphal regarded Ulrichs's

36. Westphal, "Sexualempfindung," 91.
37. Ulrichs, *Forschungen* , vol. 2.

text—a clear statement of "urning" (same-sex attraction) self-identity—it is surprising that Foucault places his own origin story with the physician Westphal. The whole idea of a circuit of identity discourse including juridical prohibition, medical diagnosis, and emancipatory self-identity comes directly out of Foucault's *History of Sexuality*, but he insistently sidelines the last, calling it, in one provocatively brief reference, "a reverse discourse."[38] Westphal, the father of the modern medico-psychiatric model of the homosexual, depended on Ulrichs and his like to provide a replacement for the visible signs that forensic physicians before him had imagined to be marked on the pederast's body. Westphal offered "contrary sexual sensibility" as the term to describe this invisible, interior stigma. Ulrichs, for his part, also shied from focusing on acts of pederasty and moved instead toward explicating the interior nature and implied community of creatures once sullied by the name. With his classicist training, he knew that "pederasty" was a calumnious misnomer from the start, and he offered not only a name for the creature he was self-describing but a way of thinking about identity and community that the new being demanded. The name he gave it, derived from classical sources, was the "urning."

### Sexual Diasporas: From Identity to Community

Already in the third paragraph of what was to become a twelve-volume treatise, Ulrichs wrote of the subjects of same-sex criminal acts as though they were a minority living among us, more like a people in diaspora than a subspecies of violent sexual delinquents:

> Several thousand urnings are living in the cities and the countryside of the lands called "Germany." They comprise the upper and lower classes, are in every occupation. There are millions all over the world. Urnings have existed in all areas, in antiquity, among uncivilized nomads, indeed, actually among the animals.[39]

---

38. Foucault, *History of Sexuality*, 101. Much more can be said about all this, but it is most important to historicize Foucault's project within his own political scene and relationship to sexual emancipation, as does Didier Eribon for instance in "Foucault's Histories of Sexuality." Sexual subjectivity is much more at issue in the second volume of the *History of Sexuality*, but to note this merely makes Foucault's sidelining of Ulrichs in the first volume even more salient. The *History* is intended as a genealogy rather than an origin story, and reading it as the latter has been the pitfall of many a critique of the whole book and its reception; see, e.g., Halperin, "Forgetting Foucault," in *History of Homosexuality*.

39. Ulrichs, *Forschungen*, 2:2. Translations are adapted from Ulrichs, *Riddle*.

In several senses, these first paragraphs of the pseudonymously published first volume of *The Riddle of "Man-Manly Love"* seems to have been a founding moment in the emergence of something like a homosexual subject. Ulrichs has thus been donned "the grandfather of gay liberation,"[40] "the first gay man of modern times."[41]

In this first section of his expansive project, Ulrichs performs several foundational acts. His first paragraph establishes a class of people whose "bodies are built like a male" but whose sexual attraction is directed toward men and not women. In the next, Ulrichs makes the first of what will be a series of proposals by jurists and scientists in the late nineteenth century to name this class of people (he proposes the term *urnings*, and hereafter in his text the quotation marks around this coinage disappear); and in the third paragraph, beginning with the above passage, he invokes the metaphor of diaspora. Such individuals are scattered around the lands called "Germany" as they have been dispersed among the peoples and periods of all history and, indeed, nature. Striking here are the quotation marks distinguishing the geographical designation "Germany," marking it as contingent and fugitive, arbitrary and unreal (recall that the text precedes the political unification of many German-speaking lands into the German Empire) next to the already naturalized, stable, unmarked term *urning*, which could not have been familiar to any reader before opening Ulrichs's pamphlet. If the urning's place within society is tenuous—indeed the need to name him attests to the stubborn avoidance to acknowledge his existence until this point—he is here established as a type of person born of nature, as an unshakable reality with deeper roots than any kingdom, culture, or system of law even if those roots are obscure. Of course, the urnings do not migrate from any originary homeland but appear among us already as foreigners within our midst. "According to some reports," Ulrichs adds ominously, "the number of urnings is constantly increasing. No father is sure if the germ of this orientation is latent in one of his sons and if it will break through at puberty."[42]

But the shadow of diaspora does not creep into the text in the third paragraph; it is already present in the very definition of the urning, the male body housing the womanly soul. In his earlier treatise on the "man love" of the Greeks, Heinrich Hössli had cited a rabbinical source describing the possibility of a female soul occupying a manly body, a circumstance he called "soul migration" (*Seelenwanderung*).[43] Even in our own bodies we are not quite at

---

40. Vern L. Bullough, "Introduction," in Ulrichs, *Riddle*, 1:21.
41. LeVay, *Queer Science*, 12.
42. Ulrichs, *Riddle*, 1:35.
43. Hössli, *Eros*, front matter and 1:295.

home. *Anima muliebris virili corpora inclusa*—the female soul enclosed in the male body—is the formula offered by Ulrichs. Urnings, as he asserts later in his book, are ill at ease in the bodies of men as in their company. Abhorring boy play as much as they will later abhor the sexual company of women, they learn at an early age what it is like to be a stranger in one's own country. In one of many comparisons of the urning to the paradigmatic figure of dias-pora, the Jew, Ulrichs describes this state in terms of inauthenticity and the dissimulation of assimilation: "we only play the man," just as a Jew raised in Germany plays the German without being one.[44]

It may be more than good fortune that all of these diverse and contradic-tory points appear in the first paragraphs of this arguably founding text. In their contradiction, these elements suggest a dual history. On the one hand, they establish a model of interior or personal homosexual identity modeled either (or even simultaneously) along the lines of more familiar identities such as gender or race, and on the other hand they introduce the notion of a homosexual community and its placement within the larger and dominant society of presumed heterosexuality.[45] In the central European fin-de-siècle political context, the immediate comparison was to Jewish communities and Jewish emancipation, a process taking place roughly contemporaneously with this emerging conception of sexuality and very much present in the minds of homosexual activists in the generations following Ulrichs (in par-ticular, perhaps, Jewish ones such as, most importantly, Magnus Hirschfeld [1868–1935]).[46] Ulrichs himself must have been instinctively aware of the

44. Ulrichs, *Riddle*, 1:58.

45. Laura Doan and Chris Waters, in their introduction to the section "Homosexualities" in a reader of translated documents of sexual science, concisely describe the controversy over the contribution of sexology in this way: "Historians are sharply divided over the question of whether the labelling of the unique identity and character of the 'homosexual' was a positive or negative development for those who experienced same-sex desires. Some welcome the sexo-logical creation of the homosexual for its powerful explanatory models of self-identity and its facilitation of a modern gay and lesbian subculture. Others, however, disparage sexology for the role it is thought to have played in the stigmatizing and pathologizing of homosexuals and homosexual desire." See Doan and Waters in Bland and Doan, *Sexology Uncensored*, 41. The conflict is thus clearly marked as one between a "positive" development for homosexual sub-jects relating to identity (in the sense of self-identity) and formation of a "subculture" on the one hand and the "negative" development of an identity from without (stigmatization, patholo-gization) on the other. Instead of taking one of these positions, one may focus on the linkages between these fields; in other words, one can avoid separation of (positive) self-identity from (negative) stigmatization.

46. James Steakley has suggestively noted that just as the second wave of gay emancipation (the American movement of the 1960s) modeled itself after the black civil rights movement,

linkage of a scientific model of homosexual identity to his explicitly juridical project, because he ventured into the terrain of medicalization in the course of his manuscripts.[47] He did this in spite of his lack of appropriate expertise, changing his mind about the origin or locus of sexual identity several times along the way. Carl Westphal and a long line of physicians to follow him, including centrally of course Richard von Krafft Ebing (1840–1902) and a host of others, would offer a broad array of origin narratives, locating the source of sexual identity on the homosexual body—in the blood, hormone system, or brain of the deviant subject. As we have seen, it is not so much the case that forensic physicians before Westphal never thought to ask about the sources of same-sex criminal behavior but that when they did it was not the core question they were asking.

The cover of Ulrichs's first pamphlet, aimed explicitly at the juridical goal of decriminalization of uranian acts, stated this goal, along with this epigraph, attributed to the author "N. Num." himself: "Give me a place to stand: And I will turn your system of persecution upside down."[48]

So did Ulrichs demand a self-grounding, a name and a "place to stand" from which to displace a world of persecution. Decidedly, the acknowledgment of a homosexual subject with natural origins does not necessarily lead to ethical acceptance. Ulrichs's early challengers already suggested that social injustice was not the only possible explanation of the discrepancy between his subjective self-understanding and the external, objective world. Ulrichs himself, an anonymous critic suggested, could be afflicted by hallucination, illusion, monomania, idée fixe.[49] Hence, it was possible to recognize the subjectivity Ulrichs claimed, but as symptom of a pathology, or simply as insanity.

In the wake of the jurist Ulrichs's rationalist text, with its expressly political aim of abolition of antisodomy penal statutes, studies of homosexuality searched for a locus of sexual deviation in various ways. At the same time as an emerging medical discourse sought the source of deviance, new urban, sociological, and criminological sciences sought to map communities of crime and

---

German-Jewish emancipation was the model of its "first wave" in Germany of this period. See Steakley, *Writings of Magnus Hirschfeld*, 1–11.

47. Hubert Kennedy considers Ulrichs to be the "first theorist of homosexuality," who was uncredited as such simply because he lacked medical credentials. Kennedy's essay, in which Michel Foucault is not mentioned, appeared in Rosario, *Science and Homosexualities*, 26–45.

48. Ulrichs, *Forschungen*, vol. 1, title page: "Gieb mir, wo ich stehe: und euer System der Verfolgung hebe ich aus seinen Angeln." See also Ulrichs, *Riddle*, 1:30n1. The reference seems to be to Archimedes: "Give me the place to stand, and a lever long enough, and I will move the earth!"

49. Anon., *Das Paradoxon*, 29.

vice within the landscape of the major city. In the last third of the nineteenth century, as we have seen, a picture of the modern city emerged in which the existence of an urban underworld—seedbed of crime, disease, prostitution, and homosexuality—was depicted in scrupulous detail. These positivist efforts in nascent realms of social science developed exactly parallel to prurient popular discourses of sexuality and crime, taking the form of sensational cases of sexuality and violence in the popular press along with the exploitation of these themes in pulp fiction and true crime genres. The figures of homosexual vice, the dark city, crime, and violence were delicately interwoven, and powerfully reinforced, through a number of discursive formations.

It is not for nothing, then, that Karl Heinrich Ulrichs was not only an outspoken advocate for recognition of the existence of homosexual selves but also, according to every report, was tireless in his efforts to establish networks of urning sociality. He made it a mission to mediate the association of homosexuals, to bring together atomized individuals in an (admittedly undercover at first) nascent public sphere. He also was the first activist to "come out of the closet"—indeed, in founding as it were both the modern concepts of gay nature and gay association, he can be said to have invented the "closet."[50] In these senses, Ulrichs's project encompassed the paradox of the two contradictory valences of the term *identity*, which in contemporary discourse refers at one and the same time to a presumed fixed, immutable, authentic selfhood at the same time that it references external representations of interiority: public identities, in other words, which can be at odds with private selves. While skeptics of the critical use of the term *identity* may object to the lack of precision implicit in such a polyvalence, the fact remains that subjects like Ulrichs do conflate these potentially contradictory meanings within their own identity projects.[51] That is to say, the coincidence of the emergences of gay identity qua essence and gay identity qua public persona is more than casual.

Ulrichs's collected pamphlets were titled the *riddle* or *puzzle* (Räthsel) of man-manly love, and this figure would be an enduring one. Ulrichs returned to it in summary statements throughout his project: "The Urning is a riddle of nature."[52] The figure appears in some of the literature proximate to and

---

50. And not without consequence—in spite of the fact that Hanover had no penal section against same-sex acts comparable to the Prussian code (which, needless to say, did not entail employment protection), his dismissal as state assessor has been documented to have been on grounds of his avowed sexuality. See Schildt, "Das Ende einer Karriere," 27–31, 32–33.

51. See, e.g., Brubaker and Cooper, "Beyond 'Identity.'"

52. See, e.g., Ulrichs, *Riddle*, 2:474.

even before Ulrichs and seems to serve as a signpost for the turn to the homosexual subject and to drives. An 1867 forensic medicine manual defines *pederasty* as "the puzzling [*räthselhaft*] impulse to seek sexual satisfaction from persons of the same sex rather than in the natural way."[53] The entry on the same term in a later medical encyclopedia offers a different kind of clue to the function of this descriptor, declaring that "pederasty is a psychological riddle [*Räthsel*] in many ways."[54] It is, the entry continues, explicable in situations of restricted access to females (at prison, or at sea) or in debauched persons seeking new excitement. It is clearly same-sex desire as orientation that is "puzzling," requiring answers of a different kind. The figure would survive the transition to the sexual knowledge system of sexology: in 1907, after two years of nearly exclusive attention to the subject, sexologist Iwan Bloch would title his own chapter "The Riddle of Homosexuality" because "to me in fact, the more precisely I have come to know it in recent years, the more I attempted to delve into it scientifically, all the more puzzling, obscure, incomprehensible it has become."[55] (Homo)sexuality as puzzle, as something to solve, or even as something insoluble is a recurring theme in the literature.

### Name-Dropping: The Real Kertbeny

As suddenly as they seem to come, all revolutionary ideas are more the product of their times than of individual innovators. As true as this proved to be for principles such as the gravitation of celestial bodies or evolution by natural selection, it was also the case for the notion of human sexuality. The history of the modern concept of homosexuality must pronounce the name of Károly Mária Kertbeny, the Pest man of letters who anonymously wrote two tracts or open letters arguing specifically against the adoption of the Prussian indecency paragraph in the penal code of the North German Confederation being formed.[56] But who was Karlóly Kertbeny?

From the first page of the first section of his first pamphlet, Karl Heinrich Ulrichs yielded to the impulse not only to speak the unspeakable act but to name the unnamable subjects of this sexuality.[57] While the name

53. Schauenstein, *Lehrbuch der gerichtlichen Medicin*, 119.

54. Hofmann, "Päderastie," in Eulenburg, *Real-Encyclopädie*, 15:144.

55. Bloch, *Das Sexualleben*, 541.

56. See Kertbeny, *Schriften*. The volume contains a biographical essay by Herzer followed by all the author's published works directly relating to homosexuality: the two 1869 tracts, the chapter from Jäger's *Die Entdeckung der Seele*, and the omitted chapter from the same, printed in 1900 in the *Jahrbuch für sexuelle Zwischenstufen*.

57. Ulrichs, *Forschungen*, 1:2, reads "These individuals I henceforward call 'Urnings.'"

he chose for it is today unknown aside from the study of Ulrichs himself, this impulse to name was shared by those who wrote on male same-sex attraction in these first years of the modern notion of sexuality. Those that followed in the latter decades of the nineteenth century chose among various terms until cognates of our word *homosexual*, adopted by Krafft-Ebing after his initial use of Westphal's *contrary sexual sensibility*, came to carry the day.

The name *homosexual* seems first to have been dropped by an Austro-Hungarian subject in whose life names, naming, and unnaming played complicated roles. If the recent secondary literature on the emergence of the term *homosexual* is riddled with apparent inconsistencies and inaccuracies, it must be said that these are legacies of the man's own feverish efforts to make a name for himself at the same time as he effaced various names given to him. These begin with his own given name, Karl-Maria Benkert, the name to which he was born in Vienna in 1824.[58] The name under which he published and by which he is known was Kertbeny, which, in spite of origins obscured by his own conflicting accounts, is an anagram of his own fashioning: an actual inversion of the syllables of the German Ben-kert with the addition of a final *y*, lending the name a distinctively aristocratic character in Hungarian. The various explanations of ancient family links to Hungarian nobility, all again Kertbeny's own accounts, tell us less than the plain fact of this and many other fabrications.[59] A name, for Kertbeny, told a story, and Kertbeny's narratives were rich in embellishment, contradiction, inversion, and dissimulation.

While some current scholarly interest may be centered on the emergence of the word *homosexual* and its context, Kertbeny never published any of his writing on sexuality under his own name. Two anonymous pamphlets of his authorship made an appeal, like Ulrichs's, for the decriminalization of homosexual acts in the penal code to be adopted by the new North German Con-

---

58. The most complete and accurate biographical account focusing particularly on Kertbeny's interest in homosexuality is Manfred Herzer, "Kertbenys Leben und Sexualitätsstudien," in Kertbeny, *Schriften*, 7–61; see also Jean-Claude Feray and M. Herzer, "Homosexual Studies and Politics in the 19th Century," 23–47, and Manfred Herzer, "Kertbeny and the Nameless Love," trans. Hubert Kennedy, *Journal of Homosexuality* 12, no. 1 (1985): 1–26; see also Katz, *Invention of Heterosexuality*.

59. Herzer, e.g., cites an 1874 letter to the poet Hermann Kletke in which he claims a grandfather's marriage to a Hungarian woman of noble title who bore his child after the death of her husband, "whereby he [the son, the author's father] was called Benkert von Kertbeny." Benkert to Kletke (November 29, 1874, Staatsbibliothek Pr. Kulturbesitz), translated and cited in Kennedy, "Kertbeny and the Nameless Love," 3.

federation.[60] One of them he signed simply (if unreliably) "ein Normalsexua-ler" (a normalsexual, as he first called heterosexuals), and he punctuated the essays with remarks about "us Germans" (*uns Deutsche*).[61] These juridical essays contrasted somewhat with the scientific tone taken in two chapters on homosexuality that he ghostwrote for Gustav Jäger. The Kertbeny name was meant to be made as a man of letters and a Hungarian patriot. Copious literary memoirs were left to posterity under this signature as well as many mediations of Hungarian national culture to a German-language audience, most notably the translation into German of Hungarian patriot poets Sandor Petöfi (1823–49) and Maurus (Mor) Jokai (1825–1904). These were contem-poraries of Kertbeny's and presumed fellow travelers in the liberal-nationalist revolution of spring 1848.

The year 1848 in fact is the year that the name Károly Kertbeny was formally adopted by the writer, and his self-image, or at least his self-representation, was deeply invested in the patriotic Hungarian culture of the "pre-March" period preceding the revolution as well as his peripatetic existence thereaf-ter. In place of diaries, Kertbeny left behind scores of little notebooks re-cording ceaseless travel from European city to city, punctuated throughout by *names*—men of letters, chiefly, or of science, politics least often of all.[62] He corresponded with as many famous people as possible and scrupulously saved any responses in case they could be of use. Where he found responses wanting, he was not above fabricating these, as well, for instance in attribut-ing praise of his work to personalities deceased or too remote to object.[63] Kertbeny was the quintessential name-dropper.

Kertbeny seemed always to be moving in the years after the revolution. It may seem—again, because that is the impression Kertbeny meant to leave—that this was the same exile enjoyed and suffered by other liberal-nationalist

---

60. [K. M. Kertbeny], ¶143 *des Preussischen Strafgesetzbuches vom 14. April 1851 und seine Au-frechterhaltung als ¶152 im Entwurfe eines Strafgesetzbuches für den Norddeutschen Bund* (Leipzig: Serbe's Commissions, 1869); *Das Gemeinschädliche des ¶143 des preussischen Strafgesetzbuches vom 14. April 1851 und daher seine nothwendige Tilgung als ¶152 im Entwurfe eines Strafgesetzbu-ches für den Norddeutschen Bund* (Leipzig: Serbe's Commissions, 1869). The rare texts have been reproduced in facsimile in K. M. Kertbeny, *Schriften*, 63–150, 151–229.

61. Kertbeny, *Schriften*, 80, 81, 206.

62. Kertbeny Károly Fond 22, 55 Duod. Hung. 9, NSL.

63. K[ároly] M[ária] Kertbeny, *Bibliographie der Werke [von K. M. Kertbeny]* [edition with extra material] (Berlin: Berliner Tageblatt, 1873), in which he attributes elaborate praise on him-self to Heine, Humboldt, Bettina von Arnim, Ludwig Uhland, Hermann Grimm, Charles Seals-field, and others. None of the claimed praise from these figures is extant in Kertbeny's preserved correspondence; see Fond 22, correspondence (ismeretlenek), NSL.

patriots in exile in the period of fierce postrevolutionary reaction. What the archives reveal, however, is that these travels were financed by the secret police, whom Kertbeny himself had approached to solicit funding for espionage activity abroad. Telling in his correspondence with the police, who never quite trusted the eccentric traveler of obscure background, is Kertbeny's insistence on erasing all trace of this activity. This is told by numerous injunctions to return correspondence, to delete his name from intrapolice memoranda, and to secure for him a passport under a false name in order to evade foreign creditors—a request with which the authorities complied, supplying him with another pseudonym, Joseph Némedy.[64]

The error produced in Hirschfeld's journal and repeatedly reproduced in the scholarship attributing the name *homosexual* to a "Hungarian physician" was again a product of Kertbeny's creative self-fashioning. In light of all of these efforts to control the reception of his identity, often by inverting apparent truths, it is surprising that time and ink have been spent taking seriously his own claims to be a "normalsexual"—but the desires the author harbored or even activities in which he "must have" engaged are not the relevant questions in this context. The search for the real Kertbeny, like Stoppard's real Inspector Hound, is a red herring, a distraction from the real mystery. What was the source of this journey of the literary critic Benkert/Kertbeny to two extensive juridical arguments arguing for removal of the prohibition against same-sex acts and the coinage of the term *homosexual*? This is no more a mystery than that surrounding the frank and open Hanoverian lawyer—the court assessor Ulrichs—whose texts immediately exceeded the juridical need to postulate on the origins of the phenomenon of urnings (beginning with theories influenced by mesmerism and moving on to more biological models in later volumes). In fact Kertbeny would prove even more influential in this field as ghostwriter of chapters on homosexuality for naturalist Gustav Jäger's *Discovery of the Soul* and would-be author of a comprehensive manuscript on human sexuality.

All of these wanderings tell us more than what we already know of the itinerant Kertbeny. They point to something about the site of imagination that was this new ground of sexuality. What was it about "sexuality" that made literary critics into jurists, jurists into physicians, physicians into philosophers?

Even before this decade, in the medico-forensic texts giving short shrift to sodomy or pederasty, reference to its prominence in classical history and literature was made; by the 1860s, such texts would expound at length about Plato's *Symposium*, with its own origin myth of sexual object choice,

64. Déak, "Translator, Editor, Publisher, Spy."

and the exploits of the Romans.[65] The literate Kertbeny, in obverse fashion, presents himself in his manuscripts on sexuality as the enlightened scientist battling the prejudice of moral distaste, religious prohibition, and other "self-deceptions" providing obstacles to science.[66] The theories of sexuality that he was attempting to hammer into a manuscript for which he had already received an advance from the publisher were based neither on scientific study nor on a review of the scientific literature that did exist on the subject, but he nonetheless understood the field to lie within the disciplines of natural science in general and medicine in particular.[67]

Kertbeny's scientific texts on homosexuality (actually "homosexualism" [Homosexualismus]) include many unpublished fragments and drafts, the expanded second juridical text and its addenda, and two chapters we know to have been authored by him to be included in naturalist Gustav Jäger's *Discovery of the Soul* (1880). One of these chapters was judged by the editor to be too potentially offensive (read censorable) to be included, but it was published later in Hirschfeld's journal. The "new field of sexuality studies" ("Die neue Lehre von der Sexualität" was the working title of his manuscript) is a taxonomy of human sexuality, surprisingly reductive, not entirely stable, and certainly worthy of critique.[68] Its coarse categories of monosexualism (masturbation), homosexualism (male-male and female-female), normalsexualism (later called heterosexualism), and heterogenalsexualism (bestiality) wander a bit throughout his drafts but remain bulky and insufficiently differentiated, disregard bisexuality, and so on. And yet it is surprising, in light of the dearth of studies of this type before him or in other languages, how "sexuality studies" emerge in these pages as a piece: legible, familiar, whole. Here are drives, object choices, gender typologies, and practices—these are fused and conflated, to be sure, but how close to the discipline of sexology that will emerge only later, how uncannily both alien and familiar.[69]

---

65. Impressive in this regard is the above-mentioned review of the forensic literature up to 1863, Ritter, *Zur Geschichte*, 326–58, with medical/biological material first following thereafter.

66. Paraphrased from Kertbeny, "Anthropologischer Gutachten. Beilage: "Der Homosexualismus," Fond 22/297, p. 377, NSL.

67. See, e.g., the correspondence with Friedrich Theodor von Frerichs, an esteemed medical and scientific expert; the extant correspondence, however, has little or no intellectual substance. See Fond 22/47, NSL. Kertbeny's claim to have sent his manuscript to Frerichs and to have received a favorable response is extremely unlikely to have been the case: see K. M. Kertbeny, *Bibliographie der Werke*, 15. The claim and the correspondence, however, do testify to the fact that this first wave of sexuality studies understood itself to be engaging a specifically medical model.

68. See manuscripts "Die neue Lehre von der Sexualität," Fond 22/296, pp. 367–89, NSL.

69. Cf. the outline of *Sexualitätsstudien*, Fond 22/296, p. 117, NSL.

As versed in literature and history as Kertbeny was, he could not have thought that the categories of sexuality he outlined were as discrete as he claimed. What must be remembered is that for the juridical argument to work, homosexual desire must be exclusive—it could not be suppressed or substituted by its "unfortunate" host; aversion to the opposite sex was as important to demonstrate as the naturalness of attraction to the same sex. Hence, Kertbeny described opposed attributes that he called *gebunden* (bound) and *ungebunden* (unbound), which applied to the categories. Homosexuality was completely exclusive or "bound" in all cases.[70] Normalsexuality, in the male particularly, was unbound. Indeed, the lascivious polysexuality of a de Sade, a Caligula, or an Alexander was indicative of a hypersexuality that was characteristic of pure masculinity. Kertbeny shared with Ulrichs and Westphal a model of gender dysphoria or inversion that mapped on to his homosexual, who was conceived as both womanish and less sexed. The reports by homosexual subjects that most of their contacts did not involve penetration or even ejaculation stood as proof of these assumptions.

The two chapters that would be published, one in *Discovery of the Soul* and one intended for that work but rejected, tacked their thesis to the zoologist Jäger's dominant theme. What the eccentric Jäger's perspective did to Kertbeny's homosexual was deliver him back to the bestial world, a hyped-up Darwinist diorama of irresistible drives and aggressions fueled by essences conveyed among animals by odor and taste.[71] The irreducible essence of these human animals, for Jäger, is this scent, this hormonal distillation (the "soul"). Kertbeny's chapters mesh well with the colorful prose of Jäger's writings, where iron laws of science etch through a landscape of fragrant essences, leading to the dissipation of scientistic reason as it spills out into the sea of instinct.[72] The texts in this manner embody both arrogant Enlightenment self-confidence and its romantic antidote. Jäger's world is one where the ice-cold gaze of modern science, free of fear and prejudice, returns the enlightened observer to the animal kingdom.

## The Subject of Violence

On the evening of January 17, 1869, while both Kertbeny and Ulrichs were in the throes of writings aimed to spare the new North German penal code from the Prussian Paragraph 143, the five-year-old Emil Hanke was found

70. See Kertbeny, *Das Gemeinschädliche*, 55–60; *Schriften*, 117–22.

71. See, e.g., Jäger, *Die Entdeckung der Seele*, 1–13.

72. Ibid., 41–9.

in critical condition in the attic of a Berlin apartment house. The boy's body displayed signs of abuse including savage bites, violation, and strangulation. The case recalled an unsolved murder of 1867, where the victim had been 15 years old but where signs of abuse had also been present. The sensational trial of a known homosexual suspected of committing both brutal crimes occupied this last year of the pivotal decade we have been examining, in which Ulrichs, Westphal, and Kertbeny confected competing but oddly complementary pictures of a kind of person: the homosexual subject. Because of the intense interest or involvement of all three, it is a prime place to examine the reciprocal effects—a kind of loop or circuit of knowledge on the homosexual person—of medico-juridical, sensational, and subjective discourses. It is also the place where the links of this peculiar sexual sensibility to violent nature are made explicit in ways that say much about the latent "animality" of normative sexuality itself.

Here is how the *Berliner Gerichts-Zeitung* (Berlin court news), speculating on proceedings in July 1869, linked licentious character (and indeed physiognomy) to homosexual milieu:

> One has to seek the authorship of both crimes in the circle of those licentious libertines of Berlin, whom—they tell us there are more than 3,000 of them!—the police characterize as having sinister, vacant looks and who stagger around the streets and promenades, averse to the fair sex, inclined to fall in love with men and boys.[73]

What is curious about this assumed convergence of a community of homosexuals to crime rings (a similar association was already familiar to public and police from the association of crime languages and networks with poorer Jewish districts) is the way in which it resonates with Ulrichs's propaganda. The excerpt marks as important precisely the features repeatedly highlighted by Ulrichs. Press, public, and police could agree on the sexual licentiousness and moral degeneracy of these types, to be sure, but even this opprobrious formulation relied on Ulrichs. For these "licentious" types have an inclination to fall in love with other males and have a visceral aversion to females. They constitute some sort of community, and that community is given concrete and alarming form by an exaggerated estimate of the number of homosexuals in Berlin. Ulrichs did react petulantly to this passage, but merely on the grounds that it demonized homosexuals. As he intuited, the report implied that homosexuals were throwbacks, even animals: "Why do they not

73. *Gerichts-Zeitung* (Berlin), July 6, 1869, translation adapted from Ulrichs, *Riddle*, 2:529.

simply portray us concealing beneath our clothing a monkey's tail and in our kid gloves?"[74]

How were (licentious) urning identity and (violent) animal nature linked in the imagination, and what does it tell us about the conceptualization of sexuality as such? The "identical origins" at play here pertain to a fanta-sized, common, primal source to both sexuality and violence. The source for homosexuality and heterosexuality, as they will come to be formulated, are similarly identical. This case marks the moment in which these to some degree unspoken understandings are implicitly acknowledged in the figure of "sexual identity" itself.

The occurrence of the alleged sadistic attack and attempted murder of a boy by a man who identified himself as an urning may be argued to fall only coincidentally in immediate proximity to Westphal's, Ulrichs's, and Kertbeny's revolutionary texts, and yet the association of homosexuality and brutal violence would endure. It had already been behind the most impor-tant precursor of Ulrichs's *Riddle*. Heinrich Hössli's *Eros: Die Männerliebe der Griechen, ihre Beziehungen zur Geschichte, Erziehung, Literatur und Gesetzge-bung aller Zeiten* (Eros: the man-love of the Greeks, its relationship to the his-tory, education, literature and legislation of all times; 1836), was a two-volume apology for same-sex love inspired directly by the gruesome execution of fel-low Swiss Franz Desgouttes, whose unrequited and passionate homosexual love had led to his murder of its object.[75] Our homosexual apologists of the 1860s similarly seized on a case calling attention to the violent nature of same-sex inclination, and their ongoing thinking about sexual nature was condi-tioned by it.

The case in question was the occasion in fact for an explosion of discourse on uranism as sexual practice, as identity, and as marked by violence. The man accused of the attack on the Hanke boy and the previous murder was a certain Lieutenant Carl von Zastrow (see fig. 13) of Berlin.[76] Zastrow was a reader of Ulrichs's pamphlets and shared with "Cajus"/von Maltzan an ap-parently unabashed identification of himself as a subject acting on his own

74. Translation from Ulrichs, *Riddle*, 2:529.

75. See Hergemöller, *Mann für Mann*, 185–86, 366–67. See also Hössli, *Eros*, vols. 13–14. On Hössli, see Karsch, *Der Putzmacher*.

76. Police materials for the Emil Hanke (in press reports and documents, sometimes spelled "Hancke" or "Handtke") attempted murder case I first viewed in sig. Rep 30 Bln C Tit 198 B 1, BBLHA; the Polizeipräsidium files have since been moved to LAB and renumbered (Repositur A Pr. Br. Rep. 030). Files that I have viewed at both archives will be listed with the current (LAB) reference.

Carl Ernst Wilhelm v. Zastrow, geb. 2. Mai 1821 zu Frankfurt a. O.

FIGURE 13. What kind of person was Zastrow? The *Berliner Gerichts-Zeitung* introduced the suspect to the reading public on January 26, 1869.

sexual nature; like Kertbeny and Ulrichs, he believed acting on this nature should be decriminalized. He also insisted on his innocence in the horrific crimes against the children.

Zastrow was known to police to have been homosexually inclined. He had been arrested and questioned before and had a record in Dresden, his previous city of residence. Like prostitutes and other habitual criminals, homosexual offenders were indexed at police headquarters and hence were the first suspects of resort in this case. The police files reveal that investigators' main criteria for identifying suspects were a known history of homosexual acts coupled with the vaguest circumstantial evidence. Early suspects included a twenty-year-old who had been arrested for such acts three months before and who was known in the neighborhood where the crime took place and a forty-five-year-old mason who lived on the same street as Hanke and sold books—the victim had reported that the attacker had lured him with the promise of a gift of books. Within weeks of the crime, Zastrow was prime suspect, and contacts between himself and these other persons of interest were explored, yielding none known.[77]

The main facts implicating Zastrow were his habitual engagement in homosexual acts and the proximity of one of his haunts to the Hanke and Corny attacks. The police file on the Hanke case included testimony taken by investigators nearly seventeen years earlier by an adult man denouncing Zastrow for making sexual advances toward him on a ferry.[78] For the case at hand, police found relevant another adult male's testimony that he had seen a man who had propositioned him in the past (possibly Zastrow) in the vicinity.[79] In this and other testimony regarding the accused's predilection to homosexual acts, investigators in the Hanke case paid particular attention to positive evidence of sexual contact with men—especially physical contact with genitals or direct propositions. Clearly for the police, this history of same-sex attraction and willingness to act on it marked Zastrow as a prime suspect. The fact that these were all aimed at adults, that they were forward but never forced or violent, and that they were passive in nature were not noteworthy, this in spite of the fact that the charge and conviction would be on the basis of a "violent exercise of indecent acts for satisfaction of the sexual drive on a person under 14 years old, connected to substantial serious bodily harm of a person." The presence of rape, of ferocious biting, and of strangling in the case at hand and the suspect's lack of any known history of attacking or even approaching a sexually immature boy were all trumped by something that was as incriminating as any of these: a self-acknowledged and unapologetic "contrary sexual sensation."

The conduit for channeling knowledge about the violent sexual subject at the center of this affair to a broad, nonprofessional public was largely a mass press that was just beginning to develop strategies for "sensationalizing" such opportunities. The term *sensation* is felicitous in that it connects the idea of a secret, inner life to a spectacular and public event. The volatile but interior life of sensibility, emotion, feeling, and so forth (as in Westphal's term for homosexuality *conträr-sexuelle Empfindung*, meaning *contrary sexual sensation* or *sensibility*), is hereby linked to the dramatic or melodramatic spectacle

77. A Pr. Br. Rep. 030–03, Nr. 1, LAB, is a document from January 21, 1869 (information on Julius Heinrich Rudolph Max Schuetze, p. 3, and Leopold Bauer, p. 4).

78. The testimony of Christian Friedrich Gille from July 1852 had been forwarded to the Berlin police headquarters by Saxon authorities for the investigation. A Pr. Br. Rep. 030–03, Nr. 1, LAB.

79. Testimony of Wilhelm Schulz, January 21, 1869, A Pr. Br. Rep. 030–03, Nr. 1, p. 1, LAB.

of social scandal. The origin of this homonym is, however, the sensations of curiosity, outrage, horror, and so on that these disclosures unleash for *readers*. In this way, an identification and even a kind of intimacy is already implied in the notion of the sensation in spite of the understandable assumption that such reports effect instead disassociation and lack of identification. What kind of tales did the press offer its eager public?

Various kinds, to be sure, but even in their variations they reveal much about an emergent paradigm of sexuality, inner nature, and violence. This is discernable already in the 1869 report quoted above, where police knowledge of circles of licentiousness—men wandering the streets with hungry, vacant visages—is shared with inhabitants of those streets who may never have noticed such faces before or known how to interpret them. Investigators' files examined above were not open to the press, of course, and still this element of an inner nature of wanton desire, rather than one of sadism or violence, is clearly the active one. Some of the more sensational press organs embraced the opportunity for prurience by focusing on the question of sexual perversity. More timid reports placed the events in a context no less sensational if less focused on deviant sex. They read like criminal stories, focusing on the shared brutality of the earlier Corny murder and the current attack on young Hanke and on the use of evidence to track down the suspect. Here the evidence in question was usually a certain ivory-handled walking stick found near the scene that several witnesses identified as the property of Zastrow, although he denied ownership of it. Another crucial detail to emerge in the course of the trial involved a curious detail in the suspect's biography. Zastrow, raised Lutheran, had converted to Catholicism some years earlier. Questioned by the prosecutor about this conversion, Zastrow supposedly replied, "Yes, sir, at that time I was bothered by my conscience." To this remark the interrogator replied dramatically that it was precisely at that time that the baker's apprentice Corny was murdered.[80]

This melodramatic narrative of the crime and its solution sidelined sexuality in any sense, even where "indecency" was referenced as a code; sadism, rape, sexual pleasure from the murder were all absent. Yet even in this sani-

---

80. This version of the sensational account of these events is paraphrased from a later review of sensational cases. See Friedlaender, *Kulturhistorische Kriminal-Prozesse*, 11–16. The court transcript is not quite this dramatic, and Zastrow did not exactly say his conscience was haunting him or anything of that sort, but the prosecutor did try to make the connection of conversion to the Corny killing. Cf. "Der Prozeß gegen den Lieutenant v. Zastrow," *Volks-Zeitung* 17, no. 54 (1867): 3. The fact of the suspect's conversion and its suspicious timing was already in the first *Gerichts-Zeitung* article identifying Zastrow, discussed below; see "Polizei- und Tages-Chronik," *Berliner Gerichts-Zeitung* 17, no. 9 (January 23, 1869): 3.

tized account, it is worth noting that the key to the truth of the crime is, again, the truth of the criminal. The key is not the physical evidence of the crime scene as much as the disclosure of the accused's inner "conscience."

When news of the crime first broke, the first suspect to be taken into custody had been the victim's father. The narrative structure of the report in the *Gerichts-Zeitung* depended on the gory disclosure of the bestial acts performed on the child, including unspeakable sexual ones, and then revealing the outraged conclusion.

> A crime recalling the Corny murder has been perpetrated with mortifying brutality. The victim is the nine-year-old boy Emil Handtke [*sic*], who was discovered close to death on the floor of the house at 45 Grüner Weg. His throat showed powerfully marked strangulation marks, leaving evidence that someone had tried to choke the child to death. In addition, traces of several stabs of a knife were found on his throat. On another part of his body the young man was mutilated. The boy was immediately rushed to Bethanien [hospital], where he was subjected to a precise medical examination. The inspection determined that in addition a further criminal act, not to be named here, had been violently exercised on him. Hence a double murder attempt: mutilation and molestation! And who is the perpetrator of these damnable crimes? The pen shudders even to write it down—the boy's *own father*.[81]

The account was prurient and sensationalist, to be sure. Its dramatic crescendo fell on the identity of the perpetrator and the horror, somehow unthinkable, that such acts could issue from the boy's own parent.[82] In the next issue of the same newspaper two days later, the item was given more attention. From a single paragraph, fourth of the list of items under the rubric "Daily Police Chronicle," a piece three times as long now led the chronicle section. The narrative strategy had changed completely, for the prime suspect had now shifted from the victim's father to an obscure stranger. The boy Emil was now identified not as nine years old but five, as "pretty as a picture."[83] The melodrama is now one of innocence endangered, through the eyes of the older brother, who spots a "somewhat corpulent figure" nearby as he heads home ahead of Emil; then the worried mother, a call to the police, and the discovery of "little Emil lying gravely wounded, with traces of the most brutal violence," along with the prime pieces of evidence, an ivory-handled cane and a soiled handkerchief, left behind. The accused—denounced by

81. "Polizei- und Tages-Chronik," *Berliner Gerichts-Zeitung*, 17, no. 7 (January 19, 1869): 2.

82. Cf. Wolff, *Postcards*, 1–6.

83. "Ein bildhübscher Knabe"; see "Polizei- und Tages-Chronik," *Berliner Gerichts-Zeitung* 17, no. 8 (January 21, 1869): 2–3.

an acquaintance as the owner of just such a cane—is incriminatingly known
to authorities as well. His name and address are in the files of the criminal
police who "for quite some time have known Zastrow as a person suspected
of such unnatural debaucheries."[84] As we have seen, debaucheries or excesses
(*Ausschweifungen*) of "this kind" (*solche*) cannot have referred to any history of violent rape, sadism, maim, or child molestation. The accused was in
police files for a history of having approached adult men for consensual sex.
The bulk of this first article introducing the suspect to readers was devoted to
a depiction of what kind of person Zastrow was, a caricature sketched from
what could be gleaned of his biography. He was an aristocrat from an esteemed line; he had dropped out of an intended military career to go on to
fail in a theatrical career, then a literary one, then to study law, until settling
on the life of an unsettled artist, frequenting every bar in the district and eager to make the acquaintance of "unmarried young men." The anonymous
reporter raised an eyebrow at Zastrow's tastes: his obsession with the ancient
Greeks (not for their art and philosophy but for their attention to the male
form); his enthusiasm for long, dramatic poetry, and for Schiller's *Don Carlos*; his peculiar attraction to the Orient, and on and on. Intriguingly, though,
when asked by the investigating magistrate whether he would confess to the
attack, the suspect also appealed to the "kind of person" he appeared to be:
"Do I look like a murderer?"[85]

Nearly six months later, visibly broken from the long stay in prison await-
ing trial, Zastrow would look quite different as he appeared before judge and
jury on the fifth of July, 1869. The trial was the occasion for open speculation
on the nature and state of the accused. If criminal responsibility, or *Zurechnungsfähigkeit*, was the fulcrum on which the competition of medical and
juridical expertises pivoted, this day in court showed that control over the
*question* of accountability was fought over by all involved: it was coveted by
the defense, the prosecutor, and the judge; the authority of adjudication of
the issue was then claimed by medical experts; finally, the defendant himself
had a crucial contribution to make about the criteria of judgment on this
issue.[86] The defense attorney brought up the issue immediately, in advance

84. "Wohl aber der Criminalpolizei bekannt, welche von Zastrow schon längst als einen
Menschen kennt, der dergleichen unnatürlicher Ausschweifungen verdächtig ist"; ibid., 3.
   85. "Polizei- und Tages-Chronik," *Berliner Gerichts-Zeitung* 17, no. 9 (January 23, 1869): 2.
   86. Most of the court records are not extant, but a virtually comprehensive account of the
testimony can be reconstructed from exhaustive reports in contemporary newspapers, notably
"Carl Friedrich Wilhelm Ernst von Zastrow vor den Geschwornen," *Berliner Gerichts-Zeitung* 17,
no. 76 (July 6, 1869): 1–2; *Vossische Zeitung: Berlinische Nachrichten von Staats- und gelehrten Sachen* (July 6, 1869), cited in Herzer, "Der Prozeß gegen den Berliner Urning Carl von Zastrow,"

of the proceedings proper, arguing that there appeared to be certain moments in which the mental competence of Zastrow was put into doubt. The state prosecutor countered that no facts suggesting the criminal unaccountability of the accused lay as yet before the court; further, no need for such a determination had been raised by any of the investigators in the course of interviews with the accused. The defense insisted that such a determination would be necessary in any case once the jury understood that both mother and grandfather of the defendant had histories of mental illness. At this point, the adjudicator intervened to ask the defendant directly whether he himself claimed *Unzurechnungsfähigkeit* in the present or the past, to which Zastrow slyly replied that he was in such a desperate and agitated state of affliction for long enough as to make him question either his own sanity or that of those accusing him.

Once the court allowed their testimony, the medical experts on hand at the trial would have the most influential say on the question of the criminal responsibility of the accused. The prestigious panel of three witnesses included Dr. Carl Westphal, whose study of two inverts had been researched and was soon to be published. Westphal responded to the question of *Zurechnungsfähigkeit* (without making a conclusive determination) by relating his experience with the two subjects of his current research. The case studies in the forthcoming "Conträre Sexualempfindung," one male and one female, were both interned in asylums.[87] The second expert was Carl Skrzeczka (1833–1902), signator of an 1869 medical testimony challenging the soundness of the criminalization of same-sex behavior, which in turn had been published by Kertbeny.[88] Skrczezka confirmed that the insane in general display a heightened sexual drive and a tendency toward excesses (*Rohheiten*), but he also reserved judgment on this particular case. The third forensic physician was Casper's nephew and successor as editor of the forensic *Handbuch,* the Berlin physician Carl Liman (1818–91). Liman noted the accused's family history, particularly the mental illness of his mother and grandfather, as a significant factor. Yet to the question of whether persons with abnormal sexual deviations of this kind could even be considered criminally responsible, the panel

---

*Capri* 2, no. 2, p. 3; "Der Prozeß gegen den Lieutenant v. Zastrow," *Volks-Zeitung: Organ für Jedermann aus dem Volke* 17, no. 54, pp. 2–3, Beilage 1.

87. "Der Prozeß gegen den Lieutenant v. Zastrow,"*Volks-Zeitung: Organ für Jedermann aus dem Volke* 17, no. 154 (July 6, 1896): 2–3, Beilage 1, see p. 3. Westphal identifies Zastrow as sharing the same "Ausschweifungen" as his male subject ("Ha——"), in spite of the focus in his article on gender dysphoria rather than sexual activity.

88. Kertbeny, ¶*143 des Preussischen Strafgesetzbuches,* 7–10, repr. in *Schriften,* 68–73. See also Kennedy, *Karl Heinrich Ulrichs,* 221–23.

was in full agreement. The presence of such inclination neither necessarily entailed nor did it exclude the mental competence underlying criminal responsibility, and each physician declared he would require further study of Zastrow before being able to make a determination.

When Zastrow himself was questioned, though, he claimed anything but incompetence. He was in a position to deny all charges, to dismiss all evidence and witness testimony. He had been falsely accused and misidentified, and the evidence found at the scene was not his property. Most important, he claimed access to knowledge that no one else present could have: self-knowledge. He was armed with an understanding of sexuality that could only have come from one source: Ulrichs's pamphlets. To be sure, those writings had been found in his apartment and seized by the police because they were incriminatory. Zastrow took the stand prepared to explain how the kind of person he was certainly did have relevance to the determination of his guilt or innocence but not in any of the ways that had been pointed to in the comments of jurists and physicians on that day.

> The accused further testified that he was far removed from that sensuality that is indicated by the name "pederasty." Yes, the preference for handsome manly forms and the desire to nestle up to them had been with him since his youth, but he had always shuddered at the thought that this would make him suspect of unnatural indecency. In this sense he agreed with conclusions of many cultured men, that besides the male and female sex there exists a third sex, "so cut by God." The accused expresses his conception of the sexual inclination of this "third sex," in which he remarks that there are further subspecies of this subspecies, which he abhors, because they are linked to excess and violence. While his own inclinations may contradict the privileged conception of the world, he has never held them as criminal, and he takes the defense of this position onto himself.[89]

Another account of Zastrow's declaration read this way:

> A preference for handsome manly forms was born in me and grew up with me, as did the drive to snuggle up to them. There are three sexes, not two; I belong to the third. The inclination of this third sex, likewise, consists of love, but not for women. It, too, is justified by nature. Legislation should never become involved in it. [90]

---

89. "Der Prozeß," *Volks-Zeitung*, 3. This paraphrase of von Zastrow's testimony is confirmed by the above-referenced accounts in the *Vossische Zeitung* and the *Gerichts-Zeitung*.

90. Cited in M. Herzer, "Das Jahr 1869," in *Eldorado: Homosexuelle Frauen und Männer in Berlin 1850–1950; Geschichte, Alltag und Kultur* (Berlin: Edition Hentrich, 1992), 11.

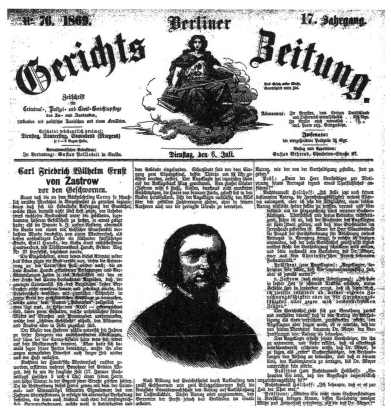

FIGURE 14. Cover story on Zastrow in the *Gerichts-Zeitung* on the occasion of his trial.

The newspapers eagerly printed these extraordinary statements of the accused not to represent his viewpoint but because their very strangeness enhanced the sensational value of the articles (fig. 14). The accused's unabashed declaration of urning identity (and hence Ulrichs's works themselves) were understood to be presented as apologia for Zastrow's horrible crimes.[91] Ulrichs's work was on trial as much as Zastrow, brought to court by revisionists of the very doctrine under fire. Ulrichs knew it, too. Reading the reports of Zastrow's bizarre theory of sexuality, Ulrichs commented, "Thus did he refer to me."

91. The Berlin *Börsenzeitung* of February 20, 1869, put it this way: "[Zastrow] publicly enjoys indulging in the acknowledgment and glorification of his love for men, a love that, according to the well-known works of the former Hanoverian lawyer Ulrichs, is to be attributed to organic reasons and psychic conditions. He often referred to the content of these writings. They discovered them . . . to be in his library as well."

After stating at the outset that he was not in the business of defending sadistic crime, Ulrichs dedicated two full pamphlets of his series of twelve to expressing outrage over the handling of the case in the courts and in the press.[92] He introduced the case with an admonition of the underground community of urnings complicit in their own persecution by virtue of keeping their identities a secret when they could have "given enlightenment"; they "should have spoken out, educating, protesting, supporting, every time uranian love was treated as unnatural," and all the more so in a case of atrocities such as this one. This promise of a self-emancipating community of urnings was thus intricately and explicitly linked to a public fantasy of a perverse urban community, and indeed to the image held by police. Ulrichs relished the idea that the Berlin police were engaged in the practice of compiling a list of Berlin urnings, just as he had done for even longer, and wished he had access to the files (if only to prove that his list was more complete).

These correspondences between Ulrichs's agenda and those of state surveillance apparatuses and the sensationalist press are typical of a pattern that emerged in the Zastrow case. First of all, through the intensity of public attention and proliferation of discourses on the homosexual, the tremendous effect of Ulrichs's project, begun five years earlier, becomes apparent. Lawyers' arguments, testimony, and newspaper reports all attested to the necessity of a language that Ulrichs had provided and over which he still claimed command. The expert witnesses were all positioned, with Ulrichs, to concede inborn homosexual identity and remove it from the domain of criminality if only to reposition it in the domain of insanity. Their recognition of Ulrichs, to whom their views were certainly indebted, was of a pathological witness; Westphal's references to him, for instance, were disparaging, as were the references in the newspapers; the next pamphlet of Ulrichs's series quoted Westphal's mentions of him in sanitized form, making it look more like academic citation than a doctor's observations of an inmate. The association of homosexual nature and violence that emerged in the professional discussions in the wake of the trial had been enabled by Ulrichs's founding doctrines on urning nature. His scathing doctrinaire critiques of the trial and its place in public read as corrections of a catechism badly learned. What is more, because the doctrine continued to be produced, with the two pamphlets released in 1869 responding to the trial and its surrounding commentary directly, there was an intensive mutual reflexivity among all these conflicting strains of dis-

---

92. Ulrichs, *Forschungen*, 9:1–154, translated in Ulrichs, *Riddle*, 2:435–540 (including book eight, *Incubus: Uranian Love and Bloodthirstiness*, and book nine, *Aronauticus: Zastrow and the Urnings of the Pietistic, Catholic, and Freethinking Parties*).

course, a structural recursivity. Ulrichs proudly quoted the *Berliner Gerichts-Zeitung*'s sensational report that "in [Zastrow's] statements he referred to the splendid (?!) writings of Ulrichs."

## The Bite of Zastrow

The accused's defense took off from these principles of natural sexuality: he is attracted by adults and not to young boys, his desire is for warmth and touching (hence not anal intercourse), and cruelties are "so contrary to my nature, that I cannot understand them." These points of defense follow Ulrichs's own interventions at certain moments. At this point in Ulrichs's changing thinking about the urning, he has complicated the model so that all urnings are not necessarily simply feminine souls in men's bodies but that urnings themselves have three genders: *Mannling* (active), *Weibling* (passive), or mixed natures. So it stands to reason that if Zastrow is a Weibling, as his carriage and personality suggest, neither anal penetration nor violent murder can be natural to him. Because the crimes in question are inseparable from the nature of urning sexuality, the usual court psychologists are simply not equipped to make these sorts of determinations—Ulrichs is.[93]

Thus, Ulrichs's specialized knowledge of uranism made him uniquely equipped to understand the subject's possible motives, coming as they must from drives particular to his type, and even to determine whether or not he was constitutionally capable of such crimes. This position, however, was at odds with a chief theme of Ulrichs's attacks on the handling of the case: that the question of Zastrow's guilt or innocence should be decoupled from his admitted uranism, and that his urning identity is not relevant in any way to the possible perpetration of any crime. These incompatible positions emerge from Ulrichs's resistance to the most malign of the revisions, popular and scientific, of Ulrichs's "urning knowledge": that "Uranian love in itself is prone to the committing of such crimes."[94] Ulrichs was not projecting this revision onto fantasized opponents: throughout his remarks, he cited examples of this assumption among jurists or physicians (one court physician states that all urnings had a preference for sadism, another physician that "people of that sort are inclined to cruelty"), newspaper reports, and ordinary people (the

---

93. Ulrichs, *Riddle*, 2:504, 528.

94. From a signed statement by Ulrichs in the Berlin *Börsenzeitung*, where he assured readers that (1) his doctrine of natural homosexuality did not gloss over uranian violence, and (2) that violent sex crimes occur "also in the love of real men" and have no special relationship to uranian nature.

new Berlin slang terms "a zastrow" and "to zastrow," conflating male-male preference and violent rape).[95] He therefore titled his eighth pamphlet *Incubus: Uranian Love and Bloodthirstiness* to address the question of the relation of urning nature and violence.

Before opening that pamphlet, we turn briefly back to Kertbeny, who, as fate would have it, was preparing his second tract on Paragraph 143 in 1869 as the Zastrow/Hanke trial broke. Just as sensationalist and scientific perspectives on homosexuality were woven into one another in the text of the trial, Kertbeny's drafts ritually repeat the elements of the case; he is concerned both with controlling the interpretation of events and also with working through what their true meaning might be in relation to sexual knowledge.[96] The archives reveal the source of the reflections. A correspondent, knowing Kertbeny to be the author of the first tract on Paragraph 143, has sent him newspaper clippings concerning the Hanke and Corny cases and challenged him to apply his logic of emancipation to these brutal acts.[97] Kertbeny argues in fits and starts against the association in spite of the lack of any evidence. The lack of evidence apart from sensationalist newspaper pieces is in fact his first argument. But gradually he turns to the theory of sexuality itself for an answer, and it finds its way into addenda to his second tract.[98] In it he begins as he began his letter to the correspondent who sent him the clippings—with the plain fact that no homosexual had ever been found to be the agent of violent crimes such as these. In all known history, such acts have been the province of normalsexuals, whether men or women. Some of them have had same-sex relations, to be sure, just as they may have with corpses or animals. The "unbound," free-floating, and hyper-potent sexual drive, we recall, is the purely *heterosexual* drive.[99] In fact sex with animals and corpses is not only by nature but by definition heterosexual,[100] he argues, and in doing so turns on its head the body of forensic medicine that, as we have seen, could never fully disaggregate pederasty, bestiality, and rape. The virility required for such acts is precisely that which is missing in the homosexual, characterized by a "certain womanishness" and "passive disposition," and therefore "no evidently

---

95. Ulrichs, *Forschungen*, 8:56.

96. Fond 22/296, NSL; see "Anthropologischer Gutachten," 384–87, and "Aus einem wissenschaftlichen Briefwechsel," 371.

97. Fond 22/296, NSL; "Aus einem wissenschaftlichen Briefwechsel," 371–2, and "Aus dem Briefwechsel zweier Naturforscher," 373r–76v.

98. See Kertbeny, *Das Gemeinschädliche*, "Ein Sondercapitel als Nachtrag," and "Der Ausgang des Processes und seine Consequenzen," 53–75; *Schriften* 207–29.

99. Kertbeny, *Das Gemeinschädliche*, 54; *Schriften* 208.

100. Kertbeny, *Das Gemeinschädliche*, 55–6; *Schriften* 209–10.

demonstrated homosexual has been known by history to practice blood-thirsty crime."[101] If the sensational version of events threatened to accept the existence of innate homosexuality and define it as bloodthirsty and publicly dangerous, Kertbeny saw things differently: the homosexually violated boys exposed nothing if not the inherent savagery of "normal sexuality" itself.

Ulrichs, in his eighth and ninth pamphlets, also turned to the Zastrow case and defended the accused in ways we have seen. In spite of all these defenses, the strongest impression one gets from a reading of these texts is that Ulrichs did assume that Zastrow had committed the sadistic crimes. Hence, an entirely different sort of defense is pursued, and it is one that is both telling and consequential. The central issue became not agency or guilt per se but criminal responsibility (*Zurechnungsfähigkeit*). If an urning were to act on the basis of a motive such as fear of discovery or escape from blackmail—were he to act out of conscious motive—he could be held responsible. But in the course of a series of related cases surveyed by Ulrichs, it emerged that "sexual pleasure can cause momentary disturbance in the emotional state"—not to put too fine a point on it, sex can be identified as a moment of madness. The crimes committed against the two boys,

> the biting and the running through with the stick, appear as totally aimless and cruel, as wild sexual rage. . . . For that reason examination must be made as to whether v. Zastrow also acted under the irresistible inner force of that emotional disturbance similar to rage.[102]

In leading up to this point, Ulrichs relied heavily on an unlikely source, cited by him no fewer than a dozen times: a treatise by Josef von Görres titled *Christian Mysticism*. "Apart from the demonological concept present in [the work], this opinion is entirely in agreement with mine; this despite the fact that its author reached it by an entirely different route than I: I by way of scientific psychology, he by mystical demonology."[103] This is a strange turn for Ulrichs's argument to take, for it seems to reverse the powerfully rationalist narrative established in the previous seven books. Görres, under the heading "Demonic Bloodthirstiness," posits that

> the desire for procreation is related to the desire to kill, which forms its reverse side: both awaken an intoxication of the blood. . . . The growing drives battle more and more against the domination of the will. Finally they sap it entirely of its power. In its inability to resist, the will becomes their slave, driven now

101. Kertbeny, *Das Gemeinschädliche*, 57–8; *Schriften* 211–12.
102. Ulrichs, *Riddle*, 2:468, 508.
103. Ulrichs, *Riddle*, see esp. 2:496–98.

from cruelty to cruelty and finally into obsession [a kind of demonic posses-
sion] . . . subjugation by the demon.[104]

Ulrichs was completely taken by this passage and this book. He included
in his further case studies stories of early modern and medieval werewolves,
werewolves from the sagas and Eddas, other tales of monstrous witches. What
are we to make of this turn of the rationalist jurist to mysticism, monsters,
and magic?

The conclusion drawn at the end of both book six and book seven is this:

> In the case of certain individuals pathological emotional disturbance appears
> to be possible—be it chronic, or only of a moment's duration . . . where the
> individual is forced into behavior of wild cruelty and bloodthirstiness by an
> unconquerable inner impulse . . . these conditions (which one could term
> "compelling intoxication of the blood") appear to have similarities to that dis-
> placement accompanying the morbid state in which persons bitten by a mad
> dog find themselves. Awareness particularly also appears to be reduced just as
> little by such emotional disturbance, as when the person bitten develops ra-
> bies. Whether they call this madness or not, responsibility for actions that arise
> from them appears to me to be exempted to the same degree as it is for the
> person who is bitten, even if the individual has behaved with full awareness.[105]

The term *intoxication of the blood* (*Blutrausch*) is drawn directly from
Görres's *Christian Mysticism*, likening, as it were, the violent sexual subject to
a demon, monster, or werewolf. The reader of book eight is suddenly trans-
ported as by magic from the relentless Enlightenment demystification of the
pamphlets into the netherworld of a madness within sexuality itself—a madness which is sexuality itself—and which "solves" the violent crimes of the
sexual subject. As in many a narrative of sensational value or fantastic nature,
this is a journey into a realm that is precivilized, intuitive, frightening, and
exciting. It is, however, not a discrete origin or natural home for urnings,
who are (Ulrichs insists) no more likely to move from sex to violence than are
"real men." It is rather the primordial place of the essence of sexuality. Only
this place, this inner sanctum of sexuality, first emerges now, after Zastrow,
after Ulrichs. It is as if the bite of Zastrow has sent us into a delirium in which
we are given a chance to escape from reason and confront the very identity
of sexuality.

All of this reminds us of that which we know but persistently work to for-

---

104. "beide wecken einen Blutrausch"; [Johann] J[osef] von Görres, *Die christliche Mystik*,
4:460–61.

105. Ulrichs, *Riddle*, 2:468, 508.

get: that discourses on and of sexual marginality are always at the same time, and perhaps mainly, explorations of "centered" sexuality. That the terms *homosexual* and *heterosexual* are diacritical, each unintelligible without constant reference to the other, is one of those truths that are so obvious that they can usually be ignored.[106] The metaphors allowing us to speak of the questions of elusive homosexual origins and diasporic communities of violence belie the ways in which the presumed heterosexual host culture is no less fugitive, incoherent, diasporic. If Numa Numantius declared a "name and a place to stand" from which to move the world, he would be moved with it; from the moment of its origin, sexuality was already on the move.

---

106. Cf. Janet E. Halley on the *Bowers v. Hardwick* case; "The Construction of Heterosexuality," in Warner, *Queer Planet*, 82–102. But this is quite different from the claim that the study of deviance was a way of defining and defending a normative masculine sexuality through bounding off its "others"; cf. Franz X. Eder, "Von 'Sodomiten' und 'Konträrsexualen': Die Konstruktion des 'homosexuellen' Subjekts im deutschsprachigen Wissenschaftsdiskurs des 18. Und 19. Jahrhunderts," in *Que(e)rdenken: Weibliche/männliche Homosexualität und Wissenschaft*, ed. Barbara Hey, Ronald Pallier, and Roswitch Roth (Innsbruck-Vienna: Studien-Verlag, 1997), 15–39.

# 3

# Sensation and Sensibility: Experts, Scandals, Subjects

What we know as the discipline of sexology would emerge in the brief half-century between the Zastrow trial and 1910.[1] Although its object was human sexuality, its focus from the start was on the deviant, and the male homosexual was given as its classic exemplar. This, as we have seen, had already been the case in Westphal's protosexological text on "contrary sexual sensibility." The subtitle of Krafft-Ebing's seminal *Psychopathia sexualis* was, in all editions from the second on, "with especial reference to the contrary sexual instinct." The special mode of production of knowledge to take this label was from the first dependent on stories provided by patients whose own self-awareness was in turn conditioned by the circulation of knowledge provided by the new science.

In this way, self-articulations or confessions of the subjective experience of sexual identity and scientific definitions of categories of sexuality worked hand in hand, but neither of these levels of discussion reached a broad general public. In fact, substantial care was taken to keep these new languages from reaching uninitiated audiences. The bridge spanning the gap from the knowledge of homosexuality as an identity commanded by experts and subjects to the consciousness of the society at large was the sex scandal. Scandal was a different register of knowledge, to be sure, but it did not innocently

---

1. A comprehensive history of sexology (or sexual science) has been lacking, although Sigusch, *Geschichte der Sexualwissenschaft*, a recent work focused on German-language sources, attempts to be one. Sigusch acknowledges the general acceptance of the initial works of the discipline at the end of the nineteenth century with Krafft-Ebing et al., or the first decade of the twentieth with Iwan Bloch, but posits instead that its original proponents are Karl-Heinrich Ulrichs and Paolo Mantegazza between 1850 and 1870.

reflect or report on the "firsthand" accounts of experts, police, legal codes, and (least of all) homosexual subjects; it was itself an active force in the constellation of representation, as had already been the case in the early example of the Zastrow trial. The genre of the high-profile homosexual sex scandal would come into its own in central Europe in the early twentieth century beginning in the wake of the Oscar Wilde trial in Britain and reaching its high-water mark in 1907 with the Harden-Eulenburg affair, a scandal involving homosexuality in the emperor's closest advisory circle that shook the imperial regime. Mainly, the spate of scandals to hit the papers in the first decade of the century were characterized by cultural fantasy involving infiltration, conspiracy, state subversion, and corruption, rather than gruesome or redemptive violence. These sensations exposed a hidden violence against society behind which lay a secret aberration.

It is no coincidence that the first years of the twentieth century, when sex scandal took on new life in central Europe in a way that the brilliant and acerbic Viennese critic Karl Kraus identified as a new order, were also the years of sexual psychiatry's florescence. The linkage was not lost on Kraus, who was the first to comment on it: "I detest psychiatry because it feeds the individual's hunger for power; and because, like journalism, it carries within itself vast potentialities for its abuse."[2] The relationship of the two realms was particularly intimate in the court cases that were so often the theater of the public affairs called scandals: psychiatric experts were called on to testify on the pathology of subjects and on their accountability, while journalists sealed their fates by different means.

Medical definitions of pathology and journalistic sex scandals worked hand in glove to set, broadcast, and enforce norms, to be sure. At the same time, paradoxically, they both produced conditions for the emergence of homosexual identity and subculture. The question of which of these presumed opposing effects was weightier than the other has been disputed and may be impossible to answer. Asking it may divert attention from other, difficult historical issues that are, however, rarely considered by historians. How did the processes producing the "homosexual subject" actually occur, and what is the nature of the link between this definition of deviance and human sexuality as such? This chapter tracks the circuit of knowledge exchange and transformation through voices of sexology, scandal, and the homosexual emancipation movement, all concerned with the nature of sexual identity and its relevance for the public sphere.

2. Kraus, *Sittlichkeit und Kriminalität*, translation taken from Szasz, *Age of Madness*, 129.

## Krafft-Ebing and the Delirious Subject

As Ulrichs's pamphlets on uranism, Westphal's article on contrary sexual
sensibility, and the Zastrow case all emerged in print, a young Richard von
Krafft-Ebing (1840–1902) was gaining experience in the field of nerve disor-
ders as an assistant physician in the mental asylum in Baden-Baden, which he
followed up by establishing a private practice in the same city. Krafft-Ebing
would enter history fifteen years after the Zastrow case with the publication
of the first edition of the *Psychopathia sexualis*, often thought of as the founding work of sexology.[3] In many ways, it followed closely on the forensic precursors discussed in the previous chapter, particularly as regards its principal
method: it was based on observation of actual subjects and incorporation of
their own self-perceptions, so the narrative of *Psychopathia sexualis* consists
in no small part of a string of citations from subjects' reports. We should not
regard it as surprising that Krafft-Ebing's background mirrors the genealogy
of sexology itself, from mental asylum to forensic medicine. His special interest in both realms was not sexuality as such but rather the altered states of
mind that he first referred to as *deliria*.

Richard Fridolin Joseph Freiherr Krafft von Festenburg auf Frohnberg
genannt von Ebing—or Richard von Krafft-Ebing, for short—was born 1840
in Mannheim in the Grand Duchy of Baden and studied medicine at Heidelberg. During his studies he lived at the home of his grandfather, who held
a chair at Heidelberg in criminal law.[4] He was inspired to specialize in psychiatry. After collecting data from observation of patients at a nearby mental asylum, he wrote his dissertation in 1863 (published 1864) on "Sensory
deliria," dedicated to his grandfather (fig. 15).[5] While the secondary literature on Krafft-Ebing (less prodigious than one might think) has not made
much of this little work, the interests that drive it are telling: hallucination,
delusion, conditions of mad excitement, and stupors of melancholy. Sex as
such—even gender—hardly merited observation for the young doctor, mes-
merized as he was by the varied border states of consciousness afflicting the
insane. When he did study people outside of the asylum, they were those

---

3. Among the precursors, it is important to include the eponymous work by Heinrich Kaan
published in 1844, which Foucault marked as the shift from the alienists to psychiatry and the
"date of birth . . . of sexuality and sexual aberrations in a psychiatric field"; see Foucault et al.,
*Abnormal*, 282. Kaan's work does not offer the enduring template of sexological research that
Krafft-Ebing would provide, but it marked a radically novel way of looking at sexual behavior;
see Henrico [Heinrich] Kaan, *Psychopathia sexualis* (Leipzig: Voss, 1844).

4. Carl Joseph Anton Mittelmaier (1787–1867). See Oosterhuis, *Stepchildren of Nature*, 77–78.

5. Krafft-Ebing, *Die Sinnesdelirien*.

Die

# Sinnesdelirien.

Inauguraldissertation

verfasst

und

mit Genehmigung einer hochlöbl. medicinischen Facultät der
Universität Heidelberg veröffentlicht

von

**Dr. med. R. v. Krafft-Ebing.**

Erlangen.
Verlag von Ferdinand Enke.
1864.

FIGURE 15. Krafft-Ebing's dissertation, "Sensory deliria," 1864.

experiencing delirium from alcohol or narcotics. Further, this interest in delirium states does not seem to be focused on disruption of the senses but on their heightening. In an early passage, he waxes eloquent in a description that weaves physiology into poetry; from impressions on ganglion cells of the corticalis to an "escalation" or even "exaltation" of imaginary power such as that described by Goethe, who could reproduce the sensory experience of a flower in bloom by closing his eyes and thinking about it. In a footnote, we learn that the author's own experience with delirium during a bout with typhoid fever the previous year has informed this observation.[6]

It was not out of any manifest interest in the reproductive instinct and its deviations that Krafft-Ebing was to come to sex. We have seen how the first glimmers of a new science of sexual identity had emerged from forensic medicine earlier in the nineteenth century, and Krafft-Ebing's path would be the same. From sensory delirium he moved in the following year to a study of "transitory manias" intended "for doctors and jurists" (a standard formula for forensic reference works), then a manual to help with the "recognition and correct forensic assessment of morbid mental conditions."[7] The following year came a study of "transitory disturbances of self-consciousness."[8] Forensic psychiatry was just one—if a chief one—of many interests pursued in his numerous publications and in professorial positions in Strasbourg and Graz and finally in Vienna.[9] In Graz, the city from which he also directed a nearby Styrian state asylum, one of his closest colleagues was the jurist and criminalist Hanns Gross. Nonetheless, his fascination with the liminal "twilight states" of consciousness was never to abate, and it played a crucial role in his work that is generally overlooked by researchers with an eye for early theories of sexuality. The persistence of this preoccupation alongside and also integrated within studies of sexuality demonstrates the continued centrality—if also different function—of delirium in the emergent psychiatric model of sexuality.[10]

6. Ibid., 5–9.

7. Krafft-Ebing, *Die Lehre von der Mania; Beiträge zur Erkennung.*

8. Krafft-Ebing, *Die transitorischen Störungen.*

9. Krafft-Ebing, *Grundzüge der Criminalpsychologie*, became a standard work.

10. Foucault argued that the early nineteenth-century alienists' conception of mental illness definitionally depended on the presence of delirium, whereas beginning with Jules Baillarger (1809–90) in France and Wilhelm Griesinger (1817–68) in Germany, the core of psychiatry is moved to the volition of the subject. See Foucault, *Abnormal*, 158–60. Arnold Davidson has noted how the "stages" of different conceptualizations (and, in his terms, styles of reasoning) relating to sexual perversion are not mapped onto historical chronology and often enough cohabit in individual scientists or even articles. See Arnold Davidson, *The Emergence of Sexuality:*

The 1880s, for example—the decade in which the first editions of the *Psychopathia* were published—was a period in which Krafft-Ebing collected a mass of material under the general heading of "trance" or "twilight state" (*Dämmerzustand*). This category included the "half-waking state" (a condition of delirium), epileptic and other seizures, amnesia, delusions of grandeur, and somnambulism. In this collection he included case histories of his and other patients, autobiographical material sent to him by subjects, and published articles and clippings.[11] There is not necessarily a connection to sexuality or to violence in these cases, although he attended to it carefully where there was one. He took copious notes, for instance, on an 1880–81 French case where a vice offense was dismissed on account of somnambulism.[12] Some of the cases and discussions of "transitory insanity" and twilight states were included in every edition of the *Psychopathia*; others were used in essays on *Dämmerzustand* written in 1875, 1877, and 1898, all of which were included along with further discussions of amnesia and other related conditions in a work appearing around this time.[13]

What were the signs of a twilight state of consciousness, and when were such signs relevant? Clues to these questions appear in Krafft-Ebing's notes to particular case studies and his markings on the actual manuscripts sent to him—letters and longer autobiographical texts sent to him from patients, case histories shared with him from other psychiatrists, as well as scholarly articles. One such autobiographical narrative runs some one hundred pages, in which Krafft-Ebing underscored or commented on points of special interest: "the sadness of my life," "mostly lethargic," "constantly displaced nature," "began to hallucinate."[14] In some, but not all of these cases, Krafft-Ebing distilled a connection to sexuality:

> Pat[ient] reports that she very often finds herself in a half-waking state in which it seems to her as though the whole world had no more than a sham existence; in these moments she has no consciousness of reality. This condition,

---

*Historical Epistemology and the Formation of Concepts* (Cambridge, MA: Harvard University Press, 2001), 3.

   11. PP-KEB/A/39, WLAM contains a sheaf of such cases, chiefly from 1899 and 1900. Krafft-Ebing's marginal notes label cases "Dämmerzustand" on the basis of particular physiological symptoms (e.g., discrepant pupil size), or more specific designations such as "Dämmerzustand mit expans. delir.," "Majestätsdelir" (delusions of grandeur), and so on.

   12. PP-KEB/A/39, WLAM; cf. Dr. A. Motet, "Accès de somnambulisme," *Annales d'hygiène publique et de médecine legale* 3, no. 5 (1881): 214–24.

   13. Krafft-Ebing, *Arbeiten aus dem Gesamtgebiet*, esp. 20–236.

   14. PP-KEB/A/12, pp. 15, 19, 25, WLAM.

she thinks, is the consequence of that which innervates her sex drive without, however, satisfying it.[15]

Another case history sent to Krafft-Ebing by an unknown colleague had been identified as a case of *Dämmerzustand* by the sender; Krafft-Ebing once again underlined the details relevant to the diagnosis: "Pat[ient] has reportedly been utterly altered in her nature over the past three days," "sporadically bursts into laughter and then falls into despair," "does not recognize her mother," and special highlighting is reserved for symptoms that might go unnoticed—"*severe headaches.*" The patient's distracted behavior is noted by the correspondent, who deems her "completely without affect" through most of the examination.[16] The inspection includes sensory tests by pinprick, measurement of pupils, and other such telltale signs of a twilight state. Another expert has provided a further assessment that the subject is half conscious (*dämmerhaft*), disoriented in terms of time and space, without affect, and laughing intermittently.[17]

The delirious subject is a fascinating paradox because she is defined as a subject who is not herself. Absence and distraction, half consciousness and lack of emotion, of connection, or of appropriate response to context are the meaningful qualities of her subjectivity. *Dämmerzustand* is the privileged diagnosis in this and all cases where subjects fail to process dates, places, and names, where they prove unable to recognize those close to them, or where they even misrecognize themselves. They live in a world of the unreal and are not equipped to articulate their own stories. The narrative compulsion of the genre of the case history is at odds with the disruption of narrative represented by these conditions to which Krafft-Ebing was demonstrably and consistently drawn.

Contemporary critics of sexology in general and of Krafft-Ebing in particular have been divided on the question of whether the categories these created served only to pathologize and stigmatize subjects falling outside the norm or instead created the ground of legitimacy for their own self-identity.[18] Both of these positions rely on the notion that these disciplines created or hailed subjects, giving them ground to stand on or consigning them to the

15. PP-KEB/A/12, WLAM, covering page in Krafft-Ebing's hand.

16. PP-KEB/A/1, WLAM. The subject is named as Maria Schebesta, washerwoman, and dated November 14, 1901.

17. PP-KEB/A/2, November 19, 1901, WLAM.

18. Paraphrasing Doan and Waters in Bland and Doan, *Sexology Uncensored*, 41 (cf. chap. 2, n41).

social margins. And yet, what was interesting to Krafft-Ebing about so many of these cases was actually the evasion of subjectivity.

Anyone who has read deeply in the primary literature will recognize that forensic medicine of the fin de siècle gave far more room to such border states of consciousness as causes of crime (and hence indicators of unaccountability, or *Unzurechnungsfähigkeit*) than one would expect. The proportion of diagnosed "epileptics" in criminal cases is extremely high (compared with 1–2 percent of the general population, which is the most generous current estimate). We have already seen how professionals considered conditions from sleepwalking to homesickness to be indicators of a pathology so great that it could render subjects helpless to control violent, sexual, or criminal urges. Alcoholism was treated just as were these other (including the arguably congenital) conditions—indeed, family histories of alcohol abuse were taken as seriously as familial insanity or other mental illness. All this points to the fact that Krafft-Ebing's special interest in *Dämmerzustände*, while clearly a particular inclination, was not out of beat with the pulse of contemporary forensics. What is arguably novel in the *Psychopathia sexualis* is what we saw already in the early pages of Krafft-Ebing's dissertation: a veritably literary eloquence pertaining to these deviations, or the poetry of pathology.

This literary quality of the *Psychopathia* is worth exploring further, but for now it is interesting to note how this is the case in spite of the predominance of the voices of patients in the text, which comes forth as a pastiche of narratives. These case histories (Krankengeschichten—literally "illness histories") sustain this literary quality in part through the way the author highlights pathological consciousness as an abstraction from reality, or as a twilight experience.[19]

The interest in the *Dämmerzustand* is not unlike Hanns Gross's interest in compulsive (motiveless) crime: it intensifies the pathology, and in doing so, it compels a peculiarly pure form of deviancy. Often enough, it seems the ground of deviant behavior itself: exhibitionists and other vice criminals showing no sign of epilepsy or degeneracy commit indecent acts once they "fall into a clouded state of consciousness," a "dreamy state," a "state of benumbed consciousness," an "imperfect state of consciousness," and so forth.[20] Consider again epilepsy, which Krafft-Ebing classifies as a "specific

19. This is not precisely what Anna Clark means with her coinage "twilight moments," referring to spaces and periods of ambiguity regarding sexuality and deviance, but it is a near relative. See Clark, "Twilight Moments," 139–60.

20. Krafft-Ebing, *Psychopathia sexualis, with Especial Reference to Contrary Sexual Instinct*, 385–90.

pathology" and allies, surprisingly, with acquired (rather than innate) states of mental feebleness.[21] Among epileptics, he contends, the sexual instinct can be especially fierce, and they may act on it compulsively and without heed of anything external to the call of the instinct. "In his exceptional psychic state the epileptic is unable to resist his instincts, on account of the disturbance of his consciousness."[22] Krafft-Ebing's interest is particularly piqued in relation to a category of person that he feels has been ignored in forensics, namely, the person who lives a normal life but who becomes something else when gripped by a spell: a boy who attacks and violates his mother, a respectable man who twice a year or so has two-week fits where he succumbs to peder- asty, a lady who has similar bouts (activated by climaxing), compelling her to fantasize about sex with young boys, and many other cases. Other instances of "periodic insanity" are likewise especially sexually intense and inclined to the perverse, unimpeded as subjects gripped by such states are from any in- terference of the consciousness.[23]

Delirium and its relatives were clearly not Krafft-Ebing's sole interests, although one could argue that he was himself at least as attentive to the cat- egory of *Dämmerzustände* as he was to the distinction of acquired and inher- ited qualities, for example. The subjects of trance states were ultimately not subjects at all, or at least they seemed to be defined by a certain resistance to subjectivity. In this they may seem rather unlike that other privileged fig- ure in Krafft-Ebing's writings, the homosexual, who emerged in texts such as Krafft-Ebing's as "a personage, a past, a case history, and a childhood," in Foucault's well-known words. Yet both these figures opened a window to the essence of sexual psychopathology and with it, to the previously hidden hu- man element that Krafft-Ebing called "the sixth sense": sexuality.

### Urning Knowledge

Sexuality scholars have taken pains to discern the fine distinctions between what Ulrichs called "urnings" and those whom Westphal identified as hav- ing "contrary sexual sensibility"—rendered into English by Havelock Ellis as "inversion"—as well as the "homosexual" of Kertbeny/Jäger's text and after. Such distinctions certainly have their uses, but they should not be

21. Krafft-Ebing, *Psychopathia sexualis*, 352–57. Most references will be to this most easily accessible volume, which is a facsimile reprint of the 14th edition.

22. Ibid., 353.

23. Krafft-Ebing, *Psychopathia sexualis*, 358–71 ("Periodisches Irresein," "Manie," etc; *Die transitorischen Störungen*).

FIGURE 16. Krafft-Ebing posing in a love seat with his wife, Maria Luise.

taken too categorically.[24] That is because what is referred to by these terms—
whether a "third-sex" model of intermediacy or gender dysphoria or prefer-

24. The gay studies literature has seen much made of these as though they were ironclad categories in light of David Halperin's important intervention in *100 Years of Homosexuality*, 16, and
Eve Kosofsky Sedgwick's use of Halperin in her classic *Epistemology of the Closet*, esp. 157–59.

ence of same-sex partner, whether the sexual "aim" or "object," passive or active, and so forth—has rarely been consistent, and even single users or coiners (as we have seen with Ulrichs and Kertbeny) slipped in their definitions sometimes from year to year.[25] There was not a single body of "urning knowledge," but rather a Venn diagram of sets of truth claims relating to the figure of sexual deviance known as urning or invert or contrary sexual or homosexual. This knowledge started with the limited if repeated claims of the early to mid-nineteenth-century forensic literature (on anal or penile shape, chiefly) based on little if any observation of actual subjects. From there, these claims came to cover the urning's entire body and psyche, his genetic history and childhood, and also the reasons for his existence. From the moment of the Baron von Malzahn's and Karl-Heinrich Ulrichs's confessions, the source of virtually all of this knowledge was to be the homosexual subject himself.

A chief vehicle delivering subjective experience to the scientist and his public was the genre of the case history (Krankengeschichte). It was not a novel form as such, but in the late nineteenth century it became exceedingly important and familiar.[26] The tension between sexology's challenge to prove itself a legitimate, scientific subdiscipline—a challenge that psychoanalysis would also face—and its unprecedented exhibition of this narrative instrument could not have been lost on its practitioners.[27] Krafft-Ebing offered rigorous instructions to physicians constructing case histories, beginning with family histories of mental illness (also alcoholism, suicide, and illnesses of arguably degenerate origin) and proceeding in biographical manner with detailed questions proscribed for each stage of life from the fetal state through childhood, adolescence, and so on up to the present; thence, the focus on physical and psychological examination of the patient.[28] This ancestor of today's medical history was a threefold story directed by the medical expert and told by the patient, the examining physician, and the patient's body. The collection of Krafft-Ebing's papers, now maintained at the Wellcome Library in London, is rich in such case histories. Recorded and sent to him by physicians

---

25. Cf. the qualifications made by Davidson, cited above.

26 See, e.g., R. Tolle, "Die Krankengeschichte in der Psychiatrie," in *Biographie und Psychologie*, ed. G. Jüttermann and H. Thomae, 36–47 (Berlin: Springer, 1987); S. Brändli, B. Lüthi, and G. Spuhler, eds., *Zum Fall Machen, Zum Fall Werden: Wissensproduktion und Patientenerfahrung in Medizin und Psychiatrie des 19. und 20. Jahrhunderts* (Frankfurt: Campus, 2009).

27. Freud, e.g., commented on this tension explicitly in the *Studies on Hysteria*; see Certeau, *Heterologies*, 19–27.

28. See the appendix to his handbook, titled "Schema zur Geisteszustandsuntersuchung"; Krafft-Ebing, *Lehrbuch der Psychiatrie*, 272–76.

from across the country and abroad, most of these texts have comments in Krafft-Ebing's hand in the margins or on the verso sides of the pages and passages that he found most relevant underscored in colored pencil. The insight that the story would reveal the disease was one that would have deep and lasting effects on Western civilization. A giant step toward these effects was taken with the publication of the first edition of *Psychopathia sexualis* in 1886, which included patient narratives verbatim for long stretches. These were offered by way of example within the ever-expanding taxonomy of sexual abnormality that was the bulk of that work, which still billed itself as a medico-forensic handbook in the sense of those that came before it in the nineteenth century. But now the question of the medical determination of the boundary of legality has clearly, and from the first edition, been replaced with the boundary of wellness, and we find ourselves squarely within the new psychiatric regime heralded by Westphal. Krafft-Ebing, like Westphal, was more interested in psychic abnormality than in illegal behavior. To get what he wanted, he was willing to listen to what his subjects had to say.

Krafft-Ebing's preface to the twelfth edition of the *Psychopathia* in 1902 presents *in nuce* the entwinement of legal, medical, and subjective registers of urning knowledge as well as moral ones:

> The universally favorable reception accorded to the book in legal circles thus far assures its author that it has not been without influence on jurisprudence and legislation, and will contribute to overcoming many centuries of error and injustice.
>
> Its unexpected commercial success is likely the best proof that there are innumerable unfortunates [*Unglückliche*] who find in this book—otherwise meant for men of science—enlightenment and relief with respect to the puzzling [*rätselhafter*] manifestations of their own *vita sexualis*. Countless missives from such stepchildren of nature that have reached the author from all over the world testify that this is the case. Compassion and sympathy are strongly evoked from a perusal of these letters, written chiefly by men of refined thought and high social and mental standing. They reveal sufferings of the soul beside which all other afflictions dealt out by Fate appear as trifles.
>
> May this book offer such unfortunates [*Unglücklichen*] some degree of solace and moral rehabilitation![29]

29. Krafft-Ebing, *Psychopathia sexualis*, vi; cf. Krafft-Ebing, *Psychopathia sexualis, with Especial Reference to the Antipathic Sexual Instinct: A Medico-forensic Study*, trans. F. J. Rebman (New York: Rebman, 1906), viii. The same two terms characterize urnings or contrary sexuals as in so many works of medicine, law, and advocacy: *unglücklich* (unhappy, unfortunate) and *Rätsel* (riddle or puzzle).

Legal knowledge submits to medical enlightenment, which promises to sweep away erroneous legislation. Yet, this foreword betrays more than the battle of medical and juridical authority on the field of forensic science. By the time this last edition of *Psychopathia sexualis* to be published during Krafft-Ebing's lifetime appeared, the author clearly recognized that the work went beyond the bounds of a "medical-forensic study." The voices of subjects poignantly confirmed the usefulness of such knowledge to themselves, even as these same voices contributed decisively to its ongoing production.

Krafft-Ebing's papers reveal the extent to which this was the case. This very case is made eloquently by Harry Oosterhuis, who made deft use of the same papers while they were still in private hands.[30] The archive consists of a dense network of correspondence from and about subjects, case histories sent to Krafft-Ebing from physicians worldwide, and finally, not least, autobiographies of subjects themselves that had been publicly solicited by the scientist, many of which would find their way into later editions of the *Psychopathia*. Those subjects, as Krafft-Ebing alluded to in his last prefaces, were themselves readers of the prime text of sexual science and in many ways spoke in its language. Autobiographies often followed the format of the case history or else in jumbled form reproduced all its elements (physical description, attending especially to physiological or developmental anomalies; family history, stressing cases of insanity, epilepsy, and alcoholism; sexual history beginning with first memories of sexual sensations, and so on). Most but not all of these reporters were highly educated; some reproduced the Latin descriptions of acts and fantasies that Krafft-Ebing had used in his text to mark it as scientific and cloak its prurient value. A Baltic aristocrat writing Krafft-Ebing, for instance, was able to invoke Latin phrases for sexual acts and to speculate on the sexological analysis of his own case; on the other hand, he conflated languages of heritability and inheritance—or genetic and environmental traits and those handed down as social privilege.[31] But the details of his perversion, beginning from what he now identified as abnormal play impulses as a very young boy through inner fantasy life up to adult proclivities, this image of a unity that is the sexual life—all this consistently if sometimes silently cites Krafft-Ebing even as the latter's further editions quote from them at length in turn.

To this circuit of scientific and subjective sexual knowledge must be added

30. Oosterhuis, *Stepchildren of Nature*.

31. P. R. Freiherr von Ringen to Krafft-Ebing, misc. correspondence, July 1900, PP-KEB/C2, WLAM. Oosterhuis begins his book with a discussion of this case and includes photographs of select pages of the long letter in the book and on the cover.

a further operating point, that of sensational knowledge. The publication of hundreds and thousands of pages of detailed descriptions of every manner of sexual diversity was, after all, not merely an exchange between sexual scientist and unfortunate subject. There was an audience. In this, as in many cases in the history of sexual science, concerns about the potential prurient function of the text were linked to the challenge to its scientific legitimacy. The two-way street that was conduit of the exchange of perverse experience and scholarly knowledge contributed to this suspicion. Like Freud after him, Krafft-Ebing's boldness of research did not make him invulnerable to these perceptions, and Latin was not the only weapon in his arsenal of defenses.

### The Countess in Trousers; or, The Fraudulent Sex

A case where all of these streams converged—providing the occasion for a landmark scientific study, a scandalous court case, and a newspaper sensation—was that of Sándor (born Sarolta) Vay (fig. 17), whom the papers would christen the Hungarian "countess in trousers." Vay was born a woman but was raised at least for some years as a boy; entering society as a man, he had wooed several women and eventually married. The case came to general attention through a fraud suit filed by Vay's father-in-law when her "true" sex was discovered. The trial was, however, also the occasion for the first sustained scientific article on lesbianism ("gynandry"), penned by Krafft-Ebing.[32] We also possess a lengthy juridical account, including medical reports, that was the key source for Krafft-Ebing as well as for the court case for which it was intended.[33] From Krafft-Ebing's initial article, his analysis passed into several editions of *Psychopathia sexualis*, so that Havelock Ellis could call the Vay case "the most fully investigated case of inversion in a woman in modern times."[34] These, juxtaposed against contemporary sensational newspaper reports, illustrate the play of understandings of sex and gender as well as the interplay of an ostensibly objective science and subjective sensibility.[35]

32. R. von Krafft-Ebing, "Gynandrie: Ein Beitrag zur conträren Sexualempfindung," *Wiener Medizinische Blätter* 13, no. 29 (July 17, 1890): 451–53.

33. C. Birnbacher, "Ein Fall von konträren Sexualempfindung vor dem Strafgericht," *Friedreichsblätter für gerichtliche Medizin* 42, no. 1 (1891): 2–42.

34. Havelock Ellis, *Studies in the Psychology of Sex*, vol. 2, *Sexual Inversion*, 3rd ed. (Philadelphia: Davis, 1921), 195.

35. An excellent account, drawn mainly from Birnbacher's article above, is by Geertje Mak, *Mannelijke vrouwen: Over grenzen van sekse in de negentiende eeuw* (Amsterdam/Meppel: Boom, 1997), 197–243; for English, see "Sandor/Sarolta Vay: From Passing Woman to Sexual Invert," *Journal of Women's History* 16, no. 1 (Spring 2004): 54–77. See also Hanna Hacker, "Edelmann

FIGURE 17. "Sandor/Sarolta Vay, Science's First Lesbian." Photo courtesy of Wellcome Library, London.

It is odd that a most perfect and prototypical example should be found in an extraordinary case of passing, where deviant gender performance is on trial, as opposed to interior sexual desire. Interesting as well is the active role played by Vay himself, who was among other things an active journalist and writer.[36]

At the center of the web of discourses spinning out from the Vay case was the long, published study by district forensic physician C. Birnbacher titled "A Case of Contrary Sexual Sensation before the Penal Court" and qualified as a forensic-medical report of Count Sandor V., rightly Countess Sarolta (Charlotte) V., in commission to the imperial royal penal court of Klagenfurt. The initial "V." might be considered to have been a standard anonymization of the subject, but it was more of a gesture to the standards of the genre of such case studies than to the subject, who was immediately a cause célèbre in Austria as well as abroad.

The legal case against Vay was complex and issued from Vay's father-in-law, an imperial forester, with whom he resided and had a financial and professional agreement; interested as any responsible investor might be in exploring the soundness of his contracts, the father-in-law began digging around only to find irregularities of the most outrageous kind. Not only the agreement itself but several other contracts and other documents, including guarantees and identity documents, were apparent forgeries. It was thus simply among a host of other fraudulent claims and documents that the accuser named "above all" the fact "that this supposed Count S. [Sándor] is no more than a female going around in public in men's clothing and named Countess Charlotte (S.) V."

The State's charge against Vay was hence not immediately or apparently related to sexual crimes as such, even though according to the terms of the penal code of the Habsburg monarchy, unlike the German Empire's Paragraph 175, homosexual sex between women was culpable. Instead, the accused was charged with contract fraud and the forgery of public documents.[37] The fascinating case would meander between a focus on Vay's gender identity (from clothing to identity papers to social role) to sexuality (desire as well as self-understanding), at times conflating the two, while at other times running

---

und Goldmarie 1890: Zum homophilen Studium einer 'Gräfin in Männerkleidung.'" *Die Schwarze Botin* 26 (March–May 1985): 16–25.

36. Birnbacher's forensic account, as Mak has noted, shifts gender pronouns in describing Vay, corresponding roughly to a distinction of gender presentation/social role (he) or biological sex (she). In this text, we follow suit.

37. This citation from the court case is published as part of Birnbacher's report; Birnbacher, "Ein Fall," 2.

into the obstinate incommensurability of external role, biological sex, object choice, and sexual aim. It is striking, in all events, that the Vay case should become a landmark case of sexual science: again, it was the basis of Krafft-Ebing's pivotal article on "gynandry" in *Psychopathia sexualis*, where the case inhabits the position of the longest and most detailed, indeed paradigmatic, case of female sexual inversion.[38] In that account, the idiosyncrasies of the subject's eccentric biography (chiefly the father's decision to raise Sarolta as a boy and his son as a girl throughout their childhoods) did not seem at all to point in a different direction from evidence of severe hereditary damage (insanity and suicide riddling the family on both sides) as well as that of the subject's own body (the genitals "completely female without a trace of her-maphroditic manifestation, but that *remained at the infantile level of a ten-year-old girl's*"). The medical testimony hence declared that in S. there was a clear instance of "inborn, morbid inversion of sexual sensation, such that was even anthropologically apparent in corporeal-developmental anomalies."[39]

But how could Vay be the prototypical lesbian when she was so unlike the vast majority of women-loving women and in fact simply identified as a man?[40] Our access to Vay's own subjective self-understanding is compromised by the fact that his self-descriptions are aimed to achieve the desirable outcomes of release and freedom, but the reports are clear that he regarded female homosexual contact as "perverse" and "disgusting." When asked what the purpose of dressing as a man was, the testiness of Vay's reply betrayed the discord of self-experience and the very question that was being suddenly and repeatedly asked: "Nothing else but the fact that I am a man, I want to be a man, and no one can forbid me that!"[41] No petulant expectoration was ever more revealing. Vay expresses what he is and what he wishes to be as a single

38. Krafft-Ebing, *Psychopathia sexualis*, 320–25 ("Beobachtung 173. Gynandrie"). The case has recently been reprinted in English in S. Stryker and S. Whittle, *The Transgender Studies Reader* (New York: Routledge, 2006), 21–27.

39. Krafft-Ebing, *Psychopathia sexualis*, 325.

40. Hacker, "Edelmann und Goldmarie 1890." Simone de Beauvoir refers to the case of "Sandor" at the beginning of her chapter on "The Lesbian" and goes a step further than Krafft-Ebing, psychoanalyzing female masculinity on the basis of his "simple statement of the facts" in *Psychopathia sexualis*; see Simone de Beauvoir, *The Second Sex*, trans. H. M. Parshley (New York: Knopf, 1952), 387–89. The excellent and detailed reading of the case by Geertje Mak contests Hacker (and de Beauvoir, implicitly) by arguing it is a founding case of medical attention to the feminine masculinity as pathological: Mak, "Sandor/Sarolta Vay," 54–77. Yet Krafft-Ebing himself identifies the case as paradigmatic of inversion in woman, as does Havelock Ellis, *Studies in the Psychology of Sex*, vol. 1, *Sexual Inversion* (Watford: The University Press, 1900), 94.

41. Vay quoted in Péter Buza, "Saroltából Sándor," *Budapest* 7 (1983): 38–41, translated and cited by Ann Borgos, "Sándor/Sarolta Vay: A Gender Bender in Fin-de-Siècle Hungary," in

thing and also as two separate things; his accusing tone is based in the fact that the question he is being asked is itself a manifestation of the prohibition he refuses. If sexology indeed created a platform from which subjects could stake novel identity claims, as has been argued, such was not the experience of Sándor Vay, who was happiest when all was just as it seemed.

The genuine sensation the case created in the European press, even making it to newspapers abroad, focused predominantly on the passing narrative—the outrageous success of the Hungarian countess to pass as a count, even to marry. In order to make the story legible, Sándor's femininity had to be brought out, or manufactured. Graphic images such as those reproduced in the satirical periodical *Der Floh* (fig. 18) and the *Wiener Tagblatt* (fig. 19), when compared with extant photographs of Vay, display a softening of the features, lengthening and curling of the hair, lengthening of the eyelashes, and so on, that must have been necessary to represent a woman in men's dress. A sensational morsel, but also a sticking point in the many sensational reports on Vay, was his happy marriage, a love match to the devoted Marie, who had had no inkling of what was now represented as a deception. Here the broadsheets could at best vaguely allude to one of the most prurient elements of the court case, namely, Vay's use of props to fill out his trousers in public and to fulfill his marital duties in the bedroom. The newspaper reports had to focus on the exterior issues of gender passing—the countess in men's clothing—and leave the hidden sex of the count/countess to the forensic physicians.

By the turn of the century, the association of inner, sexual life (or sensibility) and external scandal or sensation would become ever more familiar to central European audiences. The subjects in question were all men, and the implications were political as well as sexual.

### From Personal Fate to Public Affair; or, "Lifestyles" of the Rich and Famous

Beginning in September 1902, Karl Kraus turned his critical vision and poison pen toward what he saw as a misguided encroachment on private matters by the public organs of the state and the press. He saw it as more of an attack than an encroachment—he decried what he saw as the general campaign, conducted with "sword and fire," to battle "immorality," a charge he saw hailing from diverse if linked quarters from legislature to judiciary to the

*Comparative Hungarian Cultural Studies*, ed. Steven Tötösy de Zepetnek and Louise O. Vasvári (West Lafayette, IN: Purdue University Press, 2011), 229.

XXI. JAHRGANG NR. 46.    Preis einer Nummer 15 kr., für Deutschland 40 Pf.    WIEN. 17. NOVEMBER 1889.

Redaction:
I. Wipplingerstrasse 36.

Administration und Expedition:
I. Schulerstrasse 21.

Insertions-Preis: fr kr. ö. W.; für Deutschland
40 Pf., per Nonpareille-Zeile. Inserate übernehmen für das Deutsche Reich ausschliesslich
die Filiale des „Floh" (M. Dukes & Co.), Berlin,
Königgrätzerstrasse 19; in Paris Havas, Lafitte,
Sellier & Co.; für das übrige Ausland Haasenstein & Vogler, Rudolf Mosse, G. L. Daube.

Abonnement f. Oesterreich-Ungarn:
im Buyerzuge, Schulerstrasse 21, in allen
Buchhandlungen und bei allen Zeitungsverschleissern vierteljährig a Zustellung in's
Haus oder Versendung in die Provinz 2 fl. ö. W.

Abonnement für das Ausland:
Bei uns direct; vierteljährig für Deutschland
4 Mark; für Frankreich, Italien, Schweiz,
Belgien, England, Holland, Spanien,
Portugal, Schweden, Norwegen, Russland, Serbien, Rumänien, Bulgarien und
die Türkei 5 fl., Amerika 3 fl. 50 kr. ö. W.

Alle Rechte für sämmtliche
Artikel und Illustrationen
vorbehalten. — Nachdruck
ohne Quellenangabe wird
verfolgt.

Manuscripte werden nicht retourniert.

# DER FLOH.

ERSCHEINT JEDEN SONNTAG.

## Der Die!

Comtesse Sarolta Vay. (Text siehe Seite 2.)

FIGURE 18. "He-She!" Cover illustration of Vay on Vienna's *Der Floh*.

Comtesse Sarolta Vay
die Heldin des Klagenfurter Sittenbildes.

Gratis-Beilage des „Wiener Tagblatt".

FIGURE 19. *Wiener Tagblatt* illustration of Sarolta Vay. Photo courtesy of Wellcome Library, London.

daily newspaper of record. The whole offensive, Kraus maintained, origi-
nated in a "grandiose misunderstanding," a slip, a logical or even linguistic
fallacy: instead of protecting society from the offense of public indecency, the
crusaders inverted their task when they sought to provoke public indignation
in response to private morality.[42]

This reversal of public and private is a characteristically sly linguistic inversion in Kraus's rhetoric, where the real crusade was actually Kraus's own,
*against* morality legislation (with "fire and sword," or torch, for the crusade
took place in the pages of his journal *Die Fackel*). Kraus saw this tendency
in contemporary society to be no less fallacious than vicious, and he spared
none the hypocrisy of "the legislator as snooping reporter . . . justice as indis-
creet servant, listening at the bedroom door and spying through keyholes,"[43]
the moralizing tones of the bourgeois press in reports from court while print-
ing thinly veiled lewd personal advertisements,[44] or a society that extolled and
rewarded "good marriages" while condemning other exchanges of sex for
money.[45] Moral corruption was not irrelevant to the contemporary situation,
however, because it characterized the morality crusade itself.

The most sensational of the early twentieth-century homosexual scandals
was doubtless the Harden-Eulenburg affair in the German Empire, where
Maximilian Harden's suggestions about the perverse sexualities of members
of the Kaiser's closest advisory circle would shake press, public, and regime.[46]
The Harden-Eulenburg scandal was unique and yet also exemplary in its success in identifying a link between the realm newly conceived to be the most
private—sexuality—and the regions of concern defining the word *public*:
society and politics. The scandal is the opposite of the secret, but the relation
of these two, like that between "private" and "public," is a more complicated
one than that of simple opposition. The two contain the identical content—
and are therefore twins of sorts—while at the same time they are formal opposites of one another: one undisclosable and the other only possible within
a framework of exposure.

42. Karl Kraus, *Sittlichkeit und Kriminalität*, 14.

43. Ibid., 15.

44. Kraus collected and published such announcements, especially those appearing in the
bourgeois liberal press. See "Die Presse als Kupplerin," ibid., 33–34.

45. Ibid., 28.

46. The affair was so important that it has been recounted and analyzed many times, but a
particularly clear interpretation of its political operations emerged in Isabel V. Hull, *Entourage
of Wilhelm II*, chap. 5; "Kaiser Wilhelm II and the 'Liebenberg Circle,'" in Röhl and Sombart,
*Kaiser Wilhelm II: New Interpretations*, 193–220.

Politics and sexuality meet in these campaigns in a paradoxical way in relation to a left-socialist agenda and to associations of deviant sexuality and class. On the one hand, the Social Democratic Party (Sozialdemokratische Partei Deutschlands [SPD]) was the only major party openly to support the decriminalization of homosexuality: in 1898, August Bebel dramatically (and without European precedent) took the floor of the Reichstag to call for the abolition of Paragraph 175 of the Reich penal code. Along the lines of the homosexual emancipation movement, the Socialists argued for decriminalization on the basis of the fact that, first of all sexuality, understood as sexual orientation, was (at least in some cases) a natural, inborn and immutable thing; and second of all, that the penal code put the poor souls burdened with such an unfortunate natural sexuality at constant, real, and lifelong risk of violence and extortion. Homosexuality was hence defined as the secret that always threatened to be revealed. No one, on the other hand, could reveal it like the Socialists. Outing—or the *Weg über Leichen* (path over corpses), as it was called—seemed to be the peculiar province of progressive Socialists. Consider the following cartoon (fig. 20), appearing in January 1907 in the Socialist *Der wahre Jacob* in light of the Harden-Eulenburg scandal.[47] A woman identifiable as neither a wife nor a prostitute, but one of the type whom Alfred Schnitzler donned the "sweet girl," or lady of easy virtue, addresses a workingman who is dressing after their encounter. The surtitle reads: "Disappointed," and the caption her words, "Oh, Oscar, you really are just a common plebeian—not the least bit homosexual!"

The humor of the piece depends on several things: one was apt to giggle at the woman's use of the term *homosexual,* a scientific term that as we have seen had been coined just a generation earlier and that had only come into widespread use with this particular scandal; second, the contrast of the state indicated by the surtitle, disappointment, and that signaled by the picture, sultry satisfaction; furthermore, a similar contrast is suggested between private and public status (that is, an inverse relationship is suggested between social standing and heterosexual prowess). This message, besides being funny, could appeal to the newspaper's male working-class readership in a particular way. The lampoon is hence an example of one of the key structures

47. An early and important analysis of the Harden-Eulenburg affair was based in fact on a series of such cartoons. See Steakley, "Iconography of a Scandal." An abbreviated version appears in the now classic gay history volume *Hidden from History: Reclaiming the Gay and Lesbian Past,* ed. Martin B. Duberman, Martha Vicinus, and George Chauncey (New York: New American Library, 1989), 233–63.

FIGURE 20. From *Der wahre Jacob*, January 7, 1908, 5683.

of the scandal itself, linking the thing that defines itself as the most private sphere (sexuality) and the premier representation of one's placement in the public sphere in this time and place (class).

The first of the series of sex scandals was not in Germany or Austria at all, but it had resonance there. The Oscar Wilde trial in 1895 aroused the attention of none other than Eduard Bernstein, who in 1895 wrote two analytic editorials on the themes relating to the Wilde case.[48] The pieces, which appeared in the social democratic cultural journal *Die neue Zeit*, are nuanced and suggestive and peculiarly modern in the way that Bernstein identifies a "pederastic" habitus (*Pose*) in Wilde's modernist vision itself.[49] Bernstein's populist attack on Wilde and the "decadents" is explicit not only about the connection to pederasty but to a surplus of "civilization": "The civilization person is bound as with chains to the institutions of the modern metropolis [*Großstadt*]—he cannot go without them for very long." Bloated, sated to excess, these souls descend into ennui, seeking a substitute for natural life in "the overcivilization of the cult of the unusual, the abnormal, the substrate of art and artifice of civilization."[50] Deflecting the discussion from the fact of Wilde's deviant sexuality, Bernstein attacks instead the corrupt, cynical, and outspokenly elitist aesthetic doctrine that wishes to release art from "that which lives and should live in the body of the people [*im Volkskörper*],"[51] to declare it the autonomous province of "an aristocracy of the initiated." Hence, the secret sexuality is an unseen marker for a class of aesthetes at odds with the people.

At the turn of the century, sexual misbehavior within the powerful world of finance was in the news with the Sternberg affair, where a prominent millionaire banker was prosecuted for corruption of a minor—but while it was clearly part of the general trend Kraus decried, it involved prostitution rather than homosexuality, and the relationship to class and power were for various reasons ambiguous.[52] Homosexual scandal in Germany would really break with the sensational Krupp affair of 1902, involving the powerful Fritz (Friedrich Alfred) Krupp (1854–1902) of the Essen ironworks and artillery production, a magnate of the third generation of the Reich's leading industrial family and one whose rise was inseparable from that of Prussia and then Germany under Prussian leadership.[53] The scandal was broken in Germany chiefly by

48. Bernstein, "Aus Anlaß," 171–76; "Die Beurtheilung," 228–33.

49. Bernstein, "Aus Anlaß," esp. 173–76. The essay responds to "Zur Psychologie der Decadence" in the recently published work by Wilhelm Weigand, *Essays* (Munich: Merhoff, 1892), 165–224, as well as to the Wilde trial.

50. Bernstein, "Aus Anlaß," 172, 174.

51. Ibid., 175.

52. The "class lessons" in this case were arguably more ambiguous to contemporary audiences, due to Sternberg's own humble origins on the one hand and the status of his victims as prostitutes known to police on the other. Cf. Martin, "Zum Prozess Sternberg," 182–87.

53. See Boelcke, *Krupp und die Hohenzollern*, 98–117; cf. Steinberg, "Case of Herr Fritz Krupp."

the Socialist organ *Vorwärts*.[54] The *Vorwärts* linked Krupp's social position to his sexuality in a peculiar way, arguing that an "unfortunate tendency"— recall that the Socialists were alone among major parties in agreeing that it could be an inborn predilection—that would victimize a person without means could have a different function "under the influence of capitalist power" and become "a horrible source of corruption that then turns a personal fate into a public affair."[55] The public affair, of course, was the product of the newspaper's sensational attack itself.

Participants in the emergent homosexual emancipation movement immediately recognized the immense and complex significance of the Krupp scandal for the cause. In the months following the scandal, the Scientific-Humanitarian Committee (Wissenschaftlich-humanitäres Komitee [WhK]) was completely absorbed by it and scrambled to find a way to change the terms of the debate:

> In the wake of the Krupp affair, great demands have been made on the committee from all sides. We have generally restricted ourselves to focus more on the issue of homosexuality itself than to take a position on the person of Krupp. Nonetheless, it would be very useful if authentic material regarding Krupp's orientation or activities could be gathered and communicated to us.[56]

Scandal hence formed another component in the circuit of knowledge formed by psychiatrists, jurists, police, and homosexual activists. The Scientific-Humanitarian Committee was called on to inform the sensation and tried (in vain) to resist feeding the scandal while using the opportunity to spread enlightenment about the issue of homosexuality. Its official response, in the form of a press release, strenuously objected to the assumption, implicit and explicit in press reports on the case, that the attribution of homosexuality alone constituted a profound insult and attack on one's personal honor.[57] All this, it insisted, was irrespective of the actual fact of Krupp's sexuality, in which it took no interest. Yet as the committee's appeal to readers of its monthly report shows, it was as eager to collect salacious details as were press and police. The latter had already included

54. *Vorwärts*, November 15, 1902, p. 1.

55. Ibid.

56. Monthly report of the WhK [Monatsbericht WhK], November 1902, p. 20, Hirschfeld Collection, KIRSGR. For confirmation of this absorption see also the conference report "Bericht über die 10. Conferenz des wissensch. humani. Komitées am 11. Januar 1903," also in the Hirschfeld Collection, KIRSGR.

57. The text of the statement to the press is in Monatsbericht WhK, November 1902, p. 20, Hirschfeld Collection, KIRSGR.

Krupp in their registry of known homosexuals, although this was never intended to lead to arrest or extortion.[58] The scandal form stressed the elements of shame and dishonor that activists disputed even as other experts took it quietly for granted. Closely linked to this element of shame was the sensation's primary contribution to the circuit of knowledge about homosexuality: the centrality of exposure. One of the many ironies of the circuit of urning knowledge was that activists had advocated the making public of one's own or even others' homosexual inclination as a means to counter the assumption that the inclination was shameful. The series of exposures of homosexuality to unfold in central Europe would not be initiated by homosexual activists, and it would not have the effects they had hoped for. The implicit violence of the outing tactic was acknowledged in its name: the "path over corpses."

By the time Kraus published his collection *Sittlichkeit und Kriminalität* (Morality and crime) in 1908, the still much more sensational and consequential Harden-Eulenburg affair dominated public consciousness. This confluence of state intervention in private sexual life with press exploitation of and public interest in these formerly private affairs had reached a pitch that Kraus thought constituted a kind of new regime. One case in particular that caught his attention involved a physician and professor of physiology at the University of Vienna, Theodor Beer. Beer was from a prominent Jewish family and was accused of molesting two minors, both boys from families of similar background and station. In fact, the principal charge was that the doctor, who was also an amateur photographer, had exposed himself to the boys, asked them to expose themselves, photographed them by themselves and with him in the nude, and touched them inappropriately. Hence it is curious that the chief provision of the penal code under which he was prosecuted was Paragraph 129(b), the Austrian equivalent of the German Paragraph 175, which criminalized homosexual acts. The investigation of the case, its prosecution, and the sensation it produced in the press differ in register and to some degree in content—shielded as the public was of certain details of the case—but a particular pattern of argumentation emerged where we see the delicate network of links from the private, invisible, and undisclosed sexual identity of Dr. Beer, the utterly apparent facts of the social position of himself and others involved, and the events taking place in Beer's library—not fully private, as

---

58. The account of police commissioner Hans von Tresckow is particularly enlightening. It seems that Krupp had long been on the list of homosexuals known to police (the *Kartenregister*) without further notation. The interactions of police, politicians, and journalists come through in this account. See Tresckow, *Von Fürsten*, 126–32. See also Hall, *Scandal*, 173–87.

they involved the boys themselves, as well as various witnesses, and yet not public.

The defendant's social position was the cornerstone of his defense: his high social standing was the tangible, external manifestation of a noble character. The main witnesses against him, the children accusing him, were, in contrast, the spoiled offspring of social climbers. Interestingly, the class background of the children was used against him by the prosecuting lawyers, who argued that this choice was deliberate on his part, and this argument was underscored by the investigating magistrate, who must have found it compelling: With devilish ingenuity, the accused deliberately and specifically sought out children of good families, and he counted on the fact that if the family were to catch wind of his actions, they would forbear pressing charges for fear of scandal and concern for the affected children.[59]

The argument that the family's social humiliation was a nefarious tool of the diabolical pervert—even the phrase "with devilish ingenuity" (mit teuflischem Raffinement) inflects these "excesses" in terms of class—was particularly poignant here because Dr. Steger, the attorney making the point, was demonstrating it at the same time: he was a father of one of the two boys, hence an injured party himself. To avoid this humiliation, perhaps, he had offered Beer an alternative to prosecution before pressing charges. The alternative, surrendering his professorship and leaving the country, was what Kraus deemed nothing less than total personal destruction.[60] This collapse of notions of "personal" (privat) and social obliteration gives the lie to the discrete spheres of private and public that Kraus seemed to be trying to protect from one another. In the same month, Kraus described the two figures of his title—"morality" and "criminality," ethical expressions of personal/private and social/public realms—as "conceptual Siamese twins," aptly suggesting their inescapable unity as well as the implicit impulse to rend them from one another.[61]

This first Kraus essay on the Beer affair, in which none of the parties were yet named, took the lawyer accusing Beer to task for not knowing the law well enough to see that his offer to save social face was in literal violation of the law against extortion.[62] And here we have a hint of something strange to our perspective, and that is the suggestion that the truth of the claims against

---

59. Vienna, Landesgericht für Strafsachen 1905 4586, document of 25 April 1905 by Regierungsrat Heirich Steger, WSL. Steger was the principal plaintiff, his son Gustav being one of the boys who claimed abuse.

60. Kraus, Sittlichkeit und Kriminalität, 53.

61. Ibid., 67.

62. Ibid., 54.

Beer may be trumped by his right to privacy and the integrity of his social position. Indeed, once the facts of the case were public and Kraus discussed them outright, he even raised as a question whether, even if the professor had done everything of which he was accused, would such transgressions be comparable to the "antifamily immorality" that the sponsors of this trial have on their consciences?[63]

At trial, the question of social position played a role in Beer's defense as well as his prosecution. Even the most damning evidence against him and the occasion for sensational reportage—his several flights from the country when released on bail and the international pursuit after him—proved to be available as a proof of innocence in light of social issues. He excused his first flight to Switzerland, where he and his wife had a house on Lake Geneva, by citing his need to oversee extensive renovations to the villa. On fleeing to America before his trial, an advising attorney, a cousin of the Beers, testified that he had counseled the professor to flee at all costs, because a person of high standing was particularly vulnerable to such base attacks on character, and he should under no circumstances allow himself to stand before a jury.[64] The attorney compared Beer—significantly—to Dreyfus, promising that justice could be done only in his absence.[65]

The most compelling testimony in Beer's defense, according to the accounts of the press, was from the doctor's wife, Laura, a vision of bourgeois loveliness, wifely understanding, and composure. Her steadfast support of her husband, her manifest faith in his innocence, her insistence on the strength of their relationship, and above all, her attractive presence itself were meant to dispel accusations of her husband's perversity.[66] It was perhaps, then, a flawed strategy on the part of the defense to introduce evidence of the professor's heterosexual liaison with a mysterious woman, deceased by

63. Ibid., 168.

64. See *Neue Freie Presse*, October 27, 1905, pp. 10–11.

65. The Christian Social organ, the *Reichspost*, took a special interest in exposing lurid details of the case, sometimes referring to the accused as "der Jude Theodor Beer." See *Reichspost*, October 26, 1905, p. 9; October 27, 1905, pp. 9–10; October 28, 1905, p. 9; October 29, 1905, p. 10. See also *Das Vaterland*, October 26, 1905, p. 6; October 27, 1905, p. 5. Daniel Vyleta has broadly surveyed and analyzed other antisemitic press coverage of the Beer case; see Vyleta, "Jewish Crimes," esp. 311–16.

66. The importance of this testimony was certainly stressed more in the newspaper reports than in the court file, and it was raised to the level of overarching theme in the melodramatic recapitulation of the affair in the broadside *Das interessante Blatt*. This was due no doubt in part to the sensational end to the story offered by Laura Beer's suicide after the guilty verdict. See "Das Ende der Affäre Beer," *Das interessante Blatt*, April 12, 1906, p. 11.

the time of the trial, who seemed, however, to leave behind evidence of her partner's unnatural sexual tastes.[67]

Still other evidence of this sort was collected by investigators but kept from the public, including information from the staff at the city's central bathhouse that Beer had, some years before, been a regular customer of a particular masseur there, who was reported to have shaved Beer from head to toe and allowed himself to be shaved in the genital area by Beer, and other details of arguably sordid, if not explicitly illegal, activity.[68] Clearly, the class transgression of consorting with the bathhouse servant, a young man from the rough thirteenth district who was even invited to visit him in his villa, was an antidote to Beer's own version of his naturalist, even medical, comfort with nudity. He claimed, in defense of his having photographed partially nude children with himself and alone, that, as an amateur photographer, he was particularly interested in landscapes and, to a lesser degree, portraits and nudes. The latter genre had attracted the interest of others, including many parents who had asked him to take such photographs of their children, because they had unique usefulness in recording the physical development of the subjects. The exceptional combination in the person of Beer of both physiologist and amateur photographer was hence deeply relevant. He was also, he claimed, preparing a book on the human ideal of beauty.[69]

While there was nothing in the record to suggest any culmination of sexual gratification, the accused was argued to have corrupted at least one of the boys by enlightening him in matters of reproduction, a transgression that the victim's parents were sure was a direct cause of their child's new compulsive habit of masturbation. But the doctor espoused a more "enlightened" view of sexuality in which knowledge about sexuality might be considered to have other effects than harm. Clearly prosecution and defense, police and accused were all acutely aware that the facts themselves, such as they were, could carry completely contradictory meanings, depending on the way they were read within the context of social positions and hidden motivations.[70] Kraus was far from free from this hierarchy of interpretation, suggesting the

67. Details of testimony that had been shielded from the public are drawn from the extensive penal records, found in the two large files Landesgericht für Strafsachen 1905 4586 "Beeri [sic] Theodor Dr., par. 128, 129," WSL.

68. Strafsachen 1905 4586, document of 29 March 1904, WSL.

69. See, e.g., *Reichspost*, October 28, 1905, p. 9.

70. In fact, the focus on Beer's hidden, "true" sexual identity was necessarily more important than establishing the fact of molestation because the state prosecutor had chosen to prosecute on the basis of Paragraph 129(b)—that is, the prohibition of homosexuality—as opposed to 128, which dealt with child abuse. This was not lost on Kraus; see Kraus, *Sittlichkeit und*

inappropriateness of attending the libelous declarations of dishonest children and disingenuous parvenus. But at the same time, he positioned his
own discourse outside of that shared by accusers, investigators, prosecutors,
and, above all, the mainstream press. Reaching for a critical mode that was
literary and philosophical rather than journalistic, his attacks in the *Fackel*
dwelled less on a hidden sexual identity that would make sense of contradictory facts than on the sensational manifestation of the trial itself, the true
manifestation of ethical violation that was at once immoral and criminal. In
its perversion of justice and molestation of character, in its rude intrusion on
personal life, and in its shameless display of what should be kept private, the
case represented a transgression of greater offense and caused greater damage
than could ever occur in a gentleman's library.

### The Wrath of the Countess Merviola:
### Exposing Homosexual Subjects

Clearly the Harden-Eulenburg scandal, by the sheer magnitude of exposure,
did more to bring the existence of actually existing homosexuals into broad
public view than all previous prosecutions of Paragraph 175 in Germany and
129(b) in Austria and emancipatory efforts to reform them combined. Public
attention to the issue of homosexuality seemed at first a hopeful sign to Magnus Hirschfeld and other members of the Scientific-Humanitarian Committee calling for the repeal of Paragraph 175, but the actual effects of the attention with regard to those efforts were sooner dismal. In any event, the word
*homosexual* and the notions it evoked of both actual persons and unspeakable
acts in one's very midst were suddenly present from 1907 on in a way they had
not been before.

   In Vienna, the Harden-Eulenburg affair seemed at once so distant—so
German, so Prussian—and at the same time, it at once raised questions
about the possibility of such activity in Vienna. It is instructive to turn to a
different sort of scandal next, one not involving famous persons, where one
could argue that the notoriety of the individuals structures their behavior as
"scandalous," but anonymous (if not "ordinary") people: a series of exposés on the secret homosexual life of Vienna. These articles display some of
the same patterns that emerged in reports of the scandalous private lives of
the rich and powerful, from Krupp and Eulenburg to Vienna's own Dr. Beer.
The evolution of one particular sensationalist newspaper is offered here as an

---

*Kriminalität*, 182. This move displays nothing more clearly than the shift from harmful acts to
perverse identities.

example of an enlightened discourse on sexual scandal in order to examine its paradoxes and the dense ways in which bringing secrets to light, or offering the private to a general public, made constant reference to the visible world of public hierarchy, the "social order," in flux.

The *Oesterreichische Kriminal-Zeitung* released its first weekly issue on April 1, 1907. Ferdinand Lebzelter, former head police commissioner of Vienna, was editor. On the basis of its lead program article and the first several issues, one gets a clear image of enlightened law enforcement, where largely modern and educated judges, police, and members of the public are seen to be held hostage to an antiquated—"barbaric," "medieval"—penal code. Vowing to expose corruption and pursue enlightened reform, the paper offered different ongoing rubrics on penal reform, forensic advances, and also, more incidentally, glimpses of an exotic netherworld of crime, prostitution, and so forth relating to familiar genres of urban life.

The financial success of the newspaper seems to have been insecure, and it changed hands after a six-week run; the former commissioner tendered his polite resignation two weeks later. The following issue was already markedly more provocative than before; it was also the first of many issues to be censored. By the tenth issue (20, 1907), the big shift to tabloid journalism was apparent, with the bold headline "Sensationeller Inhalt!" blazoned on the cover (fig. 21). By August, the word *illustrated* was added to the title, and the paper resembled other European "illustrated criminal" and/or "detective" newspapers. In the wake of the Riehl affair, involving police corruption and the regulation of prostitution, the newspaper turned its focus to prostitution and, more incidentally, pederasty (fig. 22).[71] Whole districts, declared more than one article, were plagued by masses of promenading little ladies and their procurers, often endangering the general public. Respectable women could not even go out after ten o'clock at night anymore. The image, then, was of a criminal/sexual underworld run amok and threatening to consume the city. "Beyond uncontrolled hussies, the most attention is earned by their procurers as well as the ever more self-confident pederasts and their gathering places," declared the story, reminding readers that the ever-growing perverse subcultures of Vienna were also part of this picture and promising to report on this in future articles in order to "orient" the public. This at first ancillary interest turned out to be a goldmine for the paper—clearly the key to its potential success as well as to its eventual demise. Weekly reports under the heading

71. See, e.g., "Kinderspital und Nachtcafé" and "Prostitution und Polizei," *Kriminal-Zeitung*, July 18, 1907, pp. 1–4; "Die Prostitution in Wien," *Kriminal-Zeitung*, August 26, 1907, pp. 4–5; but such reports would appear in every issue around this time.

"Pederasty" were accompanied by an ever-growing set of letters to the editor spurred on by the articles, and soon the heavy hand of the censor intervened.[72] By September 1907, circulation had reached an unprecedented twenty thousand, which would become thirty thousand by the end of the year.

In keeping with its enlightened crusader self-image, the paper took an editorial stance in favor of the reform of Paragraph 129(b) on the basis of natural inclination and threat of blackmail, and at the same time, it reproduced that blackmail by making a practice of denouncing individual cafés and meeting places. The editors promised a campaign not against these pub and café owners but against "pederasty" as such to stem the tide of immorality sweeping Vienna.

The editors could never have expected that these references would elicit an immediate and unexpected response in the form of impassioned and angry anonymous letters to the editor from homosexual quarters. They moved quickly to exploit that response in a sensational way. They published the letters along with the pederasty series, and as the latter continued, the pages of letters to the editor expanded, becoming an exhibition of perversity with as much sensational power as the reports themselves. The flurry of response from the homosexual street, as it were, cued the editors of the newspaper that they were on to something—for several weeks they printed the letters unedited, until finally, under great pressure of the authorities, eliminating anonymous and outrageous contributions. The original spate of letters, however, while hardly an unproblematic source, is nonetheless a unique case where the responses of homosexual men to the initial public representations of them and their sexuality are preserved.

The issue following the original prostitution article included the first run of letters, the sensational potential of which was at once recognized by the editors. Calling attention to the section with such surtitles as "Letter-Threat of a Passive Pederast," the newspaper was more than willing to put the most hostile attacks on its own reportage on display. They printed (or claimed to print) the letters in full and unedited, including spelling and grammatical errors that betrayed the contributors' class backgrounds. The threatening letter to which the editors refer was signed by one "Countess Merviola," whose

72. See, e.g., the issues of the *Kriminal-Zeitung* beginning in August 1907, which have pederasty, the reform of Paragraph 129(b), or male prostitution as major themes. The newspaper's attention to the homosexual underworld of Vienna was among its most important editorial decisions, which contributed not only to the massive increase in its circulation but also to the regular censorship of the weekly and finally to the prosecution of its editors and the forced cessation of publication.

Bezugsbedingungen
mit Zustellung ins Haus:
Ganzjährig ..... K 5.—
Halbjährig ..... „ 2·50
Vierteljährig ..... „ 1·25
Einzelne Nummern 10 Heller.
Für die Provinz Postzuschlag.

Zu haben
in allen Tabaktrafiken, Zeitungs-
verschleißen und Bahnhofbuch-
handlungen.

# Oesterreichische
# Kriminal-Zeitung
### Wochenblatt
### für öffentliches Leben, Kriminal- und Polizeiwesen.

Redaktion
und Administration:
Wien, I., Schulerstr. 18.
Telephon 1385.
Erscheint jeden Donnerstag.
Inseratenaufträge nehmen
sämtliche Annoncenexpeditionen
und die Administration entgegen.

1. Jahrgang.     Wien, Donnerstag, den 20. Juni 1907.     Nr. 10.

## : Sensationeller Inhalt :

## Moralisch hingerichtet!

Offener Brief in Angelegenheit der vom Salzburger Kleinstadtratsch bis zum Wahnsinn
gehetzten Familie Maurer
### an Sr. Exzellenz dem Herrn Justizminister Dr. Franz Klein.

## Elsa Maurer,
die einstige Braut des zum Tode durch den Strang verurteilten Mörders Pluharsch, in Wien
als Komptoiristin der „Oesterreichischen Kriminal-Zeitung".

## Galgen oder Irrenhaus?
## Der „Kinderverzahrer" — entdeckt?

Ab nächster Nummer erscheint ein spannender Roman aus der Feder des Schriftstellers
Richard Dahl, der das tragische Schicksal der Familie Maurer, insbesondere die Tragödie
des armen Mädchens, das sich mit einer in vorliegender Nummer enthaltenen erschütternden
Zuschrift an uns um Schutz wandte, getreu nach dem Leben schildern wird.

### An unsere Leser!

Ein Diener des Verlages der „Oester-
reichischen Kriminal-Zeitung" wurde vor einigen
Tagen wegen mehrfacher Betrügereien verhaftet. Insbesondere hat der Mann auch eine
schwungvolle Bettelbrieffabrikation betrieben.
Mit Rücksicht auf den Umstand, als er hiezu
unser Firmenpapier benützte, sind wir gezwungen
Vorstehendes mitzuteilen, damit ein grober
Vertrauensmißbrauch eines Angestellten nicht
auf uns zurückfällt.

Unter einem teilen wir noch mit, daß die
angekündigte Publikation
„Anton Jenners Tragikomödie"
wegen zu großem Umfange des Aufsatzes nicht
in unserem Blatte, wohl aber Ende dieser
Woche als Broschüre zum Preise von 30 Heller
im Verlage der „Oesterreichischen Kriminal-
Zeitung" erscheint, sowie durch alle Buchhandlungen zu
beziehen sein wird.
Die Administration
der „Oesterr. Kriminal-Zeitung".

### Moralisch hingerichtet.

Offener Brief an Se. Exzellenz den Herrn
Justizminister Dr. Franz Klein.

Eure Exzellenz!

Der geehrten Redaktion kommt folgende
erschütternde Zuschrift zu, die sie im Nach-
stehenden unterbreitet, weil die Redaktion
Wert darauf legt, daß Ew. Exzellenz sich davon
überzeugen, daß in Ihrem Machtbereiche Un-
geheuerlichkeiten möglich sind, vor welchen der
menschliche Genius trauernd sein Haupt ver-
hüllt.

Die Zuschrift lautet:

Salzburg, den 15. Juni 1907.

An die löbliche Redaktion der „Oester-
reichischen Kriminal-Zeitung."

Ich beeile mich Ihr Expreßschreiben vom 14. Juni
1907 zu beantworten und danke Ihnen im voraus
für Ihr liebenswürdiges Entgegenkommen und kann ich
nur versichern, daß Sie Ihre Hilfe und Teilnahme
gewiß keiner unnahbaren Familie schenken. Gleich Ein-
gangs meines Schreibens möchte ich höflich bemerken,
daß ich um Ihren Angehörigen bis längstens 1. Juli
nach Wien zu übersiedeln gedenke, wo ich mir dann er-
lauben werde, in Ihrer Kanzlei persönlich vorzusprechen,
um Ihnen dann den Fall Pluharsch ausführlich
zu detaillieren, nachdem eine genaue Detaillierung des
Prozesses auf schriftlichem Wege zu umständlich und um-
fangreich ausfallen würde.

Meine Angehörigen und ich wurden unter dem
schweren Verdachte der „Mitschuld" an dem Morde des
Postpraktikanten Mühlberger von dessen Existenz
wir überhaupt keine Ahnung hatten, verhaftet. Im Voll-
gefühle unserer vollkommenen Unschuld sahen wir ruhig
der Entwicklung der Dinge entgegen, mit fester Zuver-
sicht hoffend, daß diese mysteriöse Fall sich in Kürze
aufklären werde. Inzwischen hatte es sich herausgestellt,
daß mein, in unserem Hause wohnhafter Bräutigam
Josef Pluharsch, der Täter sei.

Trotzdem verstrich Monat auf Monat, ohne daß
unsere Enthaftung erfolgte. Die schweren Leiden dieser
Untersuchungshaft können gar nicht im vollen Umfange
geschildert werden. Ohne Rücksicht auf tadelloses Vor-
leben und Bildung wurde ich fünf volle Monate in die
sogenannte Sammelzelle gesteckt, wo alles von der Gasse
Aufgelesene seinen Aufenthalt fand; nur meinem Charakter
und meiner guten Erziehung ist es zu danken, daß ich
daß ich während dieser Zeit nicht gänzlich verkommen
bin. — Zu den physischen Qualen kommen noch die
seelischen; nicht einmal ordentlich wissend, um was es
sich eigentlich handelt, wurde ich gleich vom ersten Tag als
überfahrten Mörderin behandelt und dies es bei meinem
ersten Verhör bereits „mitgelangen mitzugehangen"!
Nicht genug an dem, auch meine arme 80 Jahre alte
Mutter, die uns Kindern stets ein leuchtendes Vorbild
einer charaktervollen edlen Frau war, sowie mein Bruder,
der verheiratet und Familienvater ist, wurden ohne einen
besonderen Grund gefänglich eingezogen, und man hat
meines Erachtens nach auch Pluharsch den Finger-
zeig gegeben, um die Schuld so viel wie möglich von sich
abzuwälzen und auf meine armen unschuldigen Angehörigen
zu schieben. Ich habe Pluharsch jederzeit für einen
hochanständigen Menschen gehalten und es jetzt als einen
endlich gelöst! — Wie furchtbar daher die Entdeckung,
mein Ebenbild zertrümmert und als einen schweren
Verbrecher gebrandmarkt zu sehen. Alles dieses hat zu-
sammengewirkt, um mich beinahe an die Grenzen des
Wahnsinns zu bringen.

Gebrochen an Leib und Seele habe ich am 20. März
das Haus meiner schweren Leiden verlassen und daheim
wartete neuerliche Sorgen auf mich.

Durch meine mit den Kindern zurückgebliebene
Schwägerin und Schwester erfuhr ich, daß man sie nach
unserer erfolgten Verhaftung mit unausgesetzten Krän-
kungen, Beschimpfungen, Demütigungen aller Art ver-
folgte, so daß sie bereits nahe daran waren, den Tod in

FIGURES 21 AND 22. The *Kriminal-Zeitung* upon its turn to "sensational content" and to an illustrated format.

**Nach der Konfiskation zweite Auflage.**

Redaktion und Administration:
Wien, III., Ungargasse Nr. 25.
Telephon 134 — Postsparkassenkonto Nr. 200

Pränumerationen für Wien: Ganzjährig
K 5.—, halbjährig K 2.50. Für die Provinz:
Ganzjährig K 6.—, halbjährig K 3. Ein-
zelne Nummern 10 Heller, Provinz 12 Heller.

Illustrierte

# Oesterreichische Kriminal-Zeitung

### Wochenblatt für öffentliches Leben, Kriminal= und Polizeiwesen.

1. Jahrgang. Wien, Montag, den 9. September 1907. Nr. 21.

## Mädchenhandel. — Päderastie.

### Die Mordtat eines Bahnwächters. Die Wahrheit über den Prozeß Riehl.

# Die Prostitution in Wien.

Geheime Prostitution in den Wiener Nachtlokalen. — Schäferstündchen in der Wein-
loge. — Wurzenfang. — Vom Spittelberg. — Der „Strich" auf der Elisabethpromenade.

# Prostitution in der Hauptallee.

Der Text zu diesem Bilde befindet sich auf Seite 7.

letter, according to the newspaper, was received on "trollop paper," stinking of disgusting perfume. The letter reads:

> It is incredible to us the way you in your scandal sheet treat those of us who are unhappy victims by our very nature. Do you really think that the state attorney is the most appropriate expert to cure us? You find yourself in great error if you think we "warm brothers" belong in the "black house" of the Josefstadt. Every single judgment against one of our number is a horrible error of justice.[73]

In tune with much of the conventional description of homosexuality at the time, echoed in Krafft-Ebing's own preface, this reader depicted himself and his kind as "unhappy victims" of their own sexuality who could not be helped by further persecution by journalistic trash and state intervention. The effect on each convicted "warm one" is never the reversal of homosexuality, but the contrary, for

> he becomes freer and more open in his outlook because he feels himself a martyr and is also treated as such by his sexual compatriots who number many thousands just here in Vienna.[74]

A community of "martyred" homosexuals is thus a direct consequence of persecution and prosecution. The "threat" of this letter is contained in part in the suggestion that an attack on homosexuality will have the effect of galvanizing a community of homosexuals—thousands of them in Vienna— hidden so far even to themselves. This was an exaggerated restatement of the newspaper's own sensational project, which sought to make visible a social problem its readers were not even aware existed. Merviola's threat continued, making use of a more nefarious suggestion of the newspaper, that the pederast "community" included elements of great wealth and power:

> Among us we have men of resounding name who are decorated with high recognitions and offices by the State of Austria. . . . That would look quite fine if the most honored bearers of state recognition, aristocrats from the oldest lines, millionaires, and the chiefs of the most significant major firms suddenly lost all their offices and prizes and had to move to the so-called gray house [the correctional facility in the city's eighth district].[75]

Countess Merviola continued to describe her own personal presence, grace, and power in the most inflated and florid terms, then promising that the

73. *Kriminal-Zeitung* August 19, 1907, p. 7.
74. Ibid.
75. Ibid.

newspaper will receive a warning of a more official nature from the "Central Direction of the 'Warm League.'"[76]

Interestingly, the particular threat made to the newspaper was directly related to the homophobic conspiracy fantasy suggested in the offending article. The paper was able to pick up on this:

> They speak completely openly about the central office of a pederasts' league, and the gentlemen comport themselves with such self-conscious arrogance that one begins to suspect that the Viennese pederasts must enjoy some particularly highly placed protection, a protection that places them above the law. If such were not the case, these people would surely not speak so freely and openly, without any shame, about their deviations—deviations that are prosecuted as crimes under law.[77]

While the lower-class Merviola's threat was that members of Vienna's elite would be brought down along with common homosexuals, perhaps outed by the latter, the newspaper implied here and elsewhere that the toleration of the homosexual underworld was facilitated by the influence of powerful pederasts in Vienna.

The newspaper continued its pederasty series and expanded the section of letters to the editor, ostensibly in the interests of bringing the presence and aggressive stance of the inverts to the attention of the authorities. One such letter uses the ingenious strategy of asking the editor to put himself in this "unhappy place" and imagine he would be institutionalized for his own sexuality. But sympathy is not the only strategy employed by the readers. A particularly combative letter from a bold contributor reads:

> Brainless individual!
>
> In your trash rag, hopefully soon to vanish from the surface of the earth, you demonstrate very well what a godforsaken numbskull you are to judge people about whom every physician and half-thinking layman understands are not to be liable in the slightest, since they are totally innocent.[78]

This description merely reiterated the newspaper's own position as well as that of Merviola, but here the condition given by nature is not marked

---

76. Ibid. The reference is to the common name for homosexuals *avant la lettre*, "warm brothers."

77. *Kriminal-Zeitung*, August 26, 1907, p. 6.

78. Ibid., 7.

as either "morbid" or "unhappy," simply "innocent." Guilt in the letter is reserved for the newspaper editors, who cause only harm. And to what purpose, wonders the reader?

> I can imagine that all your nonsense is based entirely on blackmail, and to reach your goal you do not shy from desiring to attract denouncers who belong in prison along with *you*.[79]

Indeed it seems the writer had more than instinct at hand, as the series did in fact lead not only to heavy censorship but eventually to a blackmail case and secession of publication.[80] The articles contained denunciations, to be sure, but not so many as the letters to the editor—a point to which we will return. Another raving letter comes from the Countess Merviola, whose most intimate friend, "Princess Louse," has sent a letter to the *Kriminal-Zeitung* revealing Merviola's "intimate secrets," which, he warns, must not be published:

> Alas, hear me well, woe to you if you betray the secret proceedings of my residence; I will hereby declare war on you until one of us or the other falls to ruin. You will soon be made to feel how dangerous and powerful an opponent you have in me. . . . Since your disgusting nose cannot fancy my fine perfumed letter, so I will not forward any more perfumed luxury letter paper. Please be so kind as to avoid the term *trollop paper* in future as I am a highly respectable lady, and therefore my letter paper has not earned this expression.[81]

The drama unfolding among such characters as the Countess Merviola, the "Princess Louse von ———," the "Black Pearl," and the editors was a display that made other readers cringe. These others described themselves as physicians (unlikely, inferred the editor) or otherwise well educated professionals competing with what they see as a group of street tramps for representation of their sexual inclination.

One such reader, this one writing under the name "The Lady of the Camellias," sharply attacked the newspaper campaign and the suggestion that

---

79. Ibid.

80. The newspaper itself presented a brief (and obviously biased) report on the threats to revoke its license; see "Sittlichkeitskoller," *Kriminal-Zeitung*, September 27, 1907, p. 2. All issues from late September forward were heavily censored, including not only the letters to the editor and "Pederasty" series articles but also editorials on policy and scientific articles concerning homosexuality. State records are incomplete but leave traces of state prosecution of the editors on charges of extortion, leading to forced cessation of publication. See Allgemeine Reihe, Ministerium des Innern, 1907 Präsidiale Index Z: Zeitschriften: Wiener Schmutz-Presse, AVA; see also 1907 Materien-Index Z: Zeitungsnotizen: Kriminalzeitung.

81. *Kriminal-Zeitung*, August 26, 1907, p. 7.

homosexuality is a "so-called vice," whose victims belong in institutions.[82] Using the argument known from both the liberal camp of Hirschfeld and associates of the *Jahrbuch für sexuelle Zwischenstufen* (Yearbook for intermediary forms) as well as the conservative camp of Adolf Brand, Benedict Friedlaender, and the *Gemeinschaft der Eigenen*, Lady of the Camellias reminded the editors that this policy would have landed in asylums figures of historical greatness from Socrates and Plato to Frederick the Great and Grillparzer.[83] The letter is more original in its suggestion that homosexuality offered an alternative to the man-woman love relationship that exceeded the latter in nobility, describing the author's own six-year relationship with a certain officer in which ruled "purest harmony," enjoying full acceptance from his esteemed family, and which nonetheless allowed for a sexual freedom no wife would suffer. Merviola and other readers, while unhalting in their attacks on the campaign, nonetheless included a certain apologetics in their arguments, admitting homosexuality to be a "defect," an "unhappy predisposition," or even a "vice." The difference between these self-representations may be seen to correspond to the split between the Hirschfeld and Brand camps: the latter, explicitly misogynist and elitist, was at the same time less likely to concede to social assumptions of sexual abnormality, defect, or inferiority.[84] Whether describing themselves (or in the third person, the unlucky/unhappy ones) as burdened or not, whether aggressive or placating, rationalist or outrageous, the insistence on natural sexuality rang through the letters to the editor in ways that sometimes implicated the sexuality of the editors themselves— imagine it were you who were sent to an asylum to be healed of your own desire, suggest two different contributors.[85] In the same early September 1907 issue, the newspaper clarified (in fact revised) its editorial position on the issue of Paragraph 129(b) of the Austrian penal code, proposing that it be amended to exempt "inborn pederasty," which should be handled medically and not criminally.[86]

82. *Kriminal-Zeitung*, September 2, 1907, p. 8.

83. On the Gemeinschaft der Eigenen, see esp. Keilson-Lauritz, *Die Geschichte*, and Oosterhuis, *Homosexuality*.

84. The literature on these "two traditions" of the early homosexual emancipation movement has matured enough to already be enjoying revision. See esp. Harry Oosterhuis, "Homosexual Emancipation in Germany Before 1933: Two Traditions," in Oosterhuis, *Homosexuality*, 1–28; cf. Andrew Hewitt, *Political Inversions: Homosexuality, Fascism, and the Modernist Imaginary* (Stanford, CA: Stanford University Press, 1996), 79–170.

85. Cf. *Kriminal-Zeitung*, August 26, 1907, 7.

86. *Kriminal-Zeitung* September 2, 1907, p. 7. The editors took this to be Krafft-Ebing's own position.

It is in this context that the original "threatening pederast," Merviola, sent the following more conciliatory letter:

Esteemed Editor,

As you read these lines I do procede to pass among the living alas not in Vienna. For reasons I can not furthermore put forward I must depart Austria's metropole for indeterminant time. I undertake to the Orient, and as I have the frontiers of the monarchy behind me shall I permit myself to forward you an image of my person. I am ever much more placably inclined toward you since you have made indeed a halfway generus judgement about us unlucky warm ones in your last issue and I offer you the well-meaning advise change your tactick completely and place your self completely to our side and thousands of sincerely meant thanks from warm hearts will prove to you what a good work you have done. Fight with us on our side against the stupid prejudice of the world that can not grasp that there are warm ones and who are at the mercy of a miserable penal code demanding ruthless procedings over and above we already unlucky creatures. There is no aquired pederasty, we thousands who call ourselves "warm" are all born bourdened with this defect and no great luminery, of the medical arts and least of all the state attorny can cure us. Since it is impossible for me to speak to all like inclined so I appeal right here and now to all your warm hearts, purchase or subscrib to the Kriminal Zeitung in your own interests and right try to find other buyers in your circles That way finally for once the people will be enlightened about us, When I was just very small, I felt the need in me to get involved in talk only with gentlemen and I engaged socially with my own playmates as little as possible, whearas I was in fact happy when I was only in proximaty of a man. And as it was for me so has it gone for the thousands of others. For the acceptance of these lines in your valued paper in most polite thanks I remain

Your Countess Merviola[87]

The initial lines of the letter simply reinforce the impression of an aggressively narcissistic author left by the earlier correspondence, but the tone rapidly changes as the letter becomes a kind of negotiation. Merviola is more "placably inclined" toward the editor in light of the "halfway generus judgement" represented by the proposed exemption, and invites the newspaper to change strategy and "place yourself completely to our side" in a struggle

---

87. *Illustrierte Oesterreichische Kriminal-Zeitung* (Vienna) 1, no. 20 (September 1907): 8. The original contains grammatical and spelling errors, along with the stilted prose that this translation seeks to capture.

with an ignorant outside world that does not recognize the double burden of unlucky (*unglücklich*) souls burdened with same-sex desire and the threat of criminal prosecution for the pursuit of their natural sexuality. Merviola both reproduces and contests the medico-juridical discourse on homosexuals in presenting the empirical evidence of personal experience: there is no such thing as acquired pederasty; it is rather inborn in all cases, and medical and legal experts cannot do anything to change it. The plea that the *Kriminal-Zeitung* fight on the side of those so inclined—in fact, the whole letter—is an indication that Merviola recognizes in the newspaper the voice of another, and competing, authoritative discourse. Recognition of the tabloid's commercial motivations for the pederasty series is implicit in Merviola's strategy to win it over, as he solicits homosexual readers to support the paper by subscribing en masse.[88]

It would be an excessive claim to romanticize these few weeks of pages of readers' letters as a nascent public sphere of homosexual community or the responses contained within them as queer declarations of an autonomous and legitimate sexual identity. The forum offered by the newspaper in fact produced more intragroup conflict than it did a united front against heterosexual persecution. Each week's letters to the editor were filled with denunciations, listings of establishments missed by the newspaper articles, and even specific names of persons seen at such establishments or loitering in public parks and toilets. Even the Lady of the Camellias's proud attack on heterosexual arrogance ended with the complaint that male homosexuals were singled out in the articles and the demand that the newspaper "open the eyes of the public" to "feminine love," naming locales where they gather and suggesting, as had been suggested about the society of male homosexuals, that they were particularly powerful as a social group. Another letter writer, signing himself as "One Too," named a series of notorious homosexuals and a long list of

---

88. This is perhaps the best place to address the methodological problem of the authenticity of the letters, which naturally cannot be verified. In spite of the editors' claims to reproduce these reader letters unedited, it can never be clear how selective they were with their publication and whether or not letters were fabricated in part or entirely. In light of the absence of any similar sources before this point—the novelty of the whole genre of authorship that Merviola, Rita, Mme. Louse et al. represent—it is safe to assume the contributions were not wholly invented, but rather exploited for their sensational value. Still, a clause such as the one at issue here, where a reader openly solicits broader readership, could have been concocted by profit-motivated editors. None of this would compromise the argument put forth here, since even invented fragments would have been designed to conform to the conventions quickly established in the rush of reader responses. The discourses analyzed here are so densely recursive that the question of individual authorship moves to the background in some sense.

commercial establishments tolerating them.[89] A later respondent may well have been right that One Too was probably "None at All," or rather, that the nascent public sphere improvised in the forum paralleled that on the streets, including not only inverts, but their blackmailers as well. Some of these letters may also have been drafted by the café proprietors themselves, denouncing their own competition. More likely than this is that many of the letters written ostensibly by sympathetic heterosexual readers or even physicians were indeed by homosexuals, and this possibility was not lost on the editors.

From our contemporary perspective, the most outrageous and inflammatory of the letters correspond in many ways to a queer critique of heteronormativity, conceding to the homophobic assumptions of queer difference— even a difference ranging from "perversity" to lasciviousness—and extolling these as potential virtues in the face of a hypocritical general culture. Other letters, corresponding more clearly to the agenda of the liberal homosexual emancipation movement, stress the normality of presumed abnormal sexual orientation, pointing out (often citing Magnus Hirschfeld's own research) that perverse practices occur in homosexual and in heterosexual men in similar proportions. As one reader argued, how could he be "healed" of a drive that was natural to him, and does not even the suggestion that it require healing imply a certain brutality? With an eloquent defense of his sexuality that at the same time implicitly marginalized Merviola and her cohort, this precursor of a familiar position signed himself simply "Rita."

Finally, the *Kriminal-Zeitung*'s "pederasty" series was met by a response by "the homosexual community" in the form of a didactic and polite protest by the Vienna chapter of the Scientific-Humanitarian Committee. In their controlled and only slightly patronizing letter, the committee was selective in what it chose to discuss with regard to the scandalous articles: first, that the term *pederasty* itself, meaning boy love, was not a synonym for homosexuality, which in its adult and consensual form was not a perversion as such; second, that it was an inborn inclination and therefore could not lead to recruitment of other men of normal sexuality; and finally, the committee representatives politely suggested that homosexuality was not technically a form of insanity, and therefore decriminalization, for which the committee had so long campaigned, would be a more appropriate solution than institutionalization. To this missive was attached a friendly note from the central Scientific-Humanitarian Committee signed by Dr. Magnus Hirschfeld in which suggestions for reading up on the subject were offered. This tame intervention sealed the exchange briefly offered in the letters-to-the-editor

---

89. *Kriminal-Zeitung*, September 20, 1907, p. 8.

# Eine Nacht unter liebenden Männern.

Der Text zu diesem Bilde befindet sich auf Seite 5.

FIGURE 23. Cover story from the *Kriminal-Zeitung*, "A Night among Loving Men."

section, or was at least the newspaper's excuse to do so; in response they promised to print no more anonymous letters.

The peak of the exposé campaign was a two-part cover story titled "A Night among Loving Men" (fig. 23). Here the reporter offered a narrative account of an evening in one of the locales denounced in the newspaper. The author, entering the café, was immediately victim of a come-on in a case of mistaken "identity." Undercover, the reporter depicted the underworld of gay men as a secret society: "They greet one another with handshakes and nods or exchange certain confiding glances, all making the strong impression that all who enter here belong to a common fraternity, bound together by a secret and invisible bond."[90]

Social class reappeared in this literary exposé, where the gentlemen—largely feminized in an unflattering way as petty, vicious, and immoral—took on faux aristocratic or high bourgeois feminine identities (e.g., "Madame Kirschrot"), and waiters were called by lower-class feminine names such as Flora; soldiers (who were not feminized) were also depicted as jealous and

90. "Eine Nacht unter liebenden Männern," *Kriminal-Zeitung*, August 26, 1907, pp. 5–6.

petty. The whole scene was a grotesque parody of bourgeois social, gender, and sexual norms. It would seem from all of this that the newspaper's sensational exploitation of the homosexual subject and the self-expression of homosexual individuals self-consciously opposed and yet also reflected one another just as the echoes of the medico-juridical homosexual subject are apparent in each.

Clearly, when they began their "pederasty campaign," the editors of the *Kriminal-Zeitung* had no idea that the "pederasts" themselves would object to it in this aggressive and, to their ears, unapologetic way. At each point, they were able to turn this to their own advantage, incorporating every response into their own picture of a pathological clique endangering the general society. Just as clearly, letter writers often resorted to the same language of pathologization in use in the inflammatory articles themselves. In some ways, the newspaper's aggressive campaign simply bumped into the obstacle of actually existing homosexuals—but did its campaign have an influence on the ways in which individuals defended themselves and how they thought about their own sexualities? These articulations did not emerge merely in reply to the *Kriminal-Zeitung* and its exposés but to a couple of short decades of representations of homosexual identity, group identity, and sexual behavior. Self-understandings of homosexuals were in some sense hailed by such representations, including those in sensational news reports. However complicit with the normative ideologies to which they responded, the aggressive self-defenses printed in this newspaper—along with countless, unvocalized such responses to medical, juridical, and sensational discourses on male-to-male sex—can be seen as constitutive elements of early twentieth-century male homosexual subjectivity.

## Witnessing the Expert

Scientific expertise and subjective self-knowledge faced one another in medical offices and in the pages of sexology, but they also encountered one another in court. Many of the court transcripts of prosecutions of Paragraph 175 have not survived, although one particularly revealing case was preserved by Krafft-Ebing himself. The doctor was entreated by defense attorneys to render a professional opinion on the criminal responsibility of a homosexual; the attorneys sent him transcripts of court documents on which he took notes relating to forensic medicine.[91] He also possessed and preserved an

91. PP-KEB/A/28, "Case histories on 'conträre Sexualempfindung,'" WLAM. The initial correspondence by attorney Dr. Sello on behalf of himself and Dr. Max Silberstein is dated

autobiographical narrative by the accused, who, like so many others corresponding with the professor, was aware of the latter's work and self-identified as contrary sexual.[92] The accused was Franz Rose, the owner of the estate Charlottenhof in the East Prussian district of Osterode.[93] Several counts were being considered against him, chiefly concerning young men in his employ. The first was a servant of his from 1888 to 1890 who, as part of his duties, had to assist his master dressing and undressing in the evenings, on which occasions the accused reportedly touched him on the legs and genitals, pulled him to his bed and, opening the valet's leggings, laid himself on him and "with his stiff organ made thrusting movements *just as those accompanying intercourse [ebenso wie beim Beischlaf]* against [the servant's] bare body."[94] The valet could not testify as to whether his master achieved ejaculation during these incidents, which were frequent. A second employee boarding in a room in Rose's house, shortly after accepting the position as overseer of the estate, was roused from sleep at 3 a.m. and accosted, to which affronts he resisted, but apparently not for long: on around fifty occasions, according to the overseer's testimony, Rose pulled down the employee's trousers and rubbed against his genitals until the latter ejaculated.

These details were important in determining whether the acts were truly, as the law specified, "similar to intercourse" (*beischlafähnlich*), a term that in the past had sometimes been interpreted as referring to anal or intercrural penetration and at other times as having relied on the presence of a seminal ejaculation. Regarding these accusations, the thrusting movements of the first instance were seen to meet the standard of the term, whereas the latter case—in spite of the servant's orgasms—did not.[95] Mutual onanism was often a gray area in prosecutions of 175 (unlike the Austrian Paragraph 129(b), which did not restrict the prohibition to intercourse-like acts). This sort of

---

January 10, 1894.

92. PP-KEB/A/28, dated October 20, 1892, WLAM.

93. Rose was a successful landholder and art collector who died unmarried. See Klaus Bürger, "Franz Friedrich Adolph Rose," *Altpreussische Biographie*, Bd. 4 (Marburg: Elwert, 1995), 1148.

94. PP-KEB/A/28, transcript of hearing on July 3, 1893, WLAM (emphasis added).

95. Here the court cited several recent decisions (1890) that "according to the letter of the law, under acts of counternatural indecency are only to be understood those acts aimed at the satisfaction of the sexual instinct in a way similar to intercourse. Hence, bodily contact of the other male with the perpetrator's genitals is required, but introduction of the same into the body is not." The original summary of charges contained a more concise report of the same accusations but was inclined to see the defendant's confession of "perverse inclination" as irrelevant, and citing several 1880 decisions, assumed anal penetration (which practice was indeed rumored to take place on the estate) would be the necessary condition of "intercourse-like behavior." Ibid.

nit-picking was not atypical of legal interpretations of the statute in the nineteenth century. Yet in spite of the legal distinction based on the nature of acts, the court was also willing to see the two acts as essentially similar on the basis of intent, quickly adding, "The specific acts in each of these exchanges were driven by the concerted decision on the part of the accused continually to satisfy his genital organ on the affected person." With this sleight of hand, the analysis of the specific technicalities of particular physical contacts was trumped by the criminal subject's intention. In the course of an appeal, the court seems to have pushed this definition even further: "the physical contact of his member with the body of the other man *in the state of an intercourse-like desire* [*unter einem beischlafähnlichen Verlangen*] is sufficient cause."[96] With the word *Verlangen* (wish, demand, appetite, craving, longing), intent has become *desire*.

A further way this case was distinguished from many others, and of primary interest to Krafft-Ebing (who emphasized this passage with heavy colored wax pencil), was the defendant's own claim that he was homosexually "oriented" (*beanlagt*). Here was a clear case of a subject recognizing himself in a sexological definition laid out in the *Psychopathia sexualis* and excusing (*entschuldigt*) his actions on account of his nature. The question (here as elsewhere) for the court was whether such an "inclination" was enough to "excuse" the action. Technically, it could only be so if it were determined to be grounds for criminal irresponsibility (*Unzurechnungsfähigkeit*), which the court was in this case not willing to grant. All the language in the transcript relating to the issue of homosexuality as orientation is keyed to the legal definition of responsibility:

> The defendant excuses his acts with his "contraire sexual" [*contrair sexuell* (*sic*)] orientation but does not himself claim that he committed these [acts] while in a mental state in which he did not know what he was doing. Only true mental illness and other similar conditions disturbing mental activity and those that exclude free determination of will, such as fever delirium, epilepsy, etc. would protect the perpetrator from penalty under Par. 51 of the penal code, because his will in relation to these acts would be lacking.[97]

Instead, the judgment was that the "extraordinary" inclinations confessed by the defendant were caused by "moral weakness and a failure of energy." The exchanges in question were hence expressly intended by the perpetrator, they

96. PP-KEB/A/28, November 10, 1893, WLAM (emphasis added).
97. PP-KEB/A/28, July 3, 1893, WLAM.

had their *origin* in his own will "rather than in *some kind of an illness* that *has robbed him of his will.*" The phrases italicized here were underscored by Krafft-Ebing, who, receiving a transcript of the hearing, marked them with blue wax pencil.

One further element is of particular importance here (not only to our discussion but also to Krafft-Ebing, who emphasized this passage with vertical lines in the margin): the penalty was to be determined with consideration of the fact that the defendant belongs to the higher classes of the population, and on the basis of this and his level of education he should hold every moral high out of respectability. He is held to a higher standard, in other words, and is expected to be better equipped to "resist these inclinations," whereas instead he has confessed to them in order to excuse his actions.

The increasing public attention to the existence of subjects of contrary sexual sensibility that came with these and other cases of a sensational nature led scientist-emancipators such as Magnus Hirschfeld to the stand in court cases as expert witnesses, or *Sachverständigen*. We already know the genealogy of this practice from scientists such as Casper and Westphal. By the turn of the century, the situation had evolved substantially: the existence of a vigorous advocacy group in the Scientific-Humanitarian Committee and the combination of leading sexual scientist and sexual reform activist in a single person combined with a more modern formation of the public scandal or sensation. Furthermore, Hirschfeld's major rivals, the outspoken homophile group known as *Die Eigenen*, sought another path to emancipation. Rather than taking the stand to argue for cool science, *Eigenen* leader Adolf Brand chose the "path over corpses"—he sought to expose the hidden homosexuality of public figures, including no less a political figure than the Chancellor of the Kaiserreich, Prince Bernhard von Bülow. In a number of articles published in September of 1907, and then in a defensive statement published in November, the committee attempted to distance itself from the confrontational strategies of outing—the "path over corpses"—represented above all by Adolf Brand's comments about von Bülow.[98]

Their province, they insisted, was science, and the "objective is singularly the resolution of the homosexual question on a scientific foundation." This

---

98. "Die Homosexuelle Frage in Deutschland," *Oesterreichische Kriminal-Zeitung* 1, no. 32 (November 25, 1907): 6–7. Brand's exposure of von Bülow and others and the logic linking this tactic to decriminalization of homosexuality is all in "Fürst Bülow und die Abschaffung des § 175," *Die Gemeinschaft der Eigenen: Philosophische Gesellschaft für Sittenverbesserung und Lebenskunst*, September 10 1907, pp. 1–4.

statement of objectives is a programmatic restatement of Hirschfeld's credo, "per scientiam ad justitiam," the formula indicating the clear path to justice through science (rather than over corpses). But inasmuch as the science in question was knowledge of the sexual subject, the expertise of committee adherents could be enlisted in particular ways that they could not distance themselves from. In their statement, they tried to disaggregate intervention on behalf of individuals for their own protection from scandal from the nefarious politics of Brand and his cohort of *Eigenen*.

Magnus Hirschfeld was called to the stand in several of the individual trials that made up the Harden-Eulenburg affair. In von Bülow's libel case against Brand, he was called to the stand to support Brand's position that homosexuality was a fact of one's nature, and therefore it was not disgraceful (and therefore the statement about von Bülow could not be considered a libelous attack). Hirschfeld, embarrassingly, had to deny ever having held this position, if only to distance himself from the "zealot" Brand. But it was in the Harden-von Moltke case that Hirschfeld cemented the authority of sexual science in the twin contexts of juridical evaluation and public sensation. Hirschfeld leapt onto the chair of the court expert as a bully pulpit from which to launch the campaign against Paragraph 175 into public consciousness. In many respects, he was right about this. Who else but Hirschfeld could have anticipated the degree to which his scientific credentials and the unprecedented exposure of the case could give the love that dare not speak its own name a name, "homosexual," and place it on the tongues of a general public? How else could the arcane discussions evolving gradually from the forensic manuals called into being by specifics of the penal code transcribe themselves into common sense? Homosexuality was a medical condition, and the sexologist was the appropriate expert to consult in such cases—the secret of hidden sexuality was written on the body and in gestures, reflecting a profile of sentiment and desire, whether awakened or no. Dr. Hirschfeld diagnosed von Moltke on the basis of medical observation of his gait, his figure, and his tastes. Most important, he asserted that von Moltke's homosexuality was certain in spite of whether or not the subject had ever acted on it or even recognized it himself.

The drama of this particular trial was enhanced by the testimony of von Moltke's ex-wife, Lilly von Elbe, who offered salacious details to fuel Harden's accusations; this vicious witness was herself subject to sexological diagnosis, as Albert Moll and others, including eventually Hirschfeld himself, declared her a sexual monster. Hirschfeld was roundly attacked, misquoted, and mocked from many sides for his testimony. When the case was appealed and he was called to the stand again, he reversed his position on von Moltke, a move that only served to further discredit himself.

The Scientific-Humanitarian Committee as well as many other contemporary observers came to understand the Harden-Eulenburg scandal as the watershed setback to their campaign, and historians must concur: Paragraph 175 would famously live on through the Weimar Republic, be substantially sharpened under the National Socialist regime, and survive the war, albeit with modifications, in both German states; its full abolition was not achieved until the 1990s. In a sympathetic lecture delivered in Munich at the end of 1907, in the midst of the trials, physician and sexual researcher Leopold Loewenfeld (1847–1924) alluded defensively to what he regarded as the "current discord against the Scientific-Humanitarian Committee," whose activities have "fallen into a certain disrepute of late."[99] The confidence of the committee's enlightened members that the collection and targeted dissemination of scientific knowledge about sexuality would inevitably lead to emancipation was flawed. That knowledge, and the authority of sexologists as experts, did take on a key role in the cultural struggle for recognition of sexual variation, but not the role they had wanted or anticipated. Science did not lead an inexorable path toward justice, but it was densely entwined with legal, subjective, and sensational discourses in a cluster that produced its own, unpredictable logic.

Another parallel example of these processes concerns an index file of respected and upper-class subjects suspected of homosexuality collected by the innovator of the "criminal albums" and head of the Department of Blackmailers and Homosexuals (Erpresser- und Homosexuellendezernat) Leopold von Meerscheidt-Hüllesem (1849–1900).[100] While being responsible for the unit that was charged to make arrests under Paragraph 175, Meerscheidt-Hüllesem worked explicitly for the abolition of the paragraph.[101] In the inter-

99. L. Loewenfeld, *Homosexualität und Strafgesetz: Nach einem in der kriminalistischen Sektion des akademisch-juristischen Vereins zu München am 17. Dezember 1907 gehaltenen Vortrage* (Wiesbaden: Bergmann, 1908), 35.

100. See Jens Dobler, "Leopold von Meerscheidt-Hüllessem (1849–1900)," *Archiv für Polizeigeschichte* 9 (1998): 73–79; Benjamin Hett, *Death in the Tiergarten*, 174; Robert Beachy, "To Police and Protect: The Surveillance of Homosexuality in Imperial Berlin," in Spector, *After the History of Sexuality*, 109–23, and Beachy, *Gay Berlin*, 42–84; cf. Erwin J. Haeberle, "Justitias zweischneidiges Schwert: Magnus Hirschfeld als Gutachter in der Eulenburg-Affäre," in *Sexualität zwischen Medizin und Recht*, ed. Klaus M. Beier (Stuttgart: Fischer, 1991), 5–20.

101. See esp. the effusive obituary of von Meerscheidt-Hüllessem in Hirschfeld's journal: G, "In memoriam," *Jahrbuch für sexuelle Zwischenstufen* 4 (1902): 947–55. Cf. Gesa Lindemann,

est of this enlightened goal, he collected the names of highly placed homosexuals in a special card file (apart from and in addition to the general registry of all Berlin homosexuals that he kept along with his general "criminal album" registry). He had this index delivered into the hands of the emperor himself, in an effort to sway him; Wilhelm II reportedly did not open the packet but sent it directly to the police president.[102] The commissioner himself had committed suicide seven years before the Harden-Eulenburg affair, but when the scandal broke, the card registry would only serve to intensify the moral panic's penetration into the court, quite contrary to the emancipatory intentions of its creator. The hopes of a straight line from knowledge to justice were naive from the start, to be sure, but the dynamics created by the unanticipated and to some degree novel context of the national sensation upended the logic of enlightened emancipation.

For those who resisted such progressive ends from the start, the case was a source of disgrace for the conservative order on the one hand, and on the other an occasion for validating multiple positions at once. It gave them the space to lump together their contempt of sexuality reform, progressive science, and sensationalism, all three of which they identified with Jews. To trumpet these conclusions, they naturally engaged in the same sensational journalistic practices, if only occasionally apologizing for doing so.

> If we have instructed our readers through detailed reports on the development of the Harden affair, we have done so in recognition of our duty. Yet fulfilling that duty has not been easy. For it has required us not only to allude to but also to reproduce in detail moral transgressions that we would have preferred to pass over in strict silence. Our readers will surely grasp how thoroughly difficult this has been for a newspaper that indulges neither in the craving for sensation [*Sensationslust*] nor prurient titillation [*Sinnenkitzel*].[103]

------------

"Magnus Hirschfeld (1993)," in "*Durch Wissenschaft zur Gerechtigkeit? Textsammlung zur kritischen Rezeption des Schaffens von Magnus Hirschfeld: Geschlecht—Sexualität—Gesellschaft.* Berliner Schriften zur Sexualwissenschaft und Sexualpolitik, vol. 4 (Münster: LIT, 2003), 106.

102. Tresckow, *Von Fürsten*, 115–16. Former commissioner von Tresckow in this memoir speculates that the scandal of 1907 might have been avoided had the emperor opened the box, which included names of members of his own camarilla. Yet the political outcomes of the release of knowledge, as we have seen, were not predictable.

103. Note the scandal is named here for the Jewish journalist who penned the original exposé, and the aristocrat Eulenburg is not mentioned. The conservative organ publishing this piece was clear in its interpretation of the scandal as a conflict of estates—*Stände*; the traditional order was under attack by Jews, modern journalism, legal reformers, and social reform. See "Nachträge zum Hardenprozeß," *Neue Preussische Zeitung* (Berlin), January 6, 1908, Abend-Ausgabe, pp. 1–2.

In retrospect it is clear that Hirschfeld on the stand at the Eulenburg trials represented a climax in the symphony that had begun with Casper's and Westphal's encounter with "Cajus" and other criminal/sexual subjects. The theater of sensational scandal played to the scrutiny of a general public did not merely amplify as much as it transposed the effects of the encounter of the new sexual science with novel sensibilities of sexuality. Hirschfeld anticipated the intimate linkage of sexual science, subjectivity, and politics in the first decade of the new century, but not unlike his precursor Ulrichs, possessing this brilliant instinct did not mean he could control the ways in which the spheres would interact. Sexuality, in a word, had a life of its own.

4

# Utopian Bodies: The Sensual Woman
# and the Lust Murderer

London's "Jack the Ripper" provided sensational fodder for all of Europe and beyond. The figure also created an opportunity for a host of different kinds of narratives—suspense stories as well as melodramas focusing on the victims, to be sure, but also medical and juridical definitions of something that seemed like a new kind of killing. Whether the focus was on the murderous subject, the "lust murderer," or on his vilified object—so often, as in the Ripper cases, a prostitute or an otherwise sexualized woman—the new crime fantasy combined sexuality and violence in one gesture. The fascination provided by *Lustmord*, as German scientists and sensationalists would call it, extended to registers of culture from high to low. The bodies left in the wake of lust murderers seemed signs of something larger than themselves, but of what? Where did lust murder come from? What was its meaning?

## The Rise of the Lust Murderer

In 1890, the papers in Berlin and Vienna were buzzing with excitement about the potential for vice and violence in their respective cities. News of the Jack the Ripper murders was reported in the manner of a serial novel, where readers could be counted on for knowing the names of yesterday's suspects and last week's victims. Berlin papers defended themselves against provincial gossip that the capital was as vicious and dangerous as London and eagerly reported when a Ripper-type murder occurred somewhere far off, such as Malaga, Spain.[1] Whether relishing the lurid drama of murder in their city

---

1. A single page of a Berlin daily in fall of 1891 reported on a gruesome local murder (discussed below) while reassuring the public that lust murder was elsewhere, as in this reference

or disavowing its gravity, newspapers and police reports mirrored those in the Jack the Ripper case as well as the serial novellas and pulp fiction they inspired. Narratives began with the object that set mystery stories in motion: the victim's corpse. Such was the case for the story of 24-year-old Marie Wende, whose body was found lifeless on the so-called Waterway of the western Berlin Tiergarten park, two wounds on her breast caused by revolver shots and her throat opened by a long, deep slit wound.[2]

Just six years earlier, reports of murdered women relied on different narrative techniques to achieve sensational effects (i.e., to capture imaginations and profits). In Vienna, the convictions of the notorious Moravian-born Hugo Schenk and his main accomplice Carl Schloßarek gave rise to considerable lore after their having killed at least four in cold blood.[3] Seducing and sometimes even marrying his hapless servant-girl victims, then murdering them and making off with their life savings or dowry money, the murderer left poems behind to posterity. Schenk was a charismatic serial killer, but he was never presented in the manner that would become conventional for the lust murderer. While his victims were generally women, his motive was given as greed, and the murders hence classified as robbery killings.[4]

Back in Berlin, in the same year that Schenk and accomplices were convicted, a tale unfolded that ended with twenty knife wounds to the head and throat of a young girl, as the police report reveals, but the extensive newspaper account had a different emphasis. The seamstress Petzold had been engaged in a love affair with the married locksmith Mießner, and the tale of her murder was hence told as a love story gone awry, where passion yielded

---

to the Malaga killing. The Holzmarktgasse slashing was not a lust murder, according to police, though its similarity to the Whitechapel murders of "Jack the Ripper" led them to consult with London authorities on possible motive. Another report on the same page delivers the insights of the new science of criminalistics to demonstrate "that the vice situation in Berlin is not as bad off as the complacent provincial thinks and the conservative press makes out"; see "Lokales und Vermischtes," *Berliner Morgen-Zeitung und Tägliches Familienblatt*, October 29, 1891, p. 3.

2. "Morde im Thiergarten," *Tägliche Rundschau*, July 24, 1890, p. 169.

3. An early such account is Anon., *Prozeß des Mädchenmörders*, where the adventures of a gruesome robber band is the exploitative hook, but Schenk is not portrayed as the hero-criminal nor as a *Lustmörder* even in a nascent form. The attempt to analyze the criminal's psychopathology appears first in the 1920s in Altmann, *Hugo Schenk*; see esp. 170–71, where the author rues the lost opportunity of an "examination of mental state, since thence could have been gained a clearer look into his inner life."

4. Landesgericht für Strafsachen Vr 2362/1884, "Hugo Schenk et al." (two cartons), WSLA. Both Schenk and Schloßarek were prosecuted under Paragraphs 134 and 135 of the Austrian penal code.

to fear and anticipation of violence.[5] The centrality of the relationship over-whelmed the detail of the repetitive stabbing, as it did the personality of the murderer, his compulsive behavior, or his nature. It was only in retrospect that police officials grouped this crime with those of other "slashers."[6]

At the same time, however, slashed women's bodies began turning up in the garrison town of Cüstrin on the Oder, some fifty miles northeast of Berlin. In 1890 and 1891 there was a series of attacks on prostitutes: on December 18, 1890, while standing at the platform of the town's East Railway Station, Wilhelmine Zimmermann suffered a finger-long, deep stabbing wound to the trunk; between Christmas and New Year's Day at the same station, a similar attempt was made on Ernestine Frick and also on Louise Belgerin and Emilie Müller. On February 21, 1891, the perpetrator had more success with Pauline Wilden, leading her to a hidden place off the platform and slashing open her entire abdomen down to the navel, injuring her critically, though not fatally. All women were registered as prostitutes with the local police.[7]

On the night of October 24, 1891, another prostitute, with the name of Nitsche, was slain in a manner reminiscent of the previous attacks, and the search for an assailant became one for a murderer. Assuming the killer was the same perpetrator who had stabbed the previous four women—one of them on two occasions—this constituted a series that observers feared and relished as evocative of Jack the Ripper in London. As one newspaper reported,

> As to the motive of the murderer, in criminal police detective circles it is gen-erally held that lust murder is completely out of the question, and there re-mains only the question of whether this is a matter of the deed of an *insane* or a *superstitious* individual. It is unclear what meaning such a superstition could have. Consequentially, authorities felt encouraged to request the files from the *London police authorities* who are working on the Whitechapel woman killer *Jack the Ripper* in order to determine on the basis of these what results had emerged there regarding determination of a motive for the uncanny crimes that have such great similarity to the one exercised in the Holzmartktgasse.[8]

The secret of the series lay in motive, or rather its lack. As in criminalists' search for the pure crime, unimpeded by motive, speculation leads to ratio-

---

5. *Tägliche Rundschau*, July 30, 1884.

6. Potsdam (Orangerie), Zentralkartei für Mordsachen (1934) ZfM Rügenerstr./Pätzold, Rep 30, Bln C, Tit 198B, Nr. 12, BBLHA. The files of the *Polizeipräsidium* in these years have since been moved to LAB.

7. A Pr. Br. Rep. 030–03, Nr. 1749, LAB.

8. "Lokales und Vermischtes."

nalism's others: to insanity, superstition, or some as yet undisclosed mysterious source. The disavowal of lust murder in this report seems at odds with its easy comparison to London's Jack, but this is an artifact of a confusion surrounding the category of lust murder, which had not yet been popularized. Jack the Ripper would become the paradigmatic lust murderer, but he was not yet accepted as such.[9] If he did not murder these women after having sex with them, or if his (possibly even mad) sexual desire for them did not motivate the crime, how could it be a crime of lust? The attacks at Cüstrin on the Oder were bewildering not because they did not perfectly fit a pattern but because the pattern was not yet authoritative. If Jack the Ripper had indeed "inaugurated" an "age of sex crime," it was—like so many incipient new eras—not yet visible to its own population.[10]

To speak of modernity as the age of sex crime is not of course to claim that what we understand as sex crimes never occurred before the 1880s. The historical emergence of the recognizable figure of *Lustmord* confronts us with the problem of pinpointing the phenomenon itself. Are we speaking of the emergence of a new crime or of a new kind of criminal? Previous cases of sexual violence occur in earlier news reports, police files, and court records, to be sure. Violence accompanies the familiar category of rape; sexual coercers try to cover their tracks by killing their victims, or such deaths occur accidentally in the course of violent struggle. Arguably, the novel invention is neither the killer nor the crime nor the body of the victim; not the sophisticated forensic investigations or the competency experts, but the production of all of these in an increasingly elaborated web of discursive apparatuses. For the emergence of Ripper-like crimes and criminals cannot really be seen apart from the professional and public fascinations with them represented by the proliferation of genres and knowledges developing around the same time. *Lustmord* engaged the new science of sexology, with its systems of classification and explanation of sexual identity and diversity; criminal anthropology's focus on the criminal body itself—the physiognomy of the criminal type as well as the victim type of the prostitute; the forensic discourses of criminology accompanying the professionalization of criminal police forces; and, not

9. Still earlier reports in Germany miss the association with prostitution entirely, and the characterization of Jack the Ripper is one of a legendary monster (*Unmensch*) who preys on vulnerable women and children. See, e.g., the reports on panic in Mainz in response to rumors that Jack was in the city: *Rheinische Courier*, November 14, 1889, cited in *Berliner Gerichts-Zeitung*, November 16, 1889, p. 7.

10. The phrase is from Colin Wilson's introduction to a contemporary classic of the sensational literature, Donald Rumbelow, *The Complete Jack the Ripper* (New York: Penguin, 2004), vii, but the case was also put forcefully by feminist scholar Jane Caputi in *Age of Sex Crime*, 4.

least important, the parallel literary genres of sensationalist reportage of such crimes, true crime narratives, and crime fiction. Victims' bodies were put on display by journalists (as well as by police) as obscenely, as compulsively, and with as apparent relish as they were by the perpetrators, who left their victims opened for view and posed pornographically.[11] Already a few years before the emergence of Jack in the London crime scene in 1888, Krafft-Ebing had noted a sufficient number of cases to include in his famous catalog of sexual pathologies the new category of sex murder (*Lustmord*), the only motive of which is sexual gratification. The gratification, importantly, is not derived from a rape or any explicitly sexual act preceding or accompanying the killing, but the act of violence is itself, and for the first time, identified as a sexual act.[12] In an 1890 article on masochism, Krafft-Ebing waxes reflexively on the proximity of sexuality to violence in primitive cultures and the atavistic reappearance of these acts of brutality displacing courtship in modern perverse individuals— again, not as "preparatory" acts to coitus but as "the aim in and of itself." And then, almost casually, he extrapolates: it is just a short step from this complex of degenerate pleasures to *Lustmord*.[13] From the relative absence of discourse on sex murder some decades before, we find these most brutal murders at the heart of our understanding of sex.

So it is at the fin de siècle that we see the origins of the figure of lust murder or *Lustmord*, which has received the most attention in its incarnations in the Weimar Republic.[14] There can be no question that the radical easing of

11. Cf. Caputi, *Age of Sex Crime*, 7: "Albert DeSalvo, the 'Boston Strangler,' decorated and posed the bodies of his victims in what has been described as a parody of the gynecological exam. The victims of the 'Hillside strangler' were characteristically dumped on the hills surrounding L.A. One reporter described his reaction upon encountering the body of one of these victims: 'She was completely nude and she was sprawled out on the grass almost as if she were about to engage in an act of sex with a man. The knees were up in the air, her legs were spread apart, the hands were at about a forty-five degree angle from her sides, almost in a position of supplication.'" See also Suzanne Lacy, "In Mourning and in Rage (with Analysis Aforethought)," *Ikon* (Fall / Winter 1982–83): 60–67 (cited in Caputi, *Age of Sex Crime*).

12. Krafft-Ebing, *Psychopathia Sexualis, with especial reference to the antipathic sexual instinct*, trans. Franklin S. Klaf (New York: Stein and Day, 1965), 58–9.

13. Krafft-Ebing, "Ueber Masochismus: Aus einer neuen medizinisch-psychologischen Studie des Verfassers," *Wiener medizinische Blätter* 13, no. 52 (1890): 817–20.

14. Tatar, *Lustmord*. See also Beth Irwin Lewis, "Lustmord: Inside the Windows of the Metropolis," in Haxthausen and Suhr, *Berlin: Culture and Metropolis*, 111–40. Arne Höcker, *Epistemologie des Extremen: Lustmord in Kriminologie und Literatur um 1900* (Munich: Fink, 2012) does focus on this period from a literary perspective, stressing the rhetorics of gruesomeness and excess in criminological and literary texts. Jay Michael Layne's dissertation, "Uncanny Collapse: Sexual Violence and Unsettled Rhetoric in German-Language Lustmord Representations,

censorship in Wilhelmine Germany and post-Habsburg Austria after World War I permitted extreme visual and literary manifestations of the *Lustmord* topos, and the war itself certainly influenced these images, as critics have assumed. Yet, the conflation of sex and violence against woman was not a product of memories of the war, for it preceded it.

*Lustmord* emerges at the confluence of actively contested and reformulating conceptions of female sexuality on the one hand and of criminal psychology, motivation, and responsibility (*Zurechnung*) on the other. Both of these streams flowed from the welling spring of fascination with "other" (abnormal, eroticized, and exotic) bodies, but they led to thinking about the self.

### Otto Weininger's Two Bodies

At the symbolic center of this chapter is Otto Weininger and his influential misogynous work, *Sex and Character*, which was published in Vienna in 1903 (see fig. 24).[15] It is a matter of some debate whether the work as well as its author would have been as celebrated as they were had it not been for Weininger's dramatic end just as his opus was published. The 23-year-old scholar (fig. 25) had locked himself in Beethoven's death chamber and shot himself there. The staging of this act of violence against the backdrop of a symbol of the heights of European civilization is symptomatic for some of the relations we are examining: Weininger's fatally wounded body and the corpus of Western culture represented by the German composer were not sharing the same space by accident.

Weininger became a cause célèbre of the early twentieth century, and the text that seems today like nothing but a fanatical antifeminist diatribe was read and admired by a wide range of intellectuals in Europe and America. The author's untimely and dramatic death contributed to this phenomenon, but it does not go very far in explaining it. Thus, contemporary scholars have busily worked through Weininger's work and its reception to begin to uncover how it could have been seen to stand as a document of the times in a way that other works, such as Freud's *Interpretation of Dreams*, was not yet.[16]

---

1900–1933" (PhD diss., University of Michigan, 2008), similarly explores philosophical questions through rhetorical analysis of scientific and literary texts.

15. Weininger, *Geschlecht und Charakter*.

16. A small and provocative classic literature on Weininger and *Sex and Character* has yielded to a rather substantial interest in German studies in particular. The most important contributions, after early treatments in Lessing, *Der jüdische Selbsthaß*, and Abrahamsen, *Life and Mind*, came in the 1980s with the Munich publisher Matthes und Seitz's reprints of Weininger's work and Nike Wagner's review, "Wo Lulu war, muß Kant werden" *Die Zeit* 48 (November 21, 1980)

# GESCHLECHT

UND

# CHARAKTER

EINE PRINZIPIELLE UNTERSUCHUNG

VON

## Dr. OTTO WEININGER.

WIEN UND LEIPZIG.
WILHELM BRAUMÜLLER
K. U. K. HOF- UND UNIVERSITÄTS-BUCHHÄNDLER.
1903.

FIGURE 24. Title page of Otto Weininger's famous work, *Geschlecht und Charakter*, 1903.

FIGURE 25. Otto Weininger, 1903.

The work itself, originally a dissertation in psychology, in fact attempted to synthesize the disparate fields of human knowledge that exploded in the late nineteenth century: medical science, including biology, psychology, chemistry, endocrinology; philosophy, especially Kantian, with a powerful dose of Nietzsche; cultural history and the conservative critical practice known as "cultural criticism." The first half of the book establishes the scientific groundwork for what in the second part becomes a massive cultural critique. Before attacking modern culture, however, he turns to the individual body, positing the essential reducibility of all organic phenomena to the "principles" of "M" (for *Mann*, masculine) and "W" (for *Weib*, feminine). These principles are stored up in two different genders of plasma, arrheno- and

and references in *Geist und Geschlecht*; Le Rider, *Le Cas Otto Weininger*; Nitschke, *Männerängste, Männerwünsche*; Le Rider and Leser, *Otto Weininger*; and Rodlauer, *Von "Eros und Psyche."* In reaction to the tendency within the Weininger reception to read the thinker as symptomatic of an intensely patriarchal fin-de-siècle imaginary, Allan Janik has argued for his recuperation within a canon of neo-Kantianism, relegating the misogyny of the text to a tertiary and over-emphasized characteristic. This is obviously a hypercorrection, for misogyny is certainly and explicitly the foundation of the work, its neo-Kantianism notwithstanding. See Janik, *Essays*. Representative of the surge of interest in Weininger in German and Jewish studies in North America is the key volume edited by Harrowitz and Hyams, *Jews and Gender*. Chandok Sen-goopta's well researched study *Otto Weininger* places Weininger in the context of contemporary medical science as none other has.

thelyplasma, the former creative, productive, imaginative, individual, capable of genius, and the latter purely sexual, incapable of desiring, creating, or imagining anything beyond the realm of coitus. The balance of male and female essences in each cell of the body becomes overriding law for the content of existence. This scientific groundwork is the theology of Weininger's text: it reveals the foundation of everything else he has to say in this deepest, most essential layer of existence (indeed, the whole work is subtitled *eine prinzipielle Untersuchung*, for it is "only" an exploration of principles). Yet there is an immediate and consistent slippage in Weininger's text from a description of the principle W or "Woman" to a discussion of women: while these ideal principles are present in every organism in quantifiable admixtures, no virtue associated with the M principle is ever accessible to any woman, and even the most intellectually and artistically developed woman stands strata below the lowest man.

Hence, the search for a locus of cultural degeneracy in the principle W yields to the conclusion that there is no single locus. That is, there is no organ or gland that contains or produces masculinity or femininity—these exist in various proportions to one another in every organism in the form of plasma that resides in every cell of the body. This dispersion of the M and W principles guarantees that the whole is always represented in each part; as in the odious and ubiquitous sexuality of Woman herself, it is dispersed over her whole body, simply more "densely" located in certain regions. What we learn in the second half of Weininger's opus is that this sexuality is not only diffused over the female body—it has metastasized within the body of civilization generally and is the characterizing feature of modern culture. That is the body he was genuinely concerned about, the one he identified with—along with his other body, the one he was born in and that was also not quite the one he would have wished for himself.

Weininger's greatly admired work can thus be seen to loop around from the study of bodies to a critique of the corpus of European civilization and ultimately back to his own vessel. *W* was for "Weininger," in an important sense. And "woman" stands in for many things in Weininger's discourse, especially "man." Weininger's extended discussion of the W principle is too easily seen as a radical demarcation of the masculine self of Western civilization from the othered body of woman, the body of pure sexuality at odds with the spirit of masculine civilization. Weininger's real concern in *Sex and Character* is, after all, not this foreign, sexual, feminine body but the corpus of Western civilization that has become overtaken by the feminine principle. It was Weininger's own body, Jewish and feminized, the salvation of which he

could only find in an act of violence aimed not at the despised feminine other
but at himself.

## Woman as Question

It is often forgotten that the occasion for Weininger's synthetic innovation
(half physiology, half philosophy, with cultural critique throughout) was the
women's movement along with the general discussion it incited. The idea
of the "woman question," as it was called, is difficult to recapture entirely.
The term was meant to refer to the "issue" of women's social place generally,
including the specific question of the suffrage. At the same time, the German term for issue in this case, *Frage*, like its siblings "the social question"
and the "Jewish question," implied a nagging problem that called for some
sort of resolution. In its earliest formations, the woman question was most
closely linked to class issues (the social question), in that it encompassed concerns about women's self-fulfillment outside the domestic sphere as well as
the effects on family and society that bringing women to the workplace would
have.[17] The far-reaching ethical dimensions of the debate were sometimes
obscured by speculation about the natural capacities of women and the social outcomes of emancipation, but Weininger was not the first to identify
the problem as an ethical one. Feminists had set forth not only that social
limitations on female individuals were, as all forms of slavery, morally wrong
but that the emancipation of women would represent an ethical and moral
advance for society as a whole. Like Weininger, emancipators sometimes
couched these arguments within current thinking on degeneration, as in
the important intervention of Anita Augspurg (1857–1943), an academically

17 See Braun, *Die Frauenfrage*; cf. Bebel, *Die Frau*; Alice Salomon, "Die Arbeiterinnenfrage:
Eine Frauenfrage," *Die Nation* 24, no. 21 (February 1907): 326–327. The debates between critics
on both "sides" of the woman question make clear the focus on the single issue of women in careers or as homemakers; see Von einem Junggesellen, *Nüchterne Betrachtungen* and the response
Von einer Frau, *Auch ein paar nüchterne Betrachtungen*. Carlos von Gagern, in a somewhat patronizing lecture on the evolution of the woman question, argued that women, like slaves in
the American South, may resist their own emancipation but that it would bring not only social
equality but moral improvement to women and to society as a whole; see Gagern, *Die Entwickelung*. Key sources for this issue are Frederiksen, *Die Frauenfrage*; Canning, *Languages of Labor*;
and Evans, *Feminist Movement*. In suggesting this general trajectory, one does not mean to imply that later discussions of the woman question did not return to the narrower model of the
subset of the "social question"; see, e.g., Anna Pappritz's lead article of the special issue on the
woman question of the journal *Das Gericht: Unabhängige nationale Wochenschrift für Gerichtswesen und öffentliches Leben* 1, no. 3 (1910): 1–3.

trained activist of the so-called radical wing of the movement. In *Die ethische Seite der Frauenfrage* (The ethical side of the woman question), Augspurg accepted the cultural convention that gives woman as the bearer of morality but argued that this morality is prescribed by the other, socially and culturally hegemonic sex. She is hence neither guardian nor creator of the currently degenerate morality but she who complies with a foreign moral order.[18] Significantly, Augspurg's prime example was prostitution. This is similarly the case for Johanna Elberskirchen, another radical discussant and emancipator, who in 1896 was still a student at Zurich (the first university admitting women to graduate study and hence a center of fin-de-siècle feminism).[19] In an extended essay published that year, Elberskirchen boldly pointed to prostitution as a sign of degeneracy, but not of female degeneracy in the sense that Lombroso had or that Weininger and Möbius would; rather, it was the product of the lascivious condition of the male.[20]

Toward the turn of the century, however, the woman question drifted into another realm, which would be known, especially after the Swiss Auguste Forel's important book, as the "sexual question."[21] The question of woman's sexuality began to seem just as important—and importantly linked—to the questions of her self-actualization and social place. The medical doctor Anna Fischer-Dückelmann, who like Augspurg and Elberskirchen graduated from the pioneering University of Zurich, carried expert authority when she wrote on "the sexual life of woman," subtitled "a physiologico-social study with medical suggestions," and steadily maintained that this sexuality was the product not only of biology but of the male-dominated cultural context. Hence, she could anticipate Weininger's soon to be praised dissertation in arguing that the age was "weak" as were the morals of some women, but only because they, no more than men, were products of a weak age dominated,

18. Augspurg, *Die ethische Seite*, 31. Augspurg also states that the ethical aspects of the woman question have been overshadowed by attention to the social situation of women.

19 Meticulous research and insightful analysis of Elberskirchen's contribution can be found in the excellent dissertation by Kirsten Leng, "Contesting the 'Laws of Life': Feminism, Sexual Science and Sexual Governance in Germany and Britain, c. 1880–1914" (PhD diss., University of Michigan, 2011), and in Kirsten Leng, "Sex, Science, and Fin-de-Siècle Feminism: Johanna Elberskirchen Interprets *The Laws of Life*," *Journal of Women's History* 25, no. 3 (Fall 2013): 38–61.

20. Elberskirchen, *Die Prostitution des Mannes*. Leng persuasively specifies that Elberskirchen's use of "degeneracy" in this early text is more a marker of moral opprobrium than a reference to the biological model of degeneration that she would make use of in later texts.

21. Forel, *Die sexuelle Frage*. In other texts the term *sexual question* refers to changing mores and the perceived catastrophic rise of sexually transmitted disease, often linked back to the woman question via "sexual ethics"; see, e.g., Metta, *Wie belehren wir unsere Kinder*, 3.

after all, by the agendas of men.[22] Hanns Gross hailed expert knowledge on women by women but was alienated by what he saw as these extraneous comments on the woman question.[23]

Weininger's book was anticipated by a text as vociferously misogynistic but without the elaborate complexity of *Sex and Character*. P. J. Möbius's *Ueber den physiologischen Schwachsinn des Weibes* (Concerning the physiological feeblemindedness of the female). The pathbreaking neuropsychiatrist sought to respond to the woman question with definitive evidence of the overall psychic and physical inferiority of the female.[24] The response to the 79-page essay came fast and furious, and Möbius did not shy from including negative as well as positive responses in further editions.[25] Oda Olberg's response is particularly instructive in that it insists on a discussion of the natural sexuality (*Geschlechtsnatur*) of woman in order to move the woman question beyond the "social question."[26] Sexual nature for Olberg is gender nature more broadly, and all attempts to compare the two genders are inherently flawed in the absence of a third position from which to judge. A year before Weininger's dissertation was published, Olberg criticized a stance of cultural pessimism that identified urban intellectualism as alienated from nature and somehow feminized, and the woman question as decadent in origins.

The shift of the woman question from social place to female nature was hence not really a shift from the ethical (*ethisch*) question of social equality to the moral (*sittlich*) issues surrounding sexual nature and behavior; the two realms were delicately interwoven. This was apparent in Weininger's opus, to be sure, but it resonated just as powerfully in feminist work.[27] What counted as moral or immoral, and how these factors linked up to ethical questions, differed in the works of these women. Their own discussions dealt with these

22. Fischer-Dückelmann, *Das Geschlechtsleben des Weibes*, esp. 112. The first edition was published in 1900.

23. He can be said therefore to have been more amenable to the "physiological" analysis than the "social" one promised in the book's subtitle. Hanns Gross, "Besprechung: Das Geschlechtsleben des Weibes," *GKA* 1:370–71.

24. Möbius, *Ueber den physiologischen Schwachsinn des Weibes*. In an attempt to rehabilitate his soiled reputation, a recent article argues not only that his contributions to the history of psychiatry have been underestimated but that his views on gender in research on the etiology of hysteria were unrelated to his position in this tract. See Steinberg, Carius, and Angermeyer, "Tenth Anniversary."

25. See, e.g., P. J. Möbius, *Ueber den physiologischen Schwachsinn des Weibes*, 5th ed. (Halle: Marhold, 1905), 80–123.

26. Olberg, *Das Weib*, 10.

27. A new work offering a brilliant exploration of the field of ethics in relation to the sexual reform movement is Matysik, *Reforming the Moral Subject*.

differences explicitly, particularly in the form of a central dispute considering the fundamental virtue or corruption of the institution of marriage, linked to differing and shifting views of women's natural chastity and the conditions for her sexual and spiritual fulfillment.[28] Austrian feminist Grete Meisel-Hess found "sexual crisis" a more apt phrase than the "sexual question," and in a seminal 1907 text did much to define the agenda.[29] Radicals offered various innovative solutions to the problem left unsolved by traditional marriage—a "problem" that was defined alternatively as the sexual and spiritual unful-fillment of women, their imprisonment within one-sidedly monogamous unions, or the surplus sexual drives of men. These solutions, including pro-posals for formally open marriage, official concubinage, female same-sex relationships, and reformed and supported prostitution, were offensive to more conservative feminists and to most branches of the women's movement abroad.[30]

The maelstrom of thinking about the sexuality of woman in relation to the formally social question of women's equality was disciplined into a partic-ular stream of thought about "ethics" with the appearance of Forel's impor-tant work. Eugenics—the fruit of degeneration discourses that would grip thought about sexuality in Germany through the next half-century—was the medium binding together women's social role, physiological nature, and place in an ethical order. The place of eugenics within the sphere of women's

28. Explicit on this issue is Bäumer et al., *Frauenbewegung und Sexualethik*, where the au-thors identify a split in the women's movement between a radical minority "who sees the solu-tion of burning questions in a fundamental reformulation of the moral and juridical norms of sexual life" and the majority, with whom the authors identify, who "continue to recognize mar-riage as the highest moral norm." Cf. Evans, *Feminist Movement*, "The New Morality," 115–43.

29. Meisel-Hess, *Das Wesen der Geschlechtlichkeit*.

30. This has been well documented in the literature, particularly focusing on the career and writings of Bund für Mutterschutz leader Helene Stöcker; see, e.g., Irene Stoehr, "Fraueneinfluß oder Geschlechterversöhnung? Zur 'Sexualitätsdebatte' in der deutschen Frauenbewegung um 1900," in Geyer-Kordesch and Kuhn, *Frauenkörper*, 159–90; Evans, *Feminist Movement*, 115–43; McGuire, "Activism, Intimacy and the Politics of Selfhood"; Dickinson, *Sex, Freedom, and Power*; Repp, *Reformers, Critics, and the Paths of German Modernity*; Matysik, *Reforming the Moral Subject*. An interesting case of international feminist interface on these issues is found in the correspondence of Flora Carnegie and Auguste Fickert, I.V. 112.330–341 (October 28, 1893–February 24, 1894), WSLB. While living in Vienna, Mrs. Carnegie, an activist and associate of Josephine Butler's, was shocked at the toleration of prostitution in Europe and even more so at the failure of the members of the Allgemeiner österreichischer Frauenverein to recognize the connection of the immorality of the sex trade to feminist concerns. Fickert instead openly recognized natural sexual needs and located the problem in how society chose to organize its satisfaction, leading to a break off of the correspondence. See also Hainisch (1901); and Karin J. Jusik in Good, Gradner, and Maynes, *Austrian Women*.

sexuality and social emancipation is complex and polyvalent. It is well known by now that many of the aforementioned feminists, such as Helene Stöcker and Oda Olberg, adopted eugenic discourse to an extreme degree, as did the Austrian Grete Meisel-Hess.[31] Conservative critics could easily tar both Forel's eugenic notion of the sexual question and the radical feminists who sought to emancipate feminine sexuality with the same brush; both were "modernists" and materialists who too easily discarded traditional Christian morality and order for the flesh.[32]

## Public Bodies

The figure of the prostitute—a paradigmatic "woman in public"—seems to have been a central trope in the stories of modern urban spectatorship.[33] Prostitutes were probably the most visible signifiers of the underworld that held so much revulsion and attraction; furthermore, they embodied an amalgamation of the eroticism, crime, degeneration, private lurid desire, and public lurid display that represented that world. The prostitute is an important figure—in their words, "type"—for the growing number of scientists interested in the organic causes of criminality. By the end of the century, Lombroso had established that the prostitute was the female counterpart to the criminal "type," indeed, that "prostitution is no more than the feminine manifestation of criminality; they are analogues, parallel phenomena that are melded into one another."[34] Like male criminals, prostitutes were degenerate types predisposed toward their vice by birth and recognizable by measurable physical abnormalities: malformed ears and limbs, small or buck teeth, ab-

---

31. See esp. Grete Meisel-Hess, *Die sexuelle Krise* (Jena: Diedrichs, 1909), but this "modern" position was foreshadowed in earlier work. Meisel-Hess was the feminist to first and most directly contest Weininger's *Geschlecht und Charakter* (Sex and character), and Weininger's work was informed by earlier writing by her. See Agatha Schwartz, *Shifting Voices: Feminist Thought and Women's Writing in Fin-de-Siècle Austria and Hungary* (Montreal: McGill-Queens University Press, 2008), 84–93.

32. See F. W. Foerster, *Sexualethik und Sexualpädagogik: Eine Auseinandersetzung mit den Modernen* (Kempten: Kösel, 1907).

33. Judith Walkowitz makes these remarks in relation to late-Victorian London: "No figure was more equivocal, yet more crucial to the structured public landscape of the male flaneur, than the woman in public. In public, women were presumed to be both endangered and a source of danger to those men who congregated in the street. . . . As symbols of conspicuous display or of lower-class and sexual disorder, they occupied a multivalent symbolic position in this imaginary landscape"; Walkowitz, *City of Dreadful Delight*, 21.

34. Lombroso, *La donna delinquente*.

normalities of nostrils, skeletal abnormalities, facial and body hair, tattoos.[35] As with homosexuality, a genre of studies of prostitution arose in the fin de siècle that sought to focus on the prostitute as a type of person—the "born prostitute"—rather than as a socioeconomic manifestation. As Willy Hell- pach put it in the volume of the Moderne Zeitfragen series focused on the subject, "prostitution is not principally an anthropological or an economic manifestation, but rather a sociopsychological and perhaps—perhaps!—a sociopathic one."[36] The repeated and emphasized "perhaps" points to the fact that the inquiry into the innate nature of the prostitute was itself the marker of sensationalism and provocation, and this is quite different from a cultur- ally shared assumption of essential difference. Yet the thesis of an innate and arguably pathological personality behind the social figure of the prostitute was one that appealed to liberal and socialist reformers as well as to cultural pessimists.[37]

Otto Weininger shared the view of prostitution as "a phenomenon grounded deeply and by necessity in the nature of a being," eschewing the suggestion that economic need play a significant role in the profession at all. If men might create circumstances for prostitution, it still can only come from the nature of the human woman: "What is not, cannot become."[38] The born prostitute is compelled to "coquette" herself, with or without remu- neration but indiscriminately, wantonly. Like Hellpach, he considered the accident of birth that would place one born prostitute into a brothel and leave another to flirt a bit too shamelessly in an aristocratic or high bourgeois salon. Weininger's insight was not that prostitutes are born and not made or even that such degenerate types populate all classes. What he saw that others did not was that this character of prostitution was characteristic of the entire culture Weininger and his prostitutes inhabited.

## Other Bodies

Dwelling on the state of civilization from the vantage of fin-de-siècle Austria in a quite different way than *Sex and Character*, Robert Musil's epic *Man without Qualities* is also hailed by *Lustmord*'s utopian bodies. The characters

35. Cf. Kisch, *Die sexuelle Untreue der Frau*, 74–81.

36. Hellpach, *Prostitution und Prostituierte*.

37. To Lombroso's own sometimes liberal, sometimes socialist leanings and those of oth- ers of his cohort in central Europe, we may add Hellpach himself, who would continue stud- ies in social psychology before becoming active in the center-left German Democratic Party (Deutsche Demokratische Partei [DDP]) in the Weimar Republic.

38. Weininger, *Geschlecht und Charakter*, 280–313.

of the novel each become absorbed with the fate of a certain Moosbrugger, a presumed insane Jack the Ripper figure whose brutal attacks on prostitutes oddly gain the sympathy of the public. Moosbrugger is described as a completely masculine figure, again through a description of the killer's physical body: he is a broad-shouldered carpenter, big and silent, with huge, honest, carpenter's hands, an embodiment of simple and manly justice: "his face expressed good-hearted strength and the will to do right." He is a slasher. The corpse of his most recent victim is described in detail by reporters, and then, in turn, by Musil: "a knife wound in the throat from the larynx to the back of the neck, also the two stab wounds in the breast that penetrated the heart, and the two in the back on the left side, and how both breasts were sliced through so that they could almost be lifted off."[39]

The man without qualities, Ulrich, is touched by the tale of Moosbrugger, who sees that "this was clearly madness, and just as clearly it was no more than a distortion of our own elements of being."[40] Ulrich pleads pardon for the criminal. The violent attack on woman, on her sex, the attempt to annihilate her—to defeminize her own body (the removal of the breasts) and to eliminate her from the social body as a whole—are associated with right, nobility, and goodness. Moosbrugger's insanity is construed as an exaggerated form of justice. But the most striking thing here is the way these violent murders and their executor are presented as archetypes of the present. The enthrallment with the Moosbrugger story touches even the female characters of the novel, as if the savage attack on womanhood and sexuality addressed a common despair. "If mankind could dream as a whole," Musil ventures, "that dream would be Moosbrugger."[41]

So the fin-de-siècle fascination with other people's bodies encompassed not merely a textual interest in the sexuality of the living body (represented by the German term *Leib*) nor to the intersection of individuality and collectivity suggested by the term corpus (*Körper*) but also to the public exposure and collective examination of the bodies of victims: the corpse (*Leiche*). As the century turned, news reports as well as other texts for public consumption grew less and less shy about the exhibition of such corpses. One example can be seen in the case of one Auguste Nerger, a Berlin prostitute whose body was discovered in the last year of the century. On public announcement posts around the city, the following police report could be read:

39. Musil, *MoE*, 68; *MwQ*, 67.
40. Musil, *MoE*, 76; *MwQ*, 76.
41. Musil, *MoE*, 76; *MwQ*, 77.

On Sunday, the 14th of this month, midday at 1:30, a roughly forty-year-old *female person* was found in the cellar of the building at 7 Schulzendorferstrasse: blonde, small stature, bloated face, *dead*. Her face was fully covered and dripping with blood which had flowed from her mouth and nose. While no external wounds could be identified, it is however possible that the unknown person came to a violent death, since a bloody cloth was found in her oral cavity. . . . Apparently the dead person, who still smelled strongly of alcohol when she was discovered, was a prostitute of the lowest order.[42]

Such reports were often introduced with warnings of the unseemly nature of the explicit details that were about to be revealed at the same time as readers were made to understand the importance of their attention to details if society were to be purged of such atrocities. And yet there is an unmistakable surplus in graphic descriptions like this one, a dwelling in details that could not help the public in their exhorted role as amateur crime investigators in the service of the police. These postings were reprinted and even embellished in respectable newspapers as well as broadsides. A follow-up story in the mainstream Berlin *Tägliche Rundschau* focused on the autopsy, along with explanations of how this physical evidence could lead investigators to conclusions:

Mrs. Nerger was *killed by having a rag stuffed in her mouth*, that is, asphyxiated. The rag was stuffed down so far and so firmly that the woman could not possibly have directed it there herself. As the autopsy also reveals, this was done with such force that several of her teeth were punched out. Beyond this, the victim had some scratches on her throat and chin.[43]

Readers were invited to follow the logic of the detectives: to think of the body as physical evidence, to take a rational and detached (as opposed to a voyeuristic and involved) regard toward the opened body, to process the physical evidence to uncover the truth. These gruesome displays of bodies must have served multiple functions: prurient as well as prudent, castigating as well as cathartic. They helped draw distinctions between bad and good public persons, dividing the masses into friends and foes of the community, and in doing so projected an idealized community of participating social citizens and custodians demarcated by the bodies of bad criminals and bad victims. These lessons and others could be extrapolated from other people's bodies, and so they remained a focus of news reports of the crime investigations.

---

42. Rep 30 Bln C Tit 198B Nr. 37, BBLHA. The notice was reprinted in the *Tägliche Rundschau* (Berlin), October 15, 1900, evening ed., p. B.

43. *Tägliche Rundschau* (Berlin), October 18, 1900; cf. *Lokal-Anzeiger*, October 16, 1900.

From the victims of femmes fatales to the revived blood libel, the fin de siècle was fairly littered with bodies like these, victims of violence that defined itself as senseless and nonetheless seemed pregnant with undisclosed meaning.[44] They were bodies of others, and still they constantly threatened to breach the protective walls of the self: representing mass murderers that reflected the masses, madnesses that revealed the logic of everyday existence, or, as in Weininger's own case, a strike against the feminine intruder to Western civilization that ended up with his own corpse in Beethoven's death chamber.

## Body Boundaries

This fixation on sexualized bodies, subjects and/or objects of violence, was in fact an intensely self-reflexive preoccupation, yet one that was accompanied by deepest ambivalence.[45] The scientific, philosophical, and popular narratives of sexual danger, to paraphrase Judith Walkowitz, both incited and fed on this ambivalence, which can be understood as a radical tension between exaggerated gestures of identification and disidentification. The focus on the sexualized and violated body abetted both of these tendencies in particular ways.

In the case of Auguste Nerger, the police's notice followed up its detailed account of the violated body with a description of the way she was clothed, identifying her for possible witnesses and at the same time marking her as a prostitute. The early report quoted above noted that the corpse reeked of alcohol, and once the victim's identity was known, her alcoholism was universally reported as an important element in the story. It marked her downfall, as one newspaper put it: "Since she was given to drink, her husband divorced her. The woman alas fell ever more into decline."[46] This decline was so complete that she was barely human anymore, a degenerate embodiment of Weininger's W principle, a mere body, only interesting as a sign of something else:

---

44. A catalog of many of these markers of an obsession is Dijkstra, *Idols of Perversity*.

45. The sexual study of bodies is no less self-reflexive than the fantasy of sexual murder. Note the eerily obverse complementarity of these two statements: "I kill myself," Weininger had written in an unpublished note long before the suicide, "in order not to have to kill another." British serial killer Dennis Nilsen declared "I was always killing myself, but it was always the bystander who died." See Weininger, *Über die letzten Dinge*; Seltzer, *Serial Killers*, 20.

46. "Ein unaufgeklärtes Verbrechen beschäftigt die Criminalpolizei," *Lokal-Anzeiger* (Berlin), October 10, 1900.

An old harlot of the lowest order, a female drunkard, insufficiently clothed, homeless, dead and still stinking of rotgut. And this wench made a living of vice! What sort of men could those have been, who lay with this venus vulgivata in abandoned cellars and desolate building sites! The wench leaves behind no gap in human society, no one will mourn her, no weeping family follows her casket.[47]

If this more sensational report offered the most explicit radical disidentification, the gesture of identifying the corpse of the prostitute as a firm boundary between voyeurs and victims was typical. And yet these gestures coexisted with other kinds of identification: if these horror shows from the darkest corners of the big city were merely worthless by-products of the age, earning our attention but not our sympathy, then why did they seem an emblem of our modernity in a way that the respectable life could not?

The news report from which the above description is taken is written in the style of a dramatic narrative of modern urban decadence and danger, comparing the dark venues of the new metropolis to the deepest eastern reaches of London, home of the Jack the Ripper murders.[48] The story was accompanied by a diagram mapping this urban underworld (see fig. 2), calling attention to the world of "pimps and prostitutes who have so often played the leading roles in the murder trials of Berlin."[49] This sort of voyeuristic reportage posited the underworld as exotic at the same time as it located it domestically; it was a world apart that had nested itself in the heart of the city and was the stage of present history. Murder, Foucault reminds us, is where history and crime intersect: it is the meeting place of those outside of the power structure and the popular appropriation of control, or of the everyday anonymous persons of the city and noteworthy personages.[50] The growing fascination with the violent and erotic underbelly of the everyday city manifested itself in an explosion of new popular genres related in style to this report, including crime novels, penny dreadfuls, and the half sociological, half prurient urban explorations released by Hans Ostwald in the series *Großstadt-Dokumente* (Documents of the metropolis) discussed in chapter 1.

47. "Mord? Ein mysterioser Vorfall in dunkelsten Berlin," *Berlin Morgenpost*, October 16, 1900.

48. For the historical conditions of the textual construction of sexually dangerous social space, the best source is still Walkowitz, *City of Dreadful Delight*; on Jack the Ripper, see 191–228. A relevant work on the relation of the imagination of turn-of-the-century urban space and newspapers is Fritzsche, *Reading Berlin 1900*.

49. "Mord? Ein mysterioser Vorfall in dunkelsten Berlin," *Berlin Morgenpost* (see fig. 2).

50. Michel Foucault, "Tales of Murder," in Foucault, *I, Pierre Rivière*, 205–6.

Already in the 1890s these texts were establishing the exotic danger of
the modern urban space at the same time as they suggested that this was
the emblematic space of modernity, not indeed so far at all from the position of the bourgeois reader. Paul Born's 1893 *Berlins dunkle Existenzen* (Berlin's dark existences) asserted in its cheeky chapter "The Latest from Berlin
Pimpdom" that

> As unbelievable as it sounds, even better elements make their way into the
> swarm of the outcast and help populate Berlin in this way. No level of status
> or education is lacking there; they are simply fallen existences who maintain
> the necessary requirements of life in this manner.[51]

Margarete Böhme's 1905 *Tagbuch einer Verlorenen* (Diary of a lost woman),
which presented the "true story" of good bourgeois daughter whom fate leads
to a life of moral destitution as a courtesan and to an early tragic death, is
another example of the way the "sexual underworld" was not depicted as
beyond an impassable boundary.[52] One interpretation of this narrative pattern is that it belonged to a larger apparatus of social control, policing the
boundary between respectability and delinquency in both its tendencies toward radical stigmatization of bad citizens as well as in its ominous warning
that even the respectable might wander astray.[53] Of course an interpretation
like this one contains a potentially valuable insight, but it also forecloses the
possibility of recovering the power and complexity of these cultural fantasies
by identifying them with the deliberate ideological program of empowered
interests. Another way to begin to look at the function of concomitant radical separation and suggested identification is through the lens of the liberal
master narrative: the possibility of falling into the violent and lurid realm of
the lowest of the low was the flip side of the new promise of upward mobil-
ity. Just as education and discipline might be capable of raising anyone to a
respectable station, no privilege of birth or breeding could alone protect one
from moral destitution. But there is a third mode of interpreting this narrative strategy: there is the possibility that these invitations to join the ranks of
the debauched offered a vicarious thrill, and that readers were as engaged in

51. Born, *Berlins dunkle Existenzen*, 99–100.

52. Böhme, *Tagebuch einer Verlorenen*. The term *sexual underworld* is Richard Evans's, whose
account of the text is relevant here. See Evans, *Tales from the German Underworld*, 166–212.

53. A discourse analysis of the textual construction of the criminal in criminology, journalism, and literature is offered by Marie-Christine Leps, who always keeps an eye toward the ways
in which coherent publics are constructed through the production of deviance. See Leps, *Apprehending the Criminal*.

identification as they were in disidentification when they read long serial narratives of fallen lives and dramatic deaths.

This brings us back to Weininger and the problem of the prostitute—or rather, the question of why, if femininity is the essence of modernity, must prostitution be the quintessence of woman. Weininger's text does not merely reproduce truisms of early eugenic thinking (thinking which continued, incidentally, for decades) but again offers a model for how an essentialism as plain as this does not at all insulate the nonprostitute from her disreputable counterpart. Weininger's chapter "Motherhood and Prostitution" seeks not only to establish that maternal or coquettish nature are inborn but that they are essentially two expressions of a single thing. He offers a characterology of the Absolute Mother and the Absolute Whore in which we can see their formal resemblance: the mother is completely dependent on the child, *any* child she can have, and on *any* man that can give her one. The whore is addicted to coitus as such, where again the man she uses is insignificant.

> In relation to the *individuality* of the sexual complement, *both* are actually *indifferent*. The hussy wants *to be copulated by everything*—that is why she also coquettes when she is *alone*, and *even at inanimate objects*, at every brook, at every tree. The mother wants to be continuously and in her whole body *impregnated* by all things.[54]

This radical immersion in the body, this flight from the spirit into motherhood and into coitus, is one and the same flight. "Physical life and physical death, both so mysteriously and deeply linked in coitus, are distributed through woman as mother and as prostitute."[55]

Of course, what is really suggested goes beyond the anxiety that the sexuality of woman exceeds the body of the prostitute and touches all women; it leaves no man untouched, it reproduces itself to overflowing, and it can be contained by no corporeal boundary. Indeed, the radical segregation between M and W principles is by definition problematic for just this reason. It is true that much of *Geschlecht und Charakter* seems to be devoted to separating things that might be thought of as akin, such as love (M) and sex (W), or union (W) and wholeness (M). It is also the case that in spite of his insistence that M and W are principles and not genders, Weininger continuously argues that no virtue identified with the M principle can ever be accessible to an individual woman; *man* and *woman* are terms as alien to each other as the ideal M and W. But if indeed "W is completely occupied and engaged by

54. Weininger, *Geschlecht und Charakter*, 307.
55. Ibid., 311.

sexuality, whereas M knows a dozen other things: fighting and playing, sociability and carousing, discussion and science, commerce and politics, religion and art,"[56] then how could she be responsible for the contemporary general state of culture? Unless, of course, the absolute discretion of masculine and feminine—unless all this polarity—does not represent an unbridgeable gulf, a pathological or salutary insulation, but instead performs a dialectical tension linking the two together inextricably.

## To the Best of His Knowledge; or, "I must confess"

Musil had at least one real-life Vienna killer in mind when he dreamed up Moosbrugger, and he quoted him directly. In 1910, Christian Voigt had murdered a prostitute, Josefine Peer, in Vienna's most famous amusement space, the Prater. Her body was wrecked by knife wounds so savage that the victim's breasts were virtually lifted from her body, as was the nose from her face; her clothing had been carefully sliced open in order to expose large areas of her body to further, repeated stabbing; signs of strangulation were also apparent. The 1910–11 case was a sensational one distinguished in several ways. Paired with two earlier sexually violent attacks on young girls—acts that had landed him in asylums on the basis of expert medical testimony—and then the murder of another after escaping from the asylum, it became apparent that this was a case of serial killing reminiscent of Jack the Ripper. Modern technologies of fingerprinting detection and photographic analysis were applied in the case as had not been known before.[57] Above all, the distinguishing feature of the Voigt case was the murderer himself, who by virtue of his own eloquent self-understanding and articulations demonstrated what could only be called charisma. In addition to the usual expert analysis and testimony, Voigt delivered to his audience (and to the posterity of the archive) love letters, autobiographical musings, a richly detailed, self-analytical confession, and a companion memoir text titled "How I Became a Criminal." Seen one way, all of these articulations of pathological subjectivity did more to fortify than to

56. Ibid., 112.

57. An excellent source for the case study of Voigt is Siegfried Türkel, "Der Lustmörder Christian Voigt: Ein kriminalistisch-psychiatrischer Beitrag zur Lehre vom Lustmorde," *Archiv für Kriminal-Anthropologie und Kriminalistik* 55, no. 1/2 (1913): 47–97. For the popular legacy of the case, see Reinhard Pohanka, *Räuber, Mörder, Kindsverderber: Eine Kriminalgeschichte Wiens* (Vienna: Jugend und Volk, 1991), 95–98. A recent dissertation on *Lustmord* has a detailed chapter on Voigt: Amber Marie Aragon-Yoshida, "*Lustmord* and the Loving Other: A History of Sexual Murder in Germany and Austria (1873–1932)" (PhD diss., Washington University, 2011), 79–169.

stymie the medical, juridical, and sensational pigeonholes for which he was destined. His own texts betrayed his autodidact familiarity with all of them; instead of carving a way out, they seemed to stake a ground for the pathological subject or to insist on the author's propriety of his own liminal territory. The bodies and texts left in the destructive Voigt's wake made a claim for his own authority over his own pathological subjectivity.

Like other suspects offering accounts of their actions to police and court investigators, Voigt's first confession demonstrates competence in the case study genre and even resembles a physician's case study notes. Prompts by investigators are only partially responsible for this resemblance. They include accounts of congenital illness:

> A son of my mother's sister . . . is insane and was in the Hildburghausen asylum. . . . My father was said to have been a drinker. I am not aware of other cases of alcoholism or insanity in my family, nor any case of syphilis.[58]

The accused distanced himself from these factors by appearing unsure of his father's certain alcoholism and not mentioning the insanity closest to him, his own brother. He quickly moves on to environmental factors:

> After my father's death I attended the three-grade trade school in Tettau for seven years. Already in this period I was not living at home but at various local farms, where I had to earn my keep caring for farm animals and the like.[59]

Voigt very curtly runs through his previous arrests for murder and assault, which he sees as separate from the current charges. Two days later, in Voigt's continuation of the confession, he describes in detail his encounter with the prostitute Josefine Peer, who according to this account pursues Voigt relentlessly in spite of his protestations and apparent distaste for her. Voigt is drinking, but not excessively; Peer elicits strong reactions in him, but these have a rational basis. In particular, he attributes his revulsion for prostitutes to a case of gonorrhea he contracted from a sexual encounter with one, a fact he had placed on record in his earlier confession. The key moment occurs in the Prater, where the woman has insisted on following him as he goes to rest, lays her body on him, at which point he notes a hard object in her pocket which she claims is a scissor but is in fact a kitchen knife:

> Since her extraordinary intrusiveness already seemed so sinister to me, I thought the knife was meant for me. These thoughts caused the feeling of

---

58. Vr 7601/1910, confession part 1, 20/8/10, *Fortsetzung*, WSL, Landesgericht für Strafsachen [LfS].

59. Ibid.

disgust for her that I had felt for her all along to rise to the level of rage, and
I stabbed her in the back with the knife I held in my hand. . . . I carried her a
little out of the way and then stabbed wildly at her. . . . How many times and
where I stabbed her I could not say. I did not experience the slightest sexual
excitement in the act.[60]

In these key descriptions of the moment of crime, Voigt attempted to establish apparently contradictory things: on the one hand, a rational defense
for the crime, or the sense that a rational individual in his particular circumstance might have felt threatened by Peer; a moment of loss of reason, rage,
frenzy; and finally, an absence of both criminal intent as well as underlying
sadistic desire. He is not insane, it was not a *Lustmord*; the almost reasonable
feeling of threat from a figure of sexual danger converts in a moment to an
absence of consciousness (not epilepsy, he insists), a momentary loss of criminal responsibility. Voigt's confession reads as a condensation of study notes
of Krafft-Ebing's sexological definition of *Lustmord* and sadism, forensic psychology's definitions of trance states, and the legal debates on *Zurechnung*; its
paradoxes are those of the experts.

The experts themselves were somewhat confused by the Voigt case in
spite of the fact that the series of crimes clearly indicated pathology. Voigt
had twice before been committed to asylums in the aftermath of attempted
and successful rape and murder. But what was the nature of the pathology?
Several physicians were certain that the acts were driven by sadistic impulse
(*sadistische Antriebe*), acknowledging however that little was known to science of the precise mechanisms of *Lustmord*; other expert examination and
testimony pointed a finger to epilepsy and epileptic trance states (*epileptische
Dämmerzustände*). The latter accounts were confused because of disagreement about whether Voigt was or had ever been an epileptic, although this
diagnosis was noted in medical records. The suspect admitted that he had
feigned epilepsy to be released from military service; seizures while in custody
and in the asylum had been observed, though the question of whether these
had been simulated remained open. More significant was the possibility of
days-long trance-like states that, it was assumed, may have been combined effects of an underlying seizure disorder exacerbated by alcoholism. Indeed the
diagnosis was supported by expert testimony of one of the leading experts on
epilepsy in the world, the University of Jena neurologist Otto Binswanger.[61]

The experts vacillated between classification of the pathological crimi-

60. Vr 7601/1910, Continuation of confession 22/8/10, WSL LfS.
61. Vr 7601/1910, Befund und Gutachten, WSL LfS.

nal as epileptic or sadist (or the most extreme if also underresearched form of sadistic pathology, the *Lustmörder*). Voigt, in turn, cautiously subverted each of these diagnoses in order to leave standing only his own preferred self-diagnosis, an excusable crime of affect: a momentary "paroxysm of rage in full consciousness of the act" due to "irresistible revulsion for trollops." The police noted that this diagnosis would be the one he hoped would land him somewhere other than in lifelong custody in the asylum, which he knew well, or a sudden end on the gallows. But observers of the criminal subject noted above all another tic. Voigt's interest in the determination of his diagnosis itself had the character of an obsession. In declaring himself fundamentally untouched by epilepsy and alcoholism, but a free person capable of standing responsible for his own actions, Voigt displayed a fixation on the truth:

> V[oigt], with the most overt smugness talking himself into the role of an apostle of truth, finally asks: why should I purchase my life with a lie? Upon pertinent questioning V. explains that his fanatic love of the truth dates back to his residence in the Bayreuth asylum, where he had read so much, and thereby become a better person.[62]

The self-righteousness with which Voigt possessed his own truth was a focus of the representation of his self-defense in court and must have been striking to many a reader. Among them was Robert Musil, who seized on this element of the accused's character and representation for his Moosbrugger figure. If Voigt was a perfect criminal in terms of the aesthetic purity of his crime, he was a purist when it came to his will to truth. At the same time, the files reveal that Voigt made masterful and perhaps occasionally reckless use of the lie: his simulation of epilepsy before military authorities and in the asylum, his omission of his brother's insanity and his own heavy alcohol use in his case history of himself, not to mention the series of unlikely facts in his account of the Peer murder. Had he really convinced himself, and had he in fact persuaded many onlookers to admire his uncompromising passion for truth and right? What was it about this passion for truth that made so much sense in relation to this particular subject?

The investigation including Voigt's autobiographical statement confirmed that it was in the period of his internment, under the tutelage of a Dr. Kolb in the asylum at Bayreuth, that he began his rigorous self-education and displayed what was universally recognized as a superior intelligence for a person of his social place. The high value of the civilizing process plays a central role in another document by Voigt's hand that was an object of curiosity and

62. Ibid.

puzzlement by all kinds of experts, the autobiographical "How I Became a Criminal."[63] Neither confession nor case history nor criminal memoir, the document follows the lines of the Bildungsroman, the famed German novel of masculine self-cultivation. The attractiveness of the serial killer laid in this charismatic combination of articulate and sanctimonious self-defense; the intense violence of the crimes themselves, seemingly uncontaminated by base motive; and perhaps not least the sleight of hand through which the accused was ever ready to become the accuser of a system of knowledge and discipline that had no more moral authority than he did. The question offering its own name to this document of self-empowerment is the one of forensic psychiatry and of the detective: what is the origin of the criminal self? Voigt paid tribute to the two disciplines in his opening: "I believe to be able to answer this question today without metaphysics, basing my argument on readings of scientific literature and the precise observation of the facts." The first-person voice would not retreat from the document even as the author Voigt tried in other ways to reproduce the objective voice of the research literature on criminal responsibility:

> In my opinion there are two main categories of criminals. To the first belong those that conduct an evil act with intent and deliberation; to the other, those in whom advanced thought and reflections are lacking. In terms of penal law the re- and irresponsible. The irresponsible criminal must not always, but may be burdened with a defect, be it on hereditary basis, a temporary, or a perpetual mental disturbance. . . . Cultivation and intelligence are not always the privilege of the propertied class, although affluence may have an influence on these.[64]

The shift within the same paragraph from the discussion of criminal natures to innate mental ability would be atypical of the sort of theoretical tract Voigt was mimicking, although, as we have seen, the linkage between deep criminality and genius was a recurring theme in criminology and was not unknown in popular culture. Voigt was next interested in establishing that one's natural mental gifts may be innate and independent of station, and without the tools to develop such gifts, a talented individual could be forced to let his fertile mind go fallow and even become for all intents and purposes mentally deficient. Such a person's brain mass is virtually inactive, and the works to which it is put are of instinctive nature free of reflection, automatic

---

63. Composed between Voigt's first and second murders, the document was published in full in 1913 in Türkel, "Der Lustmörder Christian Voigt."

64. Türkel, "Der Lustmörder Christian Voigt," 57–58.

or routine acts. "I belonged to this species of individual." From this assertion, Voigt moved to his family history to show how trauma and disadvan-
tage conspired to keep his mental gifts latent for a while. The perspicacity of
the defendant would be noted by expert witnesses and was a detail picked up
on in all news reports.[65] On the one hand, this hyperdeveloped intelligence
could be seen by experts and other onlookers to be an extreme manifestation
linked to the lack of ethical consciousness; on the other hand, the rational
subjectivity stressed by these accounts and by the criminal subject himself
seemed at odds with the inherent senselessness of the shocking violence of
the crimes.

This melding of the violently irrational coupled with—even reflecting—a
will to truth and to justice is what Musil's Moosbrugger borrows from Voigt.
Yes, both are carpenters, both are serial killers, both prey on prostitutes, even
to the details of the condition of the latest victim's corpse. Moosbrugger follows the 1910 model more than he does Weimar murderer Fritz Haarmann,
whose case informed Musil as the latter was drafting the novel in 1924.[66] This
was the kernel of the elusive and ecstatic "other condition" where oppositional sides of existence unite and also demolish one another. The literary
moments where Ulrich becomes aware of this secret stratum of existence are
linked to sex (male/female or self/other); colliding in Voigt's and in Moosbrugger's confessions are the ratioïd and nonratioïd regions of life; ethics and
aesthetics; or what Musil's translator has called "precision and soul."

The public words of the condemned were those that stuck in Musil's mind
and which he adopted wholesale to be Moosbrugger's. After being convicted
and sentenced to death, both the historical murderer and the fictional character stand and declare shakingly, "I am satisfied with the sentence of the
court, even though I must confess to you that you have passed judgment on a
lunatic." Musil's first commentary on this compellingly puzzling declaration
comes through the thoughts of Ulrich, who receives it breathlessly as he sits
in the courtroom. Ulrich's thought, mentioned in the discussion above, reads
in full in the latest translation

> This was clearly madness, and just as clearly it was no more than a distortion
> of our own elements of being. Cracked and obscure it was; it somehow oc-

65. Cf. the reports in the *Neue Freie Presse*, October 22, 1911, pp. 17–18, and *Die Neue Zeitung*
4, no. 291 (October 22, 1911): 7–8.

66. This is clear from a perusal of materials in Musil, *Der literarische Nachlass.* See also
Karl Corino, "Zerstückelt und Durchdunkelt. Der Sexualmörder Moosbrugger im 'Mann ohne
Eigenschaften' und sein Modell," *Musil-Forum* 10 (1984): 105–19, and A. Höcker, *Epistemologie
des Extremen*, 189–203.

curred to Ulrich that if mankind could dream as a whole, that dream would be Moosbrugger.[67]

What is the referent of "this," what was the clear madness on display ("*Das* war deutlich Irrsinn")? Was it the case itself, the hyperrational legal process of an irrational murderer? Was it the horrific crimes of the accused? Or did it refer to the statement of the condemned man? These represent after all the three registers that we have been tracing—that of juridico-medical expertise, the sensational level of the display of horrific crimes, and, finally, the dramatically flamboyant, subjective expression of the criminal person. Ulrich sees somehow a distorted image of "our" own elements of being: cracked— "zerstückt," more "hacked" into pieces, like a victim's body—obscured, our lives are seen through a broken glass, darkly. The "dream" of Moosbrugger in this translation is dreamt by mankind "as a whole" and is hence a place where the broken is healed, the pieces brought together into a totality.

What was Voigt's intended meaning when he uttered this same, strange phrase? His was a sentence turned back from the condemned onto the court—the whole apparatus to which the court belonged, from investigators to medical experts to the magistrate as he passed sentence. It is of course not unheard of for an outraged defendant to turn the tables on his accusers, but consider the means he claims in order to do so: *confession.* He is satisfied with the sentence, even as he *is impelled to confess* ("wenn ich Ihnen auch gestehen muß") that his condemnation is itself criminal, it condemns a madman. To make this judgment on such a judgment, he must assign himself the role of self-appointed rather than court-appointed expert, declaring the defendant incompetent. If Voigt's bearing throughout the investigation and trial betrayed a coy hyperawareness of the conditions of *Zurechnung*, this dramatic flourish condensed certain paradoxes in a concentrated way. Unlike Moosbrugger, Voigt did not consider himself an arm of the terrible righteousness of God or of a transcendent moral order violated by everyday life. He understood the resounding tones of his trial, his crimes, and his confessions as the serial, distorted iterations within an echo chamber that they were. His condemnation, unjust as it was, was his truth.

### Endings and Beginnings

In light of all of these ways of talking about one's own civilization, it is arguably not unreasonable to characterize the central European fin de siècle

67. Musil, *MwQ*, 76–77.

in terms of decadence (or dystopia) rather than utopianism (or renewal). Clearly, the two may be apt characterizations of the same moment seen from different perspectives—one oriented toward a past era of enlightened optimism and progressive ideology that seemed to be winding down, and another of the promise of a new way of experiencing life that was not yet completely formed. So, decadence. But Robert Musil, an actor on the fin-de-siècle scene as well as one of its earliest and most articulate critics, had this to say:

> Recall one fact above all: around 1900 (the last spiritual and intellectual movement of great vital force in Germany), people believed in the future. In a social future. In a new art. The fin de siècle gave the period a veneer of morbidity and decadence: but both these negative definitions were only contingent expressions for the will to be different, to do things differently from the way people had done them in the past.[68]

While Musil offered this corrective in 1923, it was not much heeded (even once it was published after his death). In notes, Musil associates the fin de siècle with "truth, world building." Decadence or morbidity is a form of strength, a "specific form of thinking the world differently," an "opposition to normality." The attempt to remake humanity and the world goes astray after the fin de siècle, according to Musil. The emergence of the idea of redemption—the soul-oriented, religious outlook we associate with expressionism and the spiritual revolution in the half decade before the First World War—is "resignation," Musil tells us, "The synthesis Soul-Rationality was aborted. It leads in a direct line to the War."[69] But it could have led elsewhere.

The "aestheticist" moment as harbinger of a new social future? The revolution of 1918/19, perhaps, or the 1930s, the postwar period, maybe—but a utopian fin de siècle? As though one can forget that the end of a century is also the beginning of one. But—and here is a key and controversial point—did the actors themselves remember this?[70]

To begin to answer this, one might return to the nadir of Otto Weininger's

---

68. Robert Musil, "Der deutsche Mensch als Symptom" [1923], in Musil, *Gesammelte Werke*, 8:1353–1400 (see 1353). Translations adapted from Musil, *Precision and Soul*, 150–92.

69. Musil, *Der literarische Nachlass*, Seite VII/10/14, Kennung An 11.

70. Hermann Bahr already did, in 1890: "It may be that we are at the end, at the death of exhausted mankind and that we are experiencing mankind's last spasms. It may be that we are at the beginning, at the birth of a new humanity and that we are experiencing only the avalanches of spring. We are rising to the divine or plunging, plunging into night or destruction—but there is no standing still." Hermann Bahr, "Die Moderne," *Moderne Dichtung* (January 1, 1890), translated in Pynsent, *Decadence and Innovation*, 156.

narrative of Western civilization's decline, the much quoted ending—or near ending—of his infamous chapter, "Judaism." "Our time," Weininger indeed declared, is "not only the most Jewish, but also the most feminine of all times," and in a seventeen-line, single-sentence paragraph he laid out all of the ways in which modernity's art, culture, politics, ethics, economics, commerce, historical thought, philosophy, and scholarship had been utterly feminized and lost all cultural value. But, Weininger continued,

> in response to this new Judaism, a new Christianity is drawing into the light; humanity tarries, awaiting the new founder of religion, and the struggle demands a decision as in the Year One. Between Judaism and Christianity, between commerce and culture, between woman and man, between genus and personality, between valuelessness and value, between the earthly and higher life, between nothingness and divinity, humanity must choose.[71]

The new Christianity Weininger imagined was certainly based in antisemitism and misogyny, at least "woman" and "Jew" are the signs under which he places materialism and nihilism and against which the new world will come into being. But utopia is to be erected *against* this edifice; the formless will take form, dialectically, from *between* these two worlds. To put it another way, it is only from the ground of this nothingness, this absent subjectivity, that a new masculine subject will arise.[72] The messianic figure whom humanity awaits, as in the emergence of the "original" Christianity, will emerge from this Jewish (and feminine) world. Of course it is Weininger himself, and the holy text must be *Geschlecht und Charakter*.

As Klaus Theweleit so amply showed with regard to the right-wing Free Corps during the Weimar Republic, violent fantasies of "swarms of the outcast," mobs flooding beyond their bounds of containment, were intensely linked to a fear and hatred of women.[73] The prehistory of his provocative picture of a radically violent misogynist imaginary, however, has surprisingly not followed his 1977–78 volumes *Male Fantasies*, in spite of their broad reception. But what if the fantasies of that vanguard of Nazism—the images of feminized masses flowing blood and making bleed, the dread of women's bodies and sexuality, the panic before the prospect of being engulfed, swallowed up, annihilated—what if the history of those male fantasies did not begin with the violence of World War I, of which the Free Corps were in

71. Weininger, *Geschlecht und Charakter*, 441.

72. This is related to Slavoj Žižek's argument in his essay on Weininger, "Otto Weininger; or, 'Woman Doesn't Exist,'" in Žižek, *Metastases of Enjoyment*.

73. Theweleit, *Männerphantasien*, esp. vol. 1.

part veterans? What if the war were no more a cause than an effect of such fantasies?

## The Other Condition

By some reckoning, the unmaking of the self—the fantasy of self-annihilation—belongs to an imaginary of radical violence but also of sexuality. "Sexuality is not that which is constitutive of the self or the subject but the moment of its undoing. The mystery of sexuality lies in its inherent violence and cruelty," to paraphrase a certain psychoanalytic perspective on the relation of self to sexuality.[74] Historian Carolyn Dean, focusing on interwar France, has offered some of the richest analyses of such views in the European interwar period.[75] While some observers of the interbellum interweaving of sexuality and violence, such as Dean, acknowledge sources of such fantasies in the fin de siècle, most Weimar studies succumb to the temptation to attribute them—to the "damaged male bodies" of the First World War. But there is strong evidence to date this mapping of violence, sexuality, and loss of self earlier; and if the fin de siècle variant of this discourse is not quite as bloody as that of the 1920s, it may be that it is more *utopian*.

To see how that is the case, we turn again to Musil, who shares with Weininger (again) a universe dependent on polarities. We have seen some ways in which Weininger seems to have made an impact on Musil's epic novel, and there are many more ways in which this could be shown. Yet Musil is more explicit about the *mediation* of the two gendered spheres, which is hidden beneath the surface of Weininger's text. In the *Man without Qualities* no less than in his earlier work, and especially in his notes and essayistic work from before the war, Musil dwells on the painful irreconcilability between sensuality and reason, the passions and the intellect, artistic and scientific sensibilities, which spheres he identifies with the two genders in familiar ways. The task of philosophy, he states at several points, is to overcome this division.

---

74. Stewart-Steinberg, *Sublime Surrender*, 7. Stewart-Steinberg is here paraphrasing Leo Bersani's position in Bersani, *Freudian Body*, but similar assertions can be found in Jacques Lacan, Slavoj Žižek, Kaja Silverman, and others.

75. Dean, *Self and Its Pleasures*; see also *Frail Social Body* and *Sexuality and Modern Western Culture*. Dean's position is nuanced, acknowledging that the forms of sexually violent fantasy all prefigure the war while also thinking of the "increasingly pervasive and fundamental link between sexuality and violence [as] partly a consequence of the war" (*Frail Social Body*, 109). Suzanne Stewart-Steinberg, who shares an interest in the German-Austrian fin de siècle, also stresses that and explores how these paradigms prefigure the war to which they are so often attributed. See Stewart-Steinberg, *Sublime Surrender*.

This problem may be seen as the core of his early novellas, called "Unions," the bizarre homosexual subtext of the 1910 novel *Young Törless*, and especially his essay work. The celebrated central European anxiety about modern fragmentation and desire for completeness takes form in Musil's writings as a longing for a synthesis of feminine and masculine, aesthetics and mathematics, possibility and reality, mysticism and reason—he seeks a "daylight mysticism."[76] The myth of the incestuous Isis and Osiris was the subject of his only poem, and it can be said to make up the symbolic substructure of the second and projected third volumes of the *Man without Qualities*, where Ulrich's intense relationship with his sister Agatha develops.

To this series of dialectical pairings, Musil adds the tension between an everyday relation to experience and the heightened relation to experience characteristic of art, religion, and erotic excitement, which he called "the other condition" and described as "a deeper embedding of thought in the emotional sphere." At least one critic has pointed out that Moosbrugger's dreamlike insanity is presented in the novel as an instance of this ecstatic condition.[77]

The Moosbrugger story may seem to make obvious the place of violence in Musil's polar universe, but that is deceptive. In fact the most consistent use of the word *violence* in Musil's voluminous notes and other unpublished writings is not in the realm of the criminal dreamworld or the cultural imaginary of the fin de siècle but in its counterpole, "reality." In his notes as he was writing *The Man without Qualities*, he defined this term *reality* in opposition to the "essayism" of Ulrich, the protagonist. "The world directs itself not toward tomorrow, but toward today." It is not utopian and "cannot waver, but must be firm"; it "fears going out of joint." This description, along with a dozen scattered throughout his notes that parallel it, identifies the creative, wavering, flexible world not only of dreams but of thought (*Denkwelt*) in opposition to this, which he calls the "world of violence" (*Gewaltwelt*).[78]

## The Utopian Criminal and the Return to the Self

There are several ways in which we might identify the cultural fascination with the compulsive murderer in this period as a bridge spanning the scientific apparatus of "mathematical man" and the artistic and sensuous world of

76. Cf. Appignanesi, *Femininity and the Creative Imagination*.

77. Karthaus, *Der andere Zustand*, 62–73.

78. Musil, *Der literarische Nachlass*, Seite I/1/10, Kennung IE 7; I/I/13, IE 8; I/1/49, *IE 22; II/1/153, *II Bd. III Kapitelgruppe; II/4/26, AE 6; VII/3/34, 73/74, and 74; VII/3/69.

instinctual abandon. The figure has a special place in criminal anthropology, as indicated above. Because criminality as such is essentially a problem of eugenics, crimes involving robbery or theft for profit, organized or informal criminal networks, violence between parties known to each other, and so on, are laden with motives, causes, and meanings apart from the problem of the criminal personality or type. The compulsive murderer, in contrast, has no object in view beyond the crime itself; he is a loner, a crime artist, ingenious in his methods as he is brutal. As these features of the criminal personality became formed in the central European imaginary, the compulsive murderer became a kind of legend. It was not merely urban panic that fed the sensationalist serial reports of such killings in the press but a fascination that also created a market for crime fiction and other genres. He was a kind of hero, whether his victims were marked as debauched prostitutes or as innocent children; he was a deranged but heroic genius with extraordinary powers to outwit criminal detection forces, whose arsenal of forensic technology was constantly being perfected and yet always seemed a step behind. And this is the paradox of the compulsive murderer. For if he is, above all, a degenerate crawling up from the slime of the gene pool, than how could he be so successful against the collective participation of police and public in his apprehension?

Lombroso's chief claims about the criminal are two. First of all, he is a criminal constitutionally; his criminality is inborn and manifests itself in signs written on the body (most famously cranial shape, but also proportions of all facial and corporeal features and acquired characteristics such as tattoos). Second, what all of these signs tell the scientist is not only that this is a criminal body but that the criminal is *atavistic*, a throwback, genetic refuse from a precivilized or even animal past.[79] This is why, Lombroso reasoned, the population of criminal districts so obviously resembled savages, from their facial features and posture down to their painted bodies. As such, criminals of all kinds possess much weaker intelligence than upstanding citizens. The influential Saxon jurist and criminal psychologist Erich Wulffen put it this way:

> The criminal displays a distinct mental inferiority . . . and in sensory life an overpowering emergence of sensual, egotistical, base drives, passions, affects, dispositions, and moods. . . . Thus in intellect: deficiency of ethical feelings.[80]

The criminal psychologist is interested in mapping the criminal mind along the lines of the brain generally, as he understands it, namely in terms of

79. Lombroso, *L'uomo delinquente.*
80. Wulffen, *Gauner- und Verbrechertypen,* 8.

a division of sensory and rational functions, instinct and understanding, corresponding to criminal soul and criminal intelligence, respectively. Whether we identify this division as similar to Freud's id and superego or simply as an enlightenment opposition of instinct and reason, it is not unfamiliar. And herein lies the secret of the true criminal's wiliness. Just as Goethe was driven to write poetry in the middle of the night, as though nature herself were driving the hand of the author in his sleeplike state, the true criminal is intoxicated by his own crime; he is an "instinctual" criminal who falls into a sort of "trance state," which is the venue where the crime becomes possible. His actions are not the products of his intellect but rather of this psychic condition. Should the trance be interrupted, as by an unexpected intervention, then he becomes "insecure, awkward, careless, foolish, and just clumsy."[81] Indeed, it is only the flawed criminal reason that trips up the true "instinctual murderer," lifted to a higher plane of consciousness precisely through this immersion in a savage, dreamlike state lost to the overcivilized order of modern society. Like the artist, his destructive hand is guided as though by nature herself.[82]

Erich Wulffen devoted a full-length study to the sexual criminal that ran to several editions. He continued to write after the catastrophe of the First World War, turning his attention to art in his study *Sexualspiegel von Kunst und Verbrechen* (Sexual mirrors of art and crime). "Sexuality and crime," he writes, "extend themselves in our present ever more powerfully and knock threateningly on the thresholds of family, society, and state." The foundations of our civilization are shaken by these unshakable, anticivilizational instincts. And yet, has this civilization been erected in spite of these antediluvian forces? For in the same text Wulffen notes how history shows that

> sexuality and crime are and have always been the most powerful, necessary, driving forces of the whole of human civilization; it is first sexuality that warrants the highest and finest spirit, and without that which we call crime, no virtue, no purification, no advance would be possible. . . . It is a matter of law deeply set in the primal polarity of all creation, grounded in the organic nature of humankind. . . . We recognize and grasp how all spiritual culture of humanity has built itself on the eternal struggle of good and the virtuous with sexuality and crime, how this cyclical alternation created the mythology of all peoples, founded their religions, their wisdom and philosophy, and finally grounded all their arts and brought them to blossom.[83]

81. Ibid., 15.

82. The dialectic of nature and civilization in the "wild work" of the serial killer is analyzed in the contemporary American context in the cultural studies work by Mark Seltzer, *Serial Killers* (see esp. 79–81).

83. Wulffen, *Sexualspiegel*, vii–viii.

FIGURE 26. Otto Weininger's death portrait.

The murderous strike against sexuality and the social control of "instinctual" crime are both, then, strikes against the very origins of civilization; they are forms of violence against the violent origins of the rational subject. This circularity exposes the logic of the public fascination with the excesses of the outcast in the new big city's darkest corners as well as the new social sciences' turn to the sexual criminal as a privileged subject. These fantasies of sexualized violence were not, or at least not merely, ways to imagine a social space cleared of marginal elements but were means of self-exploration as well; they may also have been ways of beginning to imagine the euphoria of self-destruction. When the locked door was forced open, no one could doubt that Weininger's violent diatribe against woman had led all along to his own corpse.

5

# Blood Lies: The Truth about Modern Ritual Murder Accusations and Defenses

In the months following the February 1840 disappearance of a Sardinian Capuchin monk and his servant in Damascus (figs. 27, 28), rumors spread locally and abroad that the two unfortunates had fallen prey to the ancient Jewish practice of human sacrifice. These rumors took the form of the sensation as we have been discussing it. As historian Jonathan Frankel put it in his accessible volume on the "Damascus affair," Europe was engulfed by an explosion of

> polemics, fantastic theories, and strange projects. The most respected newspapers in England, France, and Germany devoted it endless space. Did the Jews really practice ritual murder and human sacrifice? Perhaps indeed they did. What kind of people was this which had survived almost two thousand years in exile, expelled from one country to another, dispersed across the globe? Was it possessed of a special destiny, providential or sinister, part of some divine pattern or satanic mystery?[1]

The Damascus case presaged and surely also prepared the ground for the sensational reemergence of the ritual murder accusation in Europe itself, specifically central Europe, beginning more than forty years after the condemnation of the Jewish community in Damascus for the murder of Father Thomas and the servant Ibrihim Amara.[2] A current historiographical cliché has it that the Jews, in the era surrounding and following their formal emancipation, were firmly associated with the modern; contemporary central European antisemitism, in this view, is clearly linked to ambivalence with modernity.

1. Frankel, *Damascus Affair*, 1.
2. See, e.g., Florence, *Blood Libel*.

FIGURE 27. Marble Commemorative Plaque, Fransciscan Church, Bab Touma.

If this is true, then what are we to make of the modern reemergence of the blood libel? Why were Jews and Jewishness depicted in their essence not only as premodern but as primordial, as ancient rather than modern, as barbaric and precivilized? In the Damascus example, the discourse can be said to have been enabled by a double displacement: it was ostensibly not a story about modern Jews but about an ancient and arcane Jewish practice that had been either retained or revived in an oriental setting. That distancing mechanism was violated, though, as later accusations and subsequent sensational cases emerged in substantial numbers in the German and Habsburg empires. The affair at Tiszaeszlár (1882) in Eastern Hungary was a particularly important

FIGURE 28. Father Thomas and Ibrahim Amara.

one, but on inspection it becomes clear that this and a few other highly publicized cases were part of a proliferation.[3] An early case in Enniger (Westphalia)
in 1873 would seem to suggest that the revival of the blood libel in central Eu-

---

3. Other cases include Lutscha (Galicia) in 1881, Polná (Bohemia) in 1899; more in other
German imperial towns, such as Breslau (1889), Xanten (1892), Kempen (Lower Rhine, 1893);
Berent (West Prussia), Burgkunstadt (Upper Franconia), and Ulm (all in 1894); Berlin in 1896;
as many as five in 1898 in East Prussia, Lower Rhine; and Silesia, Oderberg (Western Pomerania)
in 1900. Outside of these empires, but influencing the ritual murder discourse in them, was a
highly publicized case on the island of Corfu in 1891.

rope began a full decade before Tiszaeszlár, but the content and development of the case shares little with those discussed in this chapter. The archival materials themselves, and even arguably sensational newspaper reports, differ in character, and in some senses the case more closely resembles those discussed in the previous chapter yet in a time when the discourse of the *Lustmörder* was not yet articulated.[4] In fact, the number of incidents from the 1880s on is in the high dozens, accruing even more rapidly after the irregular and atypical but highly publicized case at Xanten in the last decade of the century.

Contemporary historical writing has not neglected these cases, although it has by and large focused on them as indicators of an increasingly efficient political antisemitism and the social prejudice accompanying it.[5] With their heavy concentration in central Europe, and coming as they did just on the eve of formal Jewish emancipation, it was and remains convenient to see the revival of the blood libel as the defensive reaction of a Christian society resisting social modernization represented by Jewish integration. The fantasy of this minority community as an incontrovertibly and dangerously alien and furtively savage entity, in this view, reinforced an impassable boundary between the European self and its perennial internal other that Christian acceptance and Jewish assimilation seemed to be conspiring to dissolve. Contemporaries as well as later historians have also been aware that the peculiar instrument of political antisemitism as it had developed in central Europe was an essential

4. See Sandra Lichter, ed., *Die Ermordung der Elisabeth Schütte zu Enniger betreffend* (Osnabrück: printed by author, 2010). The volume contains the full file of the case from Staatsarchiv Münster and many other relevant rare published and archival material.

5. Some work has also tried to uncover the anthropological meanings of such accusations; recently two microhistorical studies of a single, previously underresearched case track the interaction of local and larger forces in the events unfolding in the West Prussian town of Konitz (now Chojnice, Poland, discussed below): Smith, *Butcher's Tale*; Christoph Nonn, *Eine Stadt such einen Mörder: Gerücht, Gewalt und Antisemitismus im Kaiserreich* (Göttingen: Vandenhoeck und Ruprecht, 2002). A long-awaited study of the modern central European phenomenon tout court by Hillel J. Kieval is forthcoming; valuable articles relating to this project have been published, the most relevant to this argument being "Representation and Knowledge," "Importance of Place," "Neighbors, Strangers, Readers," "Ritual Murder (Modern)," "Blood Libels and Host Desecration Accusations," *YIVO Encyclopedia of East European Jewish Life*, and particularly the most recently published "The Rules of the Game: Forensic Medicine and the Language of Science in the Structuring of Modern Ritual Murder Trials," special issue, *Jewish History* 26, no. 3/4 (2012): 287–307, discussed below. See also Robert Weinberg, "The Blood Libel in Eastern Europe," special issue, *Jewish History* 26, no. 3/4 (2012): 275–285. Additional sources will be indicated throughout the chapter. Beyond the recent books by David Biale and Kenneth Stow cited below, the thinking about blood as a historical category in this chapter is indebted to Bynum, *Wonderful Blood*—in spite of its general avoidance of the ritual murder charges in its own period, and Anidjar, "Lines of Blood."

factor in the expansion of folk rumor to national sensation; the continuity of Jewish minorities in these areas, as opposed to cultures where they had been expelled or excluded for a time, guaranteed the survival of folk memory of the high medieval superstition. The rationalization argument closest to the discussion here is represented in Hillel Kieval's article on the use of forensic science in the modern ritual murder trials, arguing that the strictures of enlightened modernity constituted the "rules of the game," structuring the trials from beginning to end, and suppressing anything resembling primitive folk superstition. Certainly, all of these commonsense rationalizations of the apparently irrational outburst of the fantasy of Jewish abduction and sacrifice of human beings have validity. Notwithstanding, a different light is cast on these events and their meaning when they are looked at as another facet of the broader phenomena: European sensational culture generally and narratives of sexual danger and violence in particular; the status of evidence and the competition of various modes of expert and popular knowledge; and finally, shifting self-understandings of European "enlightenment," "civilization," or "modernity." It is these interpretive contexts that allow the ritual murder complex—including violent fantasies about Jewish individuals and communities as well as the defense of these—to be understood as a single cultural project.

## Rumblings Before the Storm

The romantic and Catholic scholar Johann Joseph von Görres does not neglect the practice in his nearly 1,000-page opus on Christian mysticism in spite of the fact that European accusations, on his account, had ceased since the mid-seventeenth century (although the Damascus affair could be seen as a recent background to his discussion).[6] He places the accusations squarely in the early modern period: he notes an alarming number of child murders during the period between the expulsion of Jews from France under Charles VI and the calamitous 1492 Spanish expulsion, the reason for which is given by the author to be the Jews' crucifixion of a kidnapped child. He describes in detail the martyrdom of the young Simon of Trent in 1472, which would remain the emblematic case of the ritual murder accusation and the example often dwelled on by believers in the practice up to the present day. While government and ecclesiastical decrees peppered throughout history had denied the veracity of the blood libel, Görres narrates his string of cases without pausing to question "the truth" about ritual murder, that

6. Görres, *Die christliche Mystik*, vol. 4, pt. 2, pp. 50–73.

is, whether ritual murder was a Jewish religious practice or an anti-Jewish rumor. Rather, the truth he is trying to get at does not seem to lie with the question of whether it was the Jewish communities or their Christian host communities that were murderous, bloody, and vengeful. Notable, too, in this description is the evaluation of the Jewish murder of Christian children as both cause of and retributive response to Christian persecution. What is more, in spite of the focus of Görres's book on Christian mysticism and the Jewish influences on it, the word *ritual* never appears in his account of the child murders. The murders are nonetheless expressly linked to the Passover celebration, which implies a ritual purpose: victims are said to be kept alive until "the particular day" they are to be killed "in the most gruesome" manner.[7]

Görres links Jewish and Christian community action and counteraction in a nearly functionalist manner, but this is not meant to rationalize and desacralize the dramatic sacrifice of Christian children. Expulsion leads to retributive murder, leading in turn to pogroms and the destruction of long-standing Jewish communities; Christian and Jew are locked together in a chain just as something larger than their own communal particularity is unleashed. The process may be unholy, but it is far from secular. It reveals a bestial truth at the heart of humanity:

> All these mutually inciting rages—the wolfish rages of Christians against Jews, and the hyena-like responses of the latter against the former—merely exposed the claw of the agitated beast that lies sleeping in man's breast; hell had expelled pure horror with its breath, and the demonic stepped into the visible world.[8]

So there is in Görres's account, preceding the reemergence of the blood libel in the 1880s, a blurring of the boundaries if not a total fusion of the retributive and the demonic. An even more interesting aspect of the ecstatic/demonic experience here associated with child murder (what Görres elsewhere in this volume referred to as a *Blutrausch*, an intoxication of the blood, a term that we recall inspired Karl-Heinrich Ulrichs in his defense of the accused homosexual sadistic murderer Zastrow) is that it is characteristic of

7. Ibid., 64.

8. "In allen diesen gegenseitig sich herausfordenden Wüthereien, den wolfsmäßigen der Christen gegen die Juden, und den hyänenartigen Rückwirkungen dieser gegen jene geübt, war die Tatze des reitzenden Thieres, das in der Brust des Menschen schläft, nur sichtbar geworden; die Hölle hatte durch seinen Athem nur Greuel ausgedampft, und das Dämonische war sichtbar in die Welt getreten." Görres, *Die christliche Mystik*, vol. 4, pt. 2, p. 68.

both Christian and Jewish experience. The wall between these is surprisingly porous as is the boundary between man and his animal nature.

This text is a prelude to the explosion of discourse on Jewish ritual murder from the 1880s through the Nazi period. For the latter, knowledge about historic Jewish murder practices would be a privileged if contested area; Julius Streicher's infamous May 17, 1934, issue of *Der Stürmer* incited international protest and, in a rare and telling moment of self-censorship, Hitler ordered cessation of publication and distribution (albeit only to be released anew in 1939, when international opinion was no longer an issue). The blood libel, as David Biale has noted, was a central myth of the Nazi worldview, although if the Nazi literalization of the figure of blood represented a culmination of the long history of the "circulation of the [blood] metaphor," it must also be seen as odd that actual cases of the ritual accusation disappeared in the Nazi period, and the number in the Weimar Republic was very few.[9] The ritual murder discourse complex heralded by Damascus and set rolling by Tiszaeszlár was, in a word, a fin-de-siècle phenomenon. It was at best a false descendent of its late medieval and early modern predecessor and no more than a rich source for later antisemitic campaigns up to the present, which differ however in volume, complexity, and kind. It should be understood as an ensemble that included ritual murder accusations and refutations, moral panics about conspiracy and violence and parallel ones about the vicious incitement of antisemitic rabble. This was a setting in which rabid adversaries could agree on more than they wished to.[10]

9. See Biale, *Blood and Belief*, 123–26.

10. In this respect, its most poignant coda must be the scandal surrounding the Italo-Israeli medievalist Ariel Toaff's *Pasque di sangue: Ebrei d'Europa e omicidi rituali* (Bologna: il Mulino, 2007). Toaff (a professor at Bar-Ilan University and son of the chief Rabbi of Italy) would seem to have suggested that there is the possibility of a factual basis of late medieval blood libel persecutions, that "a minority of fundamentalist Ashkenazis," themselves gripped in the same fantasies of superstition and violent hatred as their Christian adversaries, committed vengeful acts of ritual violence. Needless to say, the historian's willingness to consider the "truth" of late medieval blood libels has been scandalous; before the book was given broad distribution, it was removed from circulation, and the author "recanted," as one report actually put it, and promised to edit and revise the manuscript before releasing a new and more careful version. The facts that the argument must be speculative in nature, on the one hand, and that the fundament of evidence will remain transcripts of confessions made under torture, on the other, ensured that no one's mind would be changed by a revised edition. For a complete summary, see Hannah Johnson, *Blood Libel: The Ritual Murder Accusation at the Limit of Jewish History* (Ann Arbor: University of Michigan Press, 2012), 129–64. But what interests us here is not the actual text as much as the anatomy of the controversy itself, which connects in provocative ways to its fin-de-siècle ancestors. See articles in *Ha'aretz* by Ofri Ilani, February 12, 2007, and Lisa Palmiera-

The brief discussion of ritual murder in Görres's epic *Die christliche Mystik* anticipates and yet remains apart from the circuit of ritual murder accusations and responsive reactions that would begin four decades later in the 1880s. Notwithstanding his willing acceptance of the possibility of Jewish guilt, Görres was not out to seek the veracity of the accusation but instead dwelled on the world of superstition, blood fantasy, and sacral violent imaginary that Jewish and Christian communities shared. The discourse of the period of the modern ritual murder accusations themselves would be more apparently bifurcated: on the one side the Jewish accused, on the other the Christian persecutors or prosecutors; competing and mutually incompatible systems of knowledge, that is, ways of knowing, criteria of evaluating what should be asked, what can be known, and how it can be ascertained. Ritual murder, in other words (and here as always "ritual murder" refers not to a practice or a libel, but to an apparatus of knowledges and counterknowledges that helps subjects make order of their world)— became a question of *truth*.

Görres only passingly mentions the resurgence of the ritual murder charges at Damascus just before the publication of his own text. He says little about the events except to show an unveiled disdain for the modern register of sensationalism surrounding them: "a welcome opportunity for newspapers and journals to weigh in on the object with the familiar shallowness and insipidity, with use of the usual inflated verbosity, and then to leave behind forever as over and done."[11] Even before it had properly begun, he sensed that the modern revival of the blood libel was centrally characterized by the modern mass media and a particular genre special to them: the sensation. The Damascus affair, like so many affairs to follow, ostensibly concerned events in a land far away about which one knew little, but in fact they could not be separated from a very native network of contemporary newspaper reports, feuilletons and opinion pieces, penny pamphlets, and cheaply reproduced quasi-scholarly works. This network was central to the kind of knowledge produced through the topos of ritual murder. Crucial to both were the figure of the expert and the problem of expertise, specifically, the relationship of specialized expert knowledge to reportage, opinion, and publicity. Since the most scandalous of the modern ritual murder accusations came to

Billig, "Historian Gives Credence to Blood Libel," *Jerusalem Post*, February 7, 2007, citing Sergio Luzzatto's review "Those Bloody Passovers" in *Corriere della Sera*, from which the quote is drawn. Little of the storm reflected the actual text of the book with the very notable exception of historian Kenneth Stowe's review on History News Network, "Blood Libel: Ariel Toaff's Perplexing Book," February 19, 2007, http://hnn.us/articles/35496.html.

11. Görres, *Die christliche Mystik*, vol. 4, pt. 2, p. 67.

court cases—either criminal cases against Jews or libel and incitement cases against antisemites—the role of the expert and of expert testimony became ever more salient. Enlightened criminologists observed how such cases "put into motion a monstrous apparatus" relating to the long-dormant and presumed discredited blood libel.[12] This "apparatus" was a complex of different kinds of knowledge and political forces that vied for authority with forensic physicians and criminal experts.

Along with the Damascus affair, and also preceding the revival of the blood libel by some years, was a spate of European literature, much of it ideologically Catholic, theoretically supporting the reality of Jewish ritual murder.[13] The key text in this regard was published in Munster in 1871 by the tendentious Catholic academic August Rohling (1839–1931). *Der Talmudjude*, or The Talmud Jew, was a 72-page tract most of which was culled from various sources (largely mistranslated, misrepresented, or invented out of whole cloth) to show textual evidence of Jewish antipathy for Christians.[14] Ritual murder as such was raised in a short section on the present century, where the Damascus case was cited on the basis of an antisemitic French account by Achilles Laurent that would become the standard for those holding the "objective" truth of the guilt of the Jews.[15] Here the questions of evidence and suggestion are crucial. First, Laurent's account was authorized by his supposed access to official files held in the French foreign ministry in Paris. Second, he stressed the confessions of Jewish conspirators, supposedly separated from one another during questioning. Most important for Rohling was the reaction of European Jewry to the case, as it mobilized efforts by those communities "bitterly" objecting to the accusation "that nowadays a cult might exist that requires human blood."[16] If the accusations were not true, Rohling reasoned, then why would such a campaign be necessary? Why wouldn't the Jews simply produce *evidence* of Jewish innocence? And why would European

12. Kornfeld, "Gerichts-Aerzte," 191.

13. Jonathan Frankel offers an argument for the emergence of this radical ultramontanist reaction in the very decade of liberal state hegemony. See Frankel, *Damascus Affair*, 419; for another detailed review of the ultramontanist roots of the revived charges and the context of Catholic modernism, see Stow, *Jewish Dogs*, 39–48.

14. Rohling, *Der Talmudjude*.

15. Laurent, *Relation Historique*. Volume two concerned the ritual murder case, including documentary evidence from the protocols of the trial. See Frankel, *Damascus Affair*, 415–20; cf. Mary C. Wilson, "The Damascus Affair and the Beginnings of France's Empire in the Middle East," in Gershoni, Erdem, and Woköck, *Histories*, 70–71.

16. Rohling, *Talmudjude*, 56.

Jewry come rushing to aid this exotic foreign community using all their influence and, indeed, wealth?

Rohling did indicate that to his knowledge, while there had been some
isolated modern suspicions of Jewish ritual murder in the West, no confirmed
evidence of the practice had been put forward.[17] Such serious charges demanded "strict proofs" even if it might be true, as another French antisemitic
source would have it, that quite substantial numbers of people seemed to
vanish without a trace from certain metropolises in crimes that had remained
unsolved mysteries.[18] A decade after penning these suggestive rather than ac-
cusatory remarks, charges of a more substantial kind would be made; the
*Talmudjude* would qualify Rohling to be called to the stand to furnish just the
sort of proof he had lamented was lacking.

### Hungarian Rhapsody

While actual accusations were scattered and little acknowledged between the
dawn of the Enlightenment and the 1880s, the ritual murder legend had never
subsided in the popular imagination in central Europe. Rumors arose sporadically, generally in response to unsolved disappearances or killings in the
vicinity of Easter.[19] The Damascus events catapulted such local rumors to the
status of a full-blown sensation with the authorization of a public trial; accusations of furtive ritual violence by Jewish communities return to central Europe at the very moment of their legal emancipation; and the literature of the
1860s and early 1870s stressed documentary evidence of the case in ways that
seemed to give material weight to a rumor that had the flavor of a folk fable.[20]
Notwithstanding a resurgence of these accusations in light of the affair, it took
a confluence of other circumstances to produce a full-blown European sensa-

17. Ibid., 57.

18. Ibid. The source cited was a notoriously antisemitic text by Gougenot des Mousseaux,
*Le Juif,* 186.

19. Justice ministries most often showed concern about the rumors as sources of social
disorder rather than as indications of possible Jewish communal violence. See, e.g., Justiz, Acta
gener: des Justiz-Ministeriums: betreffend: die in den Rheinprovinzen gebrochenen Anrufen, I.
HA Rep. 84a Justizministerium Nr. 50231, GSPK, relating to the investigation and trial of 206
participants in excesses against members of the Jewish community and the synagogue in the
towns of Neuenholfen and Bedburdick in the summer of 1830.

20. Accusations arose in the 1860s in Cologne, Tyrolia, and, significantly, in Hungary. Kayserling, *Die Blutbeschuldigung,* 2. On the literature of the 1860s and early 1870s, see Frankel,
*Damascus Affair,* 419.

tion of the same nature, and those circumstances convened in an agricultural village in eastern Hungary in the spring of 1882. Tiszaeszlár might be thought of as a way station between the oriental displacement of the ritual murder fantasy in Damascus to the fertile ground of middle Europe. The town was indeed seen as squarely in central Europe—the Habsburg monarchy—in the first decade since the compromise producing quasi-autonomous status for the Hungarian half of the empire. The case concerned the disappearance of a fourteen-year-old peasant girl named Eszter Solymosi (fig. 29), last seen while running an errand in the late morning of April 1, 1882.[21] As fortune would have it, her last reported sighting was on a path that passed by the local synagogue; furthermore, some strangers were in town, orthodox Jews who had come to offer their services to fill the recently vacated position of *shohet*, or kosher butcher, and a few more impoverished Jewish wanderers seeking to benefit from local holiday charity.

When Eszter did not return from her errands, her mother became worried, and concern soon yielded to suspicion. By the time she got to the city clerk to request a search for her missing daughter, suspicion must have turned to certainty; she returned later that day to ask specifically for a search of the synagogue. While local authorities at first sought to dispel the thoughts of Jewish responsibility from her mind, other neighbors soon came to believe the same and began to trade in gossip; in an atmosphere of suspicion, a remark by the young son of the temple employee was enough to make the rumors full-blown in the village of Tiszaeszlár. The boy, not yet five, and then his disgruntled teenaged brother Moritz (fig. 30), were to become the star witnesses of a trial that would produce a firestorm of newspaper articles, pamphlets, and treatises across German-language central Europe and abroad.

Several other factors involving other actors contributed to the transformation of rumor to sensation. Not least of these was the context of central European political antisemitism. First, the court appointed an investigating magistrate who was young and inexperienced in light of the seriousness of the charges but who came from a family with impeccable antisemitic credentials. Most important of all, antisemites in the Hungarian Diet led by representative Geza Onódy brought up the case on the Diet floor, and it became a cause célèbre for central European antisemites. In the course of the trial, Charles University (Prague) professor Rohling himself was called as expert witness,

21. Details of the case are repeated in contemporary newspaper accounts as well as contemporary propagandistic literature both antisemitic and apologetic; they are also laid out clearly in more recent monographs of the case, including Handler, *Blood Libel at Tiszaeszlar*, Stern, *Glorious Victory*.

Efther Solymofi.

FIGURE 29. Eszter Solymosi, depicted as rustic in one of the circulating narratives (from *Blutprozeß*).

Moritz Scharf.

FIGURE 30. Accuser Moritz Scharf as country boy (from *Blutprozeß*).

and the story raced through the antisemitic press. It also raced through the liberal press, and indeed the press in general; Tiszaeszlár became a European scandal of sensational dimensions so that it has sometimes been called the Hungarian Dreyfus affair. Like Dreyfus, the case seemed to raise the specter of reaction against an inclusive liberal version of national belonging; it became a symbol of different views of modernity, civilization, and enlightenment. It produced a cacophony of discourse that could seem remarkably bifurcated—Tiszaeszlár had its Dreyfusards and anti-Dreyfusards. But when Dreyfus was tried and convicted in France just over a decade after Tiszaeszlár, suspicion about the national loyalty of a Jewish officer did not extend to fantasies of the secret maintenance by modern Jews of enduring and violent human sacrifice rituals. The Tiszaeszlár accusation itself was a source of embarrassment; it seemed a throwback that needed at times to be disavowed with the same strength that the myth of Jewish sacrificial practices must be. It is compelling, for instance, to consider that the assimilated and liberal Budapest Jew Theodor Herzl would cite Dreyfus as the turning point in his realization of the impossibility of the emancipation-assimilation contract while these events in his own country would remain unmentioned.[22]

Modernity was very much at issue in the events in that the local actors were conscious of various schemata organizing persons, communities, and ideas along an axis characterized by premodernity, barbarism, or primitivity and so forth on one end and what we might call modernity—the more active contemporary term would have been *enlightenment*—civilization, and future on the other. Clearly the initial accusations and rumors rested on a foundation of prejudice about a community of neighbors that retained about them something suspiciously alien, inscrutable, unassimilated, and nonmodern. But the accusation itself seemed to observers—not just outside the local setting, but within it—to be a symptom of the premodern: the blood libel was an embarrassing peasant legend, pointing to the ignorance of a mob that reminded internal and external observers of the medieval past. When Solymosi confessed her suspicions to the local authorities, she was referred to higher regional authorities because one was aware that the violation of the synagogue could cause communal embarrassment; the regional authorities in turn tried to assuage the panicked mother and assure her that legends of child-robbing Jews were untrue and that she should get the suspicion out of her mind. Several of the more qualified potential examining magistrates might for various reasons be seen as obliquely sympathetic to Jews. The appointment of Jószef Bary, a young functionary whose chief qualification seems to have been his

22. Herzl, *Complete Diaries.*

provenance from an antisemitic family, was fateful, because he was from the start convinced not only of the guilt of Scharf and other Jews but also of the ritual nature of the case. This very claim was the most dangerous, however, in the eyes of the state prosecutor, Ede Szeyffert. Already in his opening remarks in court, Szeyffert made sarcastic references to the absurdity of any charges suggesting the reality of the medieval superstition about Jewish ritual murders and more than obliquely ridiculing the investigating magistrate (Bary). At stake for the prosecutor as for so many talented people swept up in the swift rise of Hungarian national and imperial autonomy was the image of a secretly backward and peasant Hungary not yet ready for rule. For national antisemites, Szeyffert's unusual act of dramatically distancing himself from the position he was charged to argue was proof of a Jewish conspiracy so powerful as to control the outcome of a trial even where, finally, testimony from within the Jewish community was available. That Szeyffert's position carried the day to acquittals in both the trial and appeal only strengthened these convictions.

More than one condition helped transform antisemitic village rumor to sensation. One of these already mentioned was the emergence of anti-Judaism as a political force, identified with national parties, which were represented by a vocal minority in both the Hungarian Diet and the Austrian parliament. Equally important was the array of press organs available to all sides and with them a mass-media society in which eager readers and circulation-driven publishers forced a continuous escalation of dramatic reporting and editorializing. The image of circuits of communication among local, national, and international levels was strongly in the minds of the actors, from those giving local testimony to parliamentary speakers to readers. If such a network could serve either side of the debate, awareness of its potential penetrated the fantasies of each. One antisemitic Austrian representative announced on the floor, however implausibly, that the Vienna office of the Alliance Israélite Universelle had ordered a dedicated telegraph connection from the site of the court in Nyiregyhaza to the leaders of the Vienna Jewish community.[23] As with the ritual murder charge itself, the absurdity of this accusation paled beside the power of the image it evoked so that the truth seemed not to lay with the reality or fiction of the dedicated wire, but elsewhere.

Many other details of the case link it to the paradigm of modernity; chief

---

23. Bloch, *Talmud und Judentum*, 128. The Alliance was the international Jewish organ founded in Paris in 1860, unwittingly offering a palpable object to popular fantasies of an organized Jewish international.

among these is the status of forensic evidence and sciences of detection. This certainly also relates to the question of the constitution of truth. As a brief example, several months into the investigation, a female body was found in the Tisza river—bald and bloated, of course—yet still retaining traces of clothing belonging to Eszter Solymosi. The body was not drained of blood and showed no signs of ritual incisions. Eszter's mother insisted this unrecognizable corpse was not her daughter, and Bary indicated it was the body of an older woman with shorn hair and signs of sexual experience, hence not Eszter. The investigation took place on the cusp of the development of the "criminalistics" discussed in chapter 1, bringing knowledges of biological medicine, chemistry, and other scientific study together to solve crime. It was contemporary with Hanns Gross's fieldwork as well as with the earliest Sherlock Holmes stories.[24] In an unprecedented move, the body was later exhumed, and a second autopsy was performed by Budapest specialists, who revised the determination of age and who applied scientific forensics to the evidence provided by the hair, skin, nails, and so forth, all pointing to the fact that the bloated body was, in fact, that of Eszter Solymosi. The antisemitic press ridiculed the idea that "modern" techniques are given precedence over a mother's recognition of her own child. The intervention of outside experts from Budapest and then their authorization by Rudolph Virchow (most highly prestigious head of the University of Berlin's Pathological Institute, stigmatized by opponents as a "great friend of the Jews") naturally fed conspiratorial antisemitic thinking.[25] The identification of the Tisza corpse was hence a turning point of the case and pivot on which contradicting understandings of the case would spin.[26]

Seen one way, the testimony of witnesses with intimate knowledge of the victims and perpetrators seems to have been privileged by the local accusers, whereas for the central and enlightened authorities, the prejudice and ignorance of witnesses could be superseded by a cool examination of physical evidence by impartial experts armed with advanced forensic tools and knowledge. In this sense, the case mapped out the sections Hanns Gross would

---

24. The case is named specifically as the beginning of the "new technique of forensic autopsy that commanded justice" and as the first great building block of the science of Sherlock Holmes; see Wagner, *Science of Sherlock Holmes*, 12–15.

25. Otto Glagau, *Kulturkämpfer*, vol. 10 (Berlin, 1885), 10; in 1893 Virchow would indeed be cofounder of the Association for the Defense against Antisemitism, as later opponents would note; see Schramm, *Der jüdische Ritualmord*, 187n47.

26. See, e.g., the printed court document by Josef Scharf und Genossen, cataloged "Protest, addressed to the court" (Tisza-Eszlár, 1882), Hebrew Union College collection.

mark "subjective" and "objective" in his soon to be classic *Criminal Psychology*.[27] While some of the arguments made might seem to buttress this mental map—local actors crying foul at the intervention of unreliable outsiders, paternalistic dismissals of the ignorance of village superstition—the fact is that both sides were plugged into networks local, national, and international. Both, too, seemed obsessed with physical and with documentary evidence. Besides the body, there were the files: official documents from the case and from the historical record certifying the truth or falsehood of Jewish ritual murder practice.[28] All this evidence seemed equally available both to antisemitic crusaders exposing Jewish violence and their enlightened counterparts, sometimes furnishing identical evidence, or even borrowing from each other.[29] There might in this sense have been a circuit of knowledge between these two fronts, but it is important to note that they were not in any kind of dialogue with one another. Each text quoted its predecessors and concluded with the absurdity, in light of all this evidence, of maintaining that Jewish ritual murder did, or did not, exist. But the audiences of these literatures were generally the already faithful.[30]

When contemporaries as well as later historians looked at the Tiszaeszlár case and the spate of central European blood libels that continued in force over the next two decades, several different kinds of interpretations of the events came to mind. In light of their proximity to the formal emancipation of Jews in the German and Habsburg empires and the prospect of their further integration, the ready explanation is another form of what we have been calling the "marginalization thesis": ranks are closed on the bound-

27. See chap. 1. The reference is to Gross, *Criminalpsychologie.*

28. See, e.g., Anon., *Sechs Aktenstücke*, publishing verbatim protocols from the trial, including those focused on the Tisza corpse, with the clear purpose of exonerating the Jews; in the wake of the Xanten case, the important antisemitic reverend Josef Deckert drew on similar materials from the Trent trial to prove the opposite; see Deckert, *Ein Ritualmord.* Reference to the documentary evidence of archival files, protocols, and the like is the staple of much expert testimony, and we recall that the publication of one such collection of materials by a French antisemite under the signature of Achilles Laurent launched attention to the Damascus trial (see n. 15). The strategy is even apparent in texts preceding the efflorescence of cases, experts, and texts that are explored here. See Lippert, *Anklagen der Juden.*

29. One revealing such case is Paul Nathan, *Der Prozess von Tisza-Eszlár*, an enlightened account of the events at Tiszaeszlár a decade after the fact in light of the new sensation at Xanten, where he credits the antisemitic movement for having diligently preserved all the trial protocols and made them widely available in their party press.

30. One enlightened text, for instance, betrays that it is aimed at a Jewish readership in that it seeks to show proofs of the fictitiousness of antisemitic claims just as it implores readers not to be too zealous in their defenses.

aries of community as others are powerfully distinguished as alien, primitive, dangerous, and violent. Of course there is something to this almost commonsense observation. Yet the ways in which the rhetorics of civilization and savagery, furtive conspiracy and communal violence, and so on circulated throughout both attacks on Jews and defenses of them points to something more.

The events at Tiszaeszlár came to the national stage on the floor of the Hungarian Diet, where Geza Onódy, responding to a vitriolic letter by the local priest, raised the issue on May 23, 1882, saying, "according to the Talmud, the Jews need the blood of Christians for ritual purposes on certain festive occasions." This assertion of fact on the Diet floor can only have been verified by Rohling's recent *Der Talmudjude*, and was followed by a summary of known events and witness testimony leading to the obvious conclusion of what had happened in Tiszaeszlár.[31] The mere mention of a calumny known to be far from eradicated among common folk but not the stuff of parliamentary discussion led to a flurry of comment in newspaper articles along with, almost as immediate, published pamphlets and small books. Already in the following month, for instance, Rabbi Meyer Kayserling of the Budapest community rued the introduction on the Reichstag floor of language that brought horror to all those whose ears it reached; not only representatives in the chamber, and regardless of the auditors' confessions, everyone must be mortified by the return of "the red spook" one had long taken for utterly vanquished.[32] The lie, in Kayserling's recounting, had found no ground in Europe for many years but had reemerged forty-two years before "in Asia, into which European civilization had not yet penetrated," in Damascus. This historical geography performs the orientalist displacement we noted before, and it is an interestingly self-contradictory move in that the blood libel was a completely foreign import to the Near East. Onódy's aim, the Jewish apologist noted, seemed to be to foment the masses, a goal he apparently achieved. In fact, as we know, the local population did not require external incitement by national antisemites but instead had enlisted their aid. But it was important for the rabbi to stand on the side of those who insist on Hungary's modernity: there was for him clearly no room "on Hungary's cultivated ground" for a witch hunt against its citizens of Jewish faith; prejudice and fanaticism were, he claimed, foreign to the people's traditions; but it is sad that "the Enlightenment of our day" did not stretch far enough to render such coarse attacks completely without effect. With the return of the central role played

31. Herczl, *Christianity and the Holocaust*, 11.
32. Kayserling, *Die Blutbeschuldigung*, 1.

by juvenile witnesses, he noted, this case pushed modern Hungarians even further toward the Middle Ages than had the accusations of the 1860s.[33]

It is not necessary to strain to hear an ambivalence within this particular construction of Enlightenment and reaction: the persistent suspicion, behind the insistence of an indigenous openness and the political context of agitation, that in fact there are corners of the world less distant than Damascus where the banner of civilization had not yet firmly been planted. The Jews, here, do not stand for this Enlightenment or modernity any more than they stand for an arcane and exotic tradition (they appear in the text only as fellow citizens of other faith). Primitivity and savagery—the marks of the ritual murder accusation—are to be found elsewhere.[34] This theme is recurrent in the liberal responses to the affair, whether from Jewish quarters or not. The actions of peasant communities are called, as in a series of articles in the *Wiener Allgemeine Presse* over the next months, "mob excesses," hopefully contained but perilously reminiscent of counterparts in the Russian Empire where the same movement had been appearing "with the utter hideousness of the unbound bestiality of a brutal, uncivilized people." This feature of the liberal attack on the ritual murder charges recurs forcefully in later cases as well: the proponents of the ritual murder legend are not only less civilized, they are less human than those they attack; they are, as this article continues, "like a rabid animal whose cage has been opened for it to spring on the designated sacrifice."[35] This is nothing more than "the most brutal instinct of the masses, popular bestiality in its most primordial and gruesome form," driven by an instinct to annihilate.

This rhetoric is noteworthy because it is so common in the liberal defenses and self-defenses of Jewry in the face of ritual murder sensations over the next decades; it is no less noteworthy because of its specific similarity to the charge of ritual murder itself: the target is bestial, primordial, uncontrolled, a mass of rabid and raging animals; in a word, *savage*. Perusing the pamphlets and articles constituting the ritual murder accusations and defenses against

---

33. Ibid., 16.

34. Jews and their apologists hence persistently stressed the unenlightened state of rural Hungary in this case or stressed the Slavic milieux of Prussian or Galician villages in other cases; cf. Friedlaender, *Kulturhistorische Kriminal-Prozesse*, which focuses in detail on a paternalistic treatment of Tiszaeszlár and also the case in Skurcz, Galicia; a follow-up volume focusing on more recent cases does nonetheless include Xanten; see Friedlaender, *Interessante Kriminal-Prozesse*.

35. "Für die Juden," *Wiener Allgemeine Zeitung*, June 8, 1882, repr. in Bloch, *Gegen die Anti-Semiten*, 9–10. The text reads, "diese haben gehandelt, gewüthet und verwustet wie das rasende Their, dessen Zwinger man öffnet, damit es sich blutgierig auf das erkornene Opfer stürze."

them, this is the most striking element: without knowledge of the authors or publishers, simply reading the titles of these works, it is often impossible to know whether the object of attack is the Jews or the antisemites; whether the practice of ritual murder or the discourse of ritual murder is being decried. Both condemn radical and dangerous superstition; as an early commentator noted with more insight than most would have, it was not even much use to refute charges of the religious basis of Jewish ritual murder, but rather the superstitions themselves must be "anatomically analyzed," dissected and exposed; the legend was the object of incision and also of analysis.[36]

This was insightful in that the two camps would never really be speaking to one another, even as they seemed at times to project themselves into one another, even to covet the other's position, and to reproduce one another. As rebuttals, the points repeatedly made by Jewish authorities did anything but dispel the myth of secret and brutal Jewish rites. The irony, it seemed to Jewish supporters, was that Jewish monotheism represented precisely this turn from sacrificial violence to a system of ethics. Murder, as everyone knows, was condemned in the prime commandments of the religion. Antisemites countered with evidence from the Talmud and other writings that this and all laws applied only to Jews, and that non-Jews were indeed considered nonhuman animals by Jewish religion. Very frequently invoked in defenses were, predictably, the laws of kashruth, which strictly forbid the consumption of blood to such a degree that animals must be ritually slaughtered and drained of all blood before eating. Authors of some tracts were clever enough to note that the prohibition against blood in meat was specific to animals, and no prohibition on human blood is specified. A far stronger argument came from those who noted that the strictness and explicitness of these prohibitions merely codified and proved what people already knew to be the truth: the Jews were bloodthirsty; they were by nature driven by an unquenchable desire for blood that forced its codified restraint.

The metaphor of the rhapsody can indeed be used to describe the rants and counterrants produced in the course of the stream of narratives and polemics proceeding from the Tiszaeszlár case.[37] Yet as the musical metaphor

36. Rabbi Güdemann, "Kinderschlächter," *Wiener Allgemeine Zeitung*, July 5, 1882, in Bloch, *Gegen die Anti-Semiten*, 13.

37. The *Oxford English Dictionary* definition of *rhapsody* includes "An exalted or exaggeratedly enthusiastic expression of sentiment or feeling; an effusion (e.g. a speech, letter, poem) marked by extravagance of idea and expression, but without connected thought or sound argument."

FIGURE 31. Advertisement for the proliferation of "Educational Writings on Jewish Blood Murders!" from *Deutsch-Soziale Blätter* supplement 17, no. 713 (April 17, 1902):. 192.

also suggests, the compulsive stream of heated discourse was in some ways as harmonious as it was cacophonous: on one and then the other side of the debate, motifs were recapitulated and inverted, echoing one another in the form as well as the thematic content of their invectives. To jump from aural to visual metaphor, to read this sheaf of polemics is to find oneself in a hall of mirrors.

## Antisemitic Expertise

The exchange between two Habsburg subjects, August Rohling and his adversary Josef Samuel Bloch (1850–1923), is both emblematic and exemplary of the structure of the two modes of vociferous discourse on ritual murder: the one against Jewish violent ritual practices, and the other against vicious and dangerous antisemitic dissimulation. As a rule, as we have been arguing, the two sides reflected one another perfectly just as they remained immune to each other's attacks, because both were in a way self-contained and self-immunized conversations. The would-be collision of these early on in the confrontation of Rohling by Bloch hence displays this beautifully.[38]

Bloch, rabbi of a congregation just outside of the then borders of Vienna,

38. Hartston, *Sensationalizing the Jewish Question,* 189–204.

attacked Rohling's expertise and was sued in turn by Rohling for libel in an affair that would become known in Vienna as the Talmud Dispute. The term *roguish trickery* is used by both Bloch and Rohling, each about the other, to refer to the presumed deliberately misleading misrepresentations of the Talmud and other Jewish religious texts. At issue was the claim by Rohling (among others, including the pan-German antisemite Franz Holubek, the libel suit against whom formally launched the Dispute) that Christians were considered by Jewish law no better than animals (or, specifically, pigs, dogs, and asses), and that crimes against them from theft to murder were hence sanctioned.[39] The claim seemed to strike at the heart of the promise of emancipation and assimilation if Jewish communal law itself refused the society of gentile fellow human beings. Rohling offered a reward of 1,000 gulden to anyone who could demonstrate the error of a single citation in his *Der Talmudjude*.[40] Two very distinguished Austrian rabbis, Adolf Jellinek (1821–93) and Moritz Güdemann (1835–98) of the Vienna congregation, published just such a contestation at the end of October 1882; in December 1882 and January 1883, Bloch published several lengthy attacks on Rohling.[41] Rohling's response in two particularly ferocious pamphlets sought to dismiss the biased defenses of the rabbis as less than scholarly ("roguish tricks")—Bloch in turn ran through Rohling's misrepresentations and mistranslations, turning the same demeaning term against the good professor. He also directly challenged the scholar's ability correctly to translate a single page of scripture, offering his own reward. That the controversial *Der Talmudjude* was little more than a gloss of Johann Andreas Eisenmenger's notorious *Entdecktes Judenthum* (Judaism unmasked, 1700) was well established and often repeated, although the power of *Der Talmudjude* lay elsewhere than in its originality. Rohling sued Bloch for libel but eventually dropped the suit when, as Bloch later publicized, it would have been necessary for him actually to prove his translation abilities before the court.

Several different kinds of hierarchies were mobilized in this battle for authority. In spite of his own dubious credentials, Rohling's position as an "imperial and royal" professor at a very distinguished university could be counted on to trump the word of three very learned rabbis. When it came to the question of ritual murder, Rohling argued that the very furtiveness

---

39. See Bloch, *Acten und Gutachten*, 1–3.

40. Rohling, *Die Polemik*, 11–12, 22n.

41. "Professor Rohling und das Wiener Rabbinat oder Die arge Schelmerei, Des k.k. Prof. Rohling neuester Fälschungen," open letter to Rohling in *Wiener Allgemeine Zeitung*, January 10, 1883, etc. See Bloch, *Acten und Gutachten*, 30–89.

Rohling's Flucht.

FIGURE 32. "Rohling's Flight," shooed away by Bloch's torch of Enlightenment. From *Kikeriki*, 1885.

and conspiratorial nature of the issue tended to shield textual evidence from Christian eyes. History, however, proved that secret texts commanded the Jewish extraction and use of innocent Christian blood for Passover rituals; hence, history must needs trump text as such evidence.[42] Yet it is important to note that there are such texts—here he again claimed, as he had before, that he could find such texts if given time and funding to search. Although he had never laid hands on it, he knew the title and precise contents of one recent such text by a Kossov rabbi by the name of Mendel. Rohling claimed that the rabbi's book, *Gan Naul*, had been published in Lemberg and other such cit-

42. Rohling, *Die Polemik*, 32–33; Bloch, *Acten und Gutachten*, 157–60.

ies in twenty editions and that in it the author lamented the small numbers of observant Jews outside such places as Hungary, Galicia, and Poland who collected the prescribed blood for Passover matzohs.[43] A tale such as this one, rife enough with details to suggest to readers some sense of truth, coded the secret doctrine as oriental, if contemporary, in ways that evoked contemporary east European orthodoxy's lament of west European Jewish assimilation. Bloch's advocate drew on Rohling's rhetoric of geographies beyond civilization to remind the court that Lemberg was the capital of a Habsburg crown land and Mendel an Austrian subject.[44] This tug-of-war between associations oriental and homely, primitive and contemporary, alien and familiar, was characteristic of the whole affair; it was indeed going on within individual consciousnesses. Acculturated Jews knew more of the Talmud from Rohling's reports than from any personal knowledge, and the Talmud Dispute offered them an alien and primitive image of themselves. The daughter of the renowned German-Jewish neurologist Moriz Benedikt recalls the despair of the prominent German and Austro-Hungarian Jews in her train compartment reading the dailies, embarrassed and disgusted by this book, if these were truly its contents. Benedikt is reported to have commented, "a professor of the University of Prague wouldn't go and tell a lie like that in public."[45]

The libel case of Rohling against Bloch thus came to depend on the truthfulness of Rohling's interpretation of the Talmud passages, and so the court was faced with a particularly sticky problem of expertise. Neither judge nor jury members could be expected to read the cited passages in the original or to put them in the context of Jewish theology. The court system had at its disposal, as we have seen, a network of court experts (*Sachverständige*) in various areas of science and scholarship but unsurprisingly none in the fields of Talmudic and rabbinical literature (knowledge of Semitic languages alone would not be sufficient). Clearly the only possessors of sufficient knowledge on these matters in Austria would be students of Talmud and rabbinics at *yeshivot* in the eastern provinces, and in light of the nature of the accusations and counteraccusations, these could never be taken into court as impartial experts.[46] The court had hence to turn to Germany and to the German Oriental Society (Deutsche Morgenländische Gesellschaft [DMG]), the umbrella institution that could serve as arbiter of such knowledge. Rohling must agree to the society's authority in that he himself had stipulated that the DMG must

43. Rohling, *Die Polemik*, 22; Bloch, *Acten und Gutachten*, 158.
44. Bloch, *Acten und Gutachten*, 158.
45. Bloch, *My Reminiscences*, 64–65, 65n.
46. Bloch, *Acten und Gutachten*, 173–74.

guarantee any Jew's claim that he had falsely cited Talmud and had recognized their authority elsewhere.[47] But resorting to the DMG did not entirely solve the problem: the society was an association of scholars, but it did not proffer collective opinions. What is more, the question was raised of what to do about Jewish members of the society, or those who may be Lutheran or Catholic, but, as was sometimes the case, hailed from Jewish families?[48] The logic governing the determination of expertise hence required all sides to acknowledge rules of the game determined in significant ways and extent by the antisemites. If Bloch had been the most persistent of Rohling's attackers, the most devastating critiques came from the pen of Franz Delitzsch (1813–90), distinguished Lutheran theologian at the University of Leipzig, who was deeply involved in the mission to convert the Jews to Protestant Christianity and whose expertise in Talmudic and rabbinic literature and refutations of the blood libel had long preceded Rohling's appearance on the scene.[49] Delitzsch began his devastating attacks on the *Talmudjude* and on Rohling before the Tiszaeszlár affair, publishing what some took to be a definitive refutation in 1881; in his response to this refutation, still before the affair, Rohling played the card that was perennially to disqualify the scholar.[50] The breadth and depth of Delitzsch's knowledge had to be respected, wrote Rohling, and his commitment to the conversion of the Jews (and hence admission of inferiority of their religion) unassailable. What could explain the inconsistency of these facts with his ultimately apologetic defenses of Jewry against Rohling's charges? In his conclusion, Rohling asks "whether the Jewish origins of this scholar might not solve the inconceivable puzzle of how such a man of intelligence could write such a self-contradictory and untruthful book as Delitzsch has done."[51]

The presumed Jewish origins of Delitzsch are doubtful, but the charge stuck. More important than the specific accusation about Delitzsch is the success of the criterion of qualification manifested by a certification of lack of Jewish background, or, even better, a record of explicit antisemitic views. One incident that demonstrates this most clearly was to emerge in Silesia, in the German Empire, nearly a decade later. This case concerned a certain

47. Rohling, *Der Talmudjude*, 26; *Meine Antworten an die Rabbiner* (Prague: Zeman, 1883), 175.

48. Bloch, *Acten und Gutachten*, 176.

49. Delitzsch's translation of the New Testament into Hebrew was one of his most significant accomplishments, and he steadily worked on the salvation of the Jews. On Delitzsch's origins, see n. 55.

50. Delitzsch, *Rohling's Talmudjude*; Rohling, *Franz Delitzsch*.

51. Rohling, *Franz Delitzsch*, 154.

Max Bernstein, a rabbinical student at the Breslau yeshiva, and was not a ritual murder case per se. Early in 1889, the father of a Christian boy in Breslau noted small wounds on his son Severin Hacke's genitals, and the story emerged that Bernstein had lured the boy into his rooms with the promise of candy, then gotten the boy to undress and allow the rabbinical student to pierce his foreskin in several places, tamping the wound with blotter paper. Upon investigation it emerged that Bernstein had attempted this with other local boys.[52] In court on February 21, 1889, the accusation included a reference to "a ritual withdrawal of blood for the Israelite religious rite," although in the verdict the court avoided reference to any such motive.[53] The tribunal (which, according to the antisemites' reports, included two Jews) explicitly indicated that "the motive of the crime evokes no particular interest," and the testimony on the young man's mental capacity contained enough ambiguity to be exploited by those arguing for a cover-up of this clear case of the rabbinic need for Christian blood.

In 1889, in light of the Bernstein case, Kaiser Wilhelm II himself ordered Justice Minister Schelling to investigate and report on the truth of Jewish ritual violence practices. The investigation was delegated to Prussian Kultusminister (responsible for affairs of education and culture, including religion) Gustav von Goßler, whose task was to seek out expert testimony on the subject. On April 5, 1889, he forwarded opinions by Hermann Lebrecht Strack, Franz Delitzsch, and Paul de Lagarde.[54] As Barnet Hartston notes in his account of the case, Goßler's summary identifies Delitzsch as of Jewish origin and therefore biased, Lagarde as reliably antisemitic, and Strack as the "neutral" and therefore most reliable testimony.[55] The archives make the logic of this troika of experts explicit: "Jewish" expert testimony requires antisemitic repudiation, and a third, "neutral" confirmation of one position or the other.

52. Besides Hacke, a second boy, Michael Meyer, was identified in the investigation as Jewish. I. HA Rep. 84a Justizministerium, Nr. 56464, pp. 25–26, GSPK.

53. Quoted in Mommert, *Der Ritualmord*, 74–75.

54. I. HA Rep. 84a (Justizministerium), Nr. 56464, pp. 70–71, GSPK. The actual testimonies are not in this file, although Goßler's summaries of their contents is included.

55. Hartston, *Sensationalizing the Jewish Question*, 165n87. Crawford Howell Toy and Richard Gottheil assert that Delitzsch was actually not of Jewish descent and attribute the assumption (or, in Rohling's case, accusation) to his knowledge of Jewish sources and "a misunderstanding of his relation to his Hebrew godfather (whom he called 'uncle')"; see Adler and Singer, *Jewish Encyclopedia*, 505. This origin tale of the "misunderstanding" seems to have come from Delitzsch himself—he is credited with periodically relaying this as the source of the "fable" that his father's family was of Jewish origin: see Herzog, Hauck, and Caselmann, *Realencyklopädie für protestantische Theologie und Kirche*, 4:565–70, esp. 565–66. The fact of Jewish ancestry or not is not significant to our argument, but the need for all of this discourse on it is.

This logic was in place all along, already in the Tiszaeszlár case. Rohling's central place in the debates was not due to his masterful knowledge of Talmud (as Bloch and Delitzsch's criticisms revealed). He was called on, here as in other cases, as an expert antisemite.

Those who would defend the Jews against the uncivilized charges of ritual violence leveled against them easily conformed to this logic of expertise, always making a point to stress that they were themselves confessional Christians and not converts from Judaism.[56] Special weight was given as well to Christian sources refuting the ritual murder accusation, including repeated publications of the various papal bulls from late medieval times forward as well as anthologies of affidavits solicited from Christian biblical scholars.[57] As we observed in the Bernstein and Tiszaeszlár cases, it was a further qualification if one were not only Christian and from a family with no Jewish converts in it but if one were known to be antisemitic. Hence Paul de Lagarde was solicited for an opinion not only by the government but also by rabbis seeking to put the outrageous legend to bed.[58] While liberal rationalists might wish for credible experts to put primitive rumors and myths to rest, they would have to suffer the fact of experts who only served to summon the beast.

## The Jaws of Moloch

Concurrent with ritual murder scandals, but often without reference to them, ran a conversation about the sacrifice of children deep in the Hebrew past. Like the ritual murder discussion proper, this quasi-scholarly debate began before the ritual murder trials in the 1880s but took on special meaning thereafter. Central to the discussion was the so-called Molochistic theory, which referred to the centrality of a human sacrifice service to peoples of the Near East, including the Israelites. Indeed, biblical proscriptions of child

---

56. Strack himself certifies in his preface that all his ancestors come from "pure 'Christian-Germanic' origin," mainly ministers and teachers. The scare quotes surrounding "Christian-Germanic" only feebly indicates a skepticism toward the antisemitic category authorized by providing this qualification. Strack, *Das Blut*, v.

57. Nearly all of the countless defenses of Jews make a point to identify sources as Christian. There emerged in fact a veritable genre of anthologies of testimony certified as Christian, e.g., Lipschitz, *Christliche Zeugnisse*; *Die Blutbeschuldigung*; Baumgarten, *Die Blutbeschuldigung*; Berliner, *Gutachten Ganganelli's Clemens XIV*; Stern, *Andreas Osianders Schrift*.

58. See Lipschitz, *Christliche Zeugnisse*, 25, repr. in *Die Blutbeschuldigung*. The place of Paul Anton de Lagarde (1827–91) in the intellectual trajectory of the modern German antisemitic ideology was firmly established in Stern, *Politics of Cultural Despair*, 3–96, and Mosse, *Crisis of German Ideology*.

sacrifice to the demonic god were chief sources of the literature. The Moloch cult (or, more likely, a series of cultic practices relating to idols and gods of varied names) involved an idol made of gold in the form of a calf or a bull's head (whence the golden calf against which Moses shattered the original tablets of the Law), on the altar of which children were sacrificed to fire. In one accounted version of the practice, the figure, an upright man with a bull's head with open jaws, is hollow, and a pyre inside it is ignited; children were thought to have been roasted in the idol's arms, or "fed" to the beast through its mouth (fig. 33).

The reality of sacrificial practices in the ancient Near East was not controversial. As the biblical references confirm, a primary distinguishing feature of Jewish monotheism was its prohibition of practices that were current at the time the prohibitions were drafted. The relationship of the "Moloch service" to ancient and ongoing Jewish practice was another matter. Two scholarly texts from 1842 were important in linking child sacrifice to the Hebrews: F. W. Gillany's *Die Menschenopfer der alten Hebräer: Eine geschichtliche Untersuchung* (The human sacrifices of the ancient Hebrews) and G. F. Daumer's *Der Feuer- und Molochdienst der alten Hebräer als urväterlicher, legaler, ortho-*

*DER GÖTZE MOLOCH*
*Wie Ihme die Kinder zum Opfer in seine glüende Arme gegeben.*

FIGURE 33. Eighteenth-century image of the Moloch idol. "How children were surrendered into his smoldering arms."

*doxer Cultus der Nation* (The fire and Moloch service of the ancient Hebrews as primordial, legal, and orthodox cult of the nation).[59] Daumer in particular was invested in establishing continuity between ancient Israelite and later Judeo-Christian practice. He claimed that the Passover festival was originally a child sacrifice feast (indeed, as some authors maintained, the roasted children were eaten by the priests).

Needless to say, claims of ancient Hebrew human sacrifice and cannibalism were eagerly cited by antisemites agitating around the various ritual murder cases. Carl Mommert published a follow-up to his exposé on *Der Ritualmord bei den Talmud-Juden* (Ritual murder of the Talmud-Jews) with a book on ancient Hebrew human sacrifice for the purpose of "eliminating once and for all this barbaric and predatory cult that raises murder and killing to the level of divine commandment."[60] Scholars of ancient religion came forward in turn with evidence and arguments that the Hebrews' conception of the deity and corresponding practice represented a radical break with the cults surrounding them—the essence of Judaism was not this bloody ritual violence but the repudiation of it.[61]

In fact, Daumer's dramatic revivification of cultic cannibalistic ritual was not intended as an antisemitic distancing. For a long period of his life, the author produced critiques of Pietism, then Christian theology in general, before embracing Catholicism. The memory of primordial violence was meant to implicate a Christian present. Five years after the publication of *Der Feuer- und Molochdienst*, he made this more explicit in his scathing *Die Geheimnisse des christlichen Alterthums* (Secrets of Christian antiquity), which ascribed to the early Christians the restoration of the ancient fire and Moloch sacrifices of innocent children—it was therefore with good reason that the "dark sect" was rejected by the Jews and persecuted by the Romans.[62] It was because Christianity aimed to move "not forwards, to bring to fruition the great work of humanity that the pagans had begun, but backwards to the old, discarded and abandoned rubbish and abomination" of Judaism's primordial past.[63]

In London exile, Karl Marx reported jubilantly on Daumer's book as

59. Ghillany, *Die Menschenopfer*; Daumer, *Der Feuer- und Molochdienst.*

60. Carl Mommert, *Menschenopfer bei den alten Hebräern* (Leipzig: Haberland, 1905), cited in Mader, *Die Menschenopfer*, 13. See also the brochure published by the same house in the same year: Mommert, *Ritualmord.*

61. See Mader, *Die Menschenopfer*, 182–84; cf. Strack, *Das Blut.* Both texts, and each of the earlier and later editions of Strack's text, explicitly respond to the antisemitic literature misrepresenting the religious histories they recount.

62. Daumer, *Die Geheimnisse.*

63. Ibid., 10.

definitive evidence of the bestial early Christians' furtive and murderous
cannibalism, promising to "deal Christianity its last blow," giving certainty
that "the old society is coming to an end and that the edifice of fraud and
prejudice is collapsing."[64] Daumer was naturally more of an iconoclast than
a communist—what's more, one who would succumb to the seductions of
the Catholic faith in a very short time. Like Marx, nevertheless, he imagined
it was possible to reject that which claimed to be the essence of Western civilization (in the case of Marx) or spirituality (Daumer). Both reactions, with
Görres's of 1842, point to crucial elements of the fantasy image of ritual murder that the pugnacious ritual murder debate of the latter nineteenth century
would obscure. Conjuring a world of unspeakable violence from which we
have descended was far from the complacent self-congratulation of Christian
civilization. It was a part vicarious and prurient, part viciously self-critical
gesture of utopian hope.

## Local, National, Imperial

In the German Empire, the course of the sensations, expert testimony, the
debate of antisemites versus enlighteners, and the parallel circulation of texts
aligned with these two sides looked similar in many ways to the cases in the
Habsburg Empire. The context was different in other ways. Political antisemitism was not as advanced in the new Reich to the north as it was in the
Habsburg realm, although it was already quite strong as a cultural force—yet
we have seen how the institutional structures of political antisemitism played
a specific role in the escalation of discourse in Tiszaeszlár and other cases.
The contexts of national identities within the multinational monarchy were
clearly important to the processes of the sensations in Hungarian Tiszaeszlár
as well as in Bohemian Polná, and this would be true in different ways in the
cases in Galician Rutscha and others. On the other hand, some aspects of
these dynamics were present in cases from the areas of the German Kaiserreich with ethnically mixed populations, particularly those with mixed Slavic
populations such as Silesia, East Prussia, and West Prussia.

In the Hilsner case in Polná, Bohemia, similarly at the century's turn, the
specific context of this particular corner of central Europe would prove significant just as the pattern of the ritual murder accusation and its defenses
would be similar to the cases in the Hungarian half of the Dual Monarchy on
the one side and the Kaiserreich on the other.[65] The Hilsner affair followed

64. See Marx and Engels, "Minutes," 630.
65. Kieval, "Importance of Place."

the pattern of other ritual murder affairs in some ways and became extremely important for central Europeans, called at once the Austrian Dreyfus affair. Besides being more contemporary with Dreyfus than the earlier Tiszaeszlár case, it was alike in another respect: the accused, a Jewish ne'er-do-well named Leopold Hilsner, was convicted in court and then again on appeal; the apparent authorization by the court of the prominent prosecutor's allusions to a ritual murder motive mobilized the outrage of enlightened onlookers. Foremost among these was Tomáš Garrigue Masaryk (1850–1937), the future first Czechoslovak president and Czech national icon who had already served in the Austrian Reichsrat as a delegate for the Young Czechs. Knowing little about the culture of Polná or the Jewish religion, the philosopher and statesman's Zolaesque interventions represented a dual commitment, which he insisted must not be seen as contradictory, to Czech nationalism and to cool rationalism. In this sense, his rejection of what he saw as Czech village superstition and defense of Hilsner are comparable to his earlier support of German nationalist challenges to the authenticity of Czech medieval manuscripts.[66] Both positions drew ire from more orthodox Czech nationalists, but Masaryk was passionate about a nationalist identity that should emerge out of a modern, objectively grounded philosophical scientism—even if such a position were at odds with the prejudice of the countryside and even his own, "visceral" antisemitic feelings, as he confessed in a letter to a friend.[67] Masaryk's passion to drive out the beast of superstition and prejudice was a self-exorcism of sorts.

The belief that Jews engaged in violent anti-Christian ritual, Masaryk held, was "in fact superstition in the fullest sense of the word. This superstition is a scandal of our times . . . the open door to all other superstition, a school for national and social delusion and violence."[68] As other enlightened responses, Masaryk's treatment dwelled on the testimony of scientific and especially medical experts followed by an analysis of the logic of evidence and the subjective construction of Hilsner's guilt worthy of a student of Hanns Gross.[69] The conclusion of Hilsner's guilt could not be based on the physical evidence at all, "but on the most subjective of all grounds: antisemitism and ritual superstition."[70]

Max Grunwald, a German rabbi and folklorist from Prussian Silesia who

---

66. See Spector, *Prague Territories*, 41, 253n21.
67. Szporluk, *Political Thought of Tomáš G. Masaryk*, 61.
68. Masaryk, *Die Bedeutung*, "Vorrede"; *Die Notwendigkeit*.
69. Masaryk, *Bedeutung*, 62–78.
70. Ibid., 74.

had taken a position as rabbi in the fifteenth district in Vienna, felt he should yield to the jurists for an analysis of the "procedural monstrosities" characterizing the Hilsner case. But what expertise was he representing in his tract titled *Zur Psychologie und Geschichte des Blutritualwahnes* (On the psychology and history of the blood ritual madness)? As a rabbi he was able to assert what so many before him had asserted, namely, the incompatibility of the charge with Jewish faith and scripture, and also to stress the irony that Jewish monotheism liberated humanity from human sacrifice.[71]

The details of the case, as with each of the cases mentioned here, could fill the space of a chapter or indeed a book (and has).[72] Hilsner was accused of two murders, and in spite of a dearth of evidence was convicted twice. While the appellate court stripped reference to the ritual murder motive from its judgment, that was the foundation of the prosecutor's case. Indeed, the lawyer for the victim's family, Dr. Karel Baxa, was out for nothing less than to be at the center of this sensational case where the ritual murder charge was to be given legitimacy. He hence gave special attention to evidence and expert testimony that seemed to rule out *Lustmord*. In his closing statement he revealed these motives and called on his audience to have the courage of conviction:

> Gentlemen! The murder is not a sexual one and not a robbery murder; it was not committed out of revenge or jealousy. Let us not be afraid to say it openly, let us not fear that we will be called clerical, let us not be afraid of persecutions and attacks, let us not fear to be called reactionary and backward, but let us say clearly: it has been proven here that there are people who need the blood of our Christian girls![73]

Indeed, Baxa was perfectly justified in anticipating the hefty liberal response to the trials and convictions, which even the prosecution was unembarrassed to liken to the Dreyfus affair and which defenders of modern civilization would not hesitate to brand a witch hunt. If the unprecedented success of the ritual murder accusations was due to factors such as the rise of political antisemitism and a mass media, critics turned to another mode of understanding in light of the trial: psychology, including the branch of criminology known after Hanns Gross as "criminal psychology." Arthur Nussbaum's detailed account of the case called itself a "criminal-psychological investiga-

---

71. Grunwald, *Zur Psychologie*, 5; the disingenuous denial "lassen Sie mich schweigen" is on p. 19.

72. This particular case has recently been fictionalized, or accounted for in the manner of a novel, by Peter Zimmermann, *Die Nacht hinter den Wäldern* (Vienna: Deuticke, 2000).

73. Dr. Baxa, quoted in Paul-Schiff, *Der Prozess Hilsner*, 124.

tion" and was introduced by none less important a figure in criminal science than the Berlin professor Franz von Liszt.[74] The leader of the reform school of criminology predicted the lasting importance of the case for cultural history as well as for the criminalist in that it offered "a contribution to the psychology of testimony that puts all theoretical discussions and all experimental examinations of this subject in the shadows." Referring to Nussbaum's treatment of the case, von Liszt promised that

> In most illustrative fashion the author, on the basis of the record, shows us the power of suggestion: how fantasy images are produced in witness testimony from the source of folk superstition, how they take ever-stronger force, become more vivid and take on more numerous and detailed characteristic features; how after long months new witnesses appear and report under oath on decisive facts that they up until that point have incomprehensibly kept to themselves; how the mesh of the net being drawn about the suspect ever tightens.[75]

And to be sure, Nussbaum does recognize the role of the modern press as well as antisemitic agitation, particularly as these contribute to a sense of sensationalism that is itself the context for the psychological phenomena he is describing. Hanns Gross had already pointed out how subjective judgments can appear to the subject as facts; Schrenck-Notzing had certified that false memories or "pseudoreminiscences" were equal in power to actual memories. Research on hypnotism had moved on to the realm of psychological suggestion, for which a hypnotic state, as we learn from Freud's translation of Hippolyte Bernheim, is not necessary:

> Rather the presence of a condition of psychic agitation [*eines psychischen Erregungszustandes*] provides suggestion appropriate ground, and the more lively the agitation is, the more easily are the inhibitions overcome that interfere with the reinterpretation of the contents of the consciousness. . . . One of the most criminal-psychologically important instances of these theses is provided by the appearance of the so-called sensational trial.[76]

Schrenck-Notzing indeed explicitly noted the difficulty of obtaining unbiased jury members for such trials.[77] In ritual murder trials, Nussbaum

---

74. Nussbaum, *Der Polnaer Ritualmordprozess*.

75. Franz von Liszt, "Vorwort," in Nussbaum, *Der Polnaer Ritualmordprozess*, vi–vii.

76. Nussbaum, *Der Polnaer Ritualmordprozess*, 6–7; cf. Bernheim and Freud, *Die Suggestion*.

77. Albert von Schrenck-Notzing, "Ueber Suggestion und Erinnerungsfälschung im Berchthold-Prozess," *Zeitschrift für Hypnotismus* (1897?), cited in Nussbaum, *Der Polnaer Ritualmordprozess*, 7.

continued, agitation and hence suggestibility were whipped up as in no other time. Here the jurist Nussbaum whips his own medico-pathologizing rhetoric a lap farther, referring to the "far-reaching and dangerous symptoms" specially produced by this sort of trial, and the peculiar typologies produced by the blood libel, so that "we can therefore consider ritual murder trials to belong to a particular species of criminal psychology."[78]

## When You Believe in Things That You Don't Understand

Hanns Gross included extended discussions of two murder cases alleged to have been Jewish ritual murders—the Hilsner case in Bohemia and the murder of Ernst Winter in Konitz, West Prussia—among a set of four in an article he called "Psychopathic Superstition."[79] The mere grouping of these two with the murders of two other adult women by gentile men along with the avoidance of any mention of the charge of ritual murder, show that the father of criminalistics was deeply interested in the sensational cases but not invested in what as we have seen had become a predictable debate. His interest, instead, is methodological: he shows how a particular analysis reveals certain commonalities among these crimes and suggests an adjustment of the reigning taxonomy of violent murder. "New times bring new work," Gross begins, and the best such work is work that "comprehends what its times require."[80] The most difficult such work consists in the "putting together of what belongs together, followed by abstraction, the deduction of a rule from a series of individually identified and well observed cases."[81] As always, the disciplinary innovation Gross puts forward is both product of and response to the special conditions of modernity. He calls the new category for the family of criminality that he proposes *psychopathic superstition*, a term that is interesting for the way it seems to bear a doubled mark of difference from rational modernity. The apparent irrationality of certain violent acts is the starting point for the investigation, what makes them call for new categories and methods of interpretation: "in the appearance of criminal activities certain moments are perceived and singled out that present something or other that stands out, that cannot easily be explained, and that in some way does not seem necessarily to belong to the proceedings as a whole."[82] This ir-

78. Nussbaum, *Der Polnaer Ritualmordprozess*, 7.
79. Gross, "Psychopathischer Aberglaube."
80. Ibid., 253.
81. Ibid., 254.
82. Ibid., 253.

regularity, on the one hand, and the pattern of several such examples, on the other, together signals the need for a new category.

The much discussed case of Leopold Hilsner in Polná, Bohemia, is the first Gross discusses, and he at once casts his gaze to the apparent periphery, the details that other commentators commonly overlook: the tearing and cutting away of clothing from both victims so that they were nearly naked, with strips and articles of their clothes all around the scene of the crime. To this question, at least, the motive of the crime in profit or sexual pleasure is irrelevant; the action of scattering clothes is not clearly linked to either of these motives unless the tearing and dispersion of the victims' clothing is itself a sexual perversion, as some court experts and judges had suggested, always however without precision, explanation, and comparison to other cases. Upon hearing of these strange details, Gross responded differently, immediately recognizing a repetition of details from other cases, three of which he was able to recall after considerable effort: the 1878 murder of Th. S. by J. H., the 1894 double murder by Joseph Maier, and the Winter/Konitz case.[83]

The commonality of the six murders (presumed committed by four murderers, and Gross does not doubt this) lay in a series of details. First and most important to Gross, no ordinary motive (robbery, revenge, jealousy, sexual excitement) offered itself as an explanation for the violent acts. The removal and dispersion of clothing was common to all and remained similarly unexplained. Inexplicability, in other words, called for the creation of a category that would explain the object; collecting similar, unexplained cases was a method for solving what had been unresolved. Ironically, this had been the logic of the ritual murder accusers: the apparent absence of a profit or sexual motive opened the possibility of a motive that was coded, hidden, secret, and conspiratorial.

Gross turned next to the criminal subject and noted that in some cases, at least, the perpetrator was "a psychopathically inclined individual," a vagabond, mentally impaired, and in at least some ways inclined toward superstition.[84] Here as elsewhere (see chap. 1), Gross concluded that there would be value in maintaining an entire independent subfield of criminalistics devoted to the topic of superstition. His exposition on the subject here has two major components, one psychological or psychiatric and one sociological or cultural. The criminally superstitious subject, unlike the mentally normal individual, does not check his impulses to act on the basis of superstition at the

---

83. Gross commented on the Konitz case in the *Archiv für Kriminal-Anthropologie und Kriminalistik* 4, p. 363; 6, no. 2, pp. 216–19.

84. Gross, "Psychopathischer Aberglaube," 279.

moment when such actions would be criminal and harmful to others. Such inhibitions vanish only in the event of extreme poverty and desperation, or in the case of "morally very deeply sunken" subjects, or "if psychopathic conditions have totally compromised his ethical resistance [*Gegenvorstellungen*]."

Psychopathic superstition appears as "the only explanation for a long series of so-called horrifying crimes that are not in any case explicable to normally feeling people: murders of children, pointless or gruesome killings of adults without recognizable motive, horrible abuse and mutilation, etc."[85] Superstition of the most dangerous kind must in fact be much more widespread among ordinary people than is commonly assumed. His list of such beliefs ranges from the criminal magic he had outlined in his earlier work on criminal superstition to the popular Christian faith that innocent children who are murdered become God's angels.

In combining the psychiatric category of psychopathology with an ethnographic notion of superstition, Gross concentrated a set of crimes that were peculiarly modern, and yet in their gruesomeness and irrationality betrayed a residual resistance to modernity. While the possibility that the psychopathic superstition of a Hilsner, for example, might be linked to a Jewish folk superstition is left unspoken, Gross clearly placed the ritual murder accusation or blood libel itself in the category of superstition. As he repeated in several texts, "Superstition, and indeed blood superstition, plays a more important role in the study of penal law than we have generally recognized, but these have nothing to do with religion or with ritual."[86] Ironically, that accusation was fueled in no small part by the cultural fantasy of gruesome violence occurring with seeming randomness and without apparent grounds. More than one antisemitic text cited the unsolved mysteries of the big city, from disappearances to slashings, as evidence that Jewish ritual murder must exist. The rootless, emancipated intellect of the metropolis and the stalwart ignorance of the superstitious countryside were images that called and fed on one another just as they could not be kept apart in the imagination.

### The Anatomy of Sensation: The Ernst Winter Case in Konitz

The most recent case of the four Gross discussed in his piece on pathological superstition was "much commented," as he mentioned, but he did not in this piece refer to the controversy. He confirmed that in this case the murderer was unknown, and therefore he would have to restrict his analysis to

85. Ibid., 280.
86. Hans Gross, "Besprechung," 217.

the physical evidence rather than data about the perpetrator. In fact the details of the murder of Ernst Winter in Konitz are left out of the article with the exception of the single fact tying this case to the others: Winter's body was dismembered, and the torso, arms, thighs, and so on, were discovered in various localities around the city. This act of dispersion, so argued Gross, was the item of criminalistic interest, whereas the objects dispersed (clothing or body parts) were irrelevant.[87] In light of the furor over the case, it must be seen as noteworthy that the questions of evidence and motive raised by antisemites and their enlightened opponents fell completely beyond the bounds of Gross's discussion. The state of the victim's body was itself linked to these arguments because the expertness of its dismemberment suggested the involvement of someone in the butcher's trade.[88]

The victim in Konitz was a male, which would seem to return to the high medieval and early modern ritual murder accusation pattern, but he was no child. Ernst Winter was a student in Konitz, eighteen years of age, broad shouldered and mature, and, as all sources confirm, a bit of a lady-killer. His recent flirtation and apparent seduction of the Christian butcher's daughter made the girl's father the prime suspect until the latter's own campaign launched an explosion of antisemitic feeling in the local populace, another bout of ritual murder discourse in the press, and two parliamentary debates on the issue.[89] While the kosher *shohet* and the Jews accused of complicity were cleared of all charges, the events led to the creation of an "Association for the Solution of the Konitz Murder," meant to come up with evidence to definitively incriminate the Jewish community but which included bourgeois leaders of the community not previously identified as antisemitic, and two violent though not fatal pogroms. In his excellent analysis of the mob violence, Helmut Walser Smith touches on the communal function of the apocalyptic violence of the rioting as well as the performative dimensions of the ritual murder discourse: Christian accusers effectively "enacted and performed . . . a ritual murder."[90] This "reversal," as we have seen, ran throughout the ritual murder accusations and responses. In fact, the position that Smith takes re-

---

87. Gross, "Psychopathischer Aberglaube," 272. At the other end of the spectrum, Hett regards this action as logical and unremarkable; see Hett, *Death in the Tiergarten*, 199.

88. Hence Helmut Walser Smith's title *The Butcher's Tale*. The case was the source of another monograph from the same year, Christoph Nonn, *Eine Stadt such einen Mörder*, and two articles.

89. The discussions took place in the Prussian Abgeordnetenhaus and the Reichstag and are presented in concise detail in Groß, *Ritualmordbeschuldigungen*, 159–73. The debates followed a discussion seven years earlier in light of the Xanten case.

90. Smith, *Butcher's Tale*, 180.

produces the gesture of enlightened responses to the revived blood libel: it is the attackers who are savage, conspiratorial, and violent; their belief in Jewish ritual murder is the dangerous superstition at play. On the other hand, Smith cannot be mistaken but that the frenzy of antisemitic violence, in this moment of mirroring the fantasy of ritual human sacrifice, performed an important service for its participants: it seemed to serve a ritual function in its own right and was played out with ritual precision.

The prominence of the victim's reputation as a sexual adventurer was the source of alternative explanations of the murder, but it also foregrounds the proximity of the ritual murder claim to sexual murder claims. In Polná, while some argued the murders did not follow the patterns of *Lustmord* serial killings, elements of the erotic content of the attacks on the two young girls were impossible to quell.[91] In the case of Ernst Winter, investigators considered a linkage to prostitutes with whom the victim was thought to have had contact, and suspicion of homosexual activity with two different members of the community widely thought to have pederastic tendencies was explored by authorities.[92] Clearly it is true, as a scholar on rumor has asserted and another on Konitz has repeated, that nothing dispels rumor like more rumors; this truism, however, may mask a closer kinship of the two particular rumors in question here, one linking the Jewish community to secret, archaic savagery and the other ascribing violent sexuality to homosexuals. It is almost as if the two phantasies could stand in for one another interchangeably. As we have seen clearly before, authorities—including, in this particular case, criminal commissioner Wehn—regarded "pederasty" as reason enough for suspicion of murder.[93] This could not have been the case in quite the same way for Jews, even where the authorities (as Wehn again, in this case) were inclined to be antisemitic or suspicious of Jews qua Jews.[94] What, then, is the secret of the links between the two cultural fantasies?

At least a few contemporary observers shared the insight we are exploring that points to the genre of the sensation as the key element that requires unpacking. One of these was an anonymous respondent who delivered a

91. Motive as we know was not Gross's main interest in the above-discussed essay, but to Hilsner he does assert that "the probability is that the motive is to be sought in some sexual agitation or other"; see Gross, "Psychopathischer Aberglaube," 259.

92. Rep. 77, Tit. 500 Nr. 50 Bd. 2 Konferenz Protokoll Konitz 21.5.1900, Bl. 137, and Rep. 84a, Nr. 57471 (Bericht Kriminalkommissar Wehn), Bl. 308, GSPK, describe suspicion of the local tailor Otto Plath on the basis of some evidence and common rumor about his sexuality.

93. Rep. 84a, Nr. 57471, Bl. 312, cf. Bl. 308, GSPK.

94. Rep. 84a, Nr. 5747, B. 365, GSPK.

"contribution to a solution" of the Konitz murder even as the case labored on.[95] Hanns Gross may have found the author's facility at reasoning a "solution" (in the sense of solving the crime) artless, but the solution sought in the tract related more likely to the phenomenon of the ritual murder complex than to the crime at Konitz.[96] Beginning with the anatomy of a sensation, the anonymous author, identifying himself as a physician, describes the natural attraction people have to unfortunate incidents, a curiosity that quickly fades as they get replaced by other items of prurient interest. Not so, claims the doctor, where the images of disaster are particularly detailed and vivid—theater fires, sunken ships, or, even worse, a bestial murder followed by the dismemberment and cold distribution of the corpse around the city. In such a case, fantasy goes wild, above all when the act is as incomprehensible as it is gruesome: even the insane act of a sexually perverse killer can be grasped, but where any possible explanation of the deed is lacking, the mass gaze is held insuperably, and out of this hypnotic fascination come the fantasies that the crime comes from a brotherhood of evildoers who are likely to repeat their horrible crimes.[97] While itself reproducing a sensational register, as is so often the case, the tract outlines a particularly insightful set of characteristic features pertaining to violent events that are understood as sensations: their senselessness, obscurity, or simple lack of any conceivable motive; the suggestion of a conspiracy, a brotherhood of fiendish opposition; and finally, the promise of repetition. Like all generic conventions, this structure lends to the sensation a routine that is strikingly at odds with the irrational unpredictability that is supposed to be at the heart of its potential for suspense.

Given these "rules of sensational engagement," it is not surprising that attempts to commandeer sensational narratives and move them to more rational and enlightened conclusions were hard to carry through successfully. Another tract from 1900, for instance, labeled itself "A Call to Reason" but fashioned itself stylistically like a criminal novel, peppered with headings such as "Who Is the Murderer?" and narrating the manipulation of events by antisemitic opportunists as conspiratorial intrigue.[98]

One text that conforms to these generic conventions of the sensational

95. Dr. med. H., *Der Konitzer Mord.*

96. Hans Gross, "Besprechung," 393. Gross rejects the conclusion by "Dr. med. H.," assumed by many other commentators, that the dismemberment of the body suggested the perpetration of someone in the butcher's trade.

97. Dr. med. H., *Der Konitzer Mord,* 3–7.

98. Sutor, *Der Konitzer Mord,* 5–9, 14–23.

while attempting to commandeer the Konitz story for progressive purposes was by a certain Paul Forster and published in 1905.[99] The author, as he describes himself, has neither expertise in Jewish scripture or practice nor in criminalistics, although he does write his text as though it were a genuine criminal novel (*Kriminalroman*). His authority is meant to lie in his familiarity with the region and the city, having lived in Konitz, and he is also sure to assert that he is a Christian.[100] He recalls the reaction in town in early 1884 when the fourteen-year-old Onufri Cybalski was mysteriously murdered and found dismembered in the nearby town of Skurz (Skurcz), another occasion for charges of Jewish ritual murder, and yet the people of Konitz had commonly assumed the crime had been a *Lustmord*.[101]

With the torch of enlightenment, the reasoning of a detective, and in the style of a *Krimi*, Forster weaves a tale that might be as compelling as the legends feeding superstition itself. To the hyperrational questions of the mind of the criminalist—was Winter murdered? Was there a motive?—The masses cry, "Yes! The Jews need Christian blood for their Easter cake!" Superstition, however ungrounded, is hard to dispel.[102] Forster's solution is not much more grounded, however. After logically (if with wild presumption) dismissing the possibilities that the Winter killing was premeditated murder, then following the same procedure to dismiss manslaughter, he turns to the remarkable conclusion that the death must be related to Paragraph 175 of the penal code, and that the shame of homosexual exposure can be the only explanation for why an accidental death would need to be kept so secret. The dismemberment and dispersal of the body is for Forster, as for Gross, the salient feature of the available evidence, and the key—but for Forster, the "secretive obscurity" hovering over these acts and their apparent senselessness calls for the exposure of another secret that will allow for a reasonably probable explanation: the perpetrator is an urning.[103]

Forster spins a tale in the style of a serial novel without skipping a beat

---

99. Forster, *Mord*.

100. Ibid., 8–9.

101. Name variations include Onoph[i]rius Cybulla. Comparisons to the Skurz case in fact played an important role in the Konitz events as well as in the Prussian debates in light of the Konitz affair; the antisemitic political forces did not yet have the power and broader attention they had in the Habsburg Empire or that they would receive by the turn of the century. See Groß, *Ritualmordbeschuldigungen*, 33–50, 162; cf. Hartston, *Sensationalizing the Jewish Question*, 150–59.

102. Forster, *Mord* 11–12.

103. Ibid., 32.

from the pseudocriminological ruminations of the previous pages. The tense is indicative, as in the initial revelation that the killer "is" an urning. He and Winter are good friends, and have more than once traded sexual pleasures, which exert a magical influence over Winter that he cannot resist, although he himself is not an urning. Forster posits that Winter was so strongly inclined sexually that he could not resist sex from a man or from a woman. He draws a scene in surprising detail, still utilizing the continuous present of a serial novel:

> Furtively, he sneaks into the rooms of his urning friend. He slips in unseen. The friend, a bachelor, widow, or separated man living alone is lying stretched out on the sofa. He is dreaming of his sexual sensations. His blood courses hot through his veins. His nerves are agitated. He has desires that are hard to satisfy in Konitz.
>
> Now friend Winter comes in! Perhaps at an agreed-on time. A certain mystery is somehow present, for Winter slipped into the house carefully and *unseen.*
>
> The urning leaps to his feet.—Fiery embrace! The door latch is closed as a sign that no one is at home . . . drapes are drawn . . . the situation becomes ever more secretive.
>
> The accident!
>
> In the midst of the highest ecstasy, Winter is suffocated as the urning frantically pulls him onto himself and does not let go. The penis of the urning has closed off Winter's mouth, throat, and larynx . . . just as only a few seconds are required to bring a hanged man to death by choking, here, too, a few seconds of ecstasy were sufficient to take the life from Winter.[104]

The fantasy is extravagant, to be sure, but what message is encoded in its extravagance?

The linkages among different domains of sensational discourse are explicit here, as the author forces, or tries to force, the ritual murder tributary back into the streams of sexual scandal, urban crime drama, and criminalistic detection. In seeing these unapologetically braided together, we learn more than that rumors displace other rumors or that sensational discourses are competing and interchangeable. The moment of crime and the figure of the perpetrator are both contained in the space where these streams meet. Who is the murderer (as was asked in newspaper reports, in public postings, in criminal stories, and then, famously, in a film such as Fritz Lang's *M*)? The question becomes something more than an opportunity to choose whether it was the Christian butcher or the Jewish, the vengeful father or the duti-

104. Ibid., 34–35.

fully brutal Jew, the fanatical Jew or the desperate homosexual. What can be said about who the murderer is in a case where the murder makes no sense, where it seems to stand for so much and yet for nothing more than murder itself? To this question, Forster's account produces not answers so much as a reproduction of a certain kind of knowledge about sexuality (what was called in chap. 2 "urning knowledge"): the religion of the accidentally murderous urning cannot be determined, for they are of all faiths; the male gender is certain, but social class is uncertain, albeit that uraniandom is more developed in the better social classes, and this one was likely a local official or a tradesman. Whoever is born an urning, science has long proven, can do nothing about it. The lesson of the Konitz tragedy—both the senseless death of the victim and the violent persecution of the Jewish minority in retribution—is not, then, that mobs need to be enlightened or that communities need to be purged. The lie behind the violence is Paragraph 175.

This fantastic tale with its idiosyncratic conclusions exposes the ritual murder complex's place within a larger system of sensational narrative and fantasies of the violent self. It may seem instead to point to the lack of consensus on the meaning of the events, or the irreconcilable conflict regarding the truth about ritual murder. Yet the Winter case and others lay bare the centrality of the way in which the "truth about ritual murder" has been posited as a question throughout the ritual murder complex of accusations and counteraccusations. The question of "truth" lay all about the talk of ritual murder. While blood accusations and bloody acts of communal violence and even expulsion were ways of marking radical communal difference and rending apart categories that were threatening to lose their distinction, such gestures were also symptoms of the opposite: they represented a ritualized discourse of violence that displayed itself as the very thing it decried.

CONCLUSION

# Utopia

Robert Musil's first novel was the 1906 *The Confusions of Young Törless* (fig. 34).[1] This tale of adolescent boys engaged in an endgame of power dynamics and limit-experiences offers a crystalline model of the ways in which the definition of liminal figures may entail identification with them and how this dual process was imagined to have constructive potential. Readers of Musil may recall how throughout his work he would dwell on a concern for the duality of human experience, expressed alternately as mathematical and mystical, scientific and musical, and so on—with each of these expressions clearly gendered. His fantasy of the mystical moment of "the other condition" is sometimes mistaken for the feminine consciousness, but instead it is the moment of mutual synthesis of these spheres—art, religion, and sexual ecstasy in their most powerful moments all represent this unity. In this first novel, a clear borderline figure is "marked" early on, and that is the character Basini, the hapless thief among the boys who is then blackmailed by them and used as sexual slave and object of sadism.

Musil (fig. 35) plays out a fantasy of ecstatic fusion of opposing and gendered consciousness in this work, and it is significant that this fusion is not played out on the body of the feminized Basini but rather in the mind of the narrator and author-surrogate Törless. The narrator's identification with the buggered Basini, rather than Basini's experience, is the vehicle for the realization of his earlier fascination for the notion of the imaginary number—the insertion of the negative number into itself. Basini himself is the ideal feminine, pure object: self-centeredness, idiocy, ethical failure, without subjectivity—Weininger's W (feminine) principle at its extreme pole:

1. R. Musil, *Die Verwirrungen des Zöglings Törless* (Vienna: Wien, 1906).

FIGURE 34. Cover of Robert Musil's sensational novella, 1906.

The moral inferiority that was apparent in him and his stupidity both had a single origin. He had no power of resisting anything that happened to him and was always surprised by the consequences. In this he resembled the kind of woman, with pretty little curls on her forehead, who introduces doses of poison into her husband's food at every meal and then is amazed and horror-struck at the strange, harsh words of the public prosecutor and the death sentence pronounced on her.[2]

2. R. Musil, *Young Törless*, trans. Eithne Wilkins and Ernst Kaiser (London: Secker and Warburg, 1955), 62.

FIGURE 35. Robert Musil.

Thus not even pity is available for the contemptible figure, feminized and the object of violence, but that position retains a terse fascination for the mathematical protagonist. His ruminations about the imaginary number give way to the fantasy of projecting himself into the homosexual body; not to penetrate it, as the sadistic schoolmates are doing, but to be it, and at the same time not entirely to lose himself. Törless interrogates Basini mercilessly to get the latter to reveal the spectacular moment of crossing over, but the pitiful monster knows no such revelation. There is no membrane between self and loss of self where there was no self to begin with.

It is at this key moment that the whole "vast scientific apparatus"[3] behind Weininger's construction of W operates at once as a setup for the resistance by and overcoming of the authorial subject projected into this vessel of
the homosexual body. The moment of the breaking of this resistance would
be an ecstatic one and the place where art happens. In another coital metaphor, Musil defines this condition as "a deeper embedding of thought in the
emotional sphere." But what is the site of this permeation?

Weininger (fig. 36), for his part, did not consign the figure of the male
homosexual to the subjectless oblivion of the W principle in spite of his contempt for the degenerate feminization of all culture. The homosexual in fact
does not appear in Weininger's text as an anomaly, deformity, or exception
to the usual rules of sexual identity and attraction but rather as a special case
illustrating these. In the homosexual of either sex, Weininger finds almost
equal proportions of male and female plasma—rather than standing outside
of the spectrum of normative sexuality, the homosexual stands right in the
middle, an "intermediate form." Thus homosexuality is neither psychic, nor
acquired, but "essential" in this purest of senses.

Weininger is fascinated with the figure of the invert, as though he were a
puzzle that, if cracked, could solve some larger tangle of life. By what therapy
could the scientist masculinize the feminized male? Of course an immediate
resonance of this question is with culture as such, since *Kultur* was described
by Weininger as always only masculine, inaccessible to the W principle, and
hence the degenerate civilization of Weininger's present was not feminine but
feminized. Weininger's special interest in homosexuality is betrayed not only
by his devotion throughout the text to the question but also by the fact that
it is the only area in which Weininger moved from theory to clinical practice.
He advocated treatment of homosexuals through matchmaking with inverts
of the opposite sex (hence complementary plasmic balances) accompanied
by injections of male and female plasmic essences in the form of testicular
and ovarian extracts.[4] Beyond the formulation of this treatment, Weininger
even ventured to experimentation on a single male subject—it has been postulated that the subject was Weininger himself. In a 1901 letter to close friend
and colleague Hermann Swoboda he fairly bursts with excitement: "My agent
to combat homosexuality seems to be successful!! Even though this is only
a confirmation of my own theory, I still haven't recovered from my amaze-

3. G. Lukács, *Soul and Forms*, 25.

4. Hannelore Rodlauer, ed., *Otto Weininger, Eros und Psyche: Studien und Briefe 1899–1902*
(Vienna: Verlag der Österreichischen Akademie der Wissenschaften, 1990), 72n48.

FIGURE 36. Otto Weininger.

ment. If only I could be sure that no suggestion is involved!"[5] In this excerpt we can begin to trace the confrontation within the figure of the male homosexual of the masculine scientist subject and the feminine sexuality of the experimental subject. The physician's cool theory is face-to-face with the

5. Letter to Hermann Swoboda, April 11, 1901, in ibid., 73.

grateful amazement of the patient; the fact that they share one body (and throughout, the thesis would not even be revised by the possibility that the patient was not Weininger, but merely an anonymous subject with whom he clearly identifies) is the source of the student's particular anxiety about the possibility of autosuggestion. The letter continues, "In any case, the doses must be continued. . . . My patient is already preparing for his first coitus!"[6]

⋆

Framing the interwar period in the intellectual space of German-speaking Europe are two texts that deeply reflect on the relationship of savage violence to civilization: at one end, Sigmund Freud's *Beyond the Pleasure Principle* (1920), and at the other, Norbert Elias's *The Civilizing Process* (1939).[7] Each of these texts is considered to constitute a major turning point for its author as well as for the discipline he was influential in founding. Freud's text, in the simplest terms, was revolutionary in that, as the title suggests, it allowed a leap out of a libidinal economy where subjects are driven by the pursuit of pleasure and avoidance of its opposite—it is here, famously, that the death instinct or drive (*Thanatos*) takes on a life independent if not apart from the life of sexual fantasy. For Elias, the "civilizing process" is a history of humanity in which primal human violence is not repressed as much as sublated within a compartmentalized organization of society. This regulation and reorganization of violence assures neither that a fully evolved civilization will be free of violence nor that civilization entails a predetermined, evolutionary process at all. Rather, civilization "expresses the self-consciousness of the West," it is a diacritical concept that condemns the uncivilized periphery to beyond its borders in order to define itself. In the German-language context, the opposition between notions of "civilization" (technical, superficial, Western, modern) and "culture" (artistic, grounded, German, historical) made this concept complex in different ways, which Elias does much to outline. But we can make too much of the interwar appearance of these important texts on the place of violence within civilization (along with many others, including, temporally between them, Freud's explicit statement on this issue in *Civilization and Its Discontents*). In the same way, we may be overemphasizing the disaggregation of the sexual and death instincts/drives themselves. It is customary to think of Freud's changing thinking about the death drive in relation to the European experience of its most horrific war, and there must

6. Ibid.

7. Sigmund Freud, *Jenseits des Lustprinzips*, in Freud, *Gesammelte Werke*, 13:3–69; Norbert Elias, *Über den Prozess*.

be something right about that. At the same time, even when Freud postulated that violent gestures and fantasies derived directly from the libido, a strong awareness of this "side" of sexuality permeated his prewar texts.

At the outset of this study we established that it was only through readings of the dense constellations of material presented in the chapters that the parallel interactions of professional knowledge, self-identity, and violent cultural fantasy would come into view. Those readings and the play among them remain the best place to observe the dynamics under study in *Violent Sensations*. In sum, though, we can say more about the projected path from the conception of limit figures over fantasies of violence to an alternative future self.

The expert inquiries into the identities of figures such as the male homosexual, the eroticized woman, and the lust murderer entailed more than gestures of "marginalization" or "othering." In all of these inquiries, as well as in the sensationalizing accounts intended for broad consumption, there is a surplus of attention to such figures and a powerful tendency to associate them with lurid fantasies of savagery, abandon, and especially of violence. Yet in each of these figures, and in nearly every example that has appeared in our own inquiry, identification with these "limit figures" has cohabited with a sometimes dramatically staged disidentification (what has been called "pathologization" in the case of expert medical discourses of such figures, and which appears as moralizing disdain in melodramatic narratives from news accounts to popular fiction). Violence appears to play a key role in the relationship of an idealized subject of modern civilization to these figures, which are at once paradigmatic representatives of that modernity and its exiles. This is a relationship that, as is argued in these chapters, ought to be considered dialectical rather than diacritical. Put differently, these recurring variations function less to mark and banish those outside of the "charmed circle" of normative identity than they do to offer an occasion to imagine the possibility of recuperating a place in the "outer limits" for the rational or civilized self.

The example of sexual identity (or Dr. Westphal's "sensibility") is one where the complexity of these dynamics came into view. It may be a commonplace that sexology and its precursors from the start focused on "deviance" or "perversion"—the border cases of sexual behavior—to define the realm of sexuality generally. Yet to take this truism as a conclusion rather than a question results in missing how an image of sexuality as such is produced through a fantasy of the deviant subject. It is to miss the process whereby observers and readers posited as normal are forced to imagine their own interior lives as volatile, primal, and animalistic; as inherently violent, as excessive by nature rather than by abnormal deviation or as a result of degeneration.

Sexuality seems to have offered readers a primordial self that was paradoxically a release from selfhood (from individuality, from volition and accountability, from "identity"). This paradox of subjectivity is lost if we imagine instead an opposition of plural deviant/perverse/violent/homosexual versus normal/procreative/loving/heterosexual sexualities rather than looking at how these narratives created an identity for sexuality as such.

There are clearly compelling parallels among the constructions of various liminal figures tracked here: mad criminal, homosexual, prostitute, lust murderer, fanatic Jew. That is not to say that the figures are equivalent, or that the fantasies of violence associated with them were identical. To be sure, one interesting aspect of these cases has been their variation, or dissimilarity. The virtually universal association of these figures with violence, for example, seems to have been to some degree agnostic about whether they were subjects or objects of violence. It is true that there are no female lust murderers, and melodramas famously punish sexual indulgence with death. Yet it is more striking how often roles are reversed, as though the figures are conjured not to be expurgated as much as to release the principle of violence itself. The inclusion of a chapter on the ritual murder sensations was meant in part to highlight this through the observation of a set of representations by antisemitic accusers and enlightened Christian or Jewish respondents that reproduced one another in form (and, to a jarring degree, content). In this case, unlike that of the enlightened feminist and homosexual movements, the emancipatory discourses of Jewish communities and the self-understandings of Jewish assimilationists were not as relevant as the attacks on "savage" antisemites. The question of civilization that lay sometimes dormant in previous chapters became central in this case, where images of a ritual community harboring secret barbaric and intensely violent practices mirrored the representation of a popular ignorance and subterranean antisemitism waiting to explode violently—both sides shrouded in superstition, both bloodthirsty. As Görres's early text had anticipated, the truth of one or the other accusation paled in the face of the power of the violence released through these ritual moves.

The paradox of the metropolis framing the opening chapter turns out to have been central to the fantasies of sexuality and violence that followed. Rather than presenting an irresolvable tension, there is something productive in the suspicion that civilization itself is the source of a degeneration producing both sexual excess and violence and at the same time that both of these are escapes from the ennui of what life has become. These representations were, in other words, as deeply self-critical as they were shunning of others. Yet self-criticism on this grand (if unconscious) cultural scale was not equivalent to the cultural pessimism of certain conservative elite intellectuals or to the aesthetic pose of "decadence" by some artists and writers. As Musil revealed in a brilliant retrospective diagnosis of the age, it wore the gloss or facade of decay only to mask its utopian hope. The fantasies in play here are as much forward looking as they are reflections on decline.

The focus on "degeneration," on this view, is a call for humankind to further evolve, and the embrace of "decadence" a mask held before its future form. Aestheticism occurs in the above chapters as often as either of these other classic terms of the fin de siècle. It takes the form of a search for purity: think of the criminologist's obsession with the crime stripped of motive, the forensic psychiatrist's focus on the criminal act liberated from volition, the debates over criminal responsibility, or for that matter innate homosexuality, prostitution, or criminality. All of these were so many pieces of an imaginary that created perfect criminals and perfect victims—crime for crime's sake— and that rescued heroically staged acts of deviance from the soulless rationalization of circumstance. These particular forms of aestheticism rejected social, historical, and other contextual explanations of dissidence, but they also rejected will. Hence the consistent return to *Dämmerzustände* (Krafft-Ebing's early obsession, echoed throughout the forensic literature for decades)—the half-conscious states of sleepwalking, epilepsy, alcoholism, religious fanaticism, and sexual frenzy. The pure, compulsive, or "born" type was the key to the true nature of crime or sexuality or violence, which in turn might offer access to the secret of the self.

Instead of a utopian future, the period ended, as everybody knows, in yet unprecedented violence. The impulse toward apocalyptic violence running throughout these fantasies suggests a central European imaginary that was more closely linked to the right-wing male fantasies of the German interwar period than to a historiographical image of an aesthetic garden of ornament and pleasure. If this linkage suggests a path from nineteenth-century self-perceptions to twentieth-century violence on the ground, it is useful to recall that this was not the only possible trajectory. These self-perceptions—those proffered with scientific certainty and optimism as well as those declaring civilizational collapse—were, if we are to take them seriously, so many ways of reimagining the subject—a thing that had come to be scrupulously defined and which yet must on some level defy definition. It was a thing that must escape reason at some point and hence be left to the realm of sensation.

*Acknowledgments*

This book was researched as though it were several books. It was a long time in the writing and has been in production longer than is usual. It stands to reason that a project this long term will have incurred a commensurate share of debts. In fact I cannot name all the people and institutions I have encountered that have had an impact on this book, but I can make a gesture toward acknowledging the substance of that debt.

Thanking one's students is so routine that the gesture may seem hollow, and yet the graduate seminars devoted to topics related to this book had an influence on me as much as I hope it did on them. The topics of their own dissertations put the reciprocity of teaching, learning, and scholarship on display: Todd Ettelson's work on masculinity and National Socialism, Marti Lybeck's recent book on lesbian culture in the Weimar Republic, Kristin McGuire on German and Polish feminism, Jay Layne on the rhetoric of *Lustmord*, Ross Bowling on sensational reportage in Weimar Berlin, Kirsten Leng on sexual science and feminist activism in fin-de-siècle Germany and Britain, Sara Jackson on the performance of feminine criminality, Andy Cavin on primitivism and modernity, to name only the most relevant. Many others wrote on things much further afield but have contributed to my thinking in as many ways. I thank them first.

Through its gestation and incubation, this book has been anchored at the University of Michigan, and my friends and colleagues there have been critically important to me. Kathleen Canning, a sister in my doctoral family and in other ways, and Geoff Eley, another adopted family member, have helped me think through the questions of this book in the context of coteaching, reading groups, collaborations, jokes, and arguments. Helmut Puff has been a friend and model for many years and close to me not only as a student of

German-language culture but also in the history of sexuality. He has been one of several ideal readers for the book, and the collaboration with him as well as with Dagmar Herzog on *After the History of Sexuality* left its imprint on the manuscript. Michigan's strength in the history of sexuality has informed the text in many ways, and in addition to Helmut I must thank David Halperin, Gayle Rubin, and Valerie Traub in particular for their friendship and example. Among my many other colleagues I owe a special word to Rudolf Mrázek, my fellow Habsburg subject, more guardian angel than mentor, and comrade of sensibility.

I will not, but would have reason to name every member of the German Department, which has modeled interdisciplinary scholarship and productive collegiality for me for over two decades at this writing, and I have benefited from my appointment in the Frankel Center for Judaic Studies as well. Chapters from this book have been read in draft at colloquia in each of these units as well as at the legendary Comparative Study of Social Transformations working group and the Lesbian, Gay, Queer Research Initiative at the University of Michigan. Short pieces related to chapter 3 appeared as "Where Personal Fate Turns to Public Affair: Homosexual Scandal and Social Order in Vienna, 1900–1910" in *Austrian History Yearbook* 38 (2007): 15–24, and "The Wrath of the 'Countess Merviola': Tabloid Exposé and the Emergence of Homosexual Subjects in Vienna 1907," in *Sexuality in Austria*, ed. Günter Bischof, Anton Pelinka, and Dagmar Herzog, Contemporary Austrian Studies, vol. 15 (Edison, NJ: Transaction, 2006), 31–48; a German version of a portion of chapter 1 appeared as "Die Großstadt schreiben: Zur literarischen Unterwelt der Städte um 1900," in *Kriminalliteratur und Wissensgeschichte: Genres—Techniken—Medien*, ed. C. Peck and F. Sedlmeier (Bielefeld: Transcript 2015), 115–27.

This book is based in archival and library research, and more collections were consulted than I will name here (the bibliography includes a comprehensive list of archives). I would particularly want to thank the staffs at the Library of Congress in Washington, DC, the Austrian National Library, and the libraries of the University of Vienna and of the University of Michigan. Indispensable to me were Lesley Hall in London in the Wellcome Library's archival division, where I was given access to the Krafft-Ebing papers; Shawn C. Wilson at the Kinsey Institute archives in Bloomington, Indiana, with its Magnus Hirschfeld "scrapbook"; Ralf Dose at the Magnus Hirschfeld Society in Berlin; and the staffs of the Wiener Stadt- und Landesarchiv, giving me access to Austrian penal cases; the Berlin-Brandenburgisches Landeshauptarchiv in Potsdam, when it was still in the Orangerie of the Sanssouci palace and held Berlin police records; the Graz city, university, and Styrian State archives; the Hygiene Museum in Dresden and the Saxon State Archive; and in Hungary the National Széchényi Library manuscript collection, with its nearly comprehensive collection of Károly Kertbeny's papers. They have all made the research process possible, and also its own kind of pleasure.

Several fellowships supported the research and writing of *Violent Sensations*, including a senior fellowship at the Rutgers Center for Historical Analysis, a senior fellowship at the International Research Center for Cultural Studies (IFK) in Vienna, an American Council of Learned Societies and American Association of Universities fellowship to reside at the Library of Congress's John W. Kluge Center, a Michigan Humanities Award from the Office of the Vice President for Research at the University of Michigan, a departmental research leave sponsored by the history department, and a John Rich Faculty Fellowship at the university's Institute for the Humanities. A second stint at the wonderful IFK in 2013–14—this time funded by the Fulbright Foundation—began after the submission of this manuscript but allowed me to rescan some of the images and check a reference or two while working on forthcoming projects. Chapters of the book were presented in some form at each of the residential venues, and the intellectual exchange in all of them was a positive force. Other occasions for public lecture and discussion of this material were provided at the University of Pennsylvania, the University of Toronto, Ohio State University, the University of Cape Town, New York University, and Columbia University (thanks among others to Katherine Lebow, Jeff Peck, Paul Reitter, Liliane Weissberg, and Larry Wolff). Finally, the University of Chicago Press has an inspired editor in the person of Doug Mitchell, who has been publishing some of the best—and also some of the first—titles in the history of sexuality and related fields for decades. I met with him periodically in the years the book was being written, over music, beer, conversation. We were both lucky to have the help of Kyle Wagner to shepherd the long-grazing manuscript to the presses.

These acknowledgments would not be worthy of the name were they not to invoke the names of those who offer the most support on a daily basis. A dog's life was not long enough to support the research and writing of these pages, and so I must be grateful for both Burckhardt and Pye, who withstood every insight and revision. In so many ways, this is as much Eric's book as was my first; I can still read him on every page. Above all I feel grateful today for the closeness of my immediate family: along with Eric, for Natalie, Benjamin, Debra, and Rebecca, for Tom, Tony, Leah, and Jennifer, and for Michael, to whose memory the book is dedicated.

# Bibliography

## Archival Collections

### AUSTRIA

#### *Graz*

Archiv für die Geschichte der Soziologie in Österreich (AGSÖ)
Stadtarchiv Graz (SG)
Steiermärkisches Landesarchiv (StLA)
Universitätsarchiv Graz (UAG)

#### *Vienna*

Bundes-Polizeidirektion Wien, Archiv (BPW)
Österreichische Nationalbibliothek (ÖNB)
Österreichisches Staatsarchiv (Allgemeines Verwaltungsarchiv) (AVA)
Wiener Stadt- und Landesarchiv (WSL)
Wiener Stadt- und Landesbibliothek, manuscript division (WSLB)

### GERMANY

#### *Berlin*

Berlin-Brandenburgisches Landeshauptarchiv (BBLHA, holdings transferred to LAB)
Geheimes Staatsarchiv Preussischer Kulturbesitz (GSPK)
Landesarchiv Berlin (LAB)

#### *Dresden*

Sächsisches Staatsarchiv Dresden (SSaD)

### HUNGARY

National Széchényi Library, Manuscript Collection, Budapest (NSL)

UNITED KINGDOM

British Library Manuscripts Division, London (BLM)
Wellcome Library for the History and Understanding of Medicine, Archives and Manuscripts,
London (WLAM)


UNITED STATES

Kinsey Institute for Research in Sex, Gender, and Reproduction, Archives, Bloomington, Indiana (KIRSGR)


## Contemporary Journals and Newspapers (Selected)

NEWSPAPERS AND MAGAZINES

*Allgemeine österreichische Gerichtszeitung*
*Berliner Abendblatt*
*Berliner Gerichts-Zeitung*
*Berliner Lokal-Anzeiger*
*Berliner Morgenpost*
*Berliner Morgen-Zeitung und Tägliches Familienblatt*
*Berliner Tageblatt*
*Das Gericht: Unabhängige nationale Wochenschrift für Gerichtswesen und öffentliches Leben*
*Das interessante Blatt*
*Der Kriminalkommissär: Illustrierte Wochenschrift*
*Der Welten-Bummler. Interessante Illustrierte Zeitung*
*Deutsche Allgemeine Zeitung*
*Deutsches Volksblatt*
*Deutsch-soziale Blätter*
*Die Tribüne: Wochenschrift für Aufklärung, Belehrung und Unterhaltung* (Berlin)
*Die Zukunft* (Berlin)
*Illustrirte Wochenrundschau über das Berliner Leben*
*Morgen-Zeitung*
*Neue Detektiv-Zeitung: Illustrierte Kriminal-Wochenschrift*
*Neue Freie Presse* (Vienna)
*Neue Preussische Zeitung*
*Neues Wiener Journal: Unparteiisches Tagblatt*
*Oesterreichische Kriminal-Zeitung: Wochenblatt für öffentliches Leben, Kriminal- und Polizeiwesen*
*Oesterreichische Rundschau*
*Politisch-Anthropologische Revue: Monatsschrift für das soziale und geistige Leben der Völker*
*Tägliche Rundschau*
*Volks-Zeitung. Organ für Jedermann aus dem Volke*
*Vossische Zeitung. Berlinische Nachrichten von Staats- und gelehrte Sachen*
*Wiener Allgemeine Zeitung*
*Wiener illustrirte Kriminal-Zeitung*
*Wiener Morgen-Zeitung*
*Wiener Zeitung*

## PROFESSIONAL JOURNALS

*Archiv für Kriminal-Anthropologie und Kriminalistik*
*Archiv für Psychiatrie und Nervenkrankheiten*
*Der Irrenfreund*
*Deutsche Juristen-Zeitung*
*Deutsche Zeitschrift für die Staatsarzneikunde*
*Geschlecht und Gesellschaft*
*Jahrbuch für sexuelle Zwischenstufen*
*Monatsschrift für Kriminalpsychologie und Strafrechtsreform*
*Sexual-Probleme: Zeitschrift für Sexualwissenschaft und Sexualpolitik*
*Wiener medizinische Blätter: Zeitschrift für die gesammte Heilkunde*
*Zeitschrift für die. gesamte Strafrechtswissenschaft*
*Zeitschrift für ärztliche Fortbildung*
*Zeitschrift für Sexualforschung*
*Zeitschrift für Sexualwissenschaft*
*Zeitschrift für wissenschaftliche Zoologie*

## Contemporary Books, Pamphlets, and Articles

Adler, Cyrus, and Isidore Singer. *The Jewish Encyclopedia: A Descriptive Record of the History, Religion, Literature, and Customs of the Jewish People from the Earliest Times to the Present Day.* New York: Funk and Wagnalls, 1901–6.

Altmann, Ludwig. *Hugo Schenk und seine Genossen.* Edited by Dr. Ludwig Altmann. Vol. 3, *Aus dem Archiv des grauen Hauses: Eine Sammlung merkwürdiger Wiener Straffälle.* Vienna: Rikola, 1925.

Anon. *Das Paradoxon der Venus Urania.* Würzburg: Stuber, 1869.

———. "Die Prostitution in Wien." *Oesterreichische Kriminal-Zeitung: Wochenblatt für öffentliches Leben, Kriminal- und Polizeiwesen* 1, no. 19 (August 26, 1907): 4–5.

———. Prozess des Mädchenmörders Hugo Schenk und seiner Genossen. Linz: S. Tagwerker, 1884.

———. Sechs Aktenstücke zum Prozesse von Tisza-Eszlar. Berlin: L. Simion, 1882.

Asher, David. "Schopenhauer and Darwinism." *Journal of Anthropology* 1, no. 3 (1871): 312–32.

Augspurg, Anita. *Die ethische Seite der Frauenfrage.* Munich: Köhler, 1894.

Baer, Abraham Adolf. *Der Verbrecher in anthropologischer Beziehung.* Leipzig: Thieme, 1893.

Bäumer, Gertrud, Agnes Bluhm, Ika Freudenberg, Anna Kraußneck, Helene Lange, Anna Pappritz, Alice Salomon, and Marianne Weber. *Frauenbewegung und Sexualethik: Beiträge zur modernen Ehekritik.* Heilbronn a. N.: Salzer, 1909.

Baumgarten, Emanuel. *Die Blutbeschuldigung gegen die Juden: Von christlicher Seite beurtheilt.* 2nd ed. Vienna: Steyermühl, 1883.

Bebel, August. *Die Frau und der Sozialismus.* Zürich-Hottingen: Volksbuchhandlung, 1879.

Benedikt, Moriz. *Anatomische Studien an Verbrecher-Gehirnen: Für Anthropologen, Mediciner, Juristen und Psychologen.* Wien: Braumüller, 1879.

Berliner, A. *Gutachten Ganganelli's Clemens XIV in Angelegenheit der Blutbeschuldigung der Juden.* Berlin: Deutsch, 1888.

Bernheim, H., and Sigmund Freud. *Die Suggestion und ihre Heilwirkung.* Leipzig: Deuticke, 1889.

Bernstein, Eduard. "Aus Anlaß eines Sensationsprozesses." *Die Neue Zeit* Jg. 13, Bd. 2, no. 32 (1895): 171–76.

———. "Die Beurtheilung des widernormalen Geschlechtsverkehrs." *Die Neue Zeit* Jg. 13, Bd. 2, no. 34 (1895): 228–33.

Bertillon, Alphonse. *Identification anthropométrique: instructions signalétiques*. Melun: Impr. administrative, 1893.

Birnbaum, Karl. *Die psychopathischen Verbrecher: Die Grenzzustände zwischen geistiger Gesundheit und Krankheit in ihren Beziehungen zu Verbrechen und Strafwesen: Handbuch für Ärzte, Juristen und Strafanstaltsbeamte*. Enzyklopädie der modernen Kriminalistik 11. Berlin: Langenscheidt, 1914.

Bloch, Iwan. *Das Sexualleben unserer Zeit in seinen Beziehungen zur modernen Kultur*. Berlin: Marcus, 1907.

Bloch, Josef Samuel. *Acten und Gutachten in dem Prozesse Rohling contra Bloch*. Vol. 1. Vienna: Breitenstein, 1890.

———. *Gegen die Anti-Semiten: Eine Streitschrift*. Vienna: Löwy, 1882.

———. *My Reminiscences*. Vienna: Löwit, 1923. Reprint, New York: Arno, 1973. Citations refer to the 1973 reprint.

———, ed. *Talmud und Judentum in der Oesterr. Volksvertretung*. Documente der Aufklärung, vol. 3. [Vienna?], 1900.

Böhme, Margarete. *Tagebuch einer Verlorenen*. Berlin: Fontane, 1905.

Born, Paul. *Berlins dunkle Existenzen: Ernstes und Heiteres aus dem Leben und Treiben der Hauptstadt*. Berlin: Steinitz, 1893.

Braun, Lily. *Die Frauenfrage: Ihre geschichtliche Entwicklung und wirtschaftliche Seite*. Leipzig: Hirzel, 1901.

Bücher, Karl, Friedrich Ratzel, Georg von Mayr, Heinrich Waentig, Georg Simmel, Theodor Petermann, and Dietrich Schäfer. *Die Großstadt: Vorträge und Aufsätze zur Städteausstellung*. Jahrbuch der Gehe-Stiftung zu Dresden, Bd. 9. Dresden: Zahn und Jaensch, 1903.

Casper, Johann Ludwig. *A Handbook of the Practice of Forensic Medicine: Based upon Personal Experience*. Translated by George William Balfour, Vol. 3. London: New Sydenham Society, 1864.

———. *Klinische Novellen zur gerichtlichen Medicin: Nach eignen Erfahrungen*. Berlin: Hirschwald, 1863.

———. "Ueber Nothzucht und Päderastie und deren Ermittelung Seitens des Gerichtsarztes: Nach eigenen Beobachtung." *Vierteljahrsschrift für gerichtliche und öffentliche Medicin* 1 (1852): 21–78.

Daumer, Georg Friedrich, *Der Feuer- und Molochdienst der alten Hebräer als urväterlicher, legaler, orthodoxer Cultus der Nation*. Brunswick: Otto, 1842.

———. *Die Geheimnisse des christlichen Alterthums*. Vol. 1. Hamburg: Hoffmann und Campe, 1847.

Deckert, Joseph. *Ein Ritualmord: Aktenmässig nachgewiesen*. 3rd ed. Dresden: Glöss, 1893.

Delitzsch, Franz. *Rohling's Talmudjude beleuchtet*. Leipzig: Dörffling und Franke, 1881.

Dr. med. H. *Der Konitzer Mord: Ein Beitrag zur Klärung*. Breslau: Preuss und Jünger, 1900.

Eisler, Rudolf. *Wörterbuch der philosophischen Begriffe: Historischquellenmässig*. Berlin: Mittler, 1904.

Elberskirchen, Johanna. *Die Prostitution des Mannes: Auch eine Bergpredigt—Auch eine Frauenlektüre*. Zurich: Schabelitz, 1896.

Elias, Norbert. *Über den Prozess der Zivilisation: Soziogenetische und psychogenetische Untersu-*

*chungen.* 2 vols. Basel: Falken, 1939. Translated by Edmund Jephcott as *The Civilizing Process.* Oxford: Blackwell, 1994. Page references are to the 1994 translation.

Eulenburg, Albert. *Real-Encyclopädie der gesammten Heilkunde: Medicinisch-chirurgisches Handwörterbuch für praktische Aerzte.* Vienna: Urban und Schwarzenberg, 1894.

Ferri, Enrico, and Robert Ferri. "The Present Movement in Criminal Anthropology apropos of a Biological Investigation in the English Prisons: Charles Goring's *The English Convict: A Symposium.*" *Journal of the American Institute of Criminal Law and Criminology* 5, no. 2 (1914): 224–27.

Fischer-Dückelmann, Anna. *Das Geschlechtsleben des Weibes: Eine physiologischsoziale Studie mit ärztlichen Ratschlagen.* Berlin: Bermühler, 1901.

Foerster, Friedrich Wilhelm. *Sexualethik und Sexualpädagogik: Eine Auseinandersetzung mit den Modernen.* Kempten: Kösel'he, 1907.

Forel, Auguste. *Die sexuelle Frage: Eine naturwissenschaftliche, psychologische, hygienische und soziologische Studie für Gebildete.* Munich: Reinhardt, 1905.

Forster, Paul. *Mord, Totschlag oder Körperverletzung mit tötlichem Ausgang? Hypothesen zu dem geheimnisvollen Tode des Konitzer Gymnasiasten Winter.* Werdohl in Westfalen: Scholz, 1905.

Frederiksen, Elke. *Die Frauenfrage in Deutschland 1865–1915: Texte und Dokumente, Universal-Bibliothek.* Stuttgart: Reclam, 1981.

Freud, Sigmund. *Gesammelte Werke in achtzehn Bänden mit einem Nachtragsband.* Edited by Anna Freud, Marie Bonaparte, E. Bibring, W. Hoffer, E. Kris, and O. Osakowe. Frankfurt: Fischer, 1999.

Friedlaender, Hugo. *Interessante Kriminal-Prozesse von kulturhistorischer Bedeutung: Darstellung merkwürdiger Strafrechtsrfälle aus Gegenwart und Jüngstvergangenheit nach eigenen Erlebnissen.* Berlin: Barsdorf, 1910.

———. *Kulturhistorische Kriminal-Prozesse der letzten vierzig Jahre: Mit einem Vorwort von Rechtsanwalt Dr. jur. J. Werthauer.* Berlin: Continent, 1908.

Gagern, Carlos de. *Die Entwickelung der Frauenfrage.* Vienna: Verein Bildung, 1879.

Ghillany, Friedrich Wilhelm. *Die Menschenopfer der alten Hebräer.* Nuremberg: Schrag, 1842.

Görres, Johann Joseph von. *Die christliche Mystik.* 4 vols. Regensburg: Manz, 1842.

Gougenot des Mousseaux, R. *Le juif: Le judaïsme et la judaisation des peuples chrétiens.* Paris: Plon, 1869.

Gross, Hanns. "Besprechung: Der Blutmord in Konitz mit Streiflichtern auf die strafrechtliche Stellung der Juden im Deutschen Reich." *Archiv für Kriminal-Anthropologie und Kriminalistik* 1, no. 2 (1900): 217.

———. *Criminalpsychologie.* Graz: Leuschner und Lubensky, 1898.

———. *Gesammelte Kriminalistische Aufsätze.* 2 vols. Leipzig: Vogel, 1902–8. [*GKA*]

———. "Psychopathischer Aberglaube." *Archiv für Kriminal-Anthropologie und Kriminalistik* 9 (1902): 253–82.

Grunwald, Max. *Zur Psychologie und Geschichte des Blutritualwahnes: Der Prozess Simon von Trient und Leopold Hilsner.* Berlin: Calvary, 1906.

Hellpach, Willy. *Prostitution und Prostituierte.* Edited by Hans Landsberg. Moderne Zeitfragen 5. Berlin: Pan, 1905.

Herzl, Theodor. *Complete Diaries.* New York: Herzl Press, 1960.

Herzog, Johann Jakob, Albert Hauck, and Hermann Caselmann. *Realencyklopädie für protestantische Theologie und Kirche.* 3rd ed. Leipzig: Hinrichs, 1898.

Hirsch, William. *Genie und Entartung: Eine psychologische Studie.* Berlin: Coblentz, 1894. English translation as *Genius and Degeneration: A Psychological Study.* London: Heinmann, 1897.

Hössli, Heinrich. *Eros: Die Männerliebe der Griechen, ihre Beziehungen zur Geschichte, Erziehung, Literatur und Gesetzgebung aller Zeiten.* 1836, 1838. Reprint, Berlin: Bibliothek rosa Winkel, 1996.

Jäger, Gustav. *Die Entdeckung der Seele: Zugleich Lehrbuch der allgemeinen Zoologie.* Abt. 3, *Psychologie.* Leipzig: Günther, 1880.

Jaspers, Karl. "Heimweh und Vee brechew." *Archiv für Kriminal-Anthropologie und Kriminalistik* 35, no. 1/2 (1909): 1–116.

Karsch, Ferdinand. *Der Putzmacher von Glarus Heinrich Hössli (1784–1864), ein Vorkämpfer der Männerliebe: Ein Lebensbild, Quellenmaterial zur Beurteilung angeblicher und wirklicher Uranier.* Leipzig: Spohr, 1903. Reprint, New York: Arno, 1975.

Kayserling, Meyer. *Die Blutbeschuldigung von Tisza-Eszlár.* Budapest: Selbstverlag des Verfassers, 1882.

Kertbeny, Karl Maria, C. *Schriften zur Homosexualitätsforschung.* Edited by Manfred Herzer. Bibliothek rosa Winkel, Bd. 22. Berlin: Verlag rosa Winkel, 2000.

Kisch, E. Heinrich. *Die sexuelle Untreue der Frau. Erster Teil: Die Ehebrecherin: Eine sozialmedizinische Studie.* Bonn: Marcus und Weber, 1916.

Kornfeld, Hermann. "Gerichts-Aerzte." *Archiv für Kriminal-Anthropologie und Kriminalistik* 5, no. 2 (1900): 191–94.

Kraepelin, Emil. *Psychiatrie: Ein Lehrbuch für Studierende und Ärzte.* Leipzig: Barth, 1899.

Krafft-Ebing, Richard von. *Arbeiten aus dem Gesamtgebiet der Psychiatrie und Neuropathologie,* 3. Heft. Leipzig: Barth, 1897–99.

———. *Beiträge zur Erkennung und richtigen forensischen Beurtheilung krankhafter Gemüthszustände, für Aerzte, Richter und Vertheidiger.* Erlangen: Enke, 1867.

———. *Grundzüge der Criminalpsychologie auf Grundlage der deutschen und österreichischen Strafgesetzgebung.* Erlangen: Enke, 1872.

———. *Lehrbuch der Psychiatrie auf klinischer Grundlage für praktische Ärzte und Studirende.* 2nd ed. Stuttgart: Enke, 1883.

———. *Die Lehre von der Mania transitoria: Für Aerzte und Juristen dargestellt.* Erlangen: Enke, 1865.

———. *Psychopathia sexualis: Mit Beiträgen on Georges Bataille, Werner Brede, Albert Caraco, Salvador Dalí, Ernst Fuhrman, Maurice Heine, Julia Kristeva, Paul Kruntorad und Elisabeth Lenk.* Munich: Matthes und Seitz, 1997.

———. *Psychopathia sexualis, with Especial Reference to Contrary Sexual Instinct: A Medico-legal Study.* Translated by C. G. Chaddock from the 7th German ed. Philadelphia: Davis, 1895.

———. *Die Sinnesdelirien: Ein Versuch ihrer physiopsychologischen Begründung und klinischen Darstellung.* Erlangen: Enke, 1864.

———. *Die transitorischen Störungen des Selbstbewusstseins: Ein Beitrag zur Lehre vom transitorischen Irresein in klinisch-forensischer Hinsicht, f. Aerzte, Richter, Staatsanwälte u. Vertheidiger.* Erlangen: Enke, 1868.

Kraus, Karl. *Sittlichkeit und Kriminalität.* Vienna: Rosner, 1908. Reprint in *Schriften,* vol. 1. Frankfurt: Suhrkamp, 1987. Citations refer to the 1987 reprint.

Kurella, Hans. *Die Grenzen der Zurechnungsfähigkeit und die Kriminal-Anthropologie: Für Juristen, Ärzte und gebildete Laien dargestellt.* Halle: Gebauer-Schwetschke, 1903.

———. *Naturgeschichte des Verbrechers: Grundzüge der criminellen Anthropologie und Criminalpsychologie: Für Gerichtsärzte, Psychiater, Juristen und Verwaltungsbeamte.* Stuttgart: Enke, 1893.

Laurent, Achille. *Relation historique des affaires de Syrie: depuis 1840 jusqu'en 1842* . . . . 2 vols. Paris: Gaume Frères, 1846.

Lessing, Theodor. *Der jüdische Selbsthass.* Berlin: Jüdischer Verlag, 1930. Reprint, Munich: Matthes und Seitz, 1984.

Lippert, Robert. *Anklagen der Juden in Russland wegen Kindermords, Gebrauchs von Christenblut und Gotteslästerung.* . . . Leipzig: Engelmann, 1846.

Lipschitz, Leopold, ed. *Christliche Zeugnisse gegen die Blutbeschuldigung der Juden.* Berlin: Walther und Apolant, 1882.

———. *Die Blutbeschuldigung gegen die Juden* . . . . Vienna: Verlag von Dr. Bloch's "Oester-reichischen Wochenschrift," 1883.

Lombroso, Cesare. *Entartung und Genie.* Edited by Hans Kurella. Neue Studien, Bibliothek für Sozialwissenschaft. Leipzig: Wigand, 1894.

———. *Kerker-Palimpseste, Wandinschriften und Selbstbekenntnisse gefangener Verbrecher* . . . . Hamburg: A.-G. Königliche Hofbuchhandlung, 1899.

———. *The Man of Genius.* London: Scott, 1891.

———. *L'uomo delinquente in rapporto all'antropologia, alla giurisprudenza ed alle discipline carcerarie, 1896–1897.* Torino: Fratelli Bocca, 1896. Translated by Mary Gibson and Nicole Hahn Rafter as *Criminal Man.* Durham, NC: Duke University Press, 2006.

Lombroso, Cesare, and Guglielmo Ferrero. *La donna delinquente: la prostituta e la donna normale.* Torino: Roux, 1893. Translated by Nicole Hahn Rafter and Mary Gibson as *Criminal Woman, the Prostitute, and the Normal Woman.* Durham, NC: Duke University Press.

Lukács, György. *Soul and Form: Essays.* London: Merlin, 1974.

Mader, Evaristus. *Die Menschenopfer der alten Hebräer und der benachbarten Völker: Ein Beitrag zur alttestamentlichen Religionsgeschichte.* Edited by O. Bardenhewer. Biblische Studien, vol. 14/5–6. Freiburg: Herdersche, 1909.

Martin, Justizrat zu Nürnberg. "Zum Process Sternberg." *Archiv für Kriminal Anthropologie und Kriminalistik* 6, no. 1 (1901): 182–87.

Marx, Karl, and Friedrich Engels. "Minutes of Marx's Report to the London German Workers' Educational Society on November 30, 1847." In Collected Works. New York: International Publishers, 1975.

Masaryk, T. G. *Die Bedeutung des Polnaer Verbrechens für den Ritualaberglauben.* Berlin: Hermann, 1900.

———. *Die Nothwendigkeit der Revision des Polnaer Processes.* Vol. 9/3, Sonderabdruck aus der Wochenschrift *Die Zeit.* Vienna: Die Zeit, 1899.

Meisel-Hess, Grete. *Das Wesen der Geschlechtlichkeit: Die sexuelle Krise in ihren Beziehungen zur sozialen Frage und zum Krieg zu Moral, Rasse und Religion und insbesondere zur Monogamie.* 2 vols. Jena: Diederichs, 1916.

Metta, K. *Wie belehren wir unsere Kinder in Schule und Haus über das Geschlechtsleben? Möller's Bibliothek für Gesundheitspflege.* Berlin: Möller, 1900.

Möbius, P. J. *Ueber den physiologischen Schwachsinn des Weibes, Sammlung zwangloser Abhandlungen aus dem Gebiete der Nerven- und Geisteskrankheiten.* Halle: Marhold, 1900.

Moll, Albert. *Die conträre Sexualempfindung: Mit Benutzung amtlichen Materials.* Berlin: Fischer's Medicinische Buchhandlung, 1891.

Mommert, Carl, Dr. Theol. *Der Ritualmord bei den Talmud-Juden.* Leipzig: Haberland, 1905.

Musil, Robert. *Gesammelte Werke.* 2. vols. Edited by Adolf Frisé. Reinbek bei Hamburg: Rowohlt, 1978.

———. *Der literarische Nachlass*. Edited by Friedbert Aspetsberger, Karl Eibl, and Adolf Frisé. Reinbek: Rowohlt, 1992. CD-ROM.

———. *Der Mann ohne Eigenschaften*. Erstes und zweites Buch. 15th ed. Edited by Adolf Frisé. Reinbek bei Hamburg: Rowohlt, 2001. [*MoE*]

———. *The Man without Qualities*. 2 vols. Translated by Sophie Wilkins. New York: Knopf, 1995. [*MwQ*]

———. *Precision and Soul: Essays and Addresses*. Translated and edited by Burton Pike and David S. Luft. Chicago: University of Chicago Press, 1990.Näcke, Paul. *Verbrechen und Wahnsinn beim Weibe: mit Ausblicken auf die Criminal-Anthropologie überhaupt; klinisch-statistische, anthropologisch-biologische und craniologische Untersuchungen*. Vienna: Braumüller, 1894.

Nathan, Paul. *Der Prozess von Tisza-Eszlár: Ein antisemitisches Culturbild*. Berlin: Fontane, 1892.

Nordau, Max Simon. *Die conventionellen Lügen der Kulturmenschheit*. Leipzig: Elischer, 1883.

———. *Entartung*. 2 vols. Berlin: Duncker, 1893. Translated by [Wm. Barry] as *Degeneration*. 6th ed. New York: Appleton, 1895.

Nussbaum, Arthur. *Der Polnaer Ritualmordprozess: Eine kriminalpsychologische Untersuchung au aktenmässiger Grundlage*. 2nd ed. Berlin: Hayn's Erben, 1906.

Olberg, Oda. *Das Weib und der Intellectualismus*. Berlin: Edelheim, 1902.

Ostwald, Hans Bergmann Klaus. *Männliche Prostitution im kaiserlichen Berlin*. Berlin: Janssen, 1991.

———. *Vagabunden: Ein autobiographischer Roman*. Schriftenreihe des Instituts für Sozialhistorische Forschung. Frankfurt:Campus Verlag, 1980. First published 1900.

Ostwald, Hans, ed. *Großstadt-Dokumente*. Berlin: Seemann, 1904–8.

Paul-Schiff, Maximilian. *Der Prozess Hilsner: Aktenauszug*. Vienna: Rosner, 1908.

Prätorius, Dr. jur. N. "Die Bibliographie der Homosexualität für das Jahr 1899, sowie Nachtrag zu der Bibliographie des ersten Jahrbuchs." *Jahrbuch für sexuelle Zwischenstufen* 2 (1900): 345–445.

Rickert, Heinrich. *Die Philosophie des Lebens: Darstellung und Kritik der philosophischen Modeströmungen unserer Zeit*. Tübingen: Mohr, 1920.

Ritter, Bernhard. *Zur Geschichte der gerichtsärztlichen Ermittelung der Nothzucht, Leichenschändung, Päderastie und Sodomie*. Erlangen: Enke, 1863.

Rohling, August. *Franz Delitzsch und die Judenfrage*. Prague: Reinitzer, 1881.

———. *Die Polemik und das Menschenopfer des Rabbinismus*. Paderborn: Bonifacius, 1883.

———. *Der Talmudjude: Zur Beherzigung für Juden und Christen aller Stände*. Münster: Russell, 1873.

Schauenstein, Adolf. *Lehrbuch der gerichtlichen Medicin mit besonderer Berücksichtigung der Gesetzgebung Österreichs und deren Vergleichung mit den Gesetzgebungen Deutschlands, Frankreichs und Englands: Für Ärzte und Juristen*. Vienna: Braumüller, 1862.

Schramm, Hellmut. *Der jüdische Ritualmord: Eine historische Untersuchung*. 3rd ed. Berlin: Fritsch, 1944.

Schrenck-Notzing, Albert von. "Beiträge zur forensischen Beurteilung von Sittlichkeitsvergehen mit besonderer Berücksichtigung der Pathogenese psychosexueller Anomalien." In *Kriminalpsychologische und Psychopathologische Studien: Gesammelte Aufsätze aus den Gebieten des Psychopatia sexualis, der gerichtlichen Psychiatrie und der Suggestionslehre*. Leipzig: Barth, 1902.

Schuchardt, Ernst. *Sechs Monate Arbeitshaus: Erlebnisse eines wandernden Arbeiters, Großstadt-Dokumente*. Berlin: Seemann, 1907.

Simmel, Georg. *Einleitung in die Moralwissenschaft: Eine Kritik der ethischen Grundbegriffe.* Berlin: Hertz, 1892.

Stern, Moritz, ed. *Andreas Osianders Schrift über die Blutbeschuldigung.* Kiel: Fiencke, 1893.

Strack, Hermann Leberecht, and Edward Glaser. *Das Blut im Glauben und Aberglauben der Menschheit: mit besonderer Berücksichtigung der "Volksmedizin" und des "jüdischen Blutritus."* Schriften des Institutum Judaicum in Berlin 14. Munich: Beck, 1900.

Sutor, Gustav, ed. *Der Konitzer Mord und seine Folgen: Ein Mahnruf zur Vernunft.* Berlin: Schildberger, 1900.

Tönnies, Ferdinand. *Gemeinschaft und Gesellschaft: Grundbegriffe der reinen Soziologie.* Leipzig: Fues, 1887.

Tresckow, Hans von. *Von Fürsten und anderen Sterblichen: Erinnerungen eines Kriminalkommissars.* Berlin: Fontane, 1922.

Ulrichs, Karl Heinrich [Numa Numantius, pseud.]. *Forschungen über das Räthsel der mannmännlichen Liebe.* 12 vols. 1864–1879. Reprint, Berlin: Verlag rosa Winkel, 1994.

———. *The Riddle of "Man-Manly Love": The Pioneering Work on Male Homosexuality.* Translated by Michael A. Lombardi-Nash. 2 vols. Buffalo, NY: Prometheus Books, 1994.

Von einem Junggesellen. *Nüchterne Betrachtungen über die Frauenfrage.* Neustadt a. d. Hdt.: Gottschick-Witter, 1894.

Von einer Frau. *Auch ein paar nüchterne Betrachtungen über die Frauenfrage.* Bad Ems: Sommer, 1894.

Weininger, Otto. *Geschlecht und Charakter: eine prinzipielle Untersuchung.* Vienna: Braumüller, 1903. Reprint, Munich: Mattes und Seitz, 1980.

———. *Über die letzten Dinge.* Vienna: Braumüller, 1907.

Wilmanns, Karl. *Zur Psychopathologie des Landstreicher.* Leipzig: Barth, 1906.

Wulffen, Erich. *Gauner- und Verbrechertypen.* Berlin: Langenscheidt, 1910.

———. *Sexualspiegel von Kunst und Verbrechen.* Dresden: Aretz, 1928.

### Secondary Books, Articles, Memoirs

Abrahamsen, David *The Life and Mind of a Genius.* New York: Columbia University Press, 1946.

Anidjar, Gil. "Lines of Blood: *Limpieza de Sangre* as Political Theology." In *Blood in History and Blood Histories,* edited by Mariacarla Gadebusch Bondio. Florence: SISMEL/Edizioni del Galluzzo, 2005.

Ankum, Katharina von. *Women in the Metropolis: Gender and Modernity in Weimar Culture.* Berkeley: University of California Press, 1997.

Appignanesi, Lisa. *Femininity and the Creative Imagination: A Study of Henry James, Robert Musil and Marcel Proust.* New York: Barnes and Noble, 1973.

Bachhiesl, Christian, *Zwischen Indizienparadigma und Pseudowissenschaft: Wissenschaftshistorische Überlegungen zum epistemischen Status kriminalwissenschaftlicher Forschung.* Münster: LIT, 2012.

Bahr, Ernst, ed. *Altpreußische Biographie.* Marburg/Lahn: Elwert, 1995.

Barsch, Achim, and Peter M. Hejl. *Menschenbilder: Zur Pluralisierung der Vorstellungen von der menschlichen Natur (1850–1914).* Frankfurt: Suhrkamp, 2000.

Baumann, Imanuel. *Dem Verbrechen auf der Spur: Eine Geschichte der Kriminologie und Kriminalpolitik in Deutschland 1880 bis 1980.* Göttingen: Wallstein, 2006.

Beachy, Robert. *Gay Berlin: Birthplace of a Modern Identity.* New York: Knopf, 2014.

————. "The German Invention of Homosexuality." *Journal of Modern History* 82, no. 4 (2010): 801–38.

Becker, Peter. *Verderbnis und Entartung: Eine Geschichte der Kriminologie des 19. Jahrhunderts als Diskurs und Praxis.* Veröffentlichungen des Max-Planck-Instituts für Geschichte 176. Göttingen: Vandenhoeck und Ruprecht, 2002.

Becker, Peter, and Richard F. Wetzell. *Criminals and Their Scientists: The History of Criminology in International Perspective*, Publications of the German Historical Institute. New York: Cambridge University Press, 2006.

Beirne, Piers. *Inventing Criminology: Essays on the Rise of "Homo criminalis,"* SUNY Series in Deviance and Social Control. Albany: State University of New York Press, 1993.

Berding, Helmut, Diethelm Klippel, and Günther Lottes. *Kriminalität und abweichendes Verhalten: Deutschland im 18. und 19. Jahrhundert*, Sammlung Vandenhoeck. Göttingen: Vandenhoeck und Ruprecht, 1999.

Bersani, Leo. *The Freudian Body: Psychoanalysis and Art.* New York: Columbia University Press, 1986.

Biale, David. *Blood and Belief: The Circulation of a Symbol between Jews and Christians.* Berkeley: University of California Press, 2007.

Binder, Hartmut. *Kafka-Handbuch in zwei Bänden.* Stuttgart: Kröner, 1979.

Bland, Lucy, and Laura L. Doan. *Sexology Uncensored: The Documents of Sexual Science.* Cambridge: Polity, 1998.

Boelcke, Willi A. *Krupp und die Hohenzollern in Dokumenten: Krupp-Korrespondenz mit Kaisern, Kabinettschefs und Ministern, 1850–1918.* Frankfurt: Akademische Verlagsgesellschaft Athenaion, 1970.

Boym, Svetlana. *The Future of Nostalgia.* New York: Basic Books, 2001.

Broeckmann, Andreas. "A Visual Economy of Individuals: The Use of Portrait Photography in the Nineteenth-Century Human Sciences." PhD thesis, University of East Anglia, 1995. http://isp2.srv.v2.nl/~andreas/phd/.

Bronfen, Elisabeth. *The Knotted Subject: Hysteria and Its Discontents.* Princeton, NJ: Princeton University Press, 1998.

Brubaker, Rogers, and Frederick Cooper. "Beyond 'Identity.'" *Theory and Society* 29, no. 1 (2000): 1–47.

Burchell, Graham, Colin Gordon, and Peter Miller. *The Foucault Effect: Studies in Governmentality: With Two Lectures by and an Interview with Michel Foucault.* Chicago: University of Chicago Press, 1991.

Bynum, Caroline Walker. *Wonderful Blood: Theology and Practice in Late Medieval Northern Germany and Beyond.* Philadelphia: University of Pennsylvania Press, 2007.

Canning, Kathleen. *Languages of Labor and Gender: Female Factory Work in Germany, 1850–1914.* Ithaca, NY: Cornell University Press, 1996.

Caplan, Jane, and John C. Torpey. *Documenting Individual Identity: The Development of State Practices in the Modern World.* Princeton, NJ: Princeton University Press, 2001.

Caputi, Jane. *The Age of Sex Crime.* Bowling Green, OH: Bowling Green University Popular Press, 1987.

Certeau, Michel de. *Heterologies: Discourse on the Other.* Translated by Brian Massumi. Theory and History of Literature, vol. 17. Minneapolis: University of Minnesota Press, 1986.

————. *The Practice of Everyday Life.* Berkeley: University of California Press, 1984.

Chamberlin, J. Edward, and Sander L. Gilman. *Degeneration: The Dark Side of Progress.* New York: Columbia University Press, 1985.

Clark, Anna. "Twilight Moments." *Journal of the History of Sexuality* 114, no. 1/2 (2005): 139–60.

Cohen, Stanley. *Folk Devils and Moral Panics: The Creation of the Mods and Rockers.* Oxford: Robertson, 1980.

Cooper, Frederick. *Colonialism in Question: Theory, Knowledge, History.* Berkeley: University of California Press, 2005.

Déak, Ágnes. "Translator, Editor, Publisher, Spy: The Informative Case of Károly Kertbeny (1824–1882)." *Hungarian Quarterly* 39 (1998): 26–33.

Dean, Carolyn J. *The Frail Social Body: Pornography, Homosexuality, and Other Fantasies in Interwar France.* Berkeley: University of California Press, 2000.

———. *The Self and Its Pleasures: Bataille, Lacan, and the History of the Decentered Subject.* Ithaca, NY: Cornell University Press, 1992.

———. *Sexuality and Modern Western Culture.* Twayne's Studies in Intellectual and Cultural History. New York: Twayne, 1996.

Dean, Tim, and Christopher Lane. *Homosexuality and Psychoanalysis.* Chicago: University of Chicago Press, 2001.

Dienes, Gerhard Michael. *Gross gegen Gross: Hans und Otto Gross: ein paradigmatischer Generationenkonflikt.* Marburg: LiteraturWissenschaft, 2005.

Dienes, Gerhard Michael, and Ralf Rother. *Die Gesetze des Vaters: Problematische Identitätsansprüche: Hans und Otto Gross, Sigmund Freud und Franz Kafka.* Vienna: Böhlau, 2003.

Dijkstra, Bram. *Idols of Perversity: Fantasies of Feminine Evil in Fin-de-Siècle Culture.* New York: Oxford University Press, 1986.

Dickinson, E. Ross. *Sex, Freedom, and Power in Imperial Germany, 1880–1914.* Cambridge: Cambridge University Press, 2014.

Ellenberger, Henri F. *The Discovery of the Unconscious: The History and Evolution of Dynamic Psychiatry.* New York: Basic Books, 1970.

Eribon, Didier. "Michel Foucault's Histories of Sexuality." *GLQ* 7, no. 1 (2001): 31–86.

Evans, Richard J. *The Feminist Movement in Germany, 1894–1933.* London: Sage, 1976.

———. *The German Underworld: Deviants and Outcasts in German History.* London: Routledge, 1988.

———. *Tales from the German Underworld: Crime and Punishment in the Nineteenth Century.* New Haven, CT: Yale University Press, 1998.

Felski, Rita. *The Gender of Modernity.* Cambridge, MA: Harvard University Press, 1995.

Feray, Jean-Claude, and M. Herzer. "Homosexual Studies and Politics in the 19th Century: Karl Maria Kertbeny." *Journal of Homosexuality* 19, no. 1 (1990): 23–47.

Ferrell, Jeff, K. Hayward, W. Morrison, and M. Presdee, eds. *Cultural Criminology Unleashed.* London: GlassHouse, 2004.

Florence, Ronald. *Blood Libel: The Damascus Affair of 1840.* Madison: University of Wisconsin Press, 2004.

Foucault, Michel. *The History of Sexuality.* Translated by Robert Hurley. 3 vols. New York: Pantheon Books, 1978.

———. *I, Pierre Rivière, Having Slaughtered My Mother, My Sister, and My Brother: A Case of Parricide in the 19th Century.* Translated by Frank Jellinek. Lincoln: University of Nebraska Press, 1982.

———. *Politics, Philosophy, Culture: Interviews and Other Writings, 1977–1984.* Edited by Lawrence D. Kritzman. New York: Routledge, 1988.

Foucault, Michel, Valerio Marchetti, Antonella Salomoni, and Arnold I. Davidson. *Abnormal: Lectures at the Collège de France, 1974–1975.* New York: Picador, 2003.

Frankel, Jonathan. *The Damascus Affair: "Ritual Murder," Politics, and the Jews in 1840.* Cambridge: Cambridge University Press, 1997.

Frederiksen, Elke, ed. *Die Frauenfrage in Deutschland 1865–1915: Texte und Dokumente.* Stuttgart: Reclam, 1981.

Fritzsche, Peter. *Reading Berlin 1900.* Cambridge, MA.: Harvard University Press, 1996.

Galassi, Silviana. *Kriminologie im Deutschen Kaiserreich: Geschichte einer gebrochenen Verwissenschaftlichung.* Stuttgart: Steiner, 2004.

Gershoni, I., Y. Hakan Erdem, and Ursula Woköck. *Histories of the Modern Middle East: New Directions.* Boulder, CO: Rienner, 2002.

Geyer-Kordesch, Johanna, and Annette Kuhn. *Frauenkörper, Medizin, Sexualität: Auf dem Wege zu einer neuen Sexualmoral.* Dusseldorf: Schwann, 1986.

Gibson, Mary. *Born to Crime: Cesare Lombroso and the Origins of Biological Criminology.* Italian and Italian American Studies. Westport, CT: Praeger, 2002.

Ginzburg, Carlo. *Clues, Myths, and the Historical Method.* Translated by John Tedeschi and Anne C. Tedeschi. Baltimore: Johns Hopkins University Press, 1989.

Good, David F., Margarete Gradner, and Mary Jo Maynes. *Austrian Women in the Nineteenth and Twentieth Centuries: Cross-Disciplinary Perspectives.* Providence, RI: Berghahn, 1996.

Gould, Stephen Jay. *The Mismeasure of Man.* New York: Norton, 1996.

Groß, Johannes T. *Ritualmordbeschuldigungen gegen Juden im Deutschen Kaiserreich (1871–1914).* Zentrum für Antisemitismusforschung der Technischen Universität Berlin. Vol. 47, *Dokumente, Text, Materialien.* Berlin: Metropol, 2002.

Hall, Alex. *Scandal, Sensation, and Social Democracy: The SPD Press and Wilhelmine Germany 1890–1914.* Cambridge: Cambridge University Press, 1977.

Halperin, David M. *How to Do the History of Homosexuality.* Chicago: University of Chicago Press, 2002.

———. *One Hundred Years of Homosexuality: And Other Essays on Greek Love.* New York: Routledge, 1990.

Handler, Andrew. *Blood Libel at Tiszaeszlar.* East European Monographs. New York: Columbia University Press, 1980.

Harrowitz, Nancy A., and Barbara Hyams. *Jews and Gender: Responses to Otto Weininger.* Philadelphia: Temple University Press, 1995.

Hartston, Barnet. *Sensationalizing the Jewish Question: Anti-Semitic Trials and the Press in the Early German Empire.* Studies in Central European Histories. Leiden: Brill, 2005.

Haxthausen, Charles Werner, and Heidrun Suhr. *Berlin: Culture and Metropolis.* Minneapolis: University of Minnesota Press, 1991.

Herczl, Moshe Y. *Christianity and the Holocaust of Hungarian Jewry.* New York: New York University Press, 1993.

Hergemöller, Bernd-Ulrich. *Mann für Mann: Biographisches Lexikon.* Hamburg: Suhrkamp, 2001.

Herzog, Todd. "Crime Stories: Criminal, Society, and the Modernist Case History." *Representations* 80, no. 1 (2002): 34–61.

Hett, Benjamin. *Death in the Tiergarten: Murder and Criminal Justice in the Kaiser's Berlin.* Cambridge, MA: Harvard University Press, 2004.

Horn, David G. *The Criminal Body: Lombroso and the Anatomy of Deviance.* New York: Routledge, 2003.

Hügel, Hans-Otto. *Untersuchungsrichter, Diebsfänger, Detektive: Theorie u. Geschichte d. dt. Detektiverzählung im 19. Jh.* Stuttgart: Metzler, 1978.

Hull, Isabel V. *The Entourage of Kaiser Wilhelm II, 1888–1918.* Cambridge: Cambridge University Press, 1982.

Hundert, Gershon David. *The YIVO Encyclopedia of Jews in Eastern Europe.* New Haven, CT: Yale University Press, 2008.

Janik, Allan. *Essays on Wittgenstein and Weininger.* Studien zur österreichischen Philosophie 9. Amsterdam: Rodopi, 1985.

Jazbinsek, Dietmar. "The Metropolis and the Mental Life of Georg Simmel: On the History of an Antipathy." *Journal of Urban History* 30, no. 1 (2003): 104–6.

Johnston, William M. *The Austrian Mind: An Intellectual and Social History, 1848–1938.* Berkeley: University of California Press, 1972.

Jonsson, Stefan. *Subject without Nation: Robert Musil and the History of Modern Identity.* Durham, NC: Duke University Press, 2000.

Kaiser, Céline. *Rhetorik der Entartung: Max Nordau und die Sprache der Verletzung.* Bielefeld: Transcript, 2007.

Karthaus, Ulrich. *Der andere Zustand: Zeitstrukturen im Werke Robert Musils.* Philologische Studien und Quellen. Berlin: Schmidt, 1965.

Käser, Rudolf, and Vera Pohland. *Disease and Medicine in Modern German Cultures.* Western Societies Program occasional paper 30. Ithaca, NY: Center for International Studies, Cornell University, 1990.

Katz, Jonathan. *The Invention of Heterosexuality.* New York: Dutton, 1995.

Keilson-Lauritz, Marita. *Die Geschichte der eigenen Geschichte: Literatur und Literaturkritik in den Anfängen der Schwulenbewegung am Beispiel des Jahrbuchs für sexuelle Zwischenstufen und der Zeitschrift Der Eigene.* Homosexualität und Literatur 11. Berlin: Verlag rosa Winkel, 1997.

Kennedy, Hubert. *Karl Heinrich Ulrichs : Leben und Werk.* 2nd ed. Bibliothek rosa Winkel 27. Hamburg: MännerschwarmSkript-Verlag, 2001.

———. "Kertbeny and the Nameless Love." *Journal of Homosexuality* 12, no. 1 (1985): 1–26.

Kieval, Hillel J. "The Importance of Place: Comparative Aspects of the Ritual Murder Trial in Modern Central Europe." In *Comparing Jewish Societies*, edited by Todd M. Endelman, 135–65. Ann Arbor: University of Michigan Press, 1997.

———. "Neighbors, Strangers, Readers: The Village and the City in Jewish-Gentile Conflict at the Turn of the Nineteenth Century." *Jewish Studies Quarterly* 12 (2005): 61–79.

———. "Representation and Knowledge in Medieval and Modern Accounts of Jewish Ritual Murder." *Jewish Social Studies: History, Culture, Society* 1 (1994–95): 52–72.

———. "Ritual Murder (Modern)." In *Antisemitism: A Historical Encyclopedia of Prejudice and Persecution*, edited by Richard S. Levy, 605–8. Santa Barbara, CA: ABC-CLIO, 2005.

Krafft-Ebing, R. von. *Psychopathia sexualis: Mit Beiträgen on Georges Bataille, Werner Brede, Albert Caraco, Salvador Dalí, Ernst Fuhrman, Maurice Heine, Julia Kristeva, Paul Kruntorad und Elisabeth Lenk.* Munich: Matthes und Seitz, 1997.

Krietsch, Peter, and Manfred Dietel. *Pathologisch-Anatomisches Cabinet: Vom Virchow-Museum zum Berliner Medizinhistorischen Museum in der Charité.* Berlin: Blackwell Wissenschafts-Verlag, 1996.

LaCapra, Dominick. *History and Its Limits: Human, Animal, Violence.* Ithaca, NY: Cornell University Press, 2009.

Lamott, Franziska. *Die vermessene Frau: Hysterien um 1900.* Munich: Fink, 2001.

Leps, Marie-Christine. *Apprehending the Criminal: The Production of Deviance in Nineteenth-*

*Century Discourse*. Post-Contemporary Interventions. Durham, NC: Duke University Press, 1992.

Le Rider, Jacques. *Le cas Otto Weininger: racines de l'antiféminisme et de l'antisémitisme*. Perspectives critiques. Paris: Presses universitaires de France, 1982.

Le Rider, Jacques, and Norbert Leser. *Otto Weininger: Werk und Wirkung*. Quellen und Studien zur österreichischen Geistesgeschichte im 19. und 20. Jahrhundert 5. Vienna: Österreichischer Bundesverlag, 1984.

LeVay, Simon. *Queer Science: The Use and Abuse of Research into Homosexuality*. Cambridge, MA: MIT Press, 1996.

Lombroso, Cesare, Guglielmo Ferrero, Nicole Hahn Rafter, and Mary Gibson. *Criminal Woman, the Prostitute, and the Normal Woman*. Durham, NC: Duke University Press, 2004.

Lombroso, Cesare, Mary Gibson, and Nicole Hahn Rafter. *Criminal Man*. Durham, NC: Duke University Press, 2006.

Luft, David S. *Eros and Inwardness in Vienna: Weininger, Musil, Doderer*. Chicago: University of Chicago Press, 2003.

Matysik, Tracie. *Reforming the Moral Subject: Ethics and Sexuality in Central Europe, 1890–1930*. Ithaca, NY: Cornell University Press, 2008.

Mayhew, Henry. *London Labour and the London Poor*. Harmondsworth, Middlesex: Penguin Books, 1985.

McBride, Patrizia C. *The Void of Ethics: Robert Musil and the Experience of Modernity*, Avant-Garde and Modernism Studies. Evanston, IL: Northwestern University Press, 2006.

McGuire, Kristin M. "Activism, Intimacy and the Politics of Selfhood: The Gendered Terms of Citizenship in Poland and Germany, 1890–1918." PhD diss., University of Michigan, 2004.

Mearns, Andrew, and Anthony S. Wohl. *The Bitter Cry of Outcast London*. New York: Humanities Press, 1970.

Morrison, Wayne. "Lombroso and the Birth of Criminological Positivism: Scientific Mastery or Cultural Artifice?" In *Cultural Criminology Unleashed*, edited by Jeff Ferrell, K. Hayward, W. Morrison, and M. Presdee, 67–80. London: GlassHouse, 2004.

Mort, Frank. *Dangerous Sexualities: Medico-Moral Politics in England since 1830*. London: Routledge and Kegan Paul, 1987.

Mosse, George L. *The Crisis of German Ideology: Intellectual Origins of the Third Reich*. New York: Grosset and Dunlap, 1964.

Müller, Christian. *Verbrechensbekämpfung im Anstaltsstaat: Psychiatrie, Kriminologie und Strafrechtsreform in Deutschland 1871–1933*. Kritische Studien zur Geschichtswissenschaft 160. Göttingen: Vandenhoeck und Ruprecht, 2004.

Nitzschke, Bernd. *Männerängste, Männerwünsche*. Munich: Matthes und Seitz, 1984.

Nye, Robert A. "Heredity or Milieu: The Foundations of Modern European Criminological Theory." *Isis* 67, no. 3 (1976): 334–55.

Oosterhuis, Harry. *Homosexuality and Male Bonding in Pre-Nazi Germany: The Youth Movement, the Gay Movement, and Male Bonding before Hitler's Rise: Original Transcripts from Der Eigene, the First Gay Journal in the World*. Translated by Hubert Kennedy. New York: Harrington Park Press, 1991.

———. *Stepchildren of Nature: Krafft-Ebing, Psychiatry, and the Making of Sexual Identity*. Chicago: University of Chicago Press, 2000.

Payne-James, Jason. *Encyclopedia of Forensic and Legal Medicine*. Amsterdam: Elsevier Academic Press, 2005.

Peukert, Detlev. *The Weimar Republic: The Crisis of Classical Modernity.* New York: Hill and Wang, 1992.

Pick, Daniel. *Faces of Degeneration: A European Disorder, c.1848–c.1918.* Cambridge: Cambridge University Press, 1989.

Pynsent, Robert B. *Decadence and Innovation: Austro-Hungarian Life and Art at the Turn of the Century.* London: Weidenfeld and Nicolson, 1989.

Rémy, Jean, ed. *Georg Simmel: Ville et modernité.* Paris: L'Harmattan, 1995.

Repp, Kevin. *Reformers, Critics, and the Paths of German Modernity: Anti-politics and the Search for Alternatives, 1890–1914.* Cambridge, MA: Harvard University Press, 2000.

Rodlauer, Hannelore. *Von "Eros und Psyche" zu Geschlecht und Charakter.* Vienna: Verlag der österreichischen Akademie der Wissenschaften, 1987.

Röhl, John C. G., and Nicolaus Sombart. *Kaiser Wilhelm II, New Interpretations: The Corfu Papers.* Cambridge: Cambridge University Press, 1982.

Rosario, Vernon A. *Science and Homosexualities.* New York: Routledge, 1997.

Rowbotham, Judith, and Kim Stevenson. *Criminal Conversations: Victorian Crimes, Social Panic, and Moral Outrage.* Columbus: Ohio State University Press, 2005.

Schildt, Rudolf. "Das Ende einer Karriere: Entfernung des Amtsassessors Ulrichs aus dem Staatsdienst wegen widernatürlicher Wollust." *Capri: Zeitschrift für Schwule Geschichte,* no. 1/88 (1988): 24–33.

Schivelbusch, Wolfgang. *Disenchanted Night: The Industrialization of Light in the Nineteenth Century.* Berkeley: University of California Press, 1988.

Schorske, Carl E. *Fin-de-Siècle Vienna: Politics and Culture.* New York: Vintage Books, 1981.

Sedgwick, Eve Kosofsky. *Epistemology of the Closet.* Berkeley: University of California Press, 1990.

Sekula, Allan. "The Body and the Archive." *October* 39 (1986): 3–64.

Seltzer, Mark. *Serial Killers: Death and Life in America's Wound Culture.* New York: Routledge, 1998.

Sengoopta, Chandak. *Otto Weininger: Sex, Science, and Self in Imperial Vienna,* Chicago Series on Sexuality, History, and Society. Chicago: University of Chicago Press, 2000.

Sigusch, Volkmar, and Günter Grau. *Geschichte der Sexualwissenschaft.* Frankfurt: Campus, 2008.

Smith, Helmut Walser. *The Butcher's Tale: Murder and Anti-Semitism in a German Town.* New York: Norton, 2002.

Söder, Hans-Peter. "Disease and Health as Contexts of Modernity: Max Nordau as a Critic of Fin-de-Siècle Modernism." *German Studies Review* 14 (1991): 473–87.

Spector, Scott. *Prague Territories: National Conflict and Cultural Innovation in Franz Kafka's Fin de Siècle.* Berkeley, CA: University of California Press, 2000.

———. "Where Personal Fate Turns to Public Affair: Homosexual Scandal and Social Order in Vienna, 1900–1910." *Austrian History Yearbook* 38 (2007): 15–24.

———. "The Wrath of the 'Countess Merviola': Tabloid Exposé and the Emergence of Homosexual Subjects in Vienna 1907." In *Sexuality in Austria,* edited by Günter Bischof, Anton Pelinka, and Dagmar Herzog, 31–48. Edison, NJ: Transaction, 2006.

Spector, Scott, Helmut Puff, and Dagmar Herzog. *After the History of Sexuality: German Genealogies with and beyond Foucault.* Spektrum: Publications of the German Studies Association. New York: Berghahn Books, 2012.

Srebnick, Amy Gilman, and René Lévy. *Crime and Culture: An Historical Perspective.* Advances in Criminology. Burlington, VT: Ashgate, 2005.

Steakley, James D. "Iconography of a Scandal: Political Cartoons and the Eulenburg Affair." *Studies in Visual Communication* 9, no. 2 (1983): 20–51.

———, comp. *The Writings of Magnus Hirschfeld: A Bibliography.* Schriftenreihe der Magnus-Hirschfeld-Gesellschaft 2. Toronto: Canadian Gay Archives, 1985.

Steinberg, Holger, Dirk Carius, and Matthias C. Angermeyer. "The Tenth Anniversary of the Archives for the History of Psychiatry in Leipzig." *History of Psychiatry* 17, no. 4 (2006): 501–7.

Steinberg, Jonathan. "The Case of Herr Fritz Krupp." *Midstream: A Monthly Jewish Review* 13, no. 9 (1967): 10–19.

Stern, Edith. *The Glorious Victory of Truth: The Tiszaeszlar Blood Libel Trial, 1882–3: A Historical-Legal-Medical Research.* Jerusalem: R. Mass, 1998.

Stern, Fritz Richard. *The Politics of Cultural Despair: A Study in the Rise of the Germanic Ideology.* Berkeley: University of California Press, 1961.

Stewart-Steinberg, Suzanne. *Sublime Surrender: Male Masochism at the Fin-de-Siècle.* Ithaca, NY: Cornell University Press, 1998.

Stow, Kenneth R. *Jewish Dogs: An Image and Its Interpreters: Continuity in the Catholic-Jewish Encounter.* Stanford, CA: Stanford University Press, 2006.

Szasz, Thomas. *The Age of Madness: The History of Involuntary Mental Hospitalization, Presented in Selected Texts.* New York: Aronson, 1974.

Szporluk, Roman. *The Political Thought of Thomas G. Masaryk.* East European Monographs. New York: Columbia University Press, 1981.

Tatar, Maria M. *Lustmord: Sexual Murder in Weimar Germany.* Princeton, NJ: Princeton University Press, 1995.

Theweleit, Klaus. *Männerphantasien.* 2 vols. Frankfurt: Verlag Roter Stern, 1977–78.

Thies, Ralf. *Ethnograph des dunklen Berlin: Hans Ostwald und die "Grossstadt-Dokumente" (1904–1908).* Cologne: Böhlau, 2006.

Toaff, Ariel. *Pasque di sangue: ebrei d'Europa e omicidi rituali.* 2nd ed. Biblioteca storica. Bologna: Il mulino, 2008.

Veigl, Hans. *Morbides Wien: Die dunklen Bezirke der Stadt und ihrer Bewohner.* Vienna: Böhlau, 2000.

Verhey, Jeffrey. *The Spirit of 1914: Militarism, Myth, and Mobilization in Germany.* Cambridge: Cambridge University Press, 2000.

Verplaetse, Jan. "Moritz [sic] Benedikt's (1835–1920) Localization of Morality in the Occipital Lobes: Origin and Background of a Controversial Hypothesis." *History of Psychiatry* 15, no. 3 (2004): 305–28.

Vyleta, Dan. *Crime, Jews and News: Vienna, 1895–1914.* New York: Berghahn Books, 2007.

———. "Jewish Crimes and Misdemeanors: In Search of Jewish Criminality (Germany and Austria, 1890–1914)." *European History Quarterly* 35, no. 2 (2005): 299–325.

Wagner, E. J. *The Science of Sherlock Holmes: From Baskerville Hall to the Valley of Fear, the Real Forensics behind the Great Detective's Greatest Cases.* Hoboken, NJ: Wiley, 2006.

Wagner, Nike. *Geist und Geschlecht: Karl Kraus und die Erotik der Wiener Moderne.* Frankfurt: Suhrkamp, 1982.

Walkowitz, Judith R. *City of Dreadful Delight: Narratives of Sexual Danger in Late-Victorian London.* Women in Culture and Society. Chicago: University of Chicago Press, 1992.

Warner, Michael, and Collective Social Text. *Fear of a Queer Planet: Queer Politics and Social Theory.* Minneapolis: University of Minnesota Press, 1993.

Wetzell, Richard F. *Inventing the Criminal: A History of German Criminology, 1880–1945*. Chapel Hill: University of North Carolina Press, 2000.

Williams, Raymond. *The Country and the City*. New York: Oxford University Press, 1973.

Wiltenburg, Joy. "True Crime: The Origins of Modern Sensationalism." *American Historical Review* 109, no. 5 (2004): 1377–404.

Wolff, Kurt H. *The Sociology of Georg Simmel*. New York: Free Press, 1950.

Wolff, Larry. *Postcards from the End of the World: Child Abuse in Freud's Vienna*. New York: Atheneum, 1988.

Zimmermann, Clemens, and Jürgen Reulecke. *Die Stadt als Moloch? Das Land als Kraftquell? Wahrnehmungen und Wirkungen der Grossstädte um 1900*. Stadtforschung aktuell. Basel: Boston, 1999.

Žižek, Slavoj. *For They Know Not What They Do: Enjoyment as a Political Factor*. London: Verso, 1991.

———. *The Metastases of Enjoyment: Six Essays on Woman and Causality*. London: Verso, 1994.

# Index

criminal responsibility. See *Zurechnungsfähigkeit*
criminals: associated with genius, 191; as atavistic, 33, 37, 198; in crime fiction, 198; epileptics as, 123; expert discourses of, 31–33, 34–37, 38, 42, 50, 51–55, 62–63, 106–7, 111, 123, 188–90, 192, 193; as inborn, 32–33, 37, 50, 198, 252; influenced by homesickness, 51–52, 53–55; as instinctual, 199; literary representations of, 24–26; in Lombroso, 32–34, 38, 198; measurement of, 63–64; medicalization of, 31, 42; as modernizing agents, 65, 71; as opposite of bourgeois, 26; physiology of, 33, 35, 198; in the press, 23–24, 44; as producer of criminal law, 71; prostitutes as counterparts to, 179–80; psychological explanations for, 62, 198–99; as psychopathic, 235; readers' identification with, 26; as sensation, 32, 38; signs of degeneration in, 33, 36, 37, 191; socioenvironmental explanations of, 35–37; twilight states in, 199; typologies of, 191. See also *Zurechnungsfähigkeit*
*Criminal Woman* (Lombroso), 32
criminology: classical school, 31; connects crime with genius, 191; determinism in, 32, 33; determinists vs. socioenvironmentalists, 33, 34–37, 38; Gross's influence on, 55, 56–57; and *Lustmord*, 169; nature vs. nurture debate, 6, 32–33; as new medium, 38; origins of, 31, 33–34, 55; positive school, 31, 32–33, 34, 37, 42; relation of to criminal anthropology, 55; relation of to criminalistics, 57, 66; shift from crime to criminal, 31. See also criminal anthropology; criminalistics
Cüstrin on the Oder, 168–69
Cybalski, Onufri, 241

dactyloscopy. See fingerprinting
Damascus affair, 202–3, 206, 208–11, 219
*Dämmerzustand* (twilight or trance state), 9; case studies of, 121, 122; as ground for crime and deviancy, 123, 252; in Krafft-Ebing, 120–22, 123, 124, 252; linked with *Lustmord*, 189
*Dark Corners of Berlin* (Ostwald), 18
Darwin, Charles, 79, 80
Daumer, G. F., 229–31
Dean, Carolyn, 14n20, 196
decadence: and aesthetics, 14, 252; associated with homosexuality, 139; cultural pessimism as, 177; fin de siècle as, 1, 10, 13, 46, 194; Musil on, 194; news report as, 184; opposition to normality, 194
degeneration: ambiguous meaning of, 46; as atavism, 9, 46, 48; as autodiagnostic discourse, 49; civilization faced with, 20, 49, 50; as deviation, 46; and eugenics, 178; expert discourses on, 46–50; as fantasy, 48; genius as product of, 49; hereditary factors in, 46; linked with

crime, 49–50; linked with criminal responsibility (*Zurechnungsfähigkeit*), 45; linked with homosexuals, 100; linked with prostitution, 49–50, 176, 179, 183; within the lower classes, 36; metaphorical meanings of, 46–47; metropolis as source of, 251; Musil on, 252; Nordau on, 47–48; physiological effects of, 47, 48; as product of modernity, 47–48, 50; signs of in criminals, 33, 37
delirium: and criminal responsibility, 160; escape from reason, 114; Krafft-Ebing's research into, 120, 124
Delitzsch, Franz, 226–28
dementia, 11, 54
Department of Blackmailers and Homosexuals, Berlin (Erpresser- und Homosexuellendezernat), 163
Desgouttes, Franz, 101
deviancy, 4, 5, 250; associated with class, 137; *Dämmerzustand* as ground for, 123; expert discourses on, 6, 8, 73–74, 92–93; as fantasy, 250; focus of sexology, 116; gender performance as, 131; homosexuals associated with, 86, 92–93, 100, 116, 126, 145; and Oscar Wilde, 139; press accounts of, 104; sexual behavior linked to, 80, 82, 117
Diet, Hungary, 212, 216, 219
*Discovery of the Soul* (Jäger), 97, 98, 99
*dispositionsfähig* (capable of individual responsibility), 84
*Don Carlos* (Schiller), 106
Dreyfus, Alfred: compared to Beer, 143; to Hilsner, 232–33; to Tiszaezlár case, 215

Eisenmenger, Johann Andreas, 223
Elbe, Lilly von, 162
Elberskirchen, Johanna, 176
Elias, Norbert, 9, 249
Ellis, Havelock, 124, 129
Enlightenment, 9, 16, 18, 31, 49, 72, 99, 114, 211, 215, 219, 220
Enniger case, 204–5
*Entdecktes Judenthum* (Eisenmenger), 223
*Enzyklopädie der modern Kriminalistik* (Langenscheidt), 66–67
epilepsy, 9, 37, 42, 51, 128, 252; linked with *Lustmord*, 189, 190; as pathology, 123–24; and *Unzurechnungsfähigkeit*, 44; in Voigt case, 190
*Eros* (Hössli), 101
eugenics: crime as a problem of, 198; discourses on degeneracy, 178; in feminist discourse, 178–79; relation of to Weininger, 186
Eulenberg, Philip, Prince of, 145
experts, 6, 7; antisemites as, 227–28; competition among, 42–43, 45, 106–7; competition with press, 7; discourses about criminal